Help
- **Index**
- Keyboard
- Commands
- Procedures
- Using Help
- About...

Window
- Open Drive Window...
- Cascade — Shift+F5
- Tile — Shift+F4
- Close All
- Hide All
- Arrange Icons
- View As...
- 1. Accessories
- 2. Non-Windows Applications
- 3. Games
- 4. Main
- 5. Windows Applications
- √ 6. Norton Desktop
- 7. AutoStart
- More...

Tools
- **SuperFind**
- Calculator
- KeyFinder
- Sleeper
- Shredder
- UnErase
- Disk Doctor
- Norton Backup
- System Info
- Icon Editor
- Scheduler
- Batch Builder

Configure
- **Short Menus**
- Edit Custom Menus...
- Password...
- Preferences...
- Confirmation...
- Drive Icons...
- Button Bar...
- Shortcut Keys...
- Quick Access...
- Editor...
- Default Viewer...
- SmartErase...
- Shredder...
- Save Configuration

View
- √ Tree Pane
- √ File Pane
- View Pane
- Show Entire Drive
- Refresh — F5
- Filter...
- File Details...
- Sort By ▶
- Viewer ▶

Computer users are not all alike.
Neither are SYBEX books.

We know our customers have a variety of needs. They've told us so. And because we've listened, we've developed several distinct types of books to meet the needs of each of our customers. What are you looking for in computer help?

If you're looking for the basics, try the **ABC's** series. You'll find short, unintimidating tutorials and helpful illustrations. For a more visual approach, select **Teach Yourself**, featuring screen-by-screen illustrations of how to use your latest software purchase.

Mastering and **Understanding** titles offer you a step-by-step introduction, plus an in-depth examination of intermediate-level features, to use as you progress.

Our **Up & Running** series is designed for computer-literate consumers who want a no-nonsense overview of new programs. Just 20 basic lessons, and you're on your way.

We also publish two types of reference books. Our **Instant References** provide quick access to each of a program's commands and functions. SYBEX **Encyclopedias** and **Desktop References** provide a *comprehensive reference* and explanation of all of the commands, features and functions of the subject software.

Sometimes a subject requires a special treatment that our standard series don't provide. So you'll find we have titles like **Advanced Techniques, Handbooks, Tips & Tricks**, and others that are specifically tailored to satisfy a unique need.

We carefully select our authors for their in-depth understanding of the software they're writing about, as well as their ability to write clearly and communicate effectively. Each manuscript is thoroughly reviewed by our technical staff to ensure its complete accuracy. Our production department makes sure it's easy to use. All of this adds up to the highest quality books available, consistently appearing on best-seller charts worldwide.

You'll find SYBEX publishes a variety of books on every popular software package. Looking for computer help? Help Yourself to SYBEX.

For a complete catalog of our publications:

SYBEX Inc.
2021 Challenger Drive, Alameda, CA 94501
Tel: (510) 523-8233/(800) 227-2346 Telex: 336311
Fax: (510) 523-2373

SYBEX is committed to using natural resources wisely to preserve and improve our environment. As a leader in the computer book publishing industry, we are aware that over 40% of America's solid waste is paper. This is why we have been printing the text of books like this one on recycled paper since 1982.

This year our use of recycled paper will result in the saving of more than 15,300 trees. We will lower air pollution effluents by 54,000 pounds, save 6,300,000 gallons of water, and reduce landfill by 2,700 cubic yards.

In choosing a SYBEX book you are not only making a choice for the best in skills and information, you are also choosing to enhance the quality of life for all of us.

Understanding Norton Desktop for Windows

Understanding Norton Desktop™ for Windows™

Peter Dyson

SYBEX ®

San Francisco • Paris • Düsseldorf • Soest

Acquisitions Editor: Dianne King
Developmental Editor: Gary Masters
Editor: Stefan Grünwedel
Technical Editor: Maryann Brown
Word Processors: Ann Dunn and Susan Trybull
Chapter Art and Layout: Alissa Feinberg
Screen Graphics: Delia Brown and Thomas Goudie
Typesetter: Stephanie Hollier
Proofreaders-Production Assistants: Elizabeth Chuan and Dina F. Quan
Indexer: Tom McFadden
Cover Designer: Ingalls + Associates
Cover Photographer: Mark Johann

Norton Desktop for Windows is a trademark of Symantec/Peter Norton Computing Group

Windows is a trademark of Microsoft Corporation

SYBEX is a registered trademark of SYBEX, Inc.

TRADEMARKS: SYBEX has attempted throughout this book to distinguish proprietary trademarks from descriptive terms by following the capitalization style used by the manufacturer.

SYBEX is not affiliated with any manufacturer.

Every effort has been made to supply complete and accurate information. However, SYBEX assumes no responsibility for its use, nor for any infringement of the intellectual property rights of third parties which would result from such use.

Copyright ©1992 SYBEX Inc., 2021 Challenger Drive, Alameda, CA 94501. World rights reserved. No part of this publication may be stored in a retrieval system, transmitted, or reproduced in any way, including but not limited to photocopy, photograph, magnetic or other record, without the prior agreement and written permission of the publisher.

Library of Congress Card Number: 91-66573
ISBN: 0-89588-888-2

Manufactured in the United States of America
10 9 8 7 6 5 4

To Jane, Tony, Thomas, and Joshua

Acknowledgments

A book is never the sole product of the person whose name appears on the cover. As always, many people have worked on this project, providing technical assistance and advice.

I particularly want to thank Dianne King, acquisitions manager at SYBEX, for all her help and guidance.

Thanks to Gary Masters for the keen eye he applied through the development process, and to Stefan Grünwedel for doing an excellent job with this manuscript. Thanks also to Maryann Brown for her technical editing, Ann Dunn and Susan Trybull for word processing, Alissa Feinberg for chapter art and layout, Delia Brown and Thomas Goudie for screen graphics, Stephanie Hollier for typesetting, Elizabeth G. Chuan and Dina F. Quan for proofreading, and Tom McFadden for the index.

At Symantec/Peter Norton Computing Group, particular thanks go to J. J. Schoch and Sue Constaninides, Product Management Team for Norton Desktop for Windows, for much help and technical advice over the last year, as well as prerelease copies of the Norton Desktop software and documentation. Thanks also to Nancy Stevenson of the Symantec marketing department for all her help.

Finally, on a personal note, thanks to Nancy for all her patience, encouragement, and support; and to Gene Weisskopf for all the computer talk and good humor despite our deadlines.

Contents-at-a-Glance

	Introduction	xxvii
Part I:	**The Basics of Norton Desktop for Windows**	**1**
Chapter 1:	An Overview of Norton Desktop for Windows.	2
Chapter 2:	Installing Norton Desktop for Windows	8
Chapter 3:	Elements of Windows and the Desktop	18
Chapter 4:	How to Get Help	32
Part II:	**The Desktop**	**39**
Chapter 5:	Organization of the Desktop	40
Chapter 6:	Viewing and Printing Files	70
Chapter 7:	Launching Programs	86
Chapter 8:	Using Quick Access	102
Chapter 9:	Customizing the Desktop	120
Part III:	**The Windows Tools**	**155**
Chapter 10:	Backing Up Your System	156
Chapter 11:	Protecting Your Files	206
Chapter 12:	Examining Your System	220
Chapter 13:	Enhancing Windows	246
Chapter 14:	Advanced Desktop Utilities	286
Part IV:	**The DOS Tools**	**327**
Chapter 15:	Using the Emergency Disk	328
Chapter 16:	Diagnosing and Fixing Disk Problems	340
Chapter 17:	Optimizing Your Disk Drives	356
Chapter 18:	Recovering Files and Data.	376
Appendix:	Batch Builder Function Summary	402
	Index	467

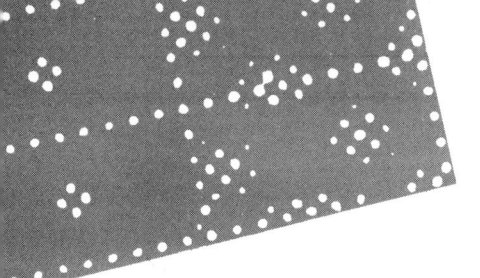

Table of Contents

Introduction   xxvii

Part One: The Basics of Norton Desktop for Windows   1

Chapter 1	**An Overview of Norton Desktop for Windows**	2
	Norton Desktop in Brief	3
	The Desktop	3
	The Windows Tools	4
	The DOS Tools	5
	Using Norton Desktop on a Network	5
	Hardware and Software Requirements for Norton Desktop	6
Chapter 2	**Installing Norton Desktop for Windows**	8
	Inspecting the Distribution Package	9
	Making Floppy-Disk Backups	10
	Making Backup Copies in DOS	10
	Making Backup Copies in Windows	11
	Installing Norton Desktop onto Your Hard Disk	11
	Using the Install Program	12
	Making a Partial Installation	15
	Using Norton Desktop on a Network	16
Chapter 3	**Elements of Windows and the Desktop**	18
	Elements of the Windows Screen	19
	Using Different Kinds of Windows	19
	The Many Parts of a Window	20

	Viewing Multiple Windows	23
	Windows Icons	24
	Windows Menus	25
	Dialog Boxes	26
	Elements of the Desktop	28
	Desktop Windows	28
	Icons on the Desktop	29
	Desktop Dialog Boxes	29
	Browsing in a Desktop Dialog Box	30
	Using Wildcards in File Names	31
Chapter 4	**How to Get Help**	**32**
	Using the Help System	33
	Keeping Help Close By	36
	Annotating the Help Text	36
	Setting and Clearing Bookmarks	37

Part Two: The Desktop — 39

Chapter 5	**Organization of the Desktop**	**40**
	Opening and Closing Your Desktop	41
	Desktop Organization	42
	Opening Drive Windows	44
	Selecting a Drive	45
	Status Bar Information	46
	Speed Searches	46
	Tree, File, and View Panes	46
	Updating, Resizing, and Closing a Drive Window	51
	Managing Your Files and Directories	52

	Selecting and Deselecting Files and Directories	52
	Browsing for Files on the Desktop....................	53
	Copying and Moving Files and Directories	54
	Renaming Files and Directories	57
	Making a New Directory	58
	Deleting Files and Directories.......................	58
	Iconizing Files on the Desktop	60
	Changing File Attributes...........................	60
	Editing Files......................................	61
	Managing Your Disks from the Desktop	62
	Copying Disks....................................	62
	Formatting Disks..................................	64
	A Note on Disk Capacity	66
	Adding a Volume Label to a Disk...................	67
	Using the Desktop with a Network....................	67
Chapter 6	**Viewing and Printing Files**	**70**
	Using the Drive Window View Pane	71
	Viewing Files with the Norton Viewer	73
	Selecting Files	74
	Arranging Viewer Windows	75
	Viewing Spreadsheet Files..........................	77
	Viewing Database Files	78
	Viewing Binary Files...............................	79
	Viewing Graphics Files	80
	Searching for Text	81
	Configuring the Viewers	83
	Printing Files from the Desktop	84
	Using the Printer Icon.............................	84
	Using the Print Command	85

Chapter 7	**Launching Programs**	**86**
	Launching Programs from the Desktop	87
	Clicking on Group Item Icons	88
	Choosing Directly from the File Pane	88
	Selecting from the Launch List	89
	Using the Run Command	90
	Using the Run DOS Command	91
	Customizing the Launch List with the Launch Manager	92
	Establishing Associations	95
	Adding and Editing Associations	96
	Deleting Associations	98
	Invoking a Custom Startup Command	98
	Launching Unassociated Documents	99
Chapter 8	**Using Quick Access**	**102**
	Working with Quick Access	103
	Running Quick Access from the Desktop	104
	Running Quick Access in Stand-Alone Mode	104
	Opening Groups and Group Items	106
	Displaying Icons	108
	Working with Quick Access Groups	109
	Creating New Groups	109
	Creating and Changing Icons	114
	Working with Passwords	115
	Changing Properties	116
	Moving, Copying, and Deleting Groups	116
	Saving Your Changes	118
	Using the AutoStart Group	118
Chapter 9	**Customizing the Desktop**	**120**
	Customizing Desktop Menus	121
	Adding Standard Desktop Commands	126

Adding Your Own Custom Commands	127
Editing Your Commands	129
Working with Passwords	130
Selecting Preferences	131
Choosing the Prompt for a File Name	132
Picking Tool Icons	133
Refining the Control Menu	133
Choosing Other Options	133
Setting Confirmation Options	134
Managing Your Drive Icons	135
Customizing the Button Bar	137
Establishing Shortcut Keys for Commands	139
Configuring the Desktop Tools	141
Configuring Quick Access	141
Configuring SmartErase	143
Configuring the Shredder	145
Specifying the Default Editor and Viewer	146
Using the Desktop as Your Windows Shell	147
What's in the NDW.INI File?	149
Saving Your Changes	152

Part Three: The Windows Tools — 155

Chapter 10 Backing Up Your System — 156

Planning Your Backups	157
Why Should You Make a Backup?	157
When Should You Make a Backup?	159
What Kind of Backup Should You Make?	159
How Is a Backup Made?	160
On-Site or Off-Site Storage?	161
Configuring Norton Backup	162
Defining Your Hardware	163

Running the Backup Compatibility Test 164
Choosing Your User Level 166
Choosing Your Floppy-Drive Configuration 167
Selecting a Disk Log Method 167
Setting the Catalog File Path...................... 168
Saving Your Configuration 168
Backing Up Your Hard Disk........................... 168
Making a Complete Backup 170
Making a Partial Backup 173
Choosing Backup Options......................... 180
Comparing Files 185
Making a Complete Comparison 187
Comparing Specific Files or Directories 189
Working with Catalogs 190
Restoring Files....................................... 192
Restoring Specific Files or Directories 194
Restoring Files after a Hard Disk Failure............ 196
Choosing Restore Options 196
Automating Your Backups 199
Using Setup Files................................ 199
Making and Using Macros 201
Using Command-Line Switches 202
Using the Scheduler 203
Running Norton Backup in the Background 204

Chapter 11 Protecting Your Files   206

Using SmartErase to Recover Deleted Files............. 207
How SmartErase and Erase Protect Work
Together.. 208
Deleting Files with SmartErase..................... 210
Recovering Erased Files 211

Listing Old Files 214
Purging Deleted Files 214
SmartErase and DOS 5.............................. 214
Using Erase Protect on a Network 215
Obliterating Files with the Shredder................... 216
Examining Shredding Methods 216
Shredding Files and Directories 217
Using the Shredder in Stand-Alone Mode 218

Chapter 12 Examining Your System   220

Using Norton Disk Doctor for Windows 221
Using System Information 224
System Summary 225
Disk Summary................................... 229
Windows Memory................................ 230
Display Summary 233
Printer Summary................................. 234
TSR Summary 234
DOS Device Drivers 237
Software Interrupts 238
CMOS Summary 240
Processor Benchmark 241
Startup Files..................................... 242
Printing and Saving the System
Information Report............................. 243

Chapter 13 Enhancing Windows   246

Using SuperFind.................................. 247
Locating Files with SuperFind 248
Searching for Text 251
Advanced File Searches........................... 251

	Tips for Optimizing a Search	254
	Creating File and Location Sets	255
	Creating Batch Files from a File List	258
Working with the Two Calculators		260
	The 10-Key Tape Calculator	260
	The Scientific Calculator	267
Using the Screen Saver		273
	Choosing the Right Sleeper Image	274
	Setting Preferences	277
	Using a Password	278
	Selecting Wake Up Settings	279
Using KeyFinder		279
	Finding and Using Special Characters	280
	Using the KeyFinder Menu	282
	Using the Edit Menu with the Clipboard	284

Chapter 14 Advanced Desktop Utilities 286

Editing Desktop Icons		287
	Using the Icon Editor Workspace	288
	Working with Icon Libraries	293
	Working with Icons in Executable Files	298
	Creating Individual Icon Files	299
Making Appointments with the Scheduler		300
	Creating a Reminder Message	304
	Scheduling a Program	305
	Scheduling a Backup	305
Creating Batch Programs		307
	What Is a Batch File?	307
	Batch Builder and Batch Runner	307
	Examining the Batch Builder Window	308

		The Batch Builder Language	314
		Batch Builder Commands and Functions............	317

Part Four: The DOS Tools   327

Chapter 15	Using the Emergency Disk	328
	Windows Incompatibilities with the Emergency Disk Programs.......................................	329
	When and How to Use the Emergency Disk	330
	Running the Emergency Disk Programs	332
	Examining the Screen Layout........................	332
	Using the Keyboard to Select Items	333
	Using the Mouse to Select Items...................	334
	How to Get Help.................................	334
	Using the Norton Disk Doctor	336
	Using Speed Disk	336
	Using UnErase	337
	Using UnFormat..................................	337

Chapter 16	Diagnosing and Fixing Disk Problems	340
	Finding Disk Problems with Diagnose Disk............	341
	Examining Your Disk with Surface Test................	343
	Reversing the Repair with Undo Changes.............	348
	Customizing the Norton Disk Doctor..................	348
	Determining the Surface Test	350
	Making a Custom Message........................	350
	Deciding Which Tests to Skip	351
	Quitting the Norton Disk Doctor	352
	Understanding Disk Errors...........................	352

Running Norton Disk Doctor from the DOS
Command Line 353

Chapter 17 Optimizing Your Disk Drives 356

Precautions to Take Before Running Speed
Disk on Your Hard Disk 358
Unfragmenting Your Hard Disk with Speed Disk 358
Choosing the Right Optimization Method 361
Configuring Speed Disk 362
Speed Disk Information 367
Running Speed Disk 372
Speed Disk and Copy-Protection Schemes 372
Running Speed Disk from the DOS Prompt 373

Chapter 18 Recovering Files and Data 376

What Really Happens When You Delete a File? 377
What Happens When You Save a File? 378
Using UnErase to Recover Deleted Files 378
    Recovering Groups of Files 382
    Finding Erased Files 382
Manually Unerasing Files 383
    Viewing Clusters 387
    Recovering Partial Files 388
    Searching for Lost Data 389
Recovering an Erased Directory 390
Unerasing Files with DOS 5 392
Using Command-Line Switches with UnErase 393
Recovering from Formatting Problems 394
    Using UnFormat 394
    Recovering Data with an IMAGE.DAT File 395
    Recovering Data without an IMAGE.DAT File 397

Using UnFormat from the DOS 5 Command Line 398
Taking Care of Your Disks 399

Apppendix: Batch Builder Function Summary 402

Running Programs 403
    Run 403
    RunHide 404
    RunIcon 405
    RunZoom 406
Asking for Input 406
    AskLine 407
    AskYesNo 407
    ItemSelect 408
    TextBox 408
Managing Information 409
    Beep 409
    DialogBox 409
    Display 410
    ItemCount 411
    ItemExtract 411
    Message 412
    Pause 412
Managing Files 413
    FileClose 413
    FileCopy 413
    FileDelete 414
    FileExist 414
    FileExtension 415
    FileItemize 415
    FileLocate 416
    FileMove 416

  FileOpen 417
  FilePath 417
  FileRead 418
  FileRename 418
  FileRoot 419
  FileSize 419
  FileWrite 419
  IniRead 420
  IniReadPvt 421
  IniWrite 421
  IniWritePvt 422
Managing Directories 422
  DirChange 422
  DirGet 423
  DirHome 423
  DirItemize 424
  DirMake 424
  DirRemove 425
  DirRename 425
Managing Disk Drives 426
  DiskFree 426
  LogDisk 426
Managing Windows 427
  WinActivate 427
  WinArrange 427
  WinClose 428
  WinCloseNot 429
  WinConfig 429
  WinExist 430
  WinGetActive 431
  WinHide 431

WinIconize	431
WinItemize	432
WinPlace	432
WinPosition	433
WinShow	434
WinTitle	434
WinWaitClose	435
WinZoom	436
Managing Strings	**436**
Char2Num	436
IsNumber	437
Num2Char	437
ParseData	437
StrCat	438
StrCmp	438
StrFill	439
StrFix	439
StrlCmp	440
StrIndex	440
StrLen	441
StrLower	442
StrReplace	442
StrScan	442
StrSub	443
StrTrim	444
StrUpper	444
Arithmetic Functions	**444**
Abs	444
Average	445
Max	445
Min	446

Random	446
Handling System Control	446
Call	447
CallExt	447
DateTime	448
Debug	448
Delay	449
DOSVersion	449
Drop	450
EndSession	450
Environment	451
ErrorMode	451
Exclusive	452
Execute	452
Exit	452
Goto	453
If...Then	453
IgnoreInput	453
IsDefined	454
IsKeyDown	454
LastError	455
Return	455
SendKey	455
SKDebug	456
Version	458
WallPaper	458
WinVersion	459
Yield	459
Windows Clipboard Functions	459
ClipAppend	460

ClipGet	460
ClipPut	460
Mathematical, Relational, and Bitwise Operators	461
Precedence and Order of Evaluation	462
Predefined Batch Builder Constants	463
Batch Runner Error Messages	465

Index 467

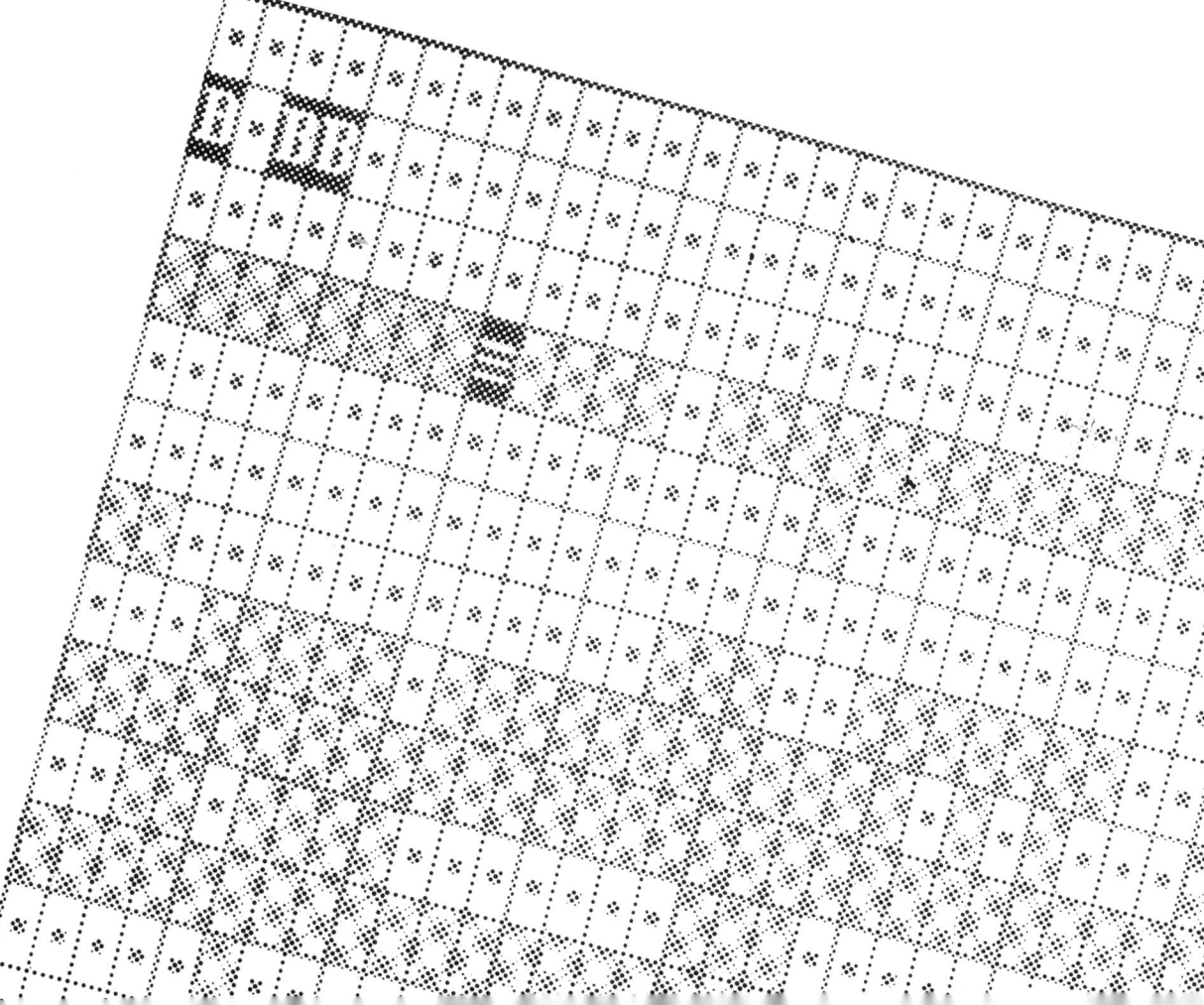

Introduction

This book is designed to help you get the most out of Norton Desktop for Windows in the shortest possible time. It is written with both the new and experienced PC user in mind and assumes a basic working knowledge of the Windows 3.0 environment, with only a modest familiarity with DOS. On the few rare occasions when you *do* have to use the DOS command line, all the steps are described in detail.

WHO SHOULD READ THIS BOOK

Understanding Norton Desktop for Windows is intended to meet the needs of a wide variety of readers. You don't have to be a computer expert to understand and use this book. Every attempt has been made to minimize jargon and present the material clearly and logically. This book will serve as your guide as you learn the fundamentals of the Desktop. All the examples are short and concise so you won't waste time trying to figure out a complex example.

You don't have to read this book from front to back in strict sequence, although you certainly can if you wish. Each of the four parts stand alone as discussions of individual components of the Norton Desktop package.

If you are new to the Norton Desktop, you should pay special attention to Part I—including the descriptions of the installation and how to get the most out of the user interface—before moving on to the more advanced material presented in later sections. If you are already familiar with Norton Desktop, you can probably move straight on to the sections describing specific problems and solutions.

HOW THIS BOOK IS ORGANIZED

This book is divided into four parts, containing a total of 18 chapters and one appendix. Each chapter provides examples on how to get the best out of your system.

Part I, "The Basics of Norton Desktop for Windows," presents essential information about the Desktop and your computer. It builds a strong foundation necessary for any user. You will learn how to install Norton Desktop on your hard disk and how to use the program interface.

Part II, "The Desktop," shows you how to use Norton Desktop to form your own personal computing environment, specifically designed to meet your day-to-day needs. Viewing and printing files, launching programs, and configuring the Desktop are also covered in detail.

Part III, "The Windows Tools," describes the extensive tool set in Windows, including how to use Norton Backup for Windows to back up essential files and directories, and how to protect files from accidental deletion. You will also learn how to examine all the dark corners of your computer to reveal both hardware and software information, how to locate lost files, and how to use the calculators, KeyFinder, and Sleeper. The last chapter in this section describes the advanced Windows tools: Batch Builder, Icon Editor, and Scheduler.

Part IV, "The DOS Tools," describes the programs you use to diagnose and fix problems with files or disks. You will learn how to rescue deleted files, how to improve the performance of your hard disk system by reducing or eliminating file fragmentation, and even how to recover the contents of your hard disk after it has been accidentally formatted.

The appendix lists all the Batch Builder commands and functions you can use to bring batch programming to Windows.

THE MARGIN NOTES

As you read through this book, you will come across margin notes that are prefaced by a symbol. There are three types of notes:

> This symbol indicates a general note about the topic under discussion. I often use it to refer you to other chapters for more information.

> This symbol denotes tips or tricks that you may find useful when using Norton Desktop. They might be shortcuts I have discovered or just important techniques that need to be emphasized.

> Pay close attention when you see this symbol in the margins. It alerts you to potential problems and often gives you methods for avoiding those problems.

THE FIGURES

The figures in this book were captured with the intention of providing the clearest possible tutorial for Norton Desktop. The default screen positions and sizes were used in most cases. Because you can configure Norton Desktop in many different ways, do not be concerned if you detect minor differences between the figures in this book and what you see on your own computer screen, particularly in the number or placement of icons.

PART ONE

The Basics of Norton Desktop for Windows

Part I introduces the Norton Desktop and describes how to install Norton Desktop on your hard disk. The Windows graphical user interface is reviewed and the additions and enhancements that the Desktop brings to Windows are also detailed. Part I closes with a description of how you can get help quickly anywhere in the Desktop.

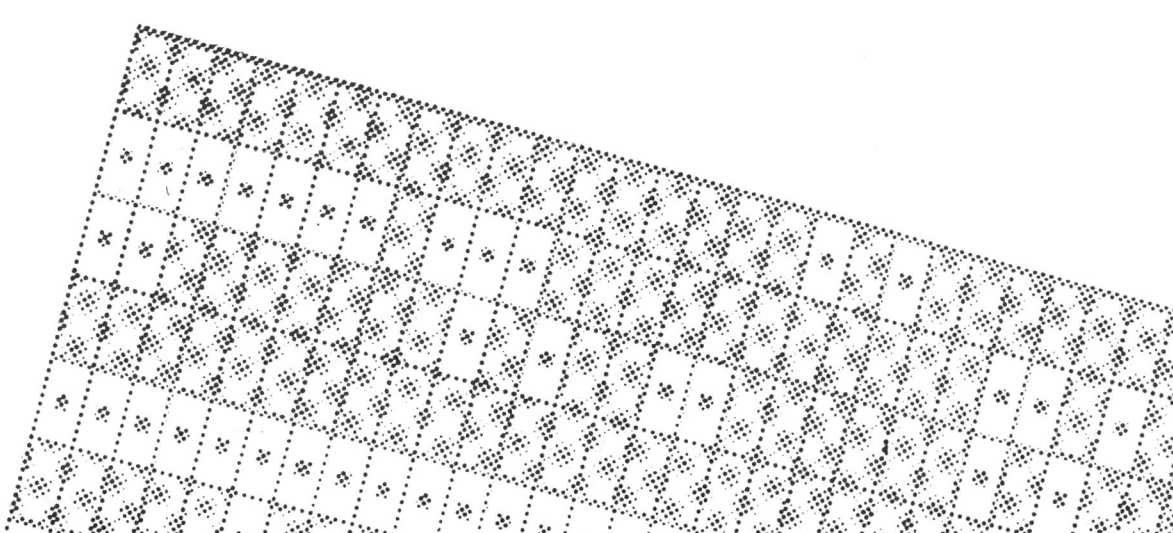

ONE

An Overview of Norton Desktop for Windows

NORTON DESKTOP FOR WINDOWS INTEGRATES THE functions found in the Windows 3 File Manager and Program Manager into a striking, integrated desktop display. Desktop for Windows also includes several important productivity tools—such as Norton Backup for Windows—and over 30 different file viewers, as well as several of the file- and data-recovery programs that have elevated the name of Norton to near-legendary proportions in the PC world. There are very few tasks in home or office Windows computing that you cannot accomplish more effectively with Norton Desktop for Windows.

NORTON DESKTOP IN BRIEF

The following sections provide a short description of the Norton Desktop package and all of the associated Windows and DOS programs.

THE DESKTOP

The Norton Desktop is a graphical environment that integrates the functions of the Windows Program Manager and File Manager, and then adds even more capabilities. Norton Desktop is not only faster and easier to use than the Windows managers, but you can use it as your normal shell in place of the Windows Program Manager. The Desktop shows disk-drive icons down the side of the screen; when you click on a drive icon, you open a window showing the disk's files and directories. You can view over 30 different kinds of files, including files made by most popular word processors, databases, and spreadsheets; you can even view .TIF graphics files. You can drag and drop documents directly onto the Desktop for fast, easy access, or drag documents to a printer icon for printing. You can also launch programs from the Desktop quickly and easily using several different methods. When you associate your document files with their application programs you need only click on the file's icon to open it.

THE WINDOWS TOOLS

In addition to the Desktop, there are several important Windows productivity tools in the package:

Norton Backup lets you back up files and directories to floppies or the hard disk, including network disk drives. You can schedule automatic, unattended backups that run while you are away from your computer, and you can view files before you back them up to make sure you have the right file.

SmartErase recovers deleted files and directories quickly and completely.

Shredder is a security program that obliterates files so that they can never be recovered. Use it to remove confidential information from your system.

Norton Disk Doctor for Windows tests your disks for problems that can cause you to lose data.

System Info lets you look into the dark corners of your computer, providing 14 screens of information on the hardware and software that make up your system.

SuperFind finds lost files and files that contain specific text.

The *Scientific* and *Tape Calculators* will stop you from reaching for your desktop calculator to perform those everyday (and sometimes not-so-everyday, highly complex) calculations.

KeyFinder displays all the characters in any given font on your system and shows you the keystrokes you need to type to generate them.

Sleeper is the Norton Desktop screen saver.

Batch Builder is a tool for creating and editing batch files.

Icon Editor creates new icons for use on the Desktop.

Scheduler lets you run programs at specified times.

All of these Windows tools can be represented as individual icons on the Desktop that you click on to start. Alternatively, you can start them from the Tools menu.

THE DOS TOOLS

Finally, there are several important DOS-based programs you can use for data and file recovery even if you cannot access Windows on your system:

Norton Disk Doctor finds and fixes all sorts of problems associated with hard or floppy disks.

Speed Disk analyzes the degree of file fragmentation on your hard disk and recommends an optimization method you can use to restore your hard-disk performance.

UnErase recovers deleted files using automatic or advanced manual recovery techniques.

UnFormat restores a hard disk when all data have been lost due to an accidental reformat.

In the chapters that follow I will explore Norton Desktop programs in detail, and—with examples where it is appropriate—show you how to use the programs in the package to get the most out of your computer.

> The programs on the Emergency Disk are essentially the same programs released as part of Norton Utilities 6 for DOS.

USING NORTON DESKTOP ON A NETWORK

You can use Norton Desktop from a networked drive, and you can use many of the more important programs on the file server itself. However, those Norton Desktop programs that are capable of modifying the file allocation table should not be run on the file server. This is particularly true of the programs found on the Emergency Disk: Norton Disk Doctor, Speed Disk, and UnFormat.

> Installing Norton Desktop on a network should be done by your network supervisor.

HARDWARE AND SOFTWARE REQUIREMENTS FOR NORTON DESKTOP

To use Norton Desktop you must have a computer capable of running Microsoft Windows 3.0 or later. This usually means a PC/AT, an IBM PS/2 286 or better, or a PC-compatible 286, 386, or 486 computer. You need 1MB of memory, although 3MB or more is recommended, along with a hard disk with at least 6MB of free space. You must also have Windows installed on your system. Norton Desktop, with its menus and dialog boxes, works best with a mouse. If you have a Microsoft mouse, you should be using Version 6.14 or higher of the mouse driver. If you have a Logitech or Dexxa mouse, check that you have Version 3.4 or higher of the device driver. Norton Desktop requires DOS 3.1 or higher, and is completely compatible with DOS 5. You can also install Norton Desktop on a Novell file server running NetWare 286 or 386 or on an IBM PC LAN server.

TWO
Installing Norton Desktop for Windows

THIS CHAPTER DESCRIBES HOW TO INSTALL NORTON Desktop for windows onto your hard disk. An essential preliminary to this installation process, however, is making backup copies of the original program disks; this protects you in case an accident occurs with the original disks.

INSPECTING THE DISTRIBUTION PACKAGE

The distribution package for Norton Desktop for Windows consists of either 5¼-inch 1.2MB floppy disks or 3½-inch 720K disks, so you can get the appropriate size for your system. Five manuals are included with the disks. *Using Norton Desktop for Windows* describes the complete Desktop package, except Norton Backup and the Batch Builder. These programs are described in separate manuals called *Using Norton Backup* and *Using Batch Builder. Using the Emergency Disk* describes the data recovery and optimization programs found on the Emergency Disk, and *Understanding the Windows Environment* is a short introduction to all the elements that make up the Windows graphical interface.

Check to see if there is a README.TXT file on the install disk. The README.TXT file contains the latest information about the package, information that may not be in the program manual. To examine this file before you install the package, open a Windows Notepad on README.TXT and maximize the window. Either read it on the screen or select Print from the File menu to send README.TXT to your printer.

You can do the same thing from the DOS prompt by using the TYPE command. Because the file is longer than one screen, use the MORE filter to display the contents of the file one screen at a time. With the install disk in drive A, type

TYPE A:README.TXT ¦ MORE

You can also use the DOS PRINT command to send README.TXT to your printer.

MAKING FLOPPY-DISK BACKUPS

As with any software you buy, the first thing you should do after taking it out of the box is make a backup copy. You should do this even if you plan to install the software on your hard disk. In the event the original disks are damaged or lost, the backups will ensure that the software is still available.

MAKING BACKUP COPIES IN DOS

To make a floppy-disk copy of the distribution package at the DOS command line:

1. Place the first distribution or *source* disk in drive A and a blank disk in drive B if you have two identical floppy-disk drives. If you have only one floppy-disk drive (or two non-identical disk drives), place the first distribution disk in drive A.

2. Type the following command at the DOS prompt if you have two drives:

   DISKCOPY A: B:

   If you have one drive, type:

   DISKCOPY A: A:

3. Follow the instructions on the screen. (With the one-drive procedure, you will have to swap disks to complete the copy.)

4. Repeat this procedure with each of the other distribution disks in the package.

MAKING BACKUP COPIES IN WINDOWS

To use the Windows File Manager to make copies of the distribution disks:

1. Insert the original disk in one drive and a blank disk in the other (it need not be formatted). If you just have one drive, insert the source disk into it.
2. Click on the source disk-drive icon.
3. Choose Copy Diskette from the Disk menu. If you are using two drives, choose the destination drive from the dialog box as well.
4. Follow the instructions on the screen; if you are using one drive, you will have to swap disks several times to complete the copy.

Repeat these steps for the other disks in the distribution set. Label the disks and put them away in a safe place.

After you finish copying the original distribution disks, you are ready to install the Norton Desktop package onto your hard disk.

INSTALLING NORTON DESKTOP ONTO YOUR HARD DISK

Do not install Norton Desktop on a hard disk that contains lost files or directories.

If you currently need to perform a recovery operation such as restoring a directory or unerasing a file, do not install the Desktop on your hard disk yet. Instead, use the Emergency Disk from the floppy-disk drive to recover the file (or directory). When the recovery is complete, you can proceed with the installation. If you were to install Norton Desktop without first recovering the file, the installation program might overwrite the area of the disk occupied by the erased file, making its recovery impossible. The following programs can be run directly from the Emergency Disk: Norton Disk Doctor, Speed Disk, UnErase, and UnFormat. They are described in Chapter 15.

USING THE INSTALL PROGRAM

Norton Desktop's installation program guides you through the installation procedure step by step, explaining the choices available at each stage. Be sure you have more than $5^1/_2$MB of free space on your hard disk if you plan to install the whole package.

> Do not attempt to install Norton Desktop while running DOS in Windows ("shelling" to DOS).

The installation program can invoke Windows as a part of the installation procedure, so if you are already in Windows, choose Run from the File menu in the Program Manager, type **A:INSTALL** into the Command Line text box, and click on OK.

If you want to install the package at the DOS command prompt, just type **A:INSTALL** and the installation program will automatically launch Windows for you.

> Don't forget to complete and send in the product registration card.

The first part of the installation process requires you to register your copy. Enter your name and company name into the two text boxes in the dialog box on the screen and click on OK. Install then searches for previous installations of the Desktop on your system.

The next window to open is shown in Figure 2.1. This window suggests the default C:\NDW directory for installation, but the choice is yours. You can use this name, or choose another that you like better. The Target Drive Status box lists the amount of disk space that is now free and estimates the space that will be free after you install Norton Desktop on the highlighted drive, assuming you make a complete installation. Percentage figures are also given. If there is insufficient space on drive C, choose another drive and the Target Drive Status window will change to reflect the space available on the new drive. Alternatively, you can choose Select to make a partial installation of the Desktop. Making a partial installation is described later in this chapter. The examples in this book assume that the Desktop is installed in a directory called NDW, so go ahead and accept the default name. To install the whole Desktop, click on OK to continue with the installation.

A small dialog box opens in the center of the screen, summarizing the files being copied and showing an analog display of the installation progress: as the programs are copied to the hard disk, the bar graph moves from the left (no files copied) to the right (all files copied). When all the files on the first floppy disk have been copied,

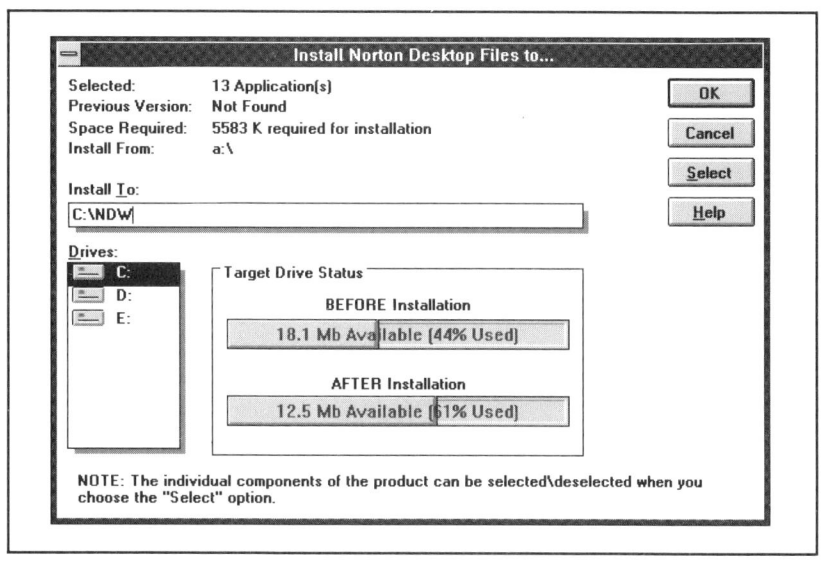

Figure 2.1: The Norton Desktop installation window, in which you choose the directory for installation

Install prompts you to insert the next disk. Don't worry, it'll know if you insert a disk out of sequence. Click on Cancel any time you want to halt the installation.

Several of the Desktop programs require you to add new commands to your AUTOEXEC.BAT file. For example, if you want to use Smart-Erase, you must add the commands EP/ON and IMAGE. The Modify AUTOEXEC.BAT File window offers you three choices:

>**Let Install modify the AUTOEXEC.BAT file.** This selection is the one you will probably choose. You can view or edit the additions to AUTOEXEC.BAT if you click on Edit or press Alt-E. This enlarges the dialog box and adds an editing window at the bottom of the screen that contains a copy of your current AUTOEXEC.BAT file. Click on OK to have Install add these changes to your file, or click on Cancel to stop editing and abandon these additions to AUTOEXEC.BAT. If you *do* have Install change your AUTOEXEC.BAT file, reboot your computer at the end of the installation process so that these changes can be implemented.

Save the required changes to a new file. Use this selection to create a new file called AUTOEXEC.NEW that contains the changes but leaves your original AUTOEXEC.BAT file unchanged. You can always rename this file later if you decide that you want to use it.

Do not make any changes. When you choose this option, no changes will be made to your AUTOEXEC.BAT file.

Click on OK when you have made your choice from this list. The install program now makes a tree file for each of your drives. This saves time and speeds up many Desktop operations that need this information.

The next window asks whether you would like to schedule automatic backups on your system. Choose Yes if you understand the Norton Backup program; otherwise choose No and refer to Chapter 10 for more information about it.

The *shell,* or user interface, of Windows is normally the Program Manager, but you don't have to use it—you can use Norton Desktop instead. By combining features from both the Program Manager and File Manager, the Desktop provides more functions, while maintaining all of your existing groups. The next window, shown in Figure 2.2, asks whether you want to use the Desktop as your shell.

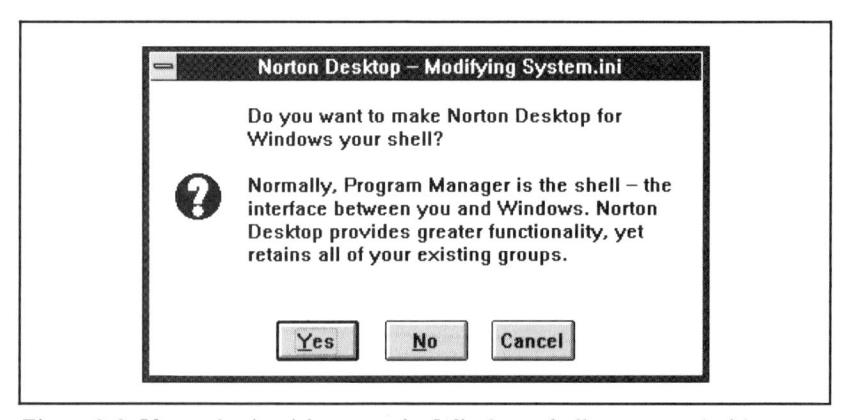

Figure 2.2: If you don't wish to use the Windows shell, you can decide to use Norton Desktop as your default shell

If you click on Yes, Install modifies your Windows SYSTEM.INI file to make Desktop your usual shell. Nothing actually happens to the Program Manager or the File Manager, but when you next start Windows, you will see the Norton Desktop rather than the Program Manager. In Chapter 9, I explain how to customize your Desktop and show you how to restore the Program Manager if you want to use it rather than the Desktop. Click on No to keep the Program Manager as your interface into Windows.

Finally, a notepad containing the README.TXT file opens so that you can check for late-breaking news that did not make it into the manuals. Your installation of the Desktop is now complete.

If you made changes to your AUTOEXEC.BAT file during this installation, you should leave Windows and reboot your computer to make sure these changes are loaded into your system.

It is a good idea to add the name of the directory you used for the Norton Desktop into your path statement. You can use the Modify AUTOEXEC.BAT File window in the Install program for this, or open a Windows notepad, or use EDLIN or EDIT in DOS 5. Edit your path statement so that it contains at least the following:

```
PATH = C:\;C:\DOS;C:\WINDOWS;C:\NDW
```

This assumes, of course, that your DOS files are in a directory on drive C called DOS, your Windows files are on the same drive in a directory called WINDOWS, and that you installed the Norton Desktop into a directory called NDW. If you are using different directory names on your system, use those names instead.

MAKING A PARTIAL INSTALLATION

If the Target Drive Status box has indicated that there is not enough room to install the complete Desktop on your system, you can make a partial installation, if you wish. If you'd rather not, you'll have to leave the installation program, delete some unwanted files to make room, and rerun the installation program.

Some of the individual applications are coupled together. For example, if you plan to make unattended backups with Norton Backup, you have to install the Scheduler.

To make a partial installation, click on Select to open the Norton Desktop Application Selection window shown in Figure 2.3. You have two options in this screen:

Select All lets you choose all the components of the Desktop for installation. This is the default setting.

Deselect All lets you choose which components to install. If you decide to install just a few pieces of the Desktop, click on Deselect All, then click on each element of the Desktop you want to install. When you have completed your selection, click on OK to continue with the installation. If you are not using a mouse, press Alt-D and press ↑ or ↓ to move through the list of applications. To choose a selection, press the spacebar when the highlight is over your choice; press the spacebar a second time on the same program to deselect it.

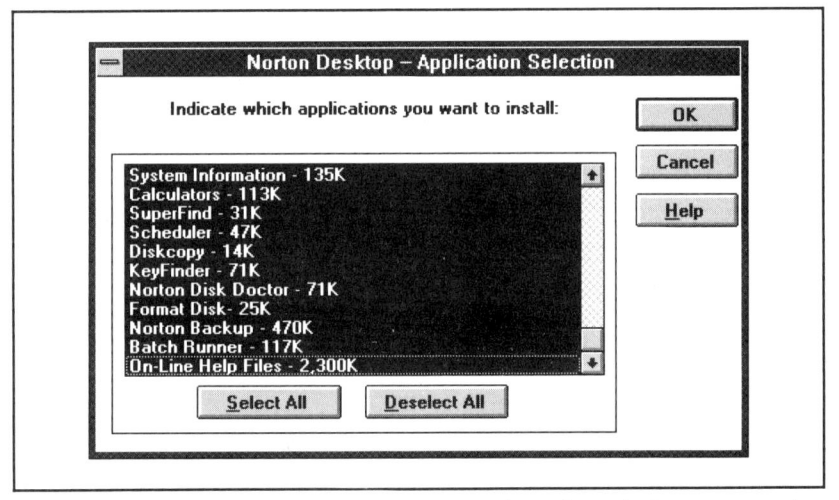

Figure 2.3: The Norton Desktop Applications Selection window

USING NORTON DESKTOP ON A NETWORK

SmartErase, Erase Protect, SuperFind, and Connect/Disconnect Net Drive all work with Novell networks. The drive windows work with all the networks supported by Windows 3.0:

- Novell NetWare
- Banyan Vines
- 3Com 3+Open and 3+Share
- IBM PC LAN
- LAN Manager

On a Novell network, make sure you are using updated versions of VPIX.386, VNETWARE.386, and NWPOPUP.EXE, all dated 9/20/90 or later.

Because networks are very reluctant to allow user files in the root directory, you will find that several Desktop files are created one level below the root to avoid this restriction. For example, the first time that Erase Protect is run on a network, it creates a hidden directory called TRASHCAN; also, tree files are located in a directory called NCDTREE. Both these directories are located one level below the root. Your system manager or network supervisor should assign the appropriate rights to users on the network; users should have all rights to the NCDTREE directory and users should have all rights except search rights to the TRASHCAN directory.

WHAT NEXT?

Now that your installation is complete, you can start to use the Norton Desktop. In the next two chapters I will complete my discussion of Desktop basics by reviewing the elements that comprise the Windows environment and describe how to use the help system.

THREE

Elements of Windows and the Desktop

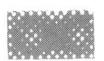

THIS CHAPTER FIRST PRESENTS A QUICK REVIEW of the major elements that make up a Windows screen. Then it goes on to describe the new elements that Norton Desktop adds to the Windows world. If you are new to a graphical user interface like Windows, the next section will be a quick introduction; if you are a seasoned Windows user, you can skip ahead to the section called "Elements of the Desktop."

ELEMENTS OF THE WINDOWS SCREEN

Windows always starts by displaying the Program Manager window. When you launch a program or open a document, a framed window opens. This is just like taking a file out of a filing cabinet, putting it on your desk, and opening it to begin work. And just as you can do at your desk, you can open several different documents at a time in Windows, first looking at one, then at another, without putting any of them away. This is in sharp contrast to normal PC work, where you have to close and put away one document before you can start another.

USING DIFFERENT KINDS OF WINDOWS

There are three kinds of window you will encounter, application windows, document windows, and group windows:

- *Application windows* contain the work area for the program that you are working with, perhaps Microsoft Word for Windows, or Write or Notepad in Windows. Most of your work will be in these windows. Figure 3.1 shows such a window from Paintbrush in Windows.

- *Document windows* are completely contained within an application window, and they share the application window's menu bar. Many Windows applications let you open several documents inside the same application window. Document windows have their own title bar, unless they are maximized, in which case the document title appears after the application title.

- *Group windows* contain icons representing application programs or documents. The Program Manager is a group window, as is the Norton Desktop.

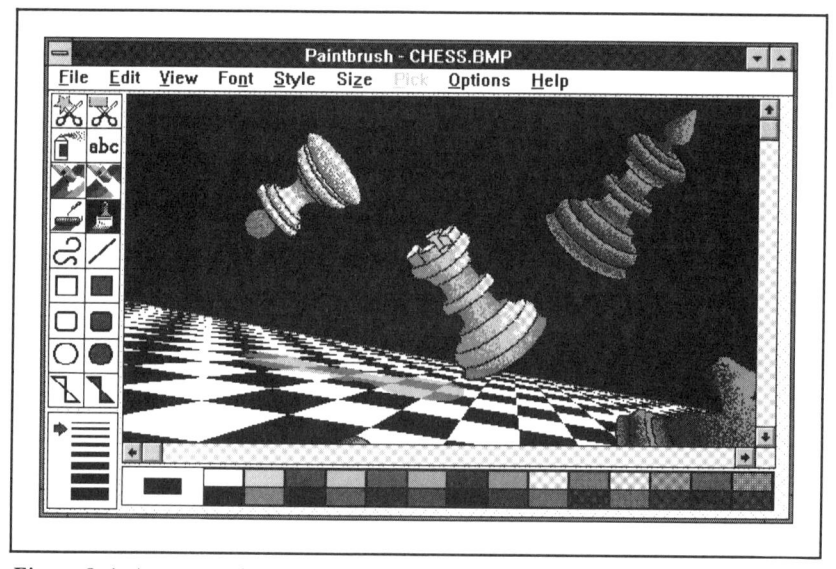

Figure 3.1: An example of an application window from Paintbrush

THE MANY PARTS OF A WINDOW

When you start Windows, the Program Manager window opens. We will use this window, shown in Figure 3.2, to help us detail the many parts of a window. Windows can contain many elements, but not every window has to contain all of them.

ELEMENTS OF WINDOWS AND THE DESKTOP   21

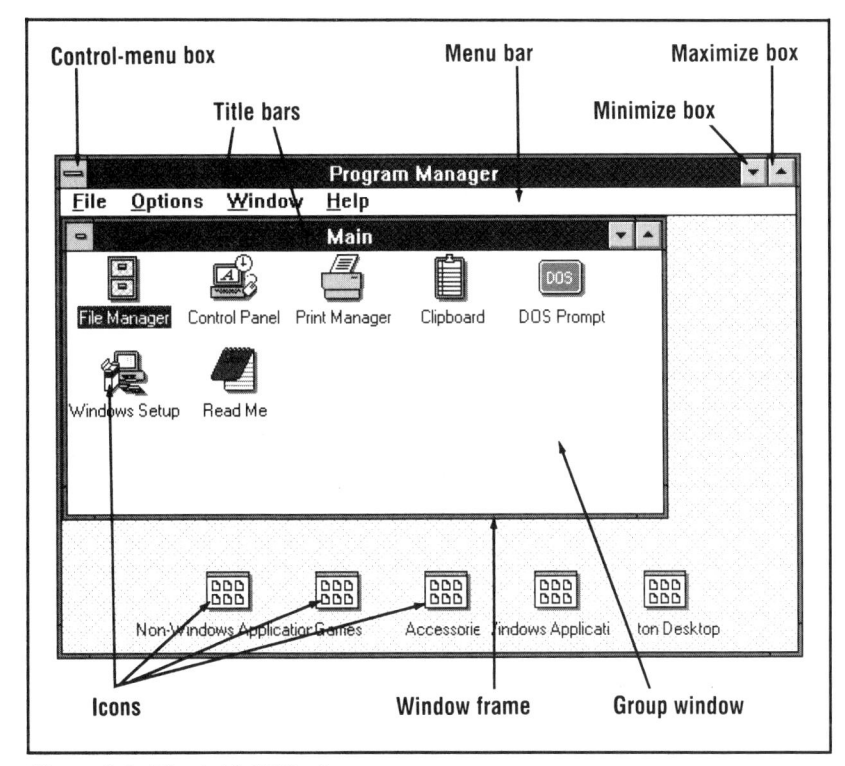

Figure 3.2: The initial Windows screen

Note that there are actually *two* windows open in Figure 3.2, the Program Manager window and the Main window. Here's a brief description of each of the main components:

- The *title bar* contains the name of the application and sometimes the name of the document or file you are working on. The title bar of the *active window* is usually a different color—or a different intensity on a monochrome screen. You may have many windows open at once, but only one of them can be active.

- *Minimize* and *maximize buttons* at the right end of the title bar are small buttons that control the size of a window. There are three main sizes for each window:

Maximized. The window takes up the whole screen. If you maximize a document window, it expands to fill the entire application window. This may or may not fill the whole screen, depending on whether the application window is maximized.

Minimized. The window shrinks to an icon. This is the smallest size a window can be, yet it can be easily opened again if you double-click on its icon.

Normal. The window is open and occupies a customized portion of the screen. This is also known as the *restored* size. When a window is maximized, the maximize button becomes the restore button.

- The *menu bar* contains the menu names, arranged across the top of the window.

- The *control-menu box* sits in the upper-left corner of each window and contains the Control menu. Click on the control box to open the Control menu—or, if you are using the keyboard, press Alt-Spacebar to open the Control menu in an application menu, or Alt-Hyphen to open it in a document window.

- The *scroll bars* are used when the entire contents of a window cannot be displayed all at once, as in the README.TXT file or in a long file listing. In this case, you will see a scroll bar down the right side of the window, with scroll buttons at either end and a scroll box in between. You may also see a horizontal scroll bar along the bottom of some windows. Click on the scroll buttons (the small arrows at the top and bottom of the scroll bar) to move through the document or list one line at a time, or hold down the mouse button to scroll continuously. The square scroll box indicates your relative position in the document or list; for instance, when it is in the middle of the scroll bar, you are positioned in the middle of the document or list.

- The entire window is contained inside a *frame*. To change the size of a window, carefully place the mouse cursor on the window frame—the cursor shape changes to that of a two-headed pointer when you are in the right place—and drag the edge of the window to a new location. You can also click the commands in the Control menu or use the minimize, maximize, or restore buttons to change the shape of a window.

VIEWING MULTIPLE WINDOWS

It is often very convenient to have several windows open at the same time. In addition to the window manipulation commands like Maximize and Minimize described previously, there are two other commands from the Desktop Window menu you can use to arrange your open windows:

> If you cascade too many windows for a single layer across the screen, another layer begins on the left side of the screen, overlapping the first layer.

Cascade aligns all the open windows so that the title bar and edge or corner of every open window is visible, like the windows shown in Figure 3.3.

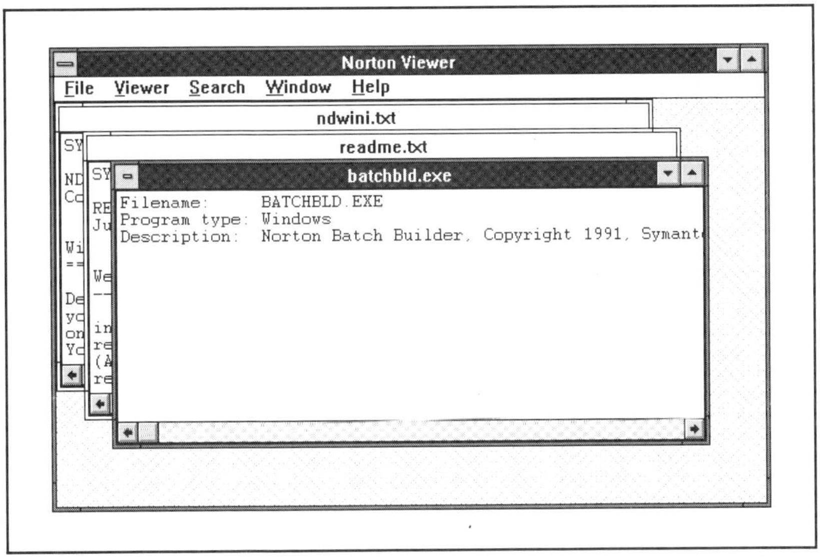

Figure 3.3: An example of cascaded windows

Tile changes the shape of all the windows so that a portion of each window is always visible, as Figure 3.4 shows.

These commands only affect the windows of the currently active application.

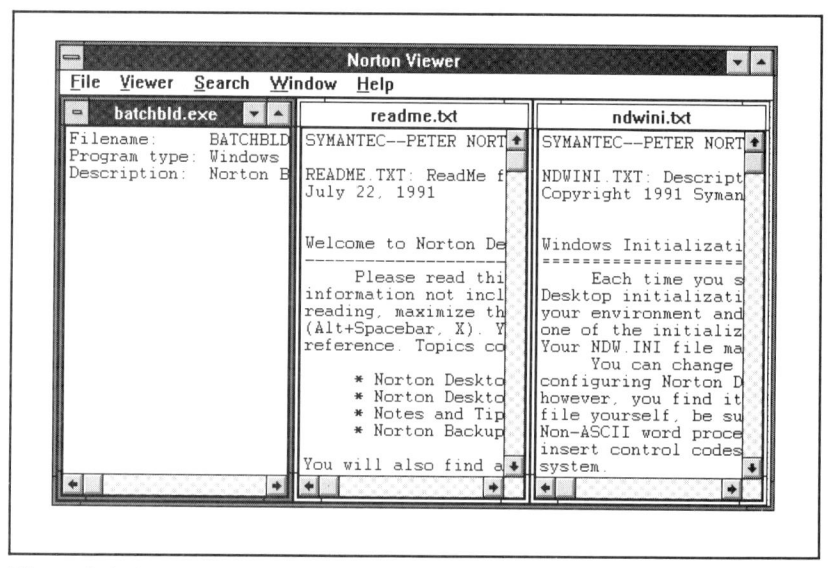

Figure 3.4: An example of tiled windows

WINDOWS ICONS

At the bottom of the Program Manager screen in Figure 3.2 you can see several small symbols with their associated names; these are called *icons*. Icons represent documents or applications that are not currently opened in a window. They might be waiting for you to work with them, or they may be applications that have been minimized or *iconized*. Icons can be associated with single application programs, or special icons called *group icons* can represent a collection of programs that you have grouped together for convenience. All of the icons in Figure 3.2 are group icons.

WINDOWS MENUS

> If a letter in a menu name or menu entry is underlined, press the Alt key and the underlined letter to select the item directly from the keyboard.

When you click on a menu name on the menu bar, a menu opens, listing the options from which you can choose. Similar functions are grouped together in a menu. For example, the File menu contains entries associated with manipulating files, while the Help menu has entries associated with using the help system, and so on. Press the Escape key, or click outside the menu area to close the menu when you have finished looking at it.

There are several indicators in menus that have a special meaning, as follows:

- *Grayed or dimmed command names.* If a command in a menu is grayed out or dimmed, it means that the command is not currently available. There can be many reasons why a menu item is dimmed; for example, if a window is already maximized, the Maximize command in the Control menu will be dimmed because it has already been selected.

- A *check mark* before a command means that the command is a *toggle*. A toggle is a special kind of command: rather like a light switch, it is alternately turned on and off each time you select it. If the check mark is present, the option is selected and turned on; if the check mark is not there, the option is not selected and it is turned off.

- An *ellipsis* (...) after a menu option indicates that you will be asked for more information—usually in a dialog box— to complete the command. (Dialog boxes are described below.)

- A *triangle* to the right of a menu option indicates that the command contains a submenu called a *cascading menu*. This cascading menu opens to the right of the current menu, so that you can select further options.

- Some of the menu options list *keyboard equivalents* to the right of the options that you can use instead of opening the menu and choosing that command. As an example, look at the File menu in the Program Manager and you will see that you can execute the Open command by pressing the Enter key, and that you can execute the Delete command by pressing the Delete key.

DIALOG BOXES

A *dialog box* opens when you select a menu command followed by an ellipsis. The dialog box may ask you to enter more information, or may post a warning message if you are about to perform a potentially dangerous operation, like deleting a file. There can be several parts to a dialog box, as follows:

- In a *text box,* you are asked to type text from the keyboard. Very often there will be text entered in already for you; if you want to keep that text, you can move on to the next element in the dialog box. To change it, just type in the new text. If the existing text is highlighted, your typing will write over the existing text; if the existing text is not highlighted, use the Backspace key first to erase it. If you click once on the highlighted text, the text cursor appears (a flashing vertical bar sometimes called an *I-beam*), which you can use to edit the existing text. Text boxes are used most often for specifying file names when you are loading or saving documents. They are also used to enter specific information, like an appointment date or the search string when you are searching a file for a particular segment of text.

- *Check boxes* usually offer a list of options that you can turn on or off. The check box itself is usually square, and when an option is selected, it contains an ×.

- A *list box* shows a column of choices. For example, when you are choosing a font for text display or printing, Windows Write shows you a list box containing all the possible selections. Click on the entry you want to use. If you are using the keyboard, use the arrow keys to highlight your choice, then press the Enter key to confirm your selection.

Information dialog boxes usually contain a large letter *i* (for *information*).

If the list box is too small to show all possible alternatives, you will see a scroll bar down the right side of the list box. Use this scroll bar to see all the selections.

- *A drop-down list box* initially appears as a box with the current or default choice highlighted. The arrow in a square box to the right of this opens up a list of choices when you click on it. If there are more selections than can be displayed at once, scroll bars are also provided.

- *Option buttons* appear in a dialog box to present a list of mutually-exclusive selections. Option buttons are round to distinguish them from check boxes, and you can only choose one from any given number at a time. Click on an option button to select it, or use the arrow keys from the keyboard. The option button that is currently selected contains a black dot; this is often the default setting. Any options that are currently unavailable will be dimmed or grayed out. Option buttons are sometimes called *radio buttons*.

- *Command buttons* make something happen immediately. The most common command buttons are OK and Cancel, found in almost all dialog boxes everywhere. One command button in a dialog box always has a thicker border; this is the selection that will be executed if you press the Enter key. Pressing the Escape key has the same effect as clicking on Cancel: the dialog box disappears and no action is taken. Some command buttons are followed by an ellipsis; if you select this button, the dialog box opens another dialog box so that you can choose more related settings. A command button that has a pair of greater-than symbols (>>) will expand the current dialog box when you select it to show more detailed options.

Not all dialog boxes have to contain all these elements, although you will find that many dialog boxes do contain most of them. For example, Figure 3.5, taken from the Printers selection in the Windows Control Panel, shows option/radio buttons, regular command buttons, a command button with an ellipsis, a command button with the two >> symbols, a dimmed command button, and a check box.

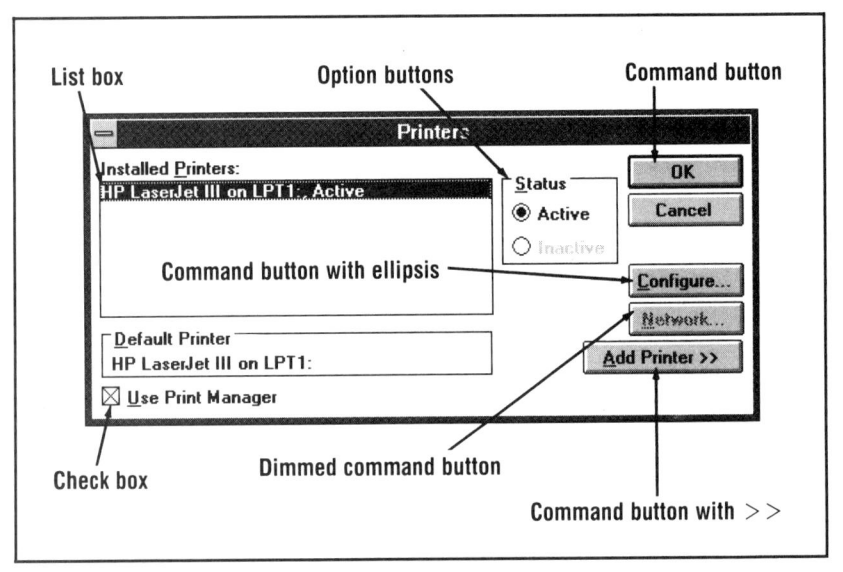

Figure 3.5: A typical dialog box

ELEMENTS OF THE DESKTOP

The Norton Desktop brings many new elements to the Windows environment, and in this next section we'll look at the most important ones.

DESKTOP WINDOWS

In addition to the normal application and document windows, Desktop adds new windows called *drive windows,* which let you access disks, directories, and files. When you open a drive window, it shows the contents, files, and directories of the drive you are working with.

Figure 3.6 shows a drive window open on drive C. The left side of the drive window shows a directory tree listing for the drive, and the right side of the window lists all the files in the highlighted directory. You can also open a view pane on a file at the bottom of a drive window, if you wish. The view pane is described in detail in Chapter 6.

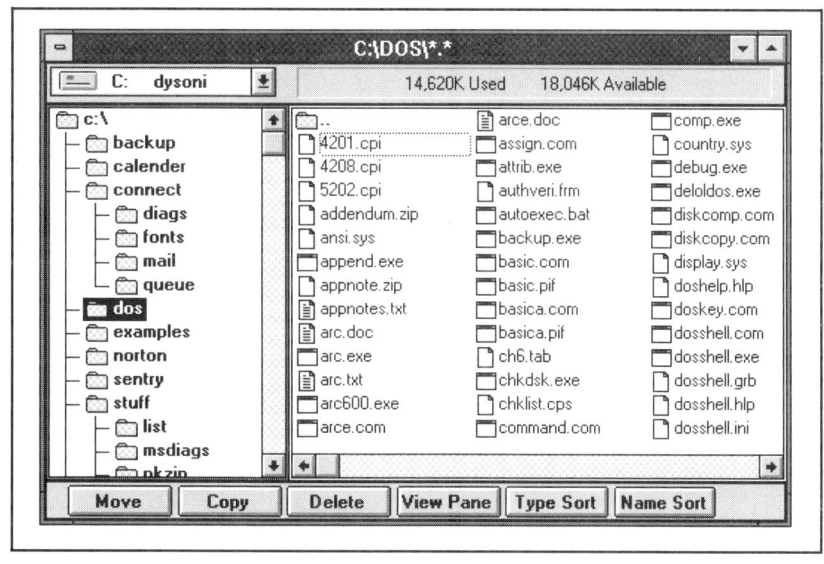

Figure 3.6: A Desktop drive window

ICONS ON THE DESKTOP

Norton Desktop introduces several new icons representing different kinds of disk drives, including both sizes of floppy disk, hard drives, RAM disks, networked drives, and CD-ROM drives. There are also icons for Desktop tools like SmartErase or the File Viewer, minimized Desktop drive windows, Quick Access objects, and other Desktop items. Many of these icons are unique to the Desktop.

DESKTOP DIALOG BOXES

In addition to the dialog box elements already described above, the Norton Desktop adds several more, as follows:

- A *spin button* is associated with a special type of text box that only accepts very specific entries. You can either enter a valid entry from the keyboard or use the spin button to cycle through the list of acceptable selections. Click on the top half of the spin button (the ↑) to move forwards through the list, or click on the lower half of the spin button (the ↓) to cycle backwards through the list. Spin buttons are often used with date or time entries, as Figure 3.7 shows.

- A *group box* helps to confine similar choices within a dialog box. Figure 3.7 shows a group box titled "Type of Action" that contains two option buttons. A group box usually contains either option buttons or check boxes.

- A *drop-down combination box* is a joint text box/drop-down list box. You can either enter your own information into the initial text box or choose from one of the default entries in the drop-down list part of the box. For instance, the Run command from the Desktop File menu includes a drop-down combination box for DOS command-line entries.

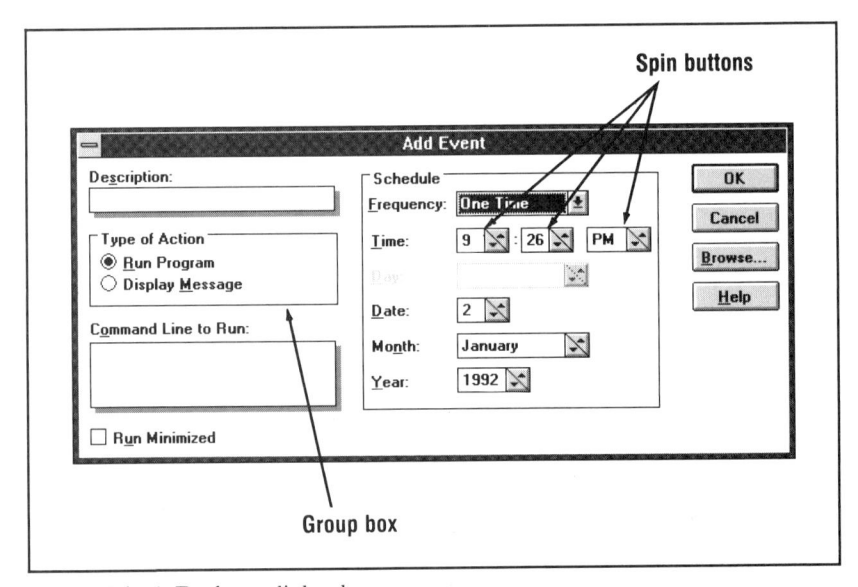

Figure 3.7: A Desktop dialog box

BROWSING IN A DESKTOP DIALOG BOX

Many of the Desktop dialog boxes contain a Browse command button. When you choose this button, the Browse dialog box opens to help you find a file to act upon. This dialog box looks slightly different, depending on the major command that it is associated with, but it always contains list boxes showing a file list, a directory list, and a drive list.

USING WILDCARDS IN FILE NAMES

You can use the DOS wildcard characters * and ? as placeholders when you want to specify a file or a group of files. These wildcard characters are most useful in text boxes when you want to select a range of files. The ? represents one character in a file name, while the * represents several characters. For example, *.TXT specifies all the text files in a directory while MEMO??.DOC specifies a numbered group of memo files.

FOUR
How to Get Help

THE NORTON DESKTOP HAS AN EXTENSIVE ONLINE
Help system that is available anytime you are using the Desktop.
There are several ways you can access it:

- Open the Help menu (press Alt-H) from the Norton Desktop menu bar, or from the menu bar of the Desktop application you are using, and select one of the options.
- Press F1 from any window to display the Help window, then choose a topic.
- Click on the Help command button available in almost every Desktop dialog box.
- Highlight a menu item that you want help with and press F1 to open a Help window that discusses it.

USING THE HELP SYSTEM

Let's start with the Help menu—it's always the menu farthest to the right on the menu bar. Open it and choose from one of the following entries:

Index lists all of the Help topics in alphabetical order.

Keyboard lists all the shortcut keystrokes you can use in the current application.

Commands summarizes the commands available in the current application.

Procedures lists the main features available in the current application.

Using Help is a guide to the Help system itself.

About shows the program version level, as well as technical information about your Windows session.

When you choose one of the selections from the Help menu (except About), the Help window opens, as in Figure 4.1.

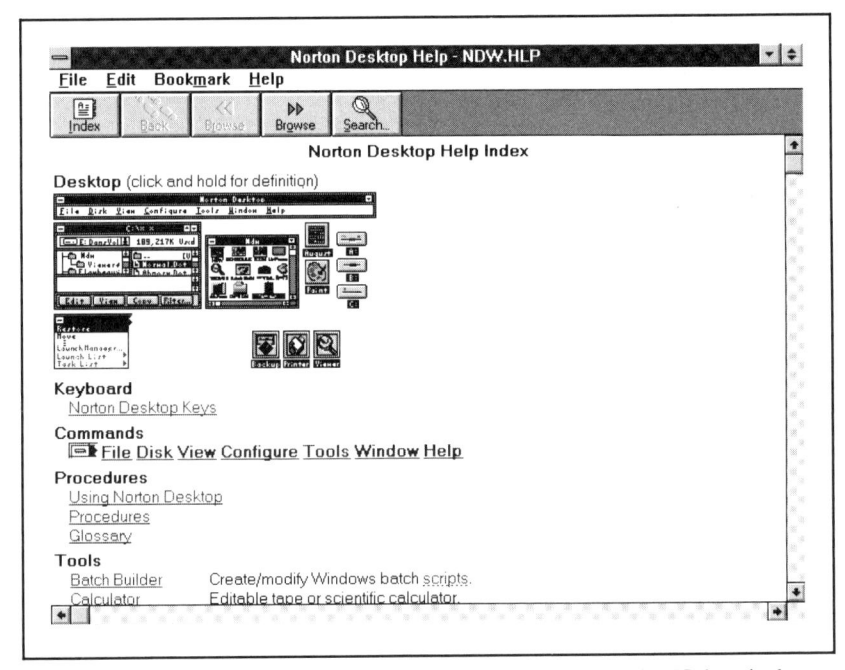

Figure 4.1: There are five buttons below the menu bar in the Help window

The Help window has several buttons across the top of the screen, used as follows:

- Choose Index to see a list of all the Help topics: Desktop, Keyboard, Commands, Procedures, and Tools. This is often the best place to start in the Help system, and is also a good place to return to when you are ready to work with the next Help subject you want to read about. When you have accessed several Help topics, one after the other, and you are several layers down in the Help system, you can always click on Index to return immediately to the top level of help.

- Click on Back or press Escape after displaying a Help entry to return to the previous topic in the Help system. The Norton Desktop keeps track of the last 15 topics you looked at. You move backwards through these topics one step at a time, each time you click on Back. Once you are at the first topic, and you cannot go any farther back and this button is dimmed.

- Click the forward and backward Browse buttons to look at the next or previous Help screen. If you have not yet chosen a Help category, Browse moves from category to category; if you have chosen a category, Browse moves from topic to topic within that category. When you reach the first or last Help screen on the current topic, the appropriate Browse button will be dimmed.

- Click the Search button to find help information on a specific subject. Enter the subject you want to search for into the text box, or choose a topic from the list box below, and then click on Search (see Figure 4.2). Each time Search finds a match, an entry is added in the Topics Found box. If more than one match is found, highlight the entry you want to look at and click on Goto to open that help.

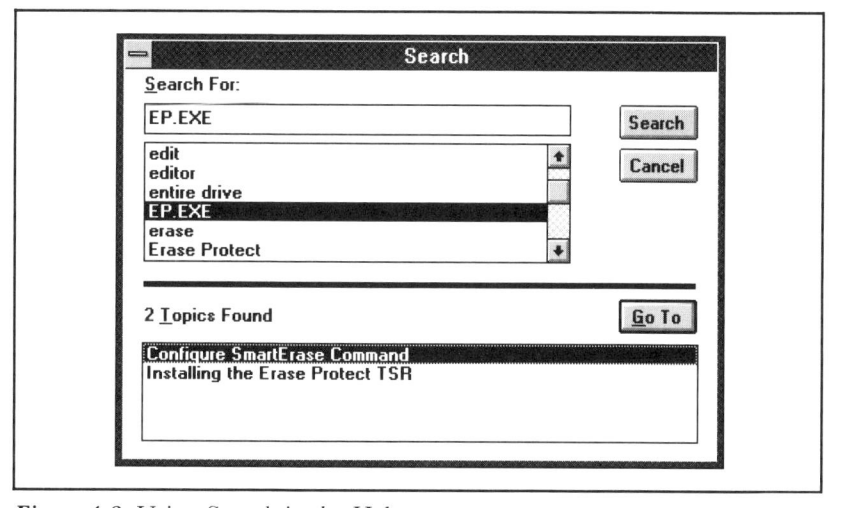

Figure 4.2: Using Search in the Help system

As you move the mouse across the Help window, the cursor may change to a pointing hand. When it does, you can click on that topic to see a related Help window. Any word underlined with a solid line is a cross reference; by clicking on it you can jump directly to the right part of the help information. If the word is underlined with a dashed line, or is a graphic, click and hold down the mouse button to see the help information displayed in a box. This box disappears as soon as you release the mouse button.

KEEPING HELP CLOSE BY

The Help system is very convenient to use and is always only a few clicks away. However, there are a couple of tricks you can use to make it even more convenient. Although it always comes up maximized, you can reduce the Help window in size and then resize or tile your other windows to fit. Alternatively, you can minimize the Help screen so that it becomes an icon at the bottom of your screen. That way, when you need to read the help information again, just double-click the Help icon to restore the Help window to its previous size. This is particularly useful to recall lists of important commands or other key information that is difficult to remember.

ANNOTATING THE HELP TEXT

You can always add a customized help note to the Help system, if you wish, such as a particularly useful piece of information you've gleaned from using the program and don't want to forget. Each Help topic can have one *annotation* attached to it, indicated by a paper-clip icon shown to the left of the Help topic title.

To add an annotation, follow these steps:

1. Select the Help topic you want to annotate from the Help Index.

2. Choose Annotate from the Edit menu in the Help system.

3. When the Help Annotation dialog box opens, type in your text. If you make a mistake, use the Backspace key to delete the unnecessary characters and continue typing until you have completed the entry. The text wraps at the end of each

line automatically, but you can end a line wherever you want by pressing Ctrl-Enter.

4. Choose OK when you are done and you will see the paper-clip icon appear to the left of the Help topic title.

To look at your annotation, click on the paper-clip icon to open the Help Annotation dialog box and read your note. If you decide to remove your annotation, click on the paper clip and select Delete when the Help Annotation dialog box opens.

If you want to leave a help note for another Desktop user, you can copy the text of a Help topic onto the Clipboard with the Copy command from the Edit menu. Then you can paste the text into a word-processing file with the Paste command in that application's Edit menu, for printing out later and distributing at your convenience.

SETTING AND CLEARING BOOKMARKS

You can mark your place in the Help system and go to it very quickly if you use a *bookmark,* in just the same way as you mark your place in a book. Use the following steps to mark an entry with a bookmark:

1. Go to the Help screen that you want to bookmark.

2. Select Define from the Bookmark menu.

3. When the Bookmark Define dialog box opens, click OK— or first edit the text in the Bookmark Name text box and then click on OK. The bookmark you have just created now appears in the Bookmark menu as bookmark number one.

To use the bookmark you have just created, open the Bookmark menu and click on the bookmark name you want to review. To remove a bookmark, select Define from the Bookmark menu, highlight the bookmark you want to remove in the list box, and click the Delete button.

To leave the Help system and close its window, click on the close box in the Help window, select Exit from the File menu, or simply press Alt-F4.

PART TWO

The Desktop

Part II shows you how to use Norton Desktop to form your own personal computing environment, specifically designed to meet your day-to-day needs. The Desktop integrates important Windows functions into a seamless operating setting. You will learn how to move, copy, delete, and rename files and directories using Desktop's drive windows. Viewing and printing files, launching programs, and using Quick Access and the Window menu are also described. The last chapter in Part II describes how to configure the Desktop.

FIVE

Organization of the Desktop

NORTON DESKTOP FOR WINDOWS IS A GRAPHICAL user interface, combining the best features of the Windows Program Manager and the Windows File Manager into a seamless whole. As a result, Norton Desktop makes managing files, directories, disks, and programs fast and easy. Although the package also includes programs for backup, file recovery, disk repair, and other important tasks, this chapter concentrates on what you see when you start Norton Desktop for Windows—the Desktop.

OPENING AND CLOSING YOUR DESKTOP

The install program loads Norton Desktop as the *shell,* or main user interface, into Windows, so that when you start Windows by typing **WIN** at the DOS prompt, what you see on the screen is the Desktop rather than the Windows Program Manager.

If you decided to keep the Program Manager as your user interface, you must type

WIN NDW

at the DOS prompt to start the Desktop. Alternatively, you can start Windows as you would normally, then double-click on the icon for Norton Desktop for Windows.

When it is time to leave the Norton Desktop, be sure that you first close all your open applications programs, then double-click on the Control-menu box or choose Exit from the File Menu. This returns you back to the DOS prompt.

42 UNDERSTANDING NORTON DESKTOP FOR WINDOWS

CH. 5

DESKTOP ORGANIZATION

When you start the Desktop, it occupies the whole of your screen, as Figure 5.1 shows. The Desktop contains many of the elements already described in Chapter 3, but we can go over them again very quickly. At the top of the screen is the title bar with the Control-menu box and the minimize button. Below is the menu bar, and below that is the desktop work area. This is where you do all your work, just like on a real desktop.

If your Desktop does not match Figure 5.1, you may have changed the configuration slightly.

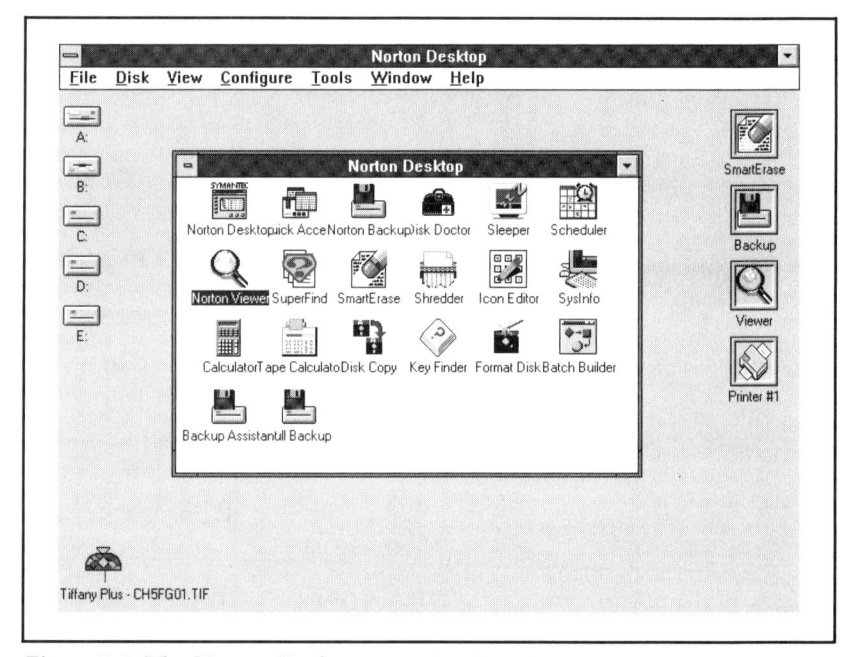

Figure 5.1: The Norton Desktop occupies the whole screen

Notice the Desktop drive icons down the (left) side of the screen. Figure 5.1 shows five drive icons; on your desktop you will see an icon for each hard and floppy drive on your system. RAM disks, network drives, and CD-ROMs, if you have them, are also indicated by icons.

Chapter 9 tells you how to manipulate these disk-drive icons.

ORGANIZATION OF THE DESKTOP 43

You may also see several program icons on the Desktop. Although it depends to some extent on which programs you told the install program to load, you may see an icon for your printer, as well as icons for some of the Desktop tools: SmartErase, Backup, and the Norton Viewer.

The Desktop contains seven menus, in addition to the Control menu, and you can configure Desktop menus as either full menus or short menus. When you start the Desktop for the first time, the short menus are selected as the default configuration; short menus contain only the most-often used commands. Full menus, on the other hand, contain *all* the options you can use on the Desktop. The left side of Figure 5.2 shows the full version of the File menu and the right side shows the short version. Use the first selection in the Configure menu to change from short to full menus. When short menus are in use the Configure menu option is called Full Menus, and when full menus are being used, it changes to Short Menus.

> You can change and customize the entries in the short menu to fit your own personal way of working; this operation is described in detail in Chapter 9.

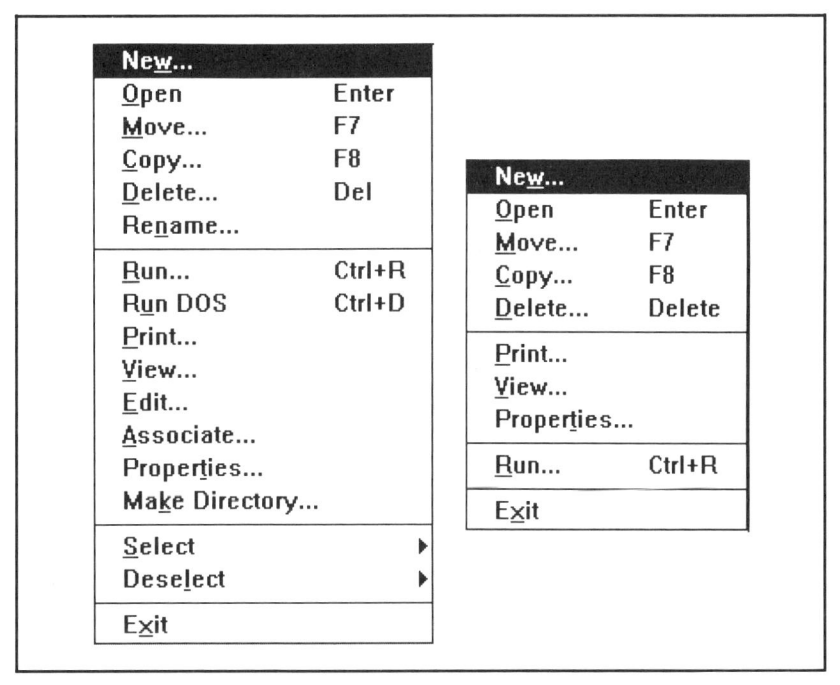

Figure 5.2: The full and short versions of the desktop File menu

CH. 5

OPENING DRIVE WINDOWS

One of the most important features of the Norton Desktop is the *drive window,* which lets you manage files, directories, and disks quickly and easily. It displays the contents of a disk as a directory tree and list of files; it may also show the contents of a specific file.

Just double-click on the icon of the drive you want to work with, and the drive window will open like the one shown in Figure 5.3. You can also open a drive window by selecting Open Drive Window from the Window menu. This opens a dialog box, which defaults to the current drive; use the Drive drop-down list box to select another drive, if you wish.

> You can have several drive windows open at the same time on the Desktop.

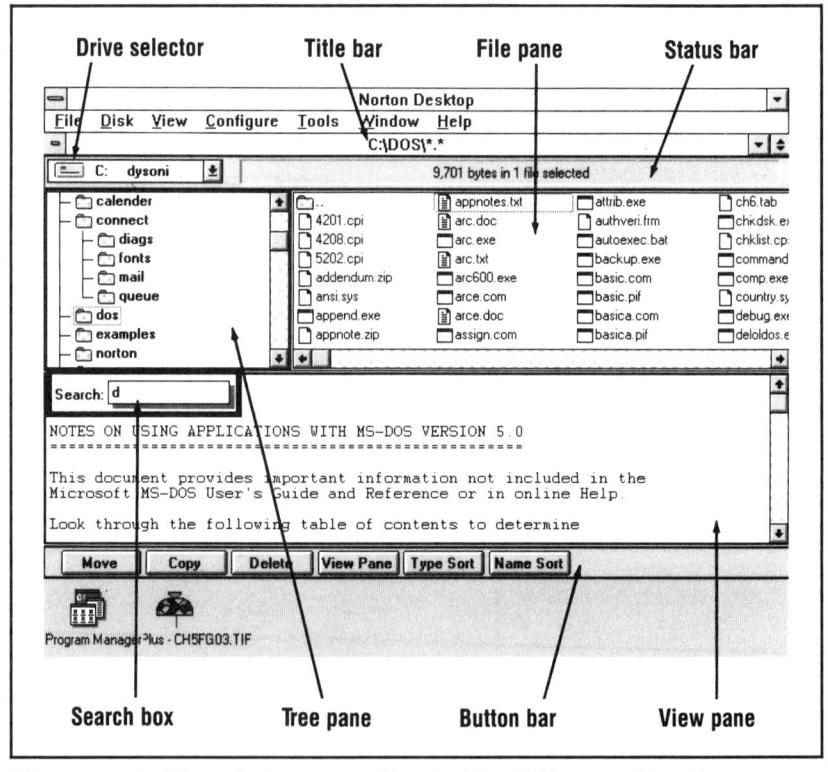

Figure 5.3: A drive window opened by double-clicking on drive C

The drive window in Figure 5.3 contains several elements not found in Windows, as well as the familiar title bar, Control-menu box, and minimize and maximize buttons:

- Use the *drive selector* to change to another drive.
- The *status bar* lists important information about the drive in the window.
- The *tree pane* lists the directories on the chosen disk.
- The *file pane* lists all the files in the chosen directory.
- The *view pane* displays the contents of the chosen file. Select a file and click on the View Pane button to open a view box across the lower portion of the drive window.
- The *button bar* at the bottom of the drive window contains six important functions for directory and file management. Using these buttons is described in the next section in this chapter. (For details on how to change these buttons, see Chapter 9.)
- Speed Search lets you go directly to the file or directory of your choice. The *Search box* appears just after you start to type a file's or directory's name (be sure the correct pane is active).

The active element of the drive window has a darker border; to move to another element, press the Tab key (to cycle through the elements) or click on it with the mouse.

SELECTING A DRIVE

The drive selector shows the letter and label (if the current drive has a label) of the *current drive,* the drive whose files and directories are listed in the tree and file panes. You can display the contents of a second disk in the current drive window; you don't have to open another drive window. Make the drive selector active, then type in the letter of the drive you want to work with. The tree and file panes are updated automatically to reflect this change. You can also make the drive selector active, then click on the drive selector prompt button (Alt-↓) and select a drive from the list.

STATUS BAR INFORMATION

The status bar lists important information about the selected drive. The default information includes the disk space used and the space available. When you select files from the file tree, the status bar changes to list the number and total size of those files; when you select directories, the status information shows the number of directories you selected.

SPEED SEARCHES

Speed Search lets you specify a directory or file quickly and easily from the keyboard. All you have to do is make the appropriate pane active—either the tree or file pane—and start typing the name you are looking for. As you start to type, the Search box opens below the active pane and the directory or file that matches the keys you have typed so far is selected. If there is no match, nothing is selected. Speed Search works by matching your keystrokes with the name in your tree or file pane. If you have many entries with similar names, you will have to enter more characters before the entry becomes unique. To find the next directory or file that matches the name you typed, press the ↓ key; to return to the previous match, press ↑. Press Enter to accept the selection and close the Search box, or press Escape to close the Search box without accepting the selection.

TREE, FILE, AND VIEW PANES

The three Pane selections in the View menu govern the current drive window, as well as all subsequent drive windows you open.

Drive windows contain tree and file panes by default—and can contain a view pane if you wish—but, as always in the Desktop, you can change this configuration to suit your needs. You might, for example, want to close one of the panes to make room for some information about another drive. You determine which pane(s) to show by selecting one of the first three entries in the View menu. Each command is a toggle: if it is on, you will see a check mark to the left of the menu item; if the command is off, there will be no check mark.

The Tree and File Panes

The *tree pane* shows a schematic drawing of your directory structure down the left side of the drive window. Simply click on a directory icon to see the files in it appear in the *file pane* to the right. Here you can select files for copying, moving, or deleting. You can also drag files from one file pane to another in a different drive window, and drag files onto the Desktop (*iconizing* them) so that you can work on them later, even if the drive window shows a different directory or is closed.

There are several selections in the View menu you can use to modify the display order or actually change which of the files are displayed in the file pane:

Filter   This opens a dialog box that lets you choose the types of files to display in the file pane, as Figure 5.4 shows. You can choose to list a particular kind of file by selecting a particular criterion:

> **All Files** displays all the files in the directory, bar none. This is the default setting.
>
> **Programs** limits the file list to displaying files that have .BAT, .COM, .EXE, or .PIF as the file-name extension. Other files are not displayed.
>
> **Documents** displays all the files associated with an applications program.
>
> **Custom** displays just about everything else. You can use wildcards in the custom box to extend the scope to groups of files. Click on the drop-down list box to see a list of the last ten custom extensions you entered.

You can also use file attributes as the basis for selecting which files to display. Files can have up to four attributes or properties, as follows:

- A *read-only* file cannot be written to or erased by the normal commands, but it can be used and read normally.

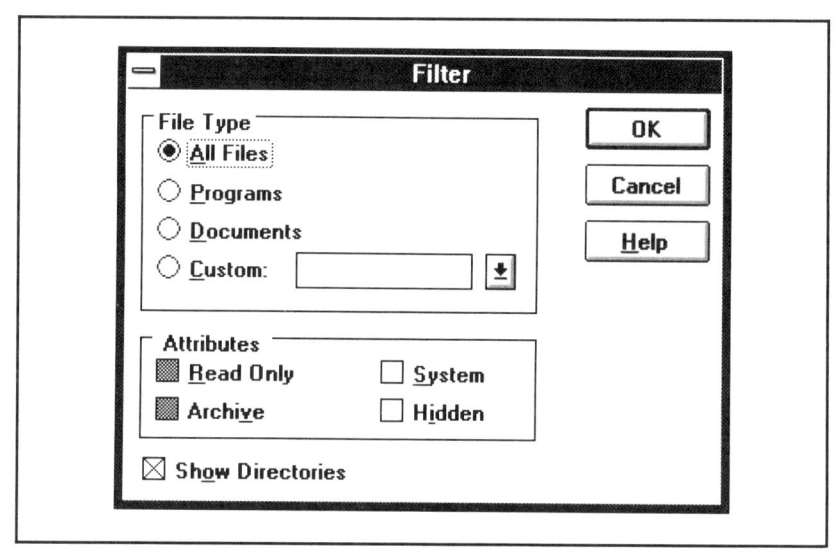

Figure 5.4: Use the Filter dialog box to choose the kinds of files you want shown in the file pane

- *Hidden* files do not appear in the usual listings, nor can they be deleted or run.

- A *system* file is a hidden, read-only file that DOS uses; it cannot be written to or erased.

- The *archive* attribute indicates that the file should be backed up; it has been changed or modified in some way since it was last backed up.

The Show Directories check box displays any subdirectory names in the file pane. Remove the check mark if you don't want to see them.

> File names are always shown in the file pane.

File Details　　This selects the amount of information shown in the file pane. The dialog box shown in Figure 5.5 contains the following selections:

> **Icon** displays a small icon to the left of each file name. Different icons represent directories, documents, text files or word-processor documents, and executable programs or batch

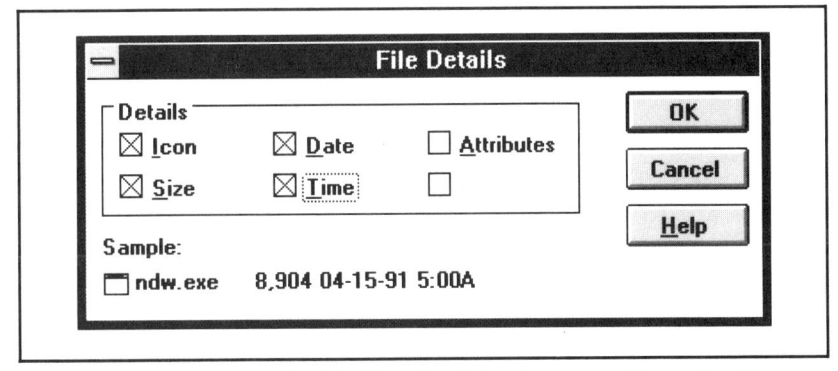

```
                    ┌─────────────────────────────────────────────┐
                    │  ═             File Details                 │
                    │  ┌Details─────────────────────────┐  ┌─────┐│
                    │  │ ☒ Icon    ☒ Date    ☐ Attributes│ │ OK  ││
                    │  │ ☒ Size    ☒ Time    ☐           │ └─────┘│
                    │  └─────────────────────────────────┘ ┌─────┐│
                    │                                      │Cancel││
                    │  Sample:                             └─────┘│
                    │  ▯ ndw.exe    8,904 04-15-91 5:00A   ┌─────┐│
                    │                                      │ Help ││
                    │                                      └─────┘│
                    └─────────────────────────────────────────────┘
```

Figure 5.5: You can use the File Details dialog box to configure the file pane display

files. If you turn the icons off, the file pane lists just the file names.

Size lists the size of each file in bytes.

Date shows the file-creation dates.

Time shows the file-creation times.

Attributes shows each file's attributes.

Directory shows the name of the directory.

A small display at the bottom of this dialog box shows you how each file will be displayed in the file pane. Making any of these selections will change the file pane from a multi-column list to a single column list.

Sort By   This determines the order in which the files in the file pane are listed, whether alphabetically or otherwise. Your choices are as follows:

Name sorts by file name. This is the same as using the Name Sort command button in the drive window.

Type sorts by file extension. This selection groups like file types together first, then sorts by file name inside the various groups. This is the same as using the Type Sort command button in the drive window.

Size sorts by file size.

Date sorts by date and time.

Unsorted displays the files as they were created, saved, or copied on your disk.

Ascending sorts files in ascending order: from *A* to *Z*, from small to large, or from old to new.

Descending is the opposite of Ascending.

Show Entire Drive This lets you see *everything*, all the files on the disk. The whole Desktop window changes into one large file pane, as Figure 5.6 shows, and the tree pane disappears. To return to the usual display, toggle Show Entire Drive off again.

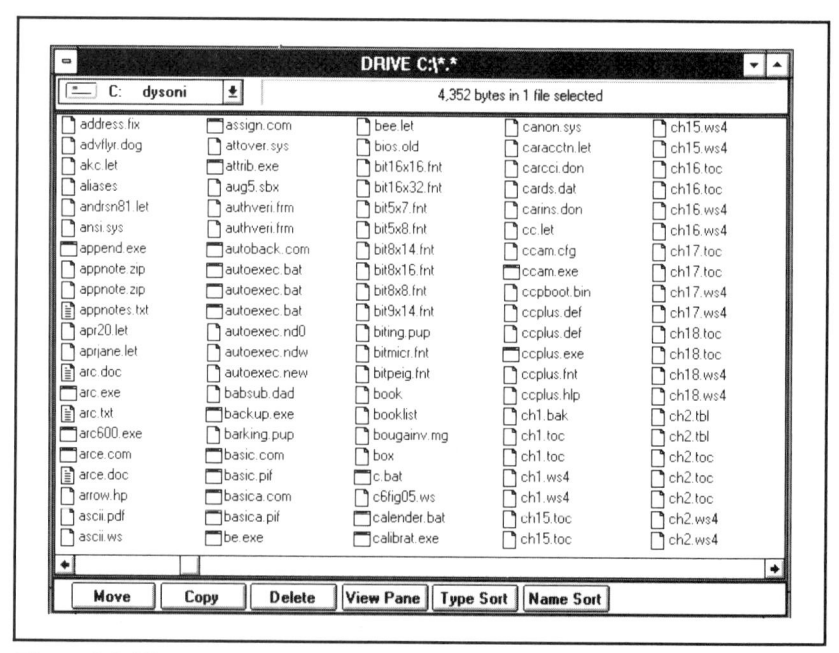

Figure 5.6: If you want to see as many files as will fit onto your screen all at once, choose Show Entire Drive

The View Pane

The *view pane* is the third component of the drive window. To use it, select a file in the file pane and click on the View Pane button or select View Pane from the View menu.

A third window opens across the lower portion of the screen, displaying the contents of the file without having to launch the application program that created that file in the first place. This means that you can examine the file to make sure that it is the one you want to work with and then launch the application program when you are sure you have the file you want. This simple operation can save you a lot of time if you work with some of the heavyweight applications programs that take a long time to start up—and if you load the wrong data file, that translates directly into wasted time.

UPDATING, RESIZING, AND CLOSING A DRIVE WINDOW

If you add or remove files or directories directly from the DOS prompt, the Desktop will not know about them, so you will have to update the display in the drive window by choosing Refresh from the View menu (or pressing F5). This operation reads the directory and file information from your disk into two files called TREEINFO .NCD and TREEINFO.DT, created in the root directory of the disk. It is much faster for Desktop to read the information it needs from those files than it is to go out and collect the information each time you open a drive window. You may also need to use the Refresh option when you change floppy disks in drive A (or B).

You can change the size of the three major components of the drive window by placing the mouse on a window border and dragging it. As you make one pane larger, the other pane will shrink because you are not changing the overall size of the window, just one of the internal components. To enlarge the whole drive window, click the maximize button; to shrink the drive window into an icon on the Desktop, click on the minimize button. When you are ready to work with the iconized drive window again, just double-click on the icon to return the drive window to its former size.

MANAGING YOUR FILES AND DIRECTORIES

Now that you understand how to work within a Desktop drive window, you can put that knowledge to work with some practical ways you can use the Desktop for file and directory management.

SELECTING AND DESELECTING FILES AND DIRECTORIES

Many times when you are using the Desktop for file or directory management, you must first select the file(s) you want to work with and then choose the operation you want to perform. The tree pane lets you work with directories and subdirectories; the file pane with subdirectories and files. To select a file, the file pane must be open.

To select a single file or subdirectory, click on the file (the icon or name) with the mouse; the highlight shows that the file is selected. To select a different file, just click on the new file and the highlight will jump to it. If you are using the keyboard, you can use the arrow keys as well as the PgUp, PgDn, Home, and End keys to move the highlight around the pane.

To select several adjacent files (or subdirectories) for an operation, just point to a file, click and hold the right button, and drag the mouse. Alternatively, select the first file in the sequence by clicking on the file, then hold down the Shift key as you click on the last file you want to include in the block. All the files in between, including the first and last files, will be highlighted to show that they have been selected. To select the same files using the keyboard, position the highlight over the first file, hold down the Shift key and use the arrow keys to move to the last file in the block, then release the Shift key. Again, all the files will be highlighted to show that they have been selected.

If you want to select several files that are not adjacent to one another, just click on each with the right mouse button. Alternatively, hold down the Ctrl key and click on each file you want to select (with either button). As you do so, each file will become highlighted in turn. With the keyboard, position the highlight over the first file you want to select, then press Shift-F8. Now use the arrow keys to move around the file pane, pressing the spacebar to toggle the highlight on and off over the file names as you go. Press Shift-F8 again to finish this selection process.

For some operations you will want to select all the files in a particular directory. The Desktop provides commands for this in the File menu. Choose Select from the File menu to open a cascading menu containing three selections:

All (Ctrl-\) selects all the files in the file pane.

Some (Ctrl-S) opens a dialog box that lets you choose the files to select by name. Enter the file names you want to select into the text box. You can also use wildcards with this box to include groups of files.

Invert reverses the current selection state; it selects those files that are not selected and deselects any that are.

To deselect all files, simply click on any file with the left mouse button.

To deselect one file from a series of selected files, either click on individual highlighted files with the right mouse button or drag the right mouse button across a group of adjacent highlighted files. Alternatively, hold down the Ctrl key and click on the file. From the keyboard, press Shift-F8, move to the file you want to deselect using the arrow keys, and press the spacebar. Repeat this process until you have deselected the right number of files, then press Shift-F8 again to end the deselection process.

There is also a cascading command called Deselect available in the File menu, with three options: All, Some, and Invert. These three commands work like the Select command described above. All deselects all the files in the file pane, Some opens a dialog box so you can specify the files you want to deselect, and Invert reverses the current selection.

BROWSING FOR FILES ON THE DESKTOP

Before we start to look at file and directory maintenance operations in detail, there is one more command button I should mention. Many of the operations described later in the chapter feature a dialog box that contains a Browse button. When you click on Browse, a version of the Browse dialog box opens on the Desktop. This dialog box may not always look the same—it depends on the command you are using it with—but it always contains three list boxes: a file list, a tree list, and a drive list. Figure 5.7 shows the Browse dialog box associated with the Run command from the File menu. You can use the Browse dialog box first to select the drive, then the directory, then finally the file that you want to work with. The file name is entered into the appropriate text box for you automatically. Click on OK or press Enter to call up the file into the dialog box you are in.

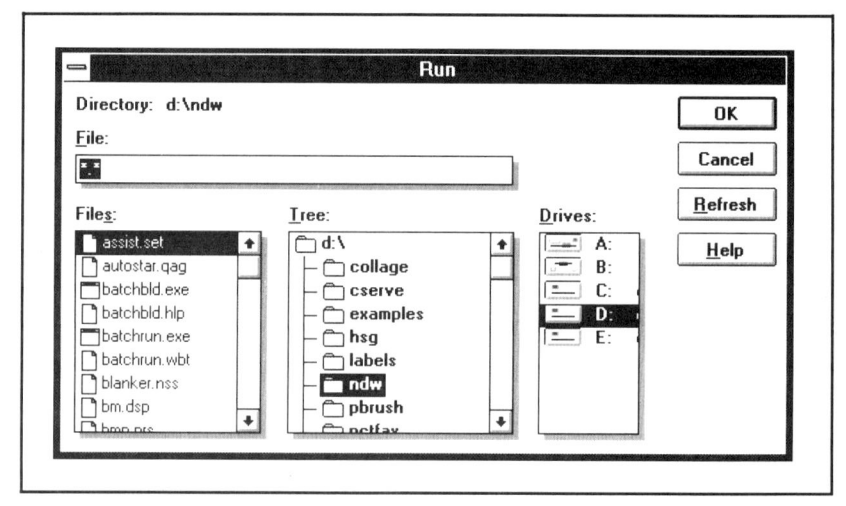

Figure 5.7: The Browse dialog box lists files, directories, and drives

COPYING AND MOVING FILES AND DIRECTORIES

You can use the Desktop to copy or move a single file or directory, but you can also use it to copy or move groups of files, or even a whole segment of your directory structure. Norton Desktop displays a warning message if you are about to overwrite a file with another file that has the same name. You can then choose whether you want to overwrite the file or cancel the move or copy operation.

Copying and Moving with the Mouse

For this example, let's assume you want to copy a directory and three associated subdirectories—along with all the files in these

> If you are moving or copying to a directory on the same drive, you may find it easier to manage the process by opening *two* drive windows, one for the source directory and another for the target directory.

directories—from drive C to the floppy disk in drive B:

1. Open a drive window for drive C and another drive window for drive B.
2. Select the directories you want to copy from drive C in the tree pane, so that you include all the files as well.
3. Drag the selected directories in the tree pane to their new location on drive B. Notice that the mouse pointer changes into a tiny directory tree as you move the mouse towards the drive B icon.
4. A dialog box opens to confirm your choice. Click on OK and a horizontal graph will show you the progress made by the copy operation. Click on Cancel any time you want to abort the copy.

> If you ever select files from the file pane, the mouse pointer will change into a single or multiple file-folder symbol, depending on whether you are copying one file or many files.

When the copy is complete, you will see that an identical directory structure has been created on the disk in drive B.

You can also copy files into the current directory on a disk by dragging the files you want to copy directly to the drive icon or minimized drive-window icon on the Desktop, without having to open the drive window for that directory. The same dialog box opens as before to confirm that you want to copy the files, and the same horizontal graph shows progress made by the copy operation. You can always open the drive window afterwards to check that the copy worked as you expected.

> Moving deletes the original, so use this operation with care.

Moving a file or directory is the same as making a copy and then deleting the original, except it is all done as a single process instead of two separate operations. To move files or directories, just follow the same steps as described above for copying, except hold down the Alt key as you perform the operation. If you don't hold down the Alt key, the move becomes a copy, and you will have to delete the original files or directories manually.

Copying and Moving from the File Menu

You can also use selections from the File menu to perform copy and move operations on files and directories. Just follow these steps

> The Copy and Move commands in the File menu refer to Quick Access objects if no drive window is open on the Desktop. See Chapter 8 for information on Quick Access.

to make a copy, substituting the Move command if you want to move them instead:

1. Either select Copy from the File menu, press F8, or click on the Copy command button at the bottom of an open drive window to open the Copy dialog box, as Figure 5.8 shows.

2. Type the name of the file you want to copy into the Copy text box; you can use wildcard characters to extend the copy to include groups of files. If you selected a file before you chose the Copy selection, its name is already entered into the text box for you. If you selected several files, the Copy text box is replaced by an entry that displays the number of files you selected.

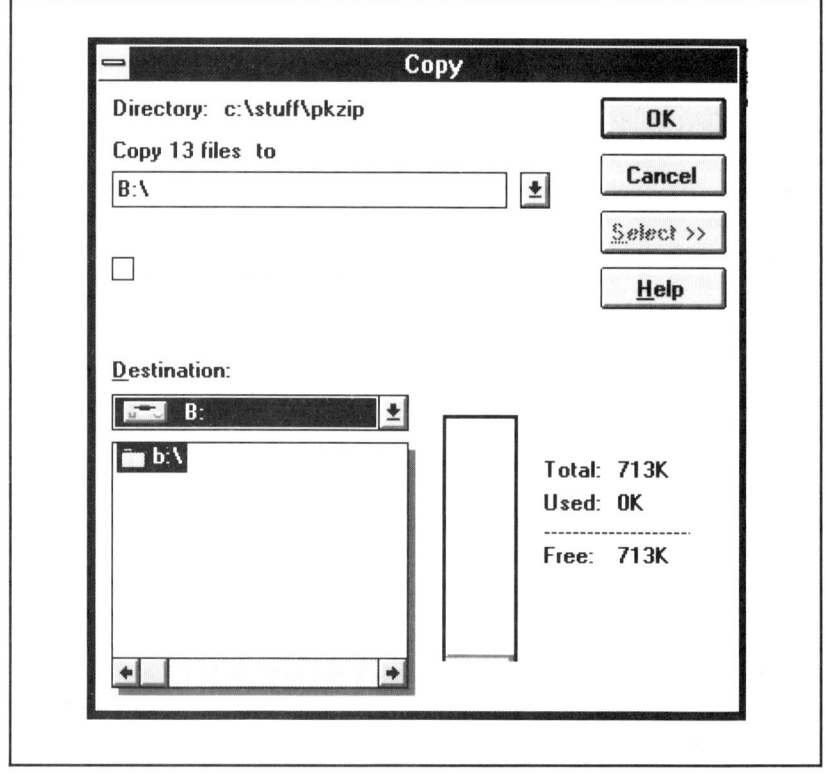

Figure 5.8: Use the Copy option from the File menu to copy files from one disk to another

ORGANIZATION OF THE DESKTOP   57

3. If you want to copy any subdirectories, click the Include Subdirectories check box.

4. Type the destination drive and directory name into the To text box. You can also open the drop-down list box to display a list of the destinations you have used most recently. This neatly allows you to avoid having to retype the destination information when you often repeat the same copy operation.

If you click on the Select button, the dialog box expands to show a drop-down list box for the destination drive and a tree list for the destination directory. A small graph indicates the amount of used and free space on the selected drive, as well.

RENAMING FILES AND DIRECTORIES

To rename a file, select the file in a file pane first, then choose Rename from the File menu. The dialog box shown in Figure 5.9 opens, showing the original file name; enter the new name you want to use into the To box, then choose OK.

A file name can contain up to eight characters before the period, and the extension can contain three characters after the period. The Rename dialog box also contains a Browse command button to help

> A file name and extension can contain any letters or numbers, except for the following characters:
> "\/[]¦<> + :*?, = ;
> or a space.

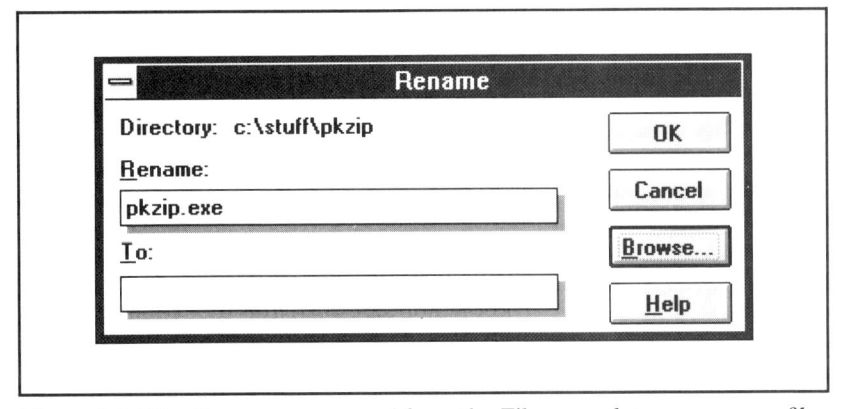

```
┌─────────────────────────────────────────────────┐
│ ─                    Rename                     │
│                                                 │
│   Directory:  c:\stuff\pkzip        ┌────────┐  │
│   Rename:                           │   OK   │  │
│   ┌─────────────────────────────┐   └────────┘  │
│   │ pkzip.exe                   │   ┌────────┐  │
│   └─────────────────────────────┘   │ Cancel │  │
│   To:                               └────────┘  │
│   ┌─────────────────────────────┐   ┌────────┐  │
│   │                             │   │Browse..│  │
│   └─────────────────────────────┘   └────────┘  │
│                                     ┌────────┐  │
│                                     │  Help  │  │
│                                     └────────┘  │
└─────────────────────────────────────────────────┘
```

Figure 5.9: The Rename command from the File menu lets you rename files or directories

you find the file to rename, in case you change your mind about your original selection.

Renaming a directory is exactly the same as renaming a file. First select the directory, choose Rename from the File menu, and type the new name into the dialog box. Directory names are also limited to eight characters before the optional extension.

MAKING A NEW DIRECTORY

You can make a new directory on any disk, as long as there is room for it, by using the Make Directory command from the File menu. Desktop, by default, creates the new directory as a subdirectory of the current directory, unless you tell it otherwise.

To make a new directory, just follow these steps:

1. Open a drive window on the drive you want to work with.
2. Select Make Directory from the File menu.
3. When the dialog box opens, type in the name you want for the new directory. The path name of the current directory is also shown in this dialog box.
4. If you want to create the directory on another drive or in a different directory, choose Select to expand the dialog box. Now you can choose the drive where you want to make the new directory and choose the parent directory from the tree display. Click on OK when you are done.

DELETING FILES AND DIRECTORIES

Deleting files and directories is an operation that you should always be careful about. It is very easy to delete a file, but not so easy to bring it back again. Norton Desktop contains several novel and creative solutions to this problem that are described in detail in later chapters: SmartErase and its companion program, Erase Protect, are described in detail in Chapter 11 along with the Shredder, while Norton's advanced file-recovery program, UnErase, is detailed in Chapter 18.

In this section I discuss deleting files using the Delete command in the File menu, which is the same as clicking the Delete button at the bottom of a drive window and pressing Delete on the keyboard. Follow these steps:

1. Select the file, group of files, or directory that you want to remove and choose Delete. When the dialog box shown in Figure 5.10 opens, the name of the file or directory is shown in the text box.
2. Click on OK to delete the file or directory.
3. A warning window opens, asking you to confirm that you want to continue with the deletion. Select Yes to continue, or—if you have selected several files for deletion—click on Yes to All. If you are absolutely positive that you want to delete all of the selected files, clicking on Yes to All avoids having to answer the same question for every file you selected. Click on No if you don't want to delete the file and click on Cancel to abort the whole delete operation.

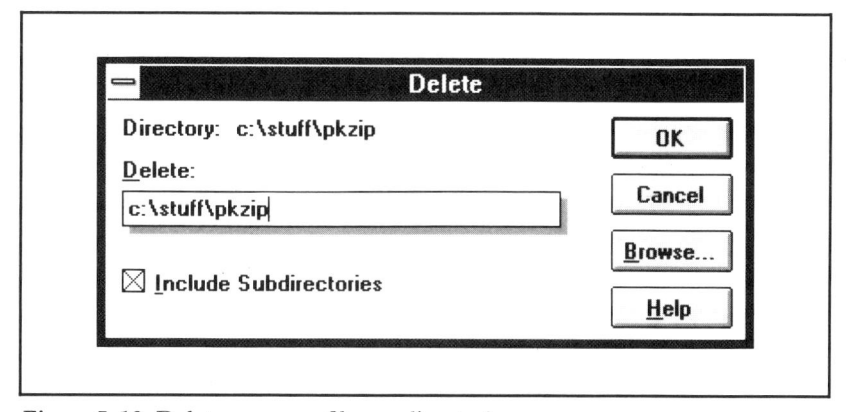

Figure 5.10: Delete removes files or directories

The Delete dialog box also contains a Browse command button so that you can search for the file you want to delete if it is not in the current directory or on the current drive.

You can also drag a file or directory directly to the SmartErase icon to delete it. The same "Are You Sure?" dialog box opens, and you must choose Yes or Yes to All to delete the file or directory. As I have already promised, there is more on SmartErase in Chapter 11.

ICONIZING FILES ON THE DESKTOP

A useful feature of Norton Desktop is being able to drag files and programs to the Desktop and leave them there as icons until you are ready to use them. For example, if it is budget time again and you know you will be using a particular Microsoft Excel spreadsheet file, drag it to the desktop so that it becomes a Desktop icon. Now when you want to access the file, just double-click on the icon. Norton Desktop will take care of launching Excel and opening the spreadsheet (but only if you have an association for the file extension).

Desktop icons stay on your Desktop until you close them; just click on the icon to open its Control menu and choose Close. This does not delete anything from the disk; it only removes the icon from the Desktop.

CHANGING FILE ATTRIBUTES

File attributes are characteristics or properties that you or DOS can assign to files. You can look at and change these attributes if you choose Properties from the File menu. A dialog box opens, showing the attributes already set for the file indicated by a check mark, along with information on the file size and the time and date it was last changed.

As an example, change to the root directory of drive C and select a file called IMAGE.DAT, then choose Properties from the File menu. You can see from Figure 5.11 that this file has the read-only attribute set, and it may or may not have the archive attribute set, depending on how often you back up your system.

Beware of changing many of these attributes, especially making too many files read-only. At first glance it may seem like a good idea because read-only files cannot be changed or deleted—right? Well, almost. Many commercial programs write the details of your computer hardware back into their own files. If you change these files to read-only and then reconfigure the program when you add new hardware to your system, the program will try to update its files, find

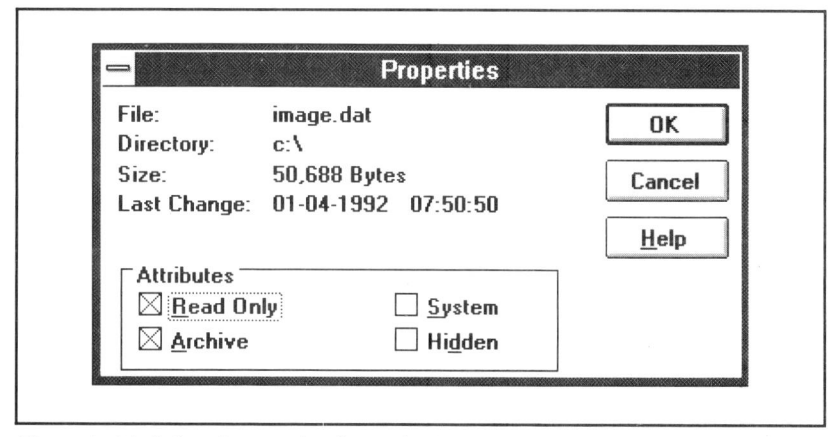

Figure 5.11: Select Properties from the File menu to look at or change a file's attributes

that they are now read-only, and report an error. Some programs display an understandable error message, but many programs are rather cryptic.

You should also resist the temptation to hide too many files, because the saying "out of sight, out of mind" is all too true. There is absolutely no point in hiding a program, because you will quickly forget that it is there—and when that happens, you will stop using it. If a directory is getting cluttered with files that you do not use often, do not hide them by setting the hidden attribute. Instead, copy them to another directory, or—better—back them up to floppy disk and keep them safe somewhere in case you change your mind.

EDITING FILES

The Edit command in the File menu launches the default text editor, which, initially at least, is Windows Notepad. This means that you can edit text files without ever leaving the Desktop. To open a file for editing, follow these steps:

1. Select the file in a drive window that you want to edit.
2. Choose Edit from the File menu to open a notepad containing the file you selected.

3. Edit the file using normal Notepad commands.

4. Save the file and exit from the text editor to return to the Desktop.

You can change this default editor to another program if you want to. I describe how to do this in Chapter 9.

MANAGING YOUR DISKS FROM THE DESKTOP

Several very important functions that were only available in the Windows File Manager are now available right from the Desktop's Disk menu. In fact, these commands have been enhanced in some ways over their File Manager counterparts. In the next few sections I will describe these commands and show you how to manage your disks.

COPYING DISKS

The Copy Diskette command in the Disk menu duplicates an original or *source* disk onto a *target* disk. This means that both disks must be of the same capacity. For instance, you cannot use Copy Diskette to copy files from a 360K floppy to a 720K floppy disk. If this is what you want to do, then you must use the Copy or Move commands and enter the wildcards *.* into the Copy text box. This specifies that you want to copy all the files from the source disk onto the target disk.

Another important factor to remember when you use Copy Diskette is that the copy process will overwrite any files that were on the target disk before you began the copy, and you will be unable to recover them. If it is important that you preserve those files, then—again—use Copy rather than Copy Diskette.

To duplicate the contents of one disk onto another of the same capacity, follow these steps:

1. Insert the source disk into the correct disk drive. If you have a dual-drive system where both drives have the same capacity, you can insert the target disk into the other disk

drive. If you have a single-drive system (or a dual-drive system where both drives have different capacities), you will be prompted to swap the source and target disks as necessary.

2. Select Copy Diskette from the Disk menu or click on the Disk Copy icon on the Desktop.

3. When the Copy Diskette dialog box opens, as shown in Figure 5.12, choose the source drive in the From drop-down list.

4. Choose the target drive from the To drop-down list box and click on OK to start copying.

5. If the target disk is formatted and contains files, a dialog box will open to give you a chance to change to another target disk and avoid overwriting these files. If you don't want to preserve the files, then continue with the copy. If the target disk is *not* formatted, a dialog box will open, giving you the chance to swap the disk for one that is. To format the target disk, click on OK. (You cannot copy files to an unformatted disk.)

When the copy is complete, a dialog box opens, asking if you want to make another copy of the same source disk. This second copy will be faster than the first because the Desktop will not have to reread the original source disk.

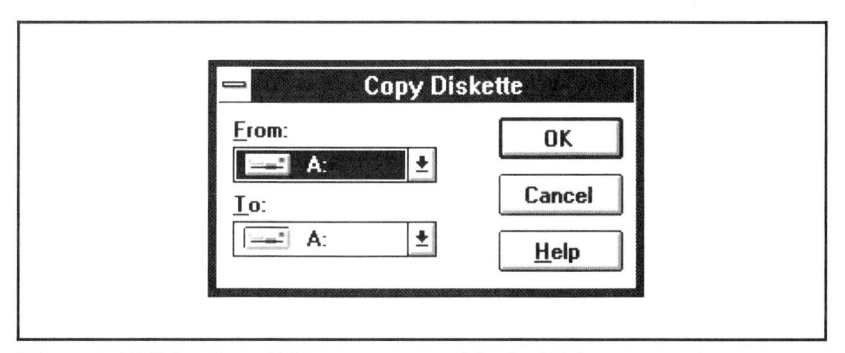

Figure 5.12: The Copy Diskette command in the Disk menu makes an exact duplicate of your original disk

CH. 5

FORMATTING DISKS

> You cannot format a hard disk with Format Diskette.

To format a blank floppy disk directly from the Desktop, follow these steps:

1. Insert a blank floppy disk of the appropriate capacity into the correct drive.
2. Choose Format Diskette from the Disk menu or click on the Format Disk icon on the Desktop.
3. When the Format Diskette dialog box opens (see Figure 5.13), select the drive letter, formatted size, and format type from the appropriate drop-down boxes. I will explain each of the three format types in a moment.
4. Click on OK to start the format.

You can make several choices when you format your disk: you can choose the format type, make the disk into a bootable disk, or save information that the UnFormat program can use in the event of an accident.

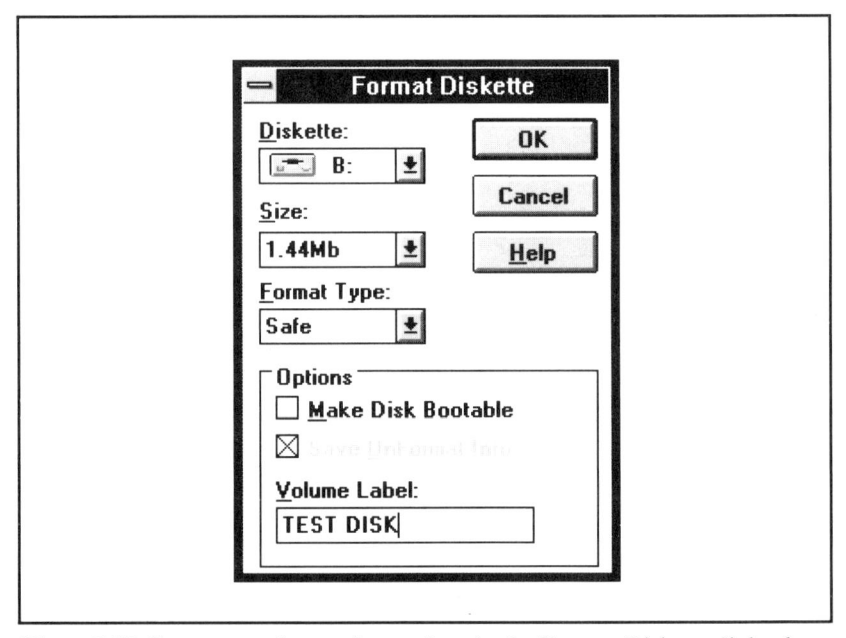

Figure 5.13: Set up your formatting options in the Format Diskette dialog box

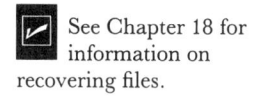

The format types are as follows:

> See Chapter 18 for information on recovering files.

Safe protects against accidental data loss because it formats the disk without overwriting the existing data on the disk. It saves information about the files on the disk in a special file that later can be used by the UnErase and UnFormat programs to reconstruct the original data on the disk before it was formatted. When you select the Safe format, the Save UnFormat Info check box is automatically checked for you. When you use this selection with a blank disk that has never been formatted before, you will be asked whether you wish to do a Destructive format.

Quick is extremely fast, because it only creates a new system area on the disk and does not overwrite the data area. You cannot use Quick on a blank disk that has never been formatted before. When you select Quick you also have the choice of saving UnFormat information or not, as you wish.

Destructive overwrites and destroys all the original data on the disk, making the data unrecoverable. This is equivalent to the standard DOS format operation.

If you are using Windows in standard mode or in 386 enhanced mode, you can switch to another application, leaving the format operation to continue in the background.

The other options include the following:

Make Diskette Bootable lets you create a bootable disk by installing the DOS system files on the disk once it has been formatted, so that you can use the disk to start your computer. This selection is optional. However, remember that the DOS files take up space on the floppy disk, so if you know you will never use the disk to start your system, there is little point in sacrificing disk space for them.

Save UnFormat Info saves information that can be used by UnErase and UnFormat in the event that you want to recover the files originally on the disk before you formatted it. This setting is not available with the Destructive format or with the Safe format option used on a new blank floppy disk.

Volume Label makes a special entry that can be up to 11 characters in length on each disk. Make the volume label descriptive: for example, you might label a floppy disk containing word-processor documents as "MEMOS," or a disk that contains spreadsheet files as "BUDGETS." This label is displayed in the drive windows on the Desktop. I describe adding a volume label to a disk later on.

A NOTE ON DISK CAPACITY

It is very important that you format disks at the appropriate capacity in your drive; otherwise, sooner or later, you will lose data. The normal capacities are as follows:

- 360K. These are the normal 5¼-inch floppies. They have a formatted capacity of 360K. Do not format these disks as 1.2MB disks or you will lose data.

- 1.2MB. These 5¼-inch disks are marked in some way as *high density*.

- 720K. This is the normal size for 3½-inch disks. They have a formatted capacity of 720K. Do not format these disks at a higher density or you will lose data.

- 1.44MB. Use this capacity for 3½-inch disks marked as high density disks. These disks have a small, square hole opposite the write-protect slide, so you can tell them apart from the 720K disks by their physical appearance. Do not format these disks at a higher capacity or you will lose data.

- 2.88MB. If you are using DOS 5 and have very high capacity 3½-inch disk drives, be sure to use disks marked in some way as *very* or *extra high density* in this drive.

Check the labeling on the outside of the disk box or on the disk label to be sure that you are using the correct capacity disk on your system.

ADDING A VOLUME LABEL TO A DISK

The Label Disk selection from the Disk menu lets you add or change a disk's volume label. A floppy disk has just one volume label, but a large hard disk that is divided into several partitions can have a volume label for each partition. To add or change a disk's volume label, follow these steps:

1. Select Label Disk from the Disk menu.

2. When the dialog box opens, the volume label, if there is one, is shown in a text box. Enter the new volume label into the text box and choose OK.

3. If you want to work with a different drive, click on the Drive prompt button to see a list of all the drives on your system and select a different drive.

USING THE DESKTOP WITH A NETWORK

If you are already logged on to the network when you start Desktop, you will see special disk-drive icons on the Desktop that represent the network disk.

The Desktop Disk menu includes the same two network commands that are in the Windows File Manager Disk menu for connecting to and disconnecting from a network. Having these commands available directly from the Desktop makes accessing your network a breeze. Just follow these steps:

1. Select Connect Net Drive in the Disk menu.

2. When the dialog box opens, the drop-down list box shows the next available drive letter because Desktop assumes you will want to use it for the file server.

3. Enter the name of the server and the network path you want to log on to. You can click on the Browse command button to see a list of file servers.

4. Enter your password, if it is required, into the Password text box and click on OK. Your password is shown as asterisks for reasons of security.

The information contained in the Browse dialog box is actually generated by the network itself, so the Browse dialog box for a Novell Network will look very different from the Browse dialog box for Microsoft's LAN Manager. Each network provides a Help function in the Browse dialog box, so use it or consult your system administrator if you need more information.

Disconnecting or logging off from the network at the end of your session is very simple. Here are the steps:

1. If your current drive is also the network drive, make a different drive current. You cannot disconnect from a drive if it is still current.

2. Choose Disconnect Net Drive from the Disk menu.

3. When the dialog box opens, choose a network disk from the list and click on OK.

By now it should be clear that you can perform all your file, disk, and directory work, as well as logging on and off the network, without ever leaving the Norton Desktop. In the next chapter we'll look at how you can print or view files from the Desktop.

SIX
Viewing and Printing Files

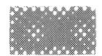

THIS CHAPTER DESCRIBES THE DIFFERENT METHODS you can use with the Desktop to view and print files. It used to be that if you wanted to check the contents of a particular file—to see whether it was worth keeping or not—you first had to load the application program that created the file and then load the file itself. With several files from big applications programs, this could take for ever. Fortunately, those days are gone. With the Desktop, you can view files in several different formats without invoking the application program that originally made them. Many different formats are available to help make sense of the data. The files are shown in what is called their *native format,* a format that closely approximates the way you are used to looking at the data. The Desktop contains formats or *viewers* for Microsoft Word, dBASE, and Excel, and you can view graphics files like CompuServe's .GIF files, Window's bitmaps, .PCX files, and even .TIF files.

USING THE DRIVE WINDOW VIEW PANE

The fastest way of looking at the contents of a single file is to use a view pane in a drive window:

1. Open a drive window for the disk.
2. Select the file you want to view from the file pane.
3. Click on the View Pane command button at the bottom of the window or select View Pane from the Desktop's View menu. The view window will open below the tree and file panes as a part of the drive window.

If the file is too large to be displayed all at once, use the horizontal or vertical scroll bars to move across the file. You can also drag the window border and make the window bigger, but this increases the size of the whole drive window, not just the view pane.

The view pane shows the contents of the file you just selected in the file pane. If you leave the view pane open and select another file, its contents will then appear in the view pane. You can only look at one file at a time, unless you open more than one drive window.

Desktop knows how to load the correct viewer format by looking at the file-name extension of the file you select. If Desktop decides that the file is a dBASE file, it will display the contents of the file in the database format; if Desktop decides that the file is a spreadsheet file, it will use the spreadsheet format; and so on. The NDW.INI file contains a list of these viewer/file-name extension associations. If the Desktop does not recognize the extension of the file you select, it uses the default viewer. You can force Desktop to use a different format by selecting Viewer from the View menu and then choosing Change Viewer from the Viewer submenu. The Set Default Viewer list box opens, containing the following selections:

> **Compressed Archives** displays files made by popular file-compression programs, such as PKZIP, PKPAK, SEA ARC, ZOO, and LHZ.
>
> **CompuServe GIF** displays .GIF (Graphics Interchange Format) files that you have downloaded from the CompuServe bulletin board.
>
> **dBASE** displays files made by dBASE or by programs that make a dBASE-compatible file format.
>
> **Documents & Text** displays text files like WIN.INI, AUTOEXEC.BAT, or CONFIG.SYS, as well as word-processor files made by Microsoft Word, Word for Windows, Windows Write and Notepad, WordPerfect, Ami, and Ami Pro. You can use it to display files made by other word processors, too, but in some cases not all formatting information in the file will be translated exactly. Non-displayable information will be represented by a solid rectangular character in the viewer.

Hex Dump can display any file, but is best suited for displaying binary files.

Lotus 1-2-3 displays the contents of files made by Lotus 1-2-3, releases 1 and 2. You can also view files made by Quattro Pro, as well as any other files from programs that make Lotus-compatible files.

Microsoft Excel displays Microsoft Excel files.

PaintBrush (PCX) displays files made by PaintBrush and many other programs that make .PCX format graphics files.

Programs displays particular information from DOS and Windows executable program files.

TIFF (Grayscale & Color) displays files in Tagged Image File format (.TIF), a versatile format for representing and transferring graphics images.

Windows Bitmaps displays Windows bitmaps; you can also look at OS/2 bitmaps using this viewer.

Windows Icons displays Windows icons. You can also view icon library files (.NIL and .ICL) with this viewer.

WordPerfect Image Graphics is specifically for WordPerfect graphics images.

Make your selection from the list and click on OK to return to the viewer. The contents of the file are now displayed in the new viewer format.

VIEWING FILES WITH THE NORTON VIEWER

The view pane is fine for some tasks, but if you want to look at more than one file at a time, the Norton Viewer is what you need. For example, you might want to open two database or spreadsheet files at the same time to be sure that they contain the information you are looking for, before you spend time working on them further.

There are several ways you can start the Norton Viewer to look at a file:

- Open a drive window, select a file, and drag it to the Viewer icon at the side of the Desktop. Release the mouse button when the document icon is over the Norton Viewer icon to open the Viewer. You can open several files by dragging them to the Viewer in this way.

- Double-click on the Norton Viewer icon in the Desktop group window and select a file using Open from the Viewer's File menu.

- Choose Run from the Desktop File menu and enter **NVIEWER** into the command-line text box, then select a file using the Viewer's File menu.

Once you have opened a view window, you can use the normal controls—like the maximize button—to open the window to full size, and you can move or resize your windows, too, if you wish.

SELECTING FILES

To select a file from inside the Norton Viewer:

1. Choose Open from the Viewer's File menu.

2. Select the file you want to work with by using the file, tree, and drive list boxes in the Open File dialog box. You can also type the name of the file directly into the File text box.

3. When you have made your choice, click on OK.

Figure 6.1 shows the Open File dialog box. If you open several files at the same time, each file is contained in its own separate window within the Viewer window. The Norton Viewer cascades these windows by default, so that the active window overlays all of the other windows. There are several commands that you can use from the Norton Viewer Window menu to manage your view windows and place them where you wish.

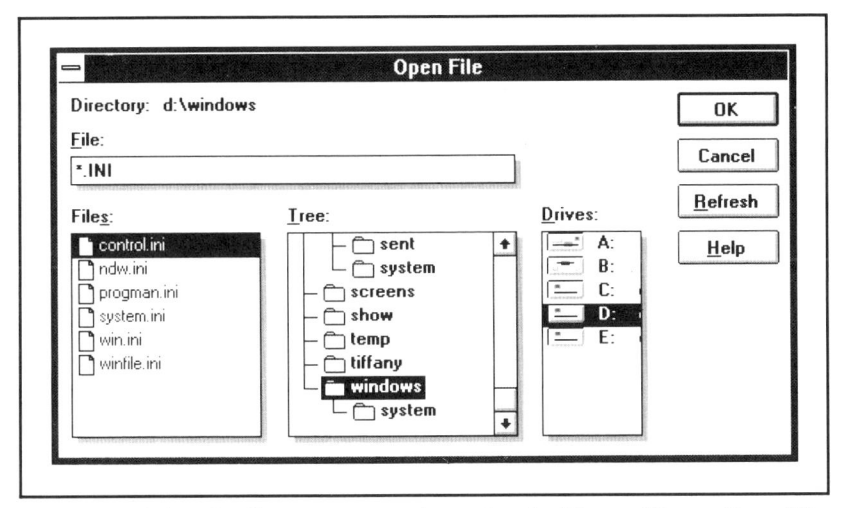

Figure 6.1: Select the file you want to view using the Norton Viewer Open File dialog box

ARRANGING VIEWER WINDOWS

The Window menu contains commands you can use to arrange your Viewer windows to your liking when you are viewing more than one file. The menu contains the following selections:

> **Cascade.** The Norton Viewer cascades windows by default. Use this command to go back to cascaded windows after you have used the next command, Tile. Figure 6.2 shows two cascaded windows.
>
> **Tile.** Use Tile if you want to see a portion of all the open files on the screen at the same time. Figure 6.3 shows two tiled windows.
>
> **Arrange Icons.** If you are not working on a window, you can make it into an icon by clicking on the minimize button; the window immediately shrinks down to an icon. You can open it up again very quickly if you double-click on the icon. Each type of file has a different kind of icon: a graphics file has a very different kind of icon from a spreadsheet file, for instance. The file name is also shown immediately under the

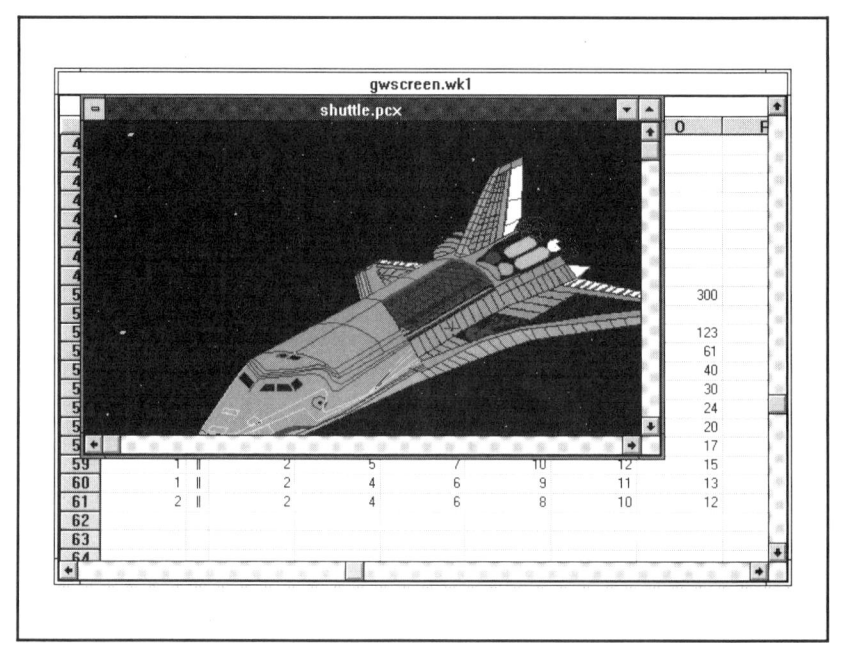

Figure 6.2: The Norton Viewer normally cascades view windows

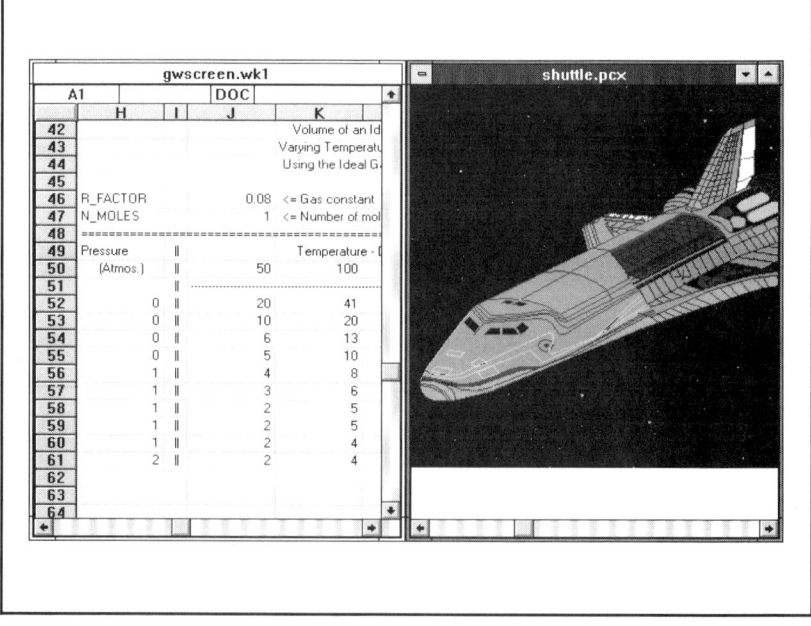

Figure 6.3: The same files shown in Figure 6.2, tiled instead of cascaded

icon at the bottom of the view window. After a while, you can end up with icons all over the viewer, so use the Arrange Icons command to put them into a neat row, from left to right, at the bottom of the Norton Viewer window. If there are too many icons to fit in one row, another row will start from the left, above the first.

Close All. Choose this selection to close all the documents open in the Norton Viewer.

At the bottom of the Viewer's Window menu you will see a list of all the files you have loaded for viewing; the active file has a check mark before its name. Just click on an entry to make it the active window.

VIEWING SPREADSHEET FILES

Figure 6.4 shows part of a spreadsheet file in the Norton Viewer. Cells in the file are arranged just as they are by the application program that created the spreadsheet in the first place. Use the arrow

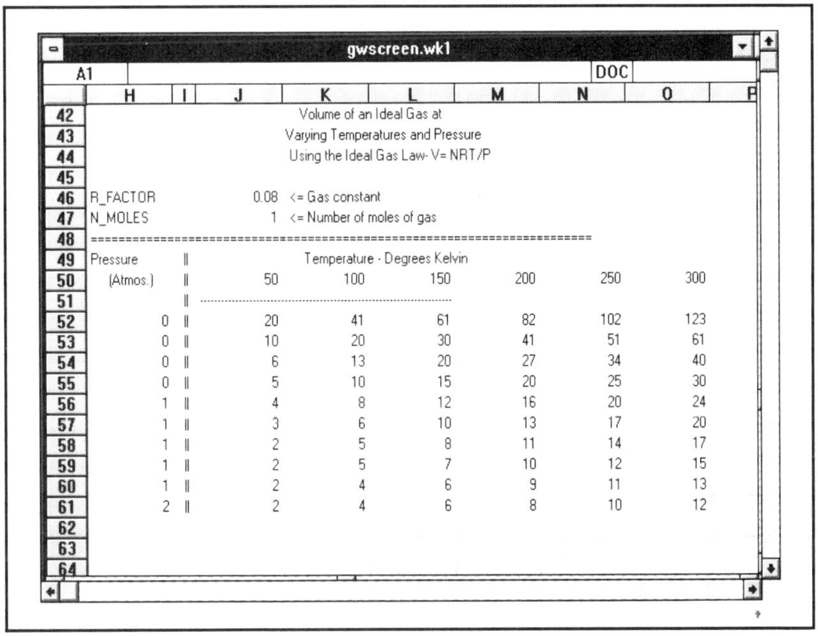

Figure 6.4: A spreadsheet file displayed in the Norton Viewer

> If you are not viewing a spreadsheet or database file, the Goto option in the Search menu is dimmed.

keys, the mouse, or the scroll bars to move around the spreadsheet. The Norton Viewer beeps when you hit the limits.

If there is a particular cell you know you want to go to directly, use the Goto selection on the Search menu to open a dialog box that contains spin buttons for row and column. Enter the appropriate entries, click on OK, and you will go straight to the right place in the spreadsheet. Using Goto can be a great timesaver if you use very large spreadsheets. The line at the top of the spreadsheet viewer, just under the menu bar, indicates the cell address, as well as the contents of the cell—whether it is a text entry, contains a formula, or is just an empty cell.

VIEWING DATABASE FILES

Figure 6.5 shows part of a database file in the Norton Viewer. The line just under the menu bar shows the database record number and the currently selected database field name.

As with the spreadsheet viewer, use the arrow keys, the mouse, or the scroll bars to move around the database. Use the Goto command from

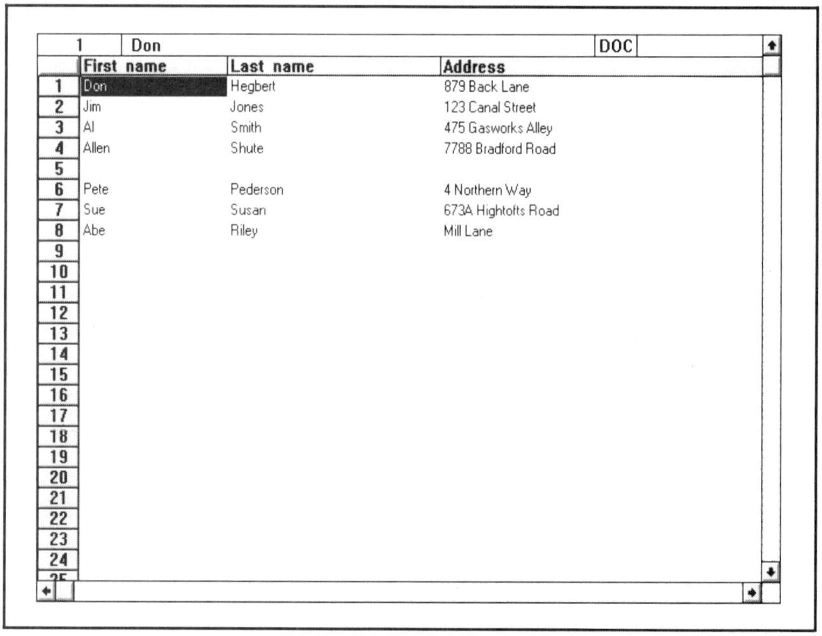

Figure 6.5: A database file in the Norton Viewer

the Search menu to go straight to a specific place in the database. A dialog box opens with a drop-down list box for database field and a spin button for record number. Select the appropriate entries, click on OK, and you will go directly to the right place in the database.

VIEWING BINARY FILES

The Hex Dump viewer displays files in a special format, as Figure 6.6 shows. It allows you to look at any kind of file, including .EXE files, files made by your word processor, even files made by your spreadsheet. In Figure 6.6, the leftmost column of hexadecimal (hex) numbers on the screen shows the location of the data in terms of a count from the beginning of the file. The central part of the window shows the actual data in the file as two-digit hex numbers. Each line displays 16 bytes of information. On the right side of the window, these same 16 bytes are shown in ASCII form.

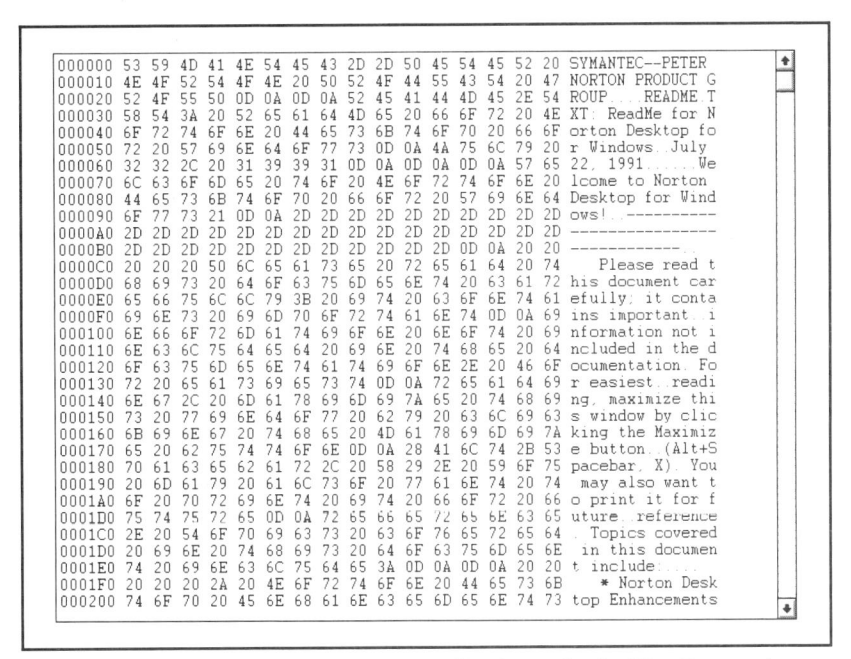

```
000000 53 59 4D 41 4E 54 45 43 2D 2D 50 45 54 45 52 20  SYMANTEC--PETER
000010 4E 4F 52 54 4F 4E 20 50 52 4F 44 55 43 54 20 47  NORTON PRODUCT G
000020 52 4F 55 50 0D 0A 0D 0A 52 45 41 44 4D 45 2E 54  ROUP....README.T
000030 58 54 3A 20 52 65 61 64 4D 65 20 66 6F 72 20 4E  XT: ReadMe for N
000040 6F 72 74 6F 6E 20 44 65 73 6B 74 6F 70 20 66 6F  orton Desktop fo
000050 72 20 57 69 6E 64 6F 77 73 0D 0A 4A 75 6C 79 20  r Windows..July
000060 32 32 2C 20 31 39 39 31 0D 0A 0D 0A 0D 0A 57 65  22, 1991......We
000070 6C 63 6F 6D 65 20 74 6F 20 4E 6F 72 74 6F 6E 20  lcome to Norton
000080 44 65 73 6B 74 6F 70 20 66 6F 72 20 57 69 6E 64  Desktop for Wind
000090 6F 77 73 21 0D 0A 2D 2D 2D 2D 2D 2D 2D 2D 2D 2D  ows!..----------
0000A0 2D 2D 2D 2D 2D 2D 2D 2D 2D 2D 2D 2D 2D 2D 2D 2D  ----------------
0000B0 2D 2D 2D 2D 2D 2D 2D 2D 2D 2D 2D 2D 0D 0A 20 20  ------------..
0000C0 20 20 20 20 50 6C 65 61 73 65 20 72 65 61 64 20 74      Please read t
0000D0 68 69 73 20 64 6F 63 75 6D 65 6E 74 20 63 61 72  his document car
0000E0 65 66 75 6C 6C 79 3B 20 69 74 20 63 6F 6E 74 61  efully; it conta
0000F0 69 6E 73 20 69 6D 70 6F 72 74 61 6E 74 20 69  ins important i
000100 6E 66 6F 72 6D 61 74 69 6F 6E 20 6E 6F 74 20 69  nformation not i
000110 6E 63 6C 75 64 65 64 20 69 6E 20 74 68 65 20 64  ncluded in the d
000120 6F 63 75 6D 65 6E 74 61 74 69 6F 6E 2E 20 46 6F  ocumentation. Fo
000130 72 20 65 61 73 69 65 73 74 0D 0A 72 65 61 64 69  r easiest..readi
000140 6E 67 2C 20 6D 61 78 69 6D 69 7A 65 20 74 68 69  ng, maximize thi
000150 73 20 77 69 6E 64 6F 77 20 62 79 20 63 6C 69 63  s window by clic
000160 6B 69 6E 67 20 74 68 65 20 4D 61 78 69 6D 69 7A  king the Maximiz
000170 65 20 62 75 74 74 6F 6E 0D 0A 28 41 6C 74 2B 53  e button..(Alt+S
000180 70 61 63 65 62 61 72 2C 20 58 29 2E 20 59 6F 75  pacebar, X). You
000190 20 6D 61 79 20 61 6C 73 6F 20 77 61 6E 74 20 74   may also want t
0001A0 6F 20 70 72 69 6E 74 20 69 74 20 66 6F 72 20 66  o print it for f
0001B0 75 74 75 72 65 0D 0A 72 65 66 65 72 65 6E 63 65  uture..reference
0001C0 2E 20 54 6F 70 69 63 73 20 63 6F 76 65 72 65 64  . Topics covered
0001D0 20 69 6E 20 74 68 69 73 20 64 6F 63 75 6D 65 6E   in this documen
0001E0 74 20 69 6E 63 6C 75 64 65 3A 0D 0A 0D 0A 20 20  t include:....
0001F0 20 20 20 2A 20 4E 6F 72 74 6F 6E 20 44 65 73 6B     * Norton Desk
000200 74 6F 70 20 45 6E 68 61 6E 63 65 6D 65 6E 74 73  top Enhancements
```

Figure 6.6: Part of the README.TXT file shown in the Hex Dump viewer

From the display of the Norton Desktop README.TXT in Figure 6.6, it is easy to see the correspondence between the hex and ASCII parts of the window. This correspondence is not so obvious when you look at an .EXE file in the Hex Dump viewer; in fact, some of the data will be completely unreadable. This is because a program file is a *binary file,* not an ASCII (text) file, and contains statements that were never intended to be read as text. These nondisplayable characters are shown as dots in the text portion of the window.

VIEWING GRAPHICS FILES

The Norton Viewer also simplifies looking at bit-mapped image files. Figure 6.7 shows a sample .PCX file containing an image of the Space Shuttle displayed in the .PCX viewer.

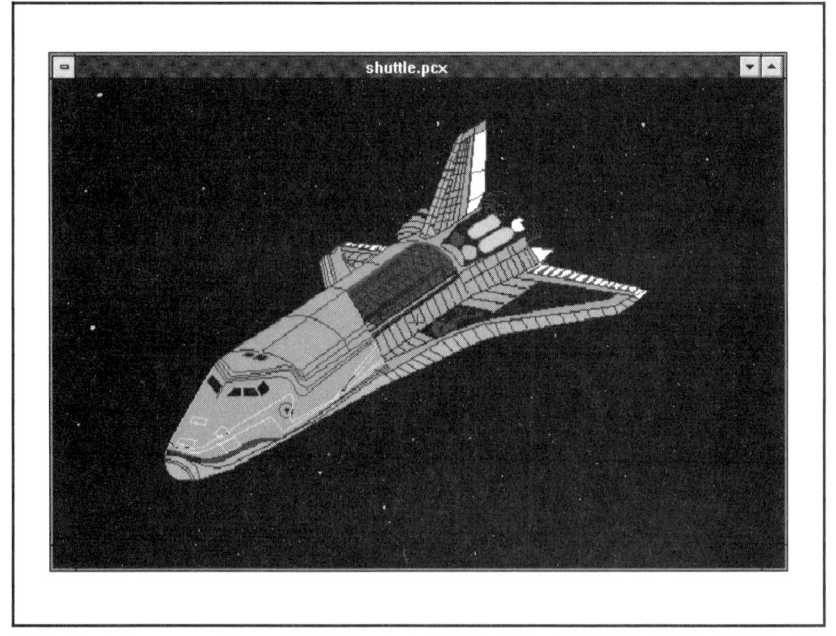

Figure 6.7: Norton Viewer can display several different kinds of bit-mapped graphics files, such as the .PCX file shown here.

To scale the graphic to the current window size, double-click on the image with the left mouse button. If the current window has a very different aspect (height-to-width) ratio you will inevitably see some distortion of your original image. Also, if the current window is very small and your original image was large, you may see some loss of detail in your image. To return the image to its original size, click the right mouse button somewhere in the image area.

The Norton Viewer makes it easy to enlarge part of a graphic, too. Move the mouse pointer to the upper-left corner of the area you want to enlarge, then hold down the left mouse button while dragging the mouse to the lower-right corner of the area. The area of the image contained inside the box will be enlarged or zoomed to fill the window. Remember to click the right mouse button to return the image to its original size.

You can also copy the current graphic displayed in the Norton Viewer to the Windows Clipboard by pressing Ctrl-Insert. This makes it very easy to paste the image into another document. If you want to copy just a piece of the image to the Clipboard:

1. Move the mouse pointer to the upper-left corner of the area.

2. Hold down the Ctrl key.

3. Hold down the left mouse button while dragging the mouse to the lower-right corner of the area. The area of the image contained inside the box will be copied to the Clipboard.

If you press the Shift key rather than Ctrl during this operation, your selected area will appear at the size of an icon and be copied to the Windows Clipboard.

SEARCHING FOR TEXT

If you want to find a particular piece of text that you think is in one of your files, open a viewer for the file and use the commands in the Search menu to look for the text or *search string*.

> If you are working with a graphics image file, all the entries in the Search menu will be dimmed because they are not available. You cannot search for text in a graphics file.

As an example, select the README.TXT file in the NDW directory and open the Norton Viewer. Now choose Find from the Search menu. When the dialog box in Figure 6.8 opens, enter the text you want to look for into the Find text box. Check the Match Upper/Lowercase box if you want to look for an exact match. If you do not check this box, Find will locate all occurrences of the letters you entered into the Find box, irrespective of case. Enter **norton** into the Find text box and make sure there is no check mark in the Match Upper/Lowercase box. Click on OK when you are ready to start.

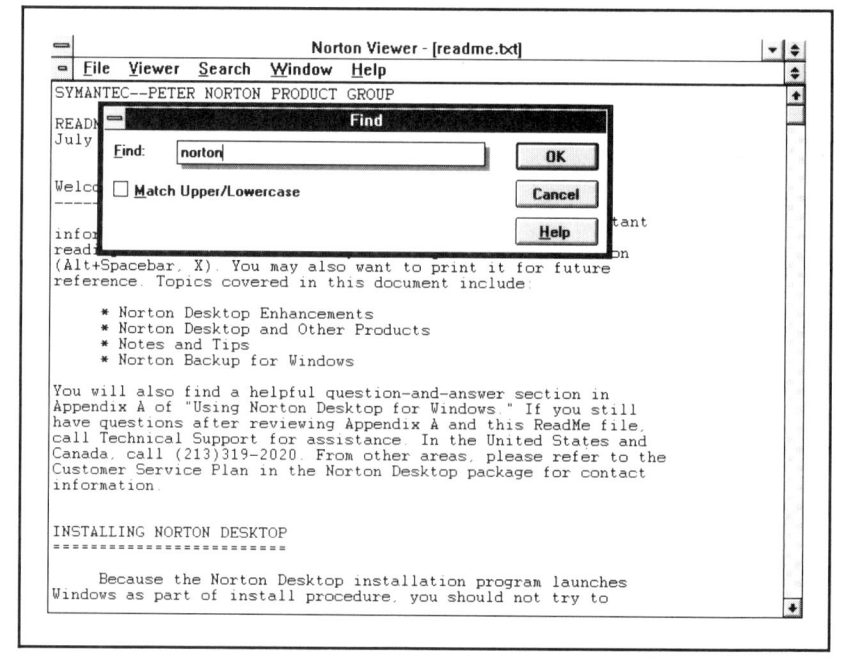

Figure 6.8: This Find dialog box will search for a text string in the README.TXT file displayed in the Norton Viewer

When a match is found, the matching text will be highlighted. Now you can use two of the commands in the Search menu to look for more matches. Select Find Next to search forwards in the file or select Find Previous if you want to search backwards through the file. If no match is found, you will see the message **No occurrences found**.

If you are working with a spreadsheet or database file, you have several more options in the Find dialog box, as follows:

Entire Document lets you search through the whole database or spreadsheet.

Partial Document allows you to restrict the search to the limits you set using the two entries below.

Column (or Field) searches just the selected column or database field.

Row (or Record) searches just the selected row or database record.

CONFIGURING THE VIEWERS

> Chapter 9 discusses NDW.INI in more detail.

When you select a file for viewing, both the view pane and the Norton Viewer look at the file-name extension to decide which viewer to open. The Desktop configuration file NDW.INI, contained in the WINDOWS directory, contains a list associating file-name extensions with specific viewers. This list is found under the heading [Viewer-Filemap] in NDW.INI. For example, NDW.INI contains the entry **TXT = DOC.PRS**. This tells the Desktop to use the document viewer for any files that have .TXT as their extension.

> Use Windows Notepad for this task; other word processors sometimes add unwanted formatting characters into files.

If you are a programmer and you want to add associations for your source files written in the C language, just use Windows Notepad to open NDW.INI and add the entry **C = DOC.PRS** at the end of the [Viewer-Filemap] list.

To make Desktop open the Hex Dump viewer rather than the Programs viewer when you select an .EXE file, change the **EXE = PROG.PRS** entry to read **EXE =HEX.PRS** instead.

You can also change the text entry associated with each of the viewers in the Select Default Viewer list, if you wish. This information is contained in NDW.INI in a section headed [Viewer-Parsers]. For example, you can use Notepad to change **Documents & Text** to read **Documents, Text, & Program Listings**.

After you have made changes to NDW.INI, remember to exit and restart the Desktop so that your changes are loaded and acted upon.

PRINTING FILES FROM THE DESKTOP

There are two easy ways to print files from the Desktop: you can drag a file to the printer icon on the Desktop or you can use the Print command from the Desktop File menu. We'll look at both these methods next.

USING THE PRINTER ICON

Using the Desktop printer icon couldn't be easier. Just follow these steps:

1. Open a drive window for the disk that contains the file you want to print.
2. Select the file from the list in the file pane.
3. Hold down the left mouse button and drag the file on top of the printer icon.
4. Release the mouse button.

> You should wait until the printer has started printing before you launch another application program; otherwise the print job may not start at all.

When you use the Desktop to print a file, the Desktop actually opens the application program that made the file in the first place and uses it to print the file. This means that the file you want to print must be properly associated with the applications program. Most of the time the associations contained in WIN.INI are sufficient, but sometimes you may want to change them. See Chapter 7 for more information on launching and associating files.

If you see either of the messages **Unable to find application** or **Print Document unformatted?** when you try to print a document, one of two things may be wrong. Either the directory containing the applications program is not in your path statement, or the path in the [Extensions] section in the Windows configuration file WIN.INI is incorrect. Chapter 7 deals with this in detail.

USING THE PRINT COMMAND

The other way you can print a document is to use the Print Command from the File menu. When the dialog box opens, enter the name of the file you want to print and choose the destination printer. If you selected a file before opening this dialog box, the file name will already be in the text box. You can also use the Browse command button to find the file you want to print.

The Setup command button in this dialog box opens the Windows Printer Setup dialog box, containing selections like choosing landscape or portrait mode for printing and selecting the graphics resolution you want. See your Windows documentation for more information on this dialog box.

SEVEN
Launching Programs

IF YOU WANTED TO START A PROGRAM RUNNING in the dark, pre-Windows days, you had to type the name of the application program at the DOS prompt. Next, you had to wait for the program to start running before telling it which document file you wanted to open.

Fortunately, we're in a bit of a Renaissance. The Norton Desktop features several easy ways to start or *launch* your applications programs, including using icons, the file pane, and the Launch Manager. Later in this chapter we will look at some more advanced topics and explore how to create associations between applications programs and the document files they create.

LAUNCHING PROGRAMS FROM THE DESKTOP

> To launch a document using an unassociated application, see "Launching Unassociated Documents" at the end of this chapter.

When you launch a document from the Desktop, you launch them using the application program that created them in the first place. Many Windows applications automatically associate files or documents according to their file-name extension. For example, documents with the .TXT extension are associated with Windows Notepad and graphics images with the .PCX extension are associated with Paintbrush. When you launch SHUTTLE.PCX, the Paintbrush program starts running and opens the SHUTTLE file.

There are several ways you can launch programs from the Desktop, including:

- clicking on group item icons
- clicking on files in the file pane of a drive window

- choosing applications from the Launch List
- using the Run or the Run DOS commands

In the next few sections, we will examine all of these methods.

CLICKING ON GROUP ITEM ICONS

Quick Access is a part of the Norton Desktop that lets you create group items representing applications programs, documents, or both applications programs and documents together. You can arrange these items together inside group windows, irrespective of where the applications programs and documents are actually located in your directory structure. This means that you can arrange your programs and documents according to the way you work, rather than have them reflect your original directory structure.

There are three ways to launch a file from a Quick Access group window:

- Double-click on the group item icon.
- Select the group item icon and choose the Open command from the File menu.
- Select the group item icon and press Enter.

Quick Access is described in detail in Chapter 8.

CHOOSING DIRECTLY FROM THE FILE PANE

When you open a drive window the file pane lists all the files and subdirectories contained in the selected directory. There are two ways to launch a program directly from the file pane:

- Double-click on the file name in the file pane.
- Highlight the file name and press the Enter key.

If you want to launch a file and them immediately minimize it, highlight the file and then hold down the Shift key as you press Enter. The application will open and then become an icon on the Desktop.

If you find that you are launching a particular application from the file pane over and over again, you can save time by dragging it to the Desktop, where it becomes an icon. Now to start the program you just double-click on the icon; the drive window does not have to be visible on the Desktop, or even open, when you do this.

SELECTING FROM THE LAUNCH LIST

The Norton Desktop features two options in the Control menu: Launch List and Launch Manager. These options are accessible from every Windows application that contains a Control menu whenever Norton Desktop is running—and that means most of them. You can launch any documents or applications programs quickly and easily from the Launch List, as long as they are on the list. You use the Launch Manager to customize the Launch List to your own requirements. The Launch Manager is detailed later in this chapter.

Figure 7.1 shows a typical Launch List made up of Norton Desktop commands; you can add your own commands to the list if you wish.

To start a program from the Launch List, select Launch List from the Control menu and choose the entry you want to run in the cascading menu. Because the Desktop adds the Launch List to the Control menu, and the Control menu is available from almost all Windows applications programs, the Launch List is available everywhere and is very easy to use.

> If the Launch List does not appear in the Desktop Control menu, select Preferences from the Configure menu and make sure there is a check mark in the Launch List check box. This also applies to the Windows Task List.

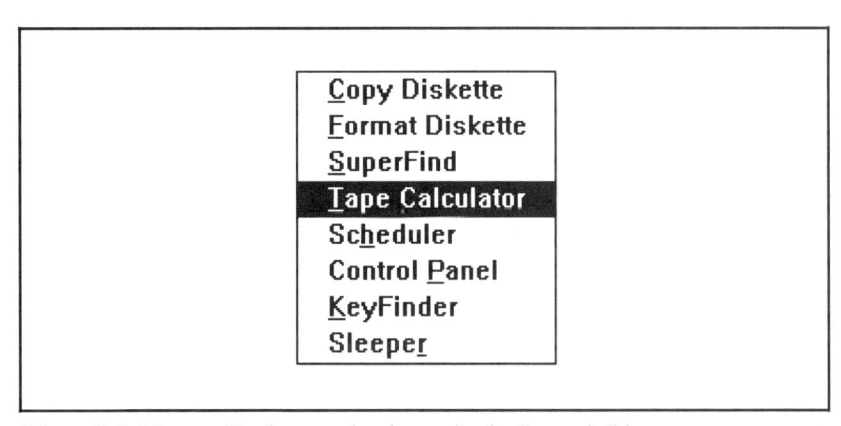

```
┌─────────────────────────────┐
│      Copy Diskette          │
│      Format Diskette        │
│      SuperFind              │
│      Tape Calculator        │
│      Scheduler              │
│      Control Panel          │
│      KeyFinder              │
│      Sleeper                │
└─────────────────────────────┘
```

Figure 7.1: Norton Desktop tasks shown in the Launch List

> To switch between applications, press Alt-Esc. To switch back to the Desktop from an application, press Alt-Tab.

Don't confuse the Launch List with the Windows Task List in the Control menu, which appears whenever you are running more than one application. There is one very important difference between these two lists that you should remember: items listed in the Task List are always programs that are running on your system *now,* while those items in the Launch List are available but are not necessarily running. The Launch List is a means for *launching* commonly used applications, whereas the Task List is a mechanism for *switching between* applications quickly.

USING THE RUN COMMAND

> You can use Run to execute any DOS command.

If you remain a devotee of the DOS command line, you can still use it from inside Windows to start your favorite programs. Here's how you can use the Run command to launch a file:

1. Select Run from the Desktop File menu

2. When the dialog box in Figure 7.2 opens, type in the correct command to start the application—and include a related data file name, too, if you wish. If the directory containing the applications program you want to use is not part of your path statement, you must include path information in the text box. For example, to start WordStar and open the file 05MAY.LET, enter

   C:\WS\WS 05MAY.LET

   into the text box. To reenter a command you recently entered into this text box, click on the drop-down list box and select the entry.

3. Select how you want the program to run using the three Run option buttons. Unless you specify to the contrary, the program will be opened in a default-sized, "normal" window. Choose Minimized if you want to minimize the program as soon as it starts, or choose Maximize to maximize it.

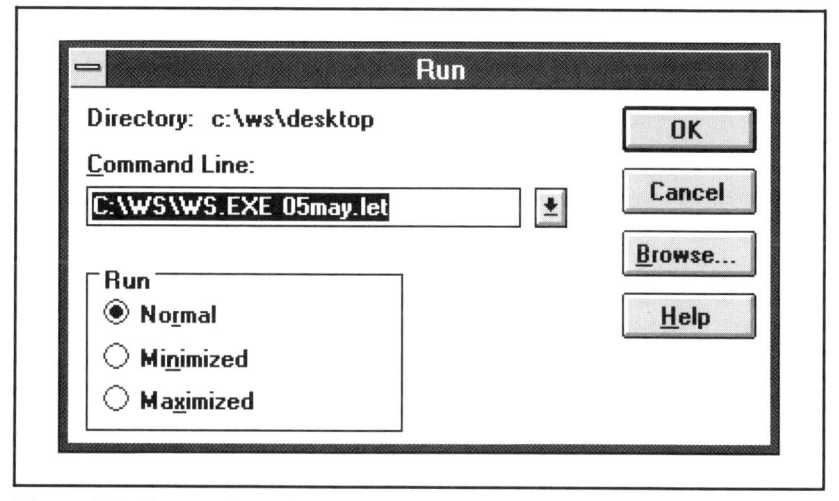

Figure 7.2: You can launch any file using Run from the Desktop File menu

USING THE RUN DOS COMMAND

Windows includes an icon for the DOS prompt in the Program Manager Main Group, but sometimes it can be inconvenient to get to and use. The Norton Desktop File menu contains the Run DOS command to save you time. When you choose Run DOS, the Desktop is cleared and the DOS prompt appears on your screen. You can now run any DOS command or run any DOS application program. To return to Windows and the Desktop, type **EXIT** at the DOS prompt and press Enter—or press Alt-Tab if you want to leave the DOS session running and switch back to the Desktop. If you do this, the Task List in the Desktop Control menu will refer to the iconized DOS command by the name COMMAND, rather than the name DOS. The icon on the Desktop is also called COMMAND.

There are some programs that should not be run in this environment, such as ones that might affect or change the file allocation table. Indeed, well engineered programs like those on the Emergency Disk will refuse to run, opening an error window instead. Programs from other suppliers may not provide such careful protection, however, so be careful.

> Avoid running another copy of Windows or Norton Desktop from this DOS prompt, because you will probably run out of memory to do anything else.

CUSTOMIZING THE LAUNCH
LIST WITH THE LAUNCH MANAGER

The Launch Manager lets you add, edit, and delete the entries that appear in your Launch List. Select the Launch Manager option from the Desktop File menu to see the dialog box shown in Figure 7.3.

In addition to the usual OK, Cancel, and Help buttons, this dialog box contains five other command buttons:

> Both Edit and Delete are dimmed until you highlight one of the entries in the Launch List.

Add. Use this command button when you want to add a new item to your Launch List.

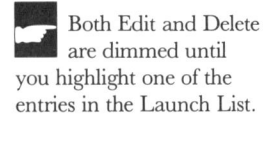

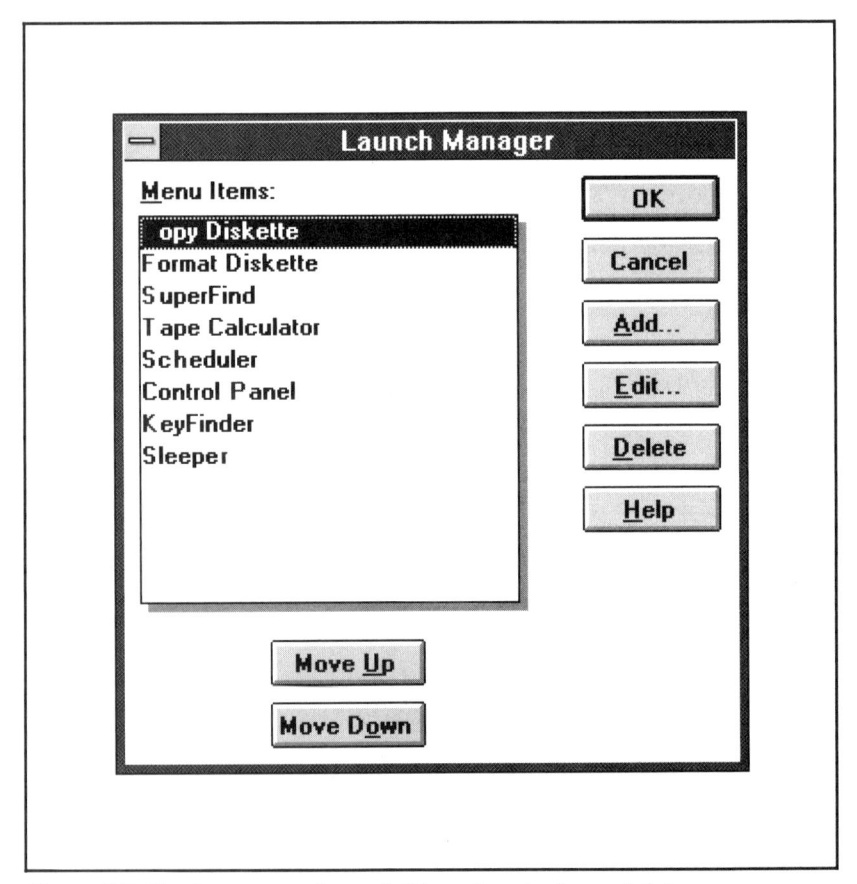

Figure 7.3: Configure your Launch List using the Launch Manager

Edit. If you want to change how one of the existing entries works, use this button.

Delete. When you decide you want to remove an entry, select this option.

Move Up. If you want to change the position of one of the entries in the Launch List, highlight the entry and click on this button to move it up the list.

Move Down. Click on this button to move an entry down the list. Alternatively, you can use the mouse to drag an entry to a new location in the Launch List.

To add a new entry to your Launch List:

1. Select Launch Manager from the Desktop Control menu.
2. When the dialog box opens, click on Add to see the dialog box shown in Figure 7.4.

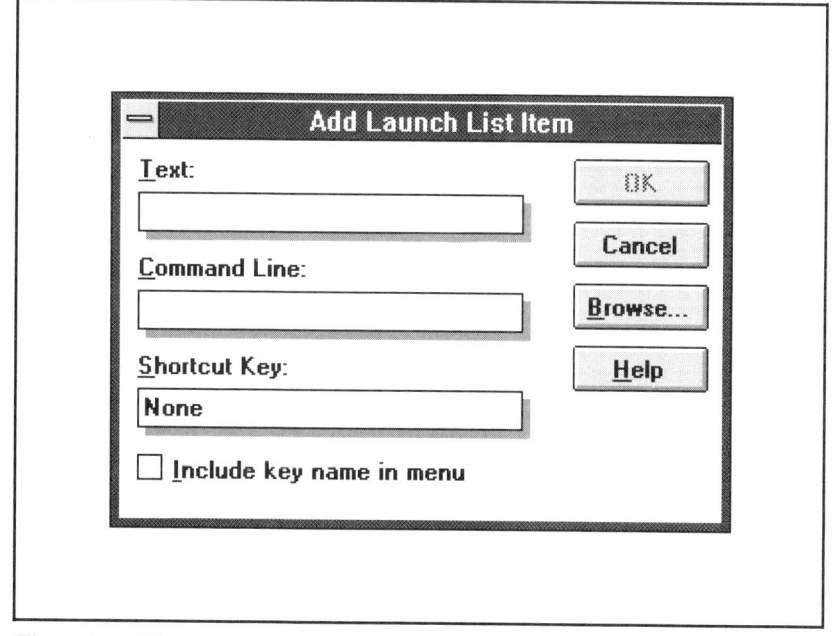

Figure 7.4: The Add Launch List Item dialog box lets you add new applications to your Launch List

3. Enter the name of the program into the text box. If you want to have one letter of the Launch List menu item appear underlined—to establish a keyboard selection for this item—place an ampersand (&) immediately before that letter. Then, when you open the Launch List cascading menu, you can type this letter rather the click on the entry. For example, if you want to add WordPerfect to your Launch List and be able to activate it by typing a *P,* enter **Word&Perfect** into the text box. It will appear as Word<u>P</u>erfect.

4. Enter the DOS command used to start the program in the Command Line text box. This may be just the name of the application program, or it may include a document name if you know the name of the file you will be working with. If the directory containing the applications program you want to work with is not part of your path statement, you must include the complete path information. In this example, the entry could be **C:\WP51\WP.EXE**.

5. If you want to establish a keyboard shortcut for this particular item, select the Shortcut Key text box and press the keystrokes you want to use. If you decide to use Alt and F11, for example, hold down the Alt key while you press the F11 function key. As long as the keystrokes you choose are valid choices, you will see them appear in the Shortcut Key text box. If you choose an invalid combination, like trying to use both of the Shift keys together, the text box won't accept it. You should only use a particular shortcut key combination for one entry in the Launch List, since two entries cannot have the same shortcut. You can use any of the following keys and combinations:

    - any function key except F1, which is always reserved for help.
    - Shift with any function key except F1, which is reserved for Windows context-sensitive help.
    - Ctrl with any function key, letter, or number.

Both Windows and the Desktop already use the Alt key in many shortcut key combinations. Do not use any of these shortcuts.

- Ctrl and Shift combined with any function key, letter, or number.
- Alt with either Ctrl, Shift, the spacebar, or Tab, along with any function key, letter, or number (e.g., Alt- Shift-F6).

6. Click on OK to add the item to your Launch List.

Editing an existing entry in the Launch List is easy, too. In fact, the dialog box used for editing an entry contains the same entries as the Add Launch List Item dialog box. Just highlight the entry you want to edit and click on Edit. Make your changes and then click on OK.

If you decide to remove an entry from your Launch List, highlight the entry in the Launch Manager Menu Items list and click on the Delete command button. You can always click on Cancel if you change your mind.

ESTABLISHING ASSOCIATIONS

The Associate command in the Desktop File menu lets you look at or change your *associations*. You can associate documents that have a given file-name extension with the application program that first created them. Most programs create these extensions automatically. For instance, the .WRI file-name extension is used by Windows Write and .TXT is used by Notepad.

When you make an association, all you have to do is double-click on a file icon to start the application program running and load the associated document into the application program's workspace. For example, if you associate file names with the .DOC extension with Microsoft Word for Windows, then when you click on any .DOC file, the Desktop will open Word and load the document you selected into the program.

These associations are made for you automatically for most of the Windows applications, and any new documents that you create with the same file-name extension will be included in the association.

Associations are contained in the Windows configuration file WIN-.INI, in the part of the file headed [Extensions]. Each time you add a new Windows application to your system, the installation program adds any additional file-name extensions that may be required into the right place in the WIN.INI file.

ADDING AND EDITING ASSOCIATIONS

Most of the time there is no need to make these associations manually. But if there ever is such a need, or you just want to look at the associations, select the Associate command from the Desktop File menu. The dialog box shown in Figure 7.5 opens, listing all your associations. There are two option buttons at the bottom of this dialog box that you can use to display your association in two different ways:

> **Programs.** Choose Programs to see your associations listed alphabetically by application program name. Note that some programs, like Windows Paintbrush (PBRUSH.EXE), have two or more file-name extensions associated with them. In

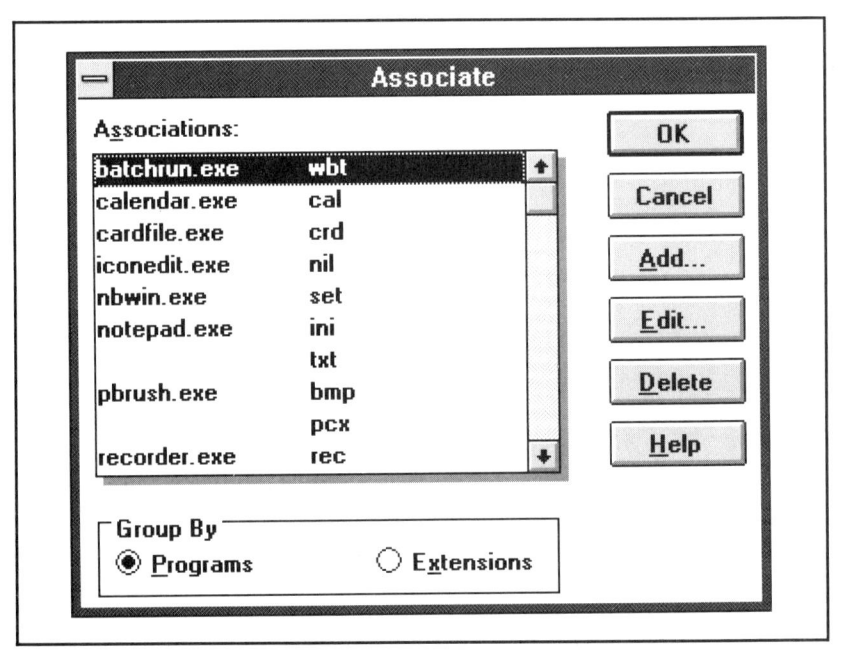

Figure 7.5: You can examine or change your associations using the Associate command

Figure 7.5, both .BMP and .PCX are associated with Paintbrush.

Extensions. Select Extensions to see your extensions listed alphabetically.

If you just want to look at the existing associations on your system, this is as far as you need to go. Use the scroll bars or the arrow keys to move through the list shown in the Associations list box. Adding or changing associations is for advanced users, because most of the time Windows does a good job of taking care of these associations for you.

To create a new association between an application program and a file-name extension, choose the Add command button from this dialog box. If you want to modify an existing association, highlight it and then click on Edit. The Add Extension dialog box shown in Figure 7.6 is very similar to the Edit Extension dialog box.

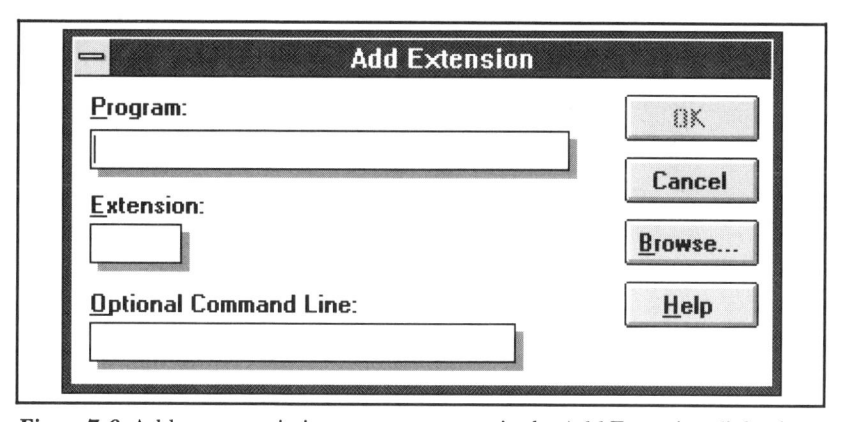

Figure 7.6: Add new associations to your system in the Add Extension dialog box

There are three text boxes in this dialog box. To create a new association:

1. Enter the full path name of the application program into the Program text box, including drive letter and directory name, if this information is not already part of your DOS path statement.

2. Enter the file-name extension you want to associate with this application program into the Extension text box. An

extension can be one, two, or three characters; do *not* enter the leading period that precedes the extension. Remember that you can only associate a particular extension with one application program at a time (for example, TXT only with Notepad), although an application program can have several extensions associated with it (for example, Paintbrush with PCX and BMP).

3. Any text you enter into the Optional Command Line text box is appended to the program name at the time you actually double-click on the document to start the program running. This can be used when opening non-Windows applications programs that take DOS command-line arguments or switches. You can also use a special character as a *placeholder,* or substitute, for the file name. For instance, add the sequence ^.*EXT* to indicate that the document's file name and extension should be passed to the application program and the document opened.

This dialog box also contains a Browse command button. When you select a file using this particular Browse dialog box, the path and file name are placed into the Program text box.

DELETING ASSOCIATIONS

If you have removed a Windows application program from your system because you don't plan to use it any more, you can delete any residual associations that remain. Open the Associate dialog box, highlight the entry you want to remove, and click on the Delete command button.

INVOKING A CUSTOM STARTUP COMMAND

You can use the Optional Command Line text box in the Add or Edit Extension dialog boxes to open your application program in a particular way. For example, if your application program supports macros, and you always use the same macro with your files, add its name to the Optional Command Line text box and it will be executed as the application program starts running.

You can include any normal DOS command-line entry in this text box. For example, if you are a WordPerfect user and you share a computer with other users, you might want to add the /X startup option for WordPerfect. This tells WordPerfect to restore all the default values that you can change with the Setup key (Shift-F1). By using this /X option, you can be sure that the regular default values are in effect, not those of any previous user.

LAUNCHING UNASSOCIATED DOCUMENTS

There may be times when you want to open a document using a program that did not create it originally, and therefore does not have the appropriate association in place. This is very straightforward:

1. Open a drive window for the disk that contains the document you want to open.

2. Open another drive window for the directory containing the application program you want to use to look at the document.

3. Highlight the document you want to look at in the first file pane and drag the document to the application program in the second file pane. When the document icon is directly over the application program name, release the mouse button.

When you release the mouse button, a dialog box opens, asking you to confirm that you want to use the application program to open the document. When you click on Yes, the application program starts and opens the document that you selected. When you exit from the application program, you return immediately to the Desktop.

An example will make this clearer. For the sake of argument, let's say you want to look at the Windows configuration file WIN.INI using the non-Windows word processor WordStar, and that no associations exist for WordStar documents on your system. First open a drive window for your Windows directory and locate WIN.INI.

Then open another drive window for the directory containing WordStar and find the file WS.EXE. Now drag the WIN.INI document icon from the first file pane until it is on top of the WS.EXE file in the second file pane. Release the mouse button. The WordStar program starts running and opens the WIN.INI document. When you have finished looking at WIN.INI and you exit WordStar, you return straight back to the Desktop.

EIGHT
Using Quick Access

QUICK ACCESS IS NORTON DESKTOP'S GRAPHICAL menuing system. It lets you create and manage your own application program groups so that you can move from one to another with a minimum number of keystrokes. Quick Access also lets you arrange groups within other groups, so that you can manage your work rather than having your work manage you. If you have used the Windows Program Manager, you will understand just how powerful an enhancement Quick Access is.

WORKING WITH QUICK ACCESS

Quick Access provides the following major enhancements over the Windows Program Manager. You can:

- create groups that contain related applications programs and documents, as well as include groups inside other groups.

- run Quick Access from the Desktop, or run it in stand-alone mode.

- define an AutoStart Group window, which runs all the applications in it every time you start Quick Access.

- specify a keyboard shortcut to open a group or group item.

- choose your own icons for your groups and group items from any icon available on your system.

- add password protection at the group and item level.

- arrange group items in a menu list format—showing the item title, a complete description, and any shortcut key—or in an icon format like that of the Program Manager.

- place Quick Access windows and icons directly on the Desktop.
- specify the directory to use. When you start an application program using the Windows Program Manager, by contrast, you are changed to the directory where that application program's files are located—which is not always convenient.

RUNNING QUICK ACCESS FROM THE DESKTOP

If you made a full installation of the whole Desktop package, you loaded Quick Access at that time, so it is now configured as a part of the Desktop. In this mode, you control Quick Access using selections from the File menu, the Configure menu, and from the Window menu. The selections from the File menu include some of the commands you have already used in a drive window; but when no drive window is open, these commands work with Quick Access items instead.

Start Quick Access by double-clicking its icon in the Norton Desktop group window.

> If you made a partial installation and did not choose Quick Access, do so now (see Chapter 2).

RUNNING QUICK ACCESS IN STAND-ALONE MODE

You can also run Quick Access in a rather different mode, independent of the Desktop and as a replacement for the Windows Program Manager, if you type

WIN QACCESS

at the DOS prompt.

When Quick Access starts running, you will notice that the main title bar reads **Quick Access** rather than **Norton Desktop**, and that the menu bar contains the following selections: File, Options, Window, and Help, rather than the usual Desktop menus. From a functional point of view, you can do everything you need to do using these menus or using the menus in the Desktop; there is no difference, apart from their arrangement. Figure 8.1 shows the File menu and Quick Access window.

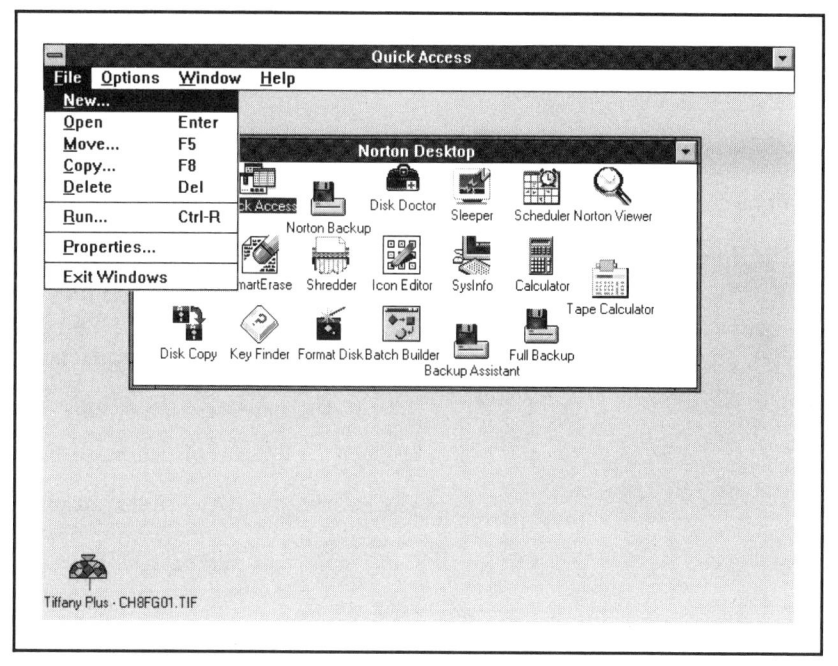

Figure 8.1: The menu bar contains slightly different options when you run Quick Access in stand-alone mode

If you decide that you like using Quick Access this way, rather than from the Desktop, you can alter your Windows SYSTEM.INI file so that Quick Access is always loaded. Use Notepad to change the line that reads

SHELL = PROGMAN.EXE

to read

SHELL = QACCESS.EXE

Now when you start Windows, Quick Access will open, instead of the Program Manager.

Throughout the rest of this chapter I assume that you are using Quick Access from the Desktop, rather than in this stand-alone mode. This way I can refer to the menu commands used to configure Quick Access in a consistent way.

OPENING GROUPS AND GROUP ITEMS

There are two kinds of objects in Quick Access: *groups* and *group items*. When you open a group, the appropriate group window opens, but when you open a group item, you actually launch that program and also open any associated document that is included in that group item's definition.

To open a group, do one of the following:

- Double-click on the group icon.
- Select the icon and then choose Open from the File menu.
- Select the icon and press the Enter key.
- Select the Window menu in either Desktop or Quick Access, if you are running in stand-alone mode, and choose the group title that you are interested in from the list in the menu.

To open a group item, do one of the following:

- Double-click on the group item icon.
- Select the icon and then choose Open from the File menu.
- Select the icon and press Enter.

To show how Quick Access can help you, suppose you decide that you want open Windows Notepad. You have to find a way of getting to the Windows Accessories group, because that's where you'll find Notepad. To do this, just double-click on the Quick Access icon. When the Quick Access group icons appear, double-click on the Accessories group icon. When the Accessories window opens, double-click on the Notepad icon to open that application.

Another way of accomplishing the same end is to use the Window menu, shown in Figure 8.2. At the bottom of the Window menu you will see a set of numbered entries, 1 through 7. These entries correspond to the group icons in Quick Access, which you can open by selecting from this menu. The currently selected group shows a check mark to the left of its menu entry. To open a notepad, for instance,

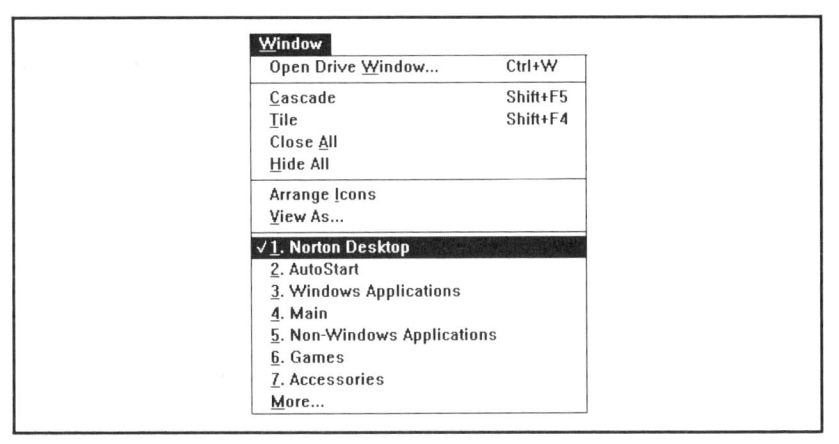

Figure 8.2: Select another group from the numbered list in the Window menu

open the menu, click on the Accessories entry to open the Accessories group window, and then double-click on the Notepad icon.

If you have more than seven groups, you will see a check mark by the last item in the Window menu, called More. Select this option to open the More Windows dialog box shown in Figure 8.3. This dialog box lets you open any group window, or restore it to its full size if it is currently minimized. It also lists all your open drive windows; if they are iconized, you can restore them by selecting them from this list.

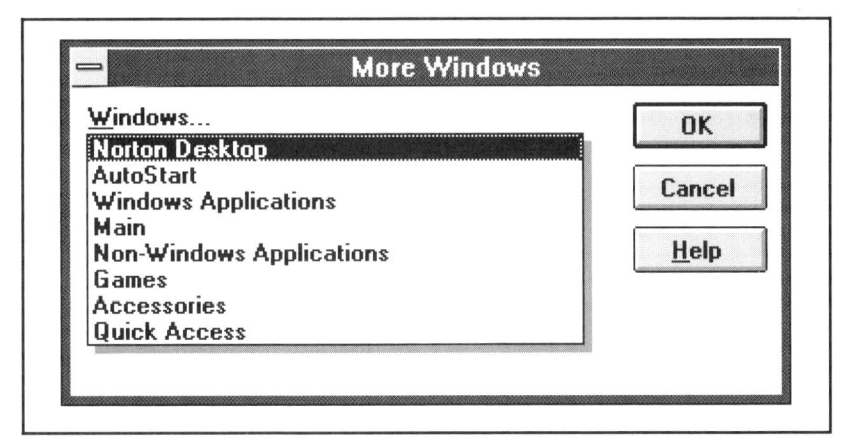

Figure 8.3: Choose More from the Window menu to open the More Windows dialog box

Use the arrow keys or the mouse and the scroll bars to locate the selection you are interested in, and either press the Enter key or double-click on the appropriate entry with the mouse. Your selection, group window or drive window, will appear on the Desktop.

DISPLAYING ICONS

You can choose to display group icons or group item icons either in the traditional array of icons or in a list format. In icon format, items are arranged with the icons above their names; additional descriptive text and shortcut keys do not appear. In list format, items are arranged vertically, with the icons appearing to the left of their names; additional descriptive text and any shortcut keys may appear to the right, as well.

To select the style you want to use on your system, choose View As from the Window menu. You will see the dialog box shown in Figure 8.4. The name of the group you are working with appears in the top left corner of this dialog box. There are two option buttons and a check box in the dialog box, as follows:

> Choose **Icon** to see icons on your system in the traditional style.
>
> Choose **List** if you prefer to see them arranged in list format.
>
> Click **Change All Groups** if you want to extend this format to cover all the groups on your system; otherwise the icon format will only apply to the currently active group.

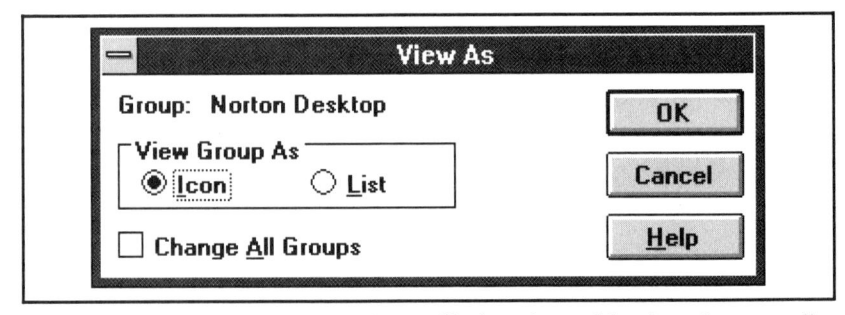

Figure 8.4: Choose the display style you like best from either icon format or list format

The option button that is selected when you first open this dialog box denotes the style that is currently in effect on your system.

Figure 8.5 shows an example of both arrangements: the top window is in list format and the bottom window is in icon format. When you use the icon format, there are two ways to position or space the icons. You can either drag each individual icon with the mouse to a new location more to your liking, or you can use the Arrange Icons command from the Windows menu to rearrange the icons for you. After you rearrange your icons, remember to select Save Configuration in the Configure menu, otherwise your changes will be lost when you quit Quick Access.

Icon spacing in Quick Access groups is governed by a pair of settings in the Desktop configuration file, NDW.INI. These settings are in the section of NDW.INI called [Quick Access] and are called IconSpacingX and IconSpacingY. They determine, respectively, the spacing between icons in the x and y dimensions in *pixels* or picture elements. The default for x is 60 pixels and the default for y is 58. Since each icon is a square 32 pixels by 32 pixels, these defaults leave room for the icon title. If you want to change these settings, open NDW.INI in Windows Notepad.

> You can make Quick Access rearrange your icons automatically when you resize a window if you check the Auto Arrange Icons check box in the Configure Quick Access selection from the Configure menu. More on this particular topic in Chapter 9.

WORKING WITH QUICK ACCESS GROUPS

This part of the chapter describes how to manage Quick Access groups and group items, and how to specify which group items are opened each time you start Quick Access. We will also look at maintaining the various properties of groups or group items, such as icons, passwords, shortcut keys, startup directories, and application program file names.

CREATING NEW GROUPS

You can use Quick Access to make new groups, to add group items to existing groups, and create subgroups inside other groups. Quick Access also preserves the groups you originally created when you first installed Windows. If you create more groups or add to existing

> In fact, all these groups are subgroups of the Quick Access group.

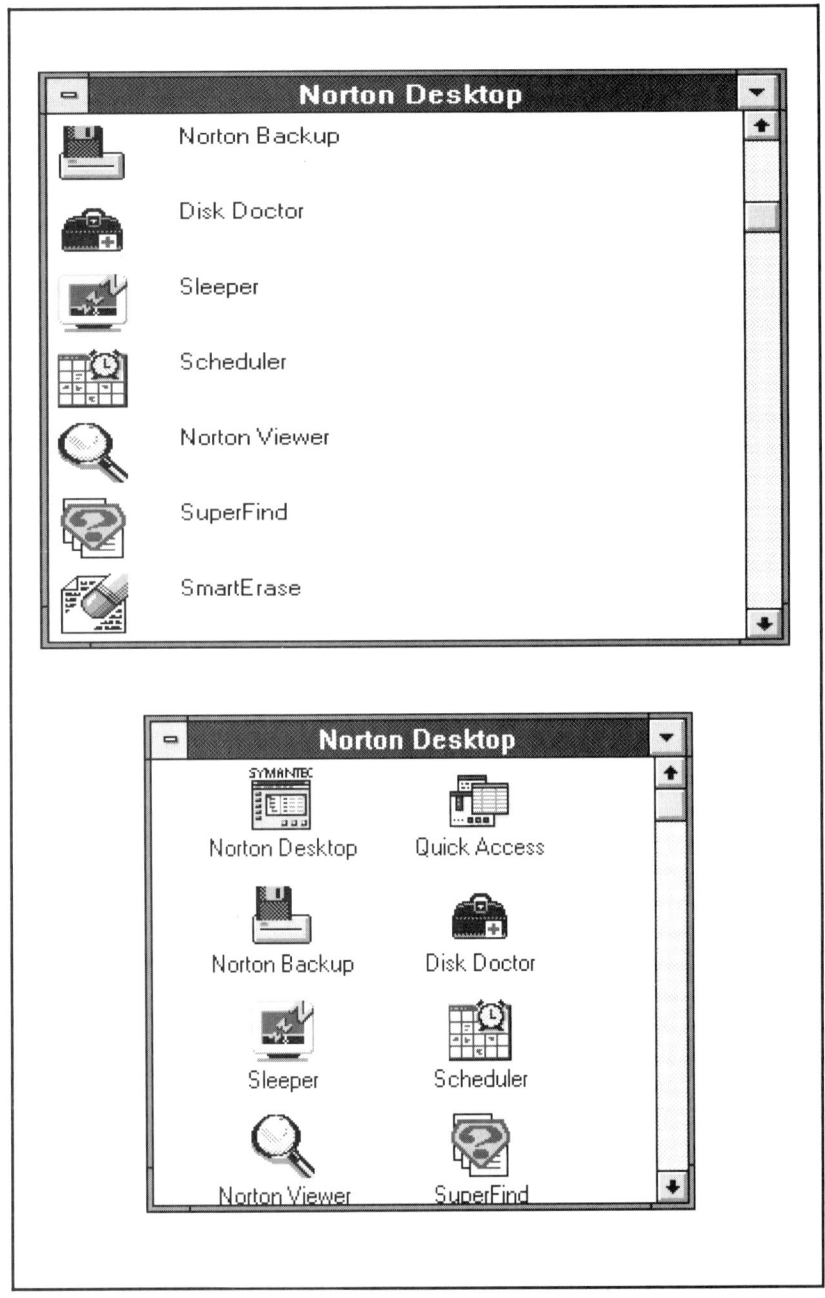

Figure 8.5: The top window is in list format, the bottom in icon format

groups using Windows Setup, Quick Access will intercept these additions and make sure that they are added to your Quick Access groups.

To create a new group or add a group item to a group, follow these steps:

1. Open the group window you want to work with and make sure it is the active window. To create a top-level group, make sure you select the Quick Access main group; if you want to create a subgroup in an existing group, select that group. If you want to create a group item, select the group to which you want the item to belong.

2. Select New from the File menu to open the New dialog box, shown in Figure 8.6.

3. Choose the Group option button if you want to create a new group, or the Item option button if you are adding a program or document icon. The object you create will be

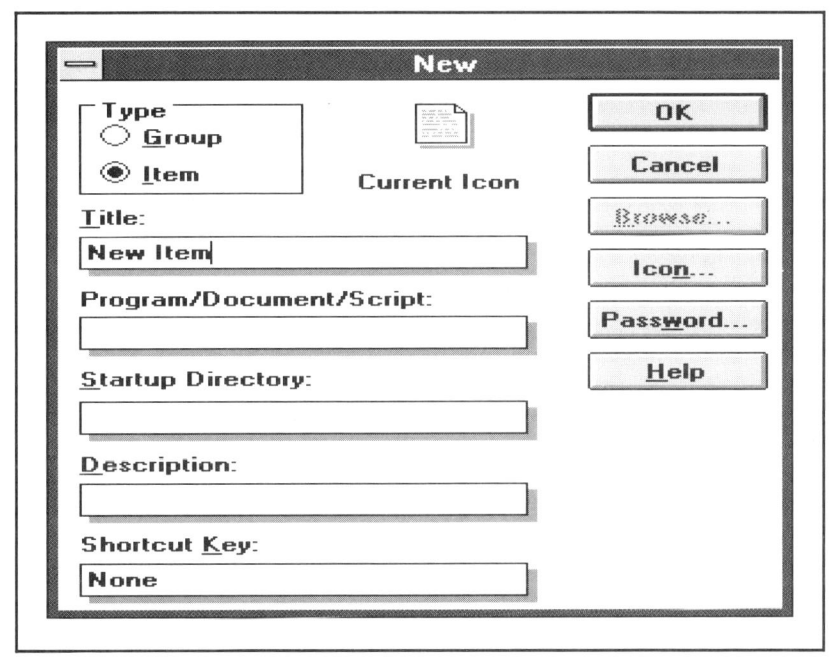

Figure 8.6: Create new groups or group items using New from the File menu

CH. 8

part of the active group window, whether it is a group or an icon. As you switch from one choice to another, notice that the Current Icon also changes from a group icon to a group item icon.

4. Enter a title into the Title text box. You can type as many as 64 characters into this text box, but you should try to keep the title as short as possible to prevent it from overwriting the titles or nearby icons on the screen. This title is placed underneath the icon if you are in icon mode and next to the icon if you are in list mode. If you are making a group item and you leave this text box blank, Quick Access will assign a title for you automatically. If the item is an application program, Quick Access uses the program file name (without the extension) as the title; if the item is a document, it uses the full file name.

5. Enter a file name into the next text box, or use the Browse command button to select a file name. If you are working with a group, this text box is called Group File Name and the text box called Startup Directory is dimmed out. If you are working with a group item, this text box is called Program/Document/Script and the Startup Directory text box is not dimmed out.

> You must add full path details for the application program and document you want to use, unless it is already part of the path statement established in your AUTOEXEC.BAT file.

6. If you are working with a group item, enter the file name you want executed when this item is opened. If the program file name has an .EXE, .COM, .BAT, or .PIF extension, you don't need to specify the extension here. If you always want to work with a specific document, enter the application program name, press the spacebar, then add the document name. If an association already exists for this program and the document you want to open, you don't have to specify the program name at all; Desktop takes care of it for you. See Chapter 7 for more details on associations.

To change to a specific directory when Quick Access starts your group item, enter that directory name and path information into the

> Certain applications have to run from specific directories where all their related files and font information is located. In this case, you may see an error message if you specify a different directory here.

Startup Directory text box. Remember, if you are creating a group, this text box has no meaning and is dimmed out.

The Description text box is optional. If you work in list mode, the text you enter here is displayed below the text you entered into the Title text box. In icon mode, this description is ignored and is never displayed.

Every group or group item is assigned a particular icon, and sample icons are displayed at the top of the New dialog box. To change the icon, click on the Icon command button. This procedure is described in detail in the next section, "Creating and Changing Icons."

If you want to add password protection to the group or icon, click on the Password command button. This procedure is also described in detail later in this chapter.

To use a keyboard shortcut, press the actual keys you want to use into the Shortcut Key text box. If you press Ctrl and A, for example, the key combination will appear in the text box. If you use a combination that is not valid, nothing will appear in the text box.

You can use any of the following keys and key combinations: any function key except F1; any combination of the Shift key and a function key (except F1); Ctrl with any letter, number or function key; Shift and Ctrl with any letter, number, or function key; Alt with either Ctrl, Shift, the spacebar, or Tab, and any letter, number, or function key.

Remember that the Launch Manager lets you assign shortcut key combinations to applications, as described in Chapter 7. Desktop does not check whether you are using the same combination in both Quick Access and the Launch Manager; if you are, the Launch Manager will take precedence. Shortcut key combinations in group windows are displayed when you choose list format, but are not shown if you use icon format.

Using the New command is the only way to create a new group—and it seems like a long, complex procedure—but it really becomes straightforward once you have gone though the process a couple of times.

> You can add any program whose file-name extension is either .EXE, .COM, .BAT, or .PIF to a group, and you can add any document for which an association already exists on the Desktop.

Once the group exists, however, you can use New again to add items to the group that you just created, or you can just add them by dragging them with the mouse. Here's how with the mouse:

1. Open a drive window for the drive that contains the application program you want to add to the group. Locate the appropriate file in the file pane.

2. Open the group window to which you want to add this item. Resize or tile the two windows so that they both fit on the screen at the same time.

3. Drag the application program or document file name from the drive window to its new location on the group window.

CREATING AND CHANGING ICONS

Icons are one of the elements that make the Windows environment so popular. People understand and like the concept of clicking on a picture to start a program running.

> If you want to make your own icons, or edit an existing icon, use the Desktop Icon Editor from the Tools menu, described in Chapter 14.

When you create a new group in Quick Access you have the opportunity of changing the default icon. But you don't have to do it then; you can change the icon at any time. I don't recommend that you change or edit the group icon; keep the normal icon for all your new and existing groups. This way you can tell at a glance whether the icon represents a group or an individual application program.

Select the Icon command button from the New dialog box if you are creating a new group or item, or choose the Properties command from the File menu if you want to change an existing icon. You can also drag an icon from its group window to the Desktop, then choose Icon from its Control menu. In any case, the Choose Icon dialog box opens, as shown in Figure 8.7.

The current icon is displayed in the Choose Icon dialog box, and you can click on the drop-down list box to see other icons. Select your icon from the drop-down list. Icons are stored in several ways; they can be contained in icon libraries like the Norton Icon Libraries (file-name extension .NIL), or they may be part of an executable file, or even stored as a single icon file with a file-name extension of .ICO or .ICN.

If you want to look at other icons, enter an icon file name into the Icon File text box and click on the View command button. For example,

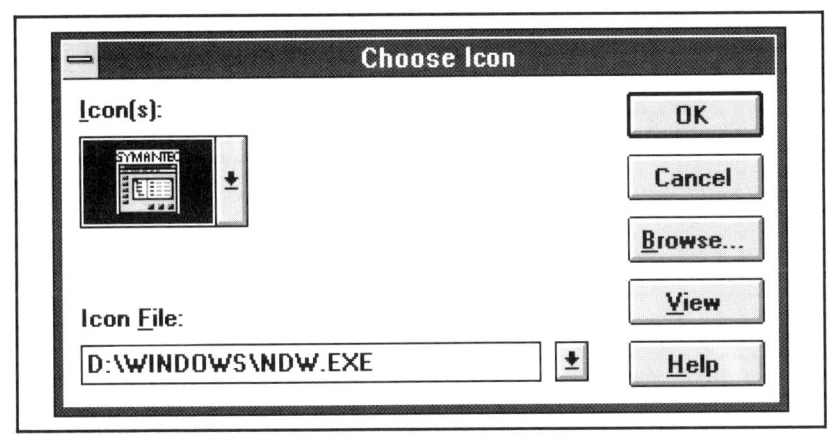

Figure 8.7: Changing icons is easy with the Choose Icon dialog box

the Norton Desktop icon is located in the file NDW.EXE and the Windows Solitaire game icon is in the file called SOL.EXE in your Windows directory. If you enter an icon file name into the text box, its icon is shown in the Icon(s) list box; if you enter the name of an .EXE file, all the icons in that file can be accessed from the list box. To look for icon files on your system, use the Browse command button.

When the Icon drop-down list box displays the icon you want to use, click on OK to accept the icon and close the dialog box.

WORKING WITH PASSWORDS

If you want to password-protect a group or group item, select New from the File menu and click on the Password command button in the New dialog box to open the Enter New Password dialog box. The password can be up to 20 characters in length and you can use any of the keys on the main part of the computer keyboard, including letters, numbers, and the symbols (like !, @, #, and $) that appear when you shift a number key. Make your password longer than six characters, because passwords of fewer characters are easy to guess—and don't choose obvious passwords like initials, dates, place names, or people's names. As you type the password, all you see in the dialog box is a series of asterisks, for reasons of security. You will be asked to type it a second time to confirm your choice of password.

To change an existing password, select the item you want to work with and choose Properties in the File menu to open the Properties dialog box. Click on the Password command button. When the Enter New Password dialog box opens, type in your new password and click on OK. When the Confirm Password dialog box opens, type in your new password a second time to confirm it.

Unless you use Save Changes in the Configure menu, your password will not take effect when you quit Quick Access.

If you start by using a password and then decide you don't want to use any password protection at all, you can quickly disable the password:

1. Select Properties from the File menu.

2. Enter the password into the Password text box and click on OK.

3. When the Confirm Disable Password dialog box opens, click on OK without entering anything from the keyboard, then click on OK to confirm that you want to disable password protection.

CHANGING PROPERTIES

Once you have created a group or group item, you can change any of the original settings you made by selecting Properties from the File menu. This command opens the Properties dialog box, which is identical to the New dialog box you used to create the group in the first place. The only limitations on the changes you can make are the following: you cannot change a group into a single item or a single item into a group, and you cannot change a group file name. You also cannot change any of the properties of the Quick Access main window, apart from the name. I describe how to do this in Chapter 9.

MOVING, COPYING, AND DELETING GROUPS

Inevitably there will come a time when you want to move or copy a group or group item from one place to another on your system. There are two commands in the File menu for these operations—Move and

Moving transfers the single copy of the group or item to another location. *Copying* duplicates the original in a different location so that two or more copies exist at the same time.

If you want several copies of items on your system, go ahead and create them, because they do not take up a significant amount of additional disk space. Only the information about the groups is duplicated, not the actual programs or documents.

Copy—or you can use the mouse if you prefer. When you move or copy a group, you also include all of the subgroups and group items in the operation, but you cannot move or copy to a subgroup that is below the one you want to work with.

To move or copy using the mouse, select Tile from the Window menu to arrange on the Desktop both the group window that contains the item you want to move or copy and the window that you want to move or copy the item to. Drag the group icon or group item icon from its current location to a new location in the new window. If you want to make this a copy operation rather than a move, hold down the Ctrl key while you drag the object you want to copy.

To move or copy using the File menu is also simple, and the two dialog boxes used for these operations are virtually identical:

1. Select Move from the File menu (or press F7) to open the Move dialog box shown in Figure 8.8. To copy, select Copy or press F8. The From scrolling list on the left displays all the Quick Access groups, subgroups and program items. The To list only shows groups, because you cannot move or copy a group to a group item.

2. Highlight the object you want to move or copy in the From list box.

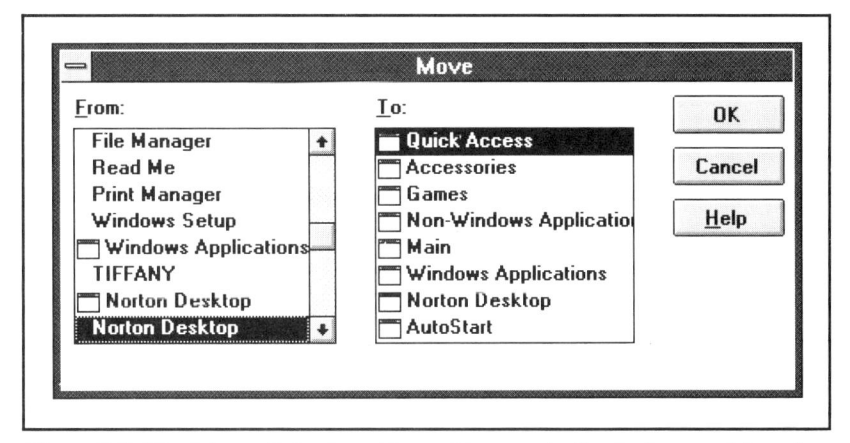

Figure 8.8: The Move dialog box (shown) is very similar in form and function to the Copy dialog box

3. Highlight the group you want to move or copy the item to in the To list box and click on OK.

If you are no longer using a group because it has outlived its usefulness, you can delete it whenever you like. This operation does *not* remove any programs or documents from your system, it just deletes an icon from a window. To delete a group or group item:

1. Open the appropriate group window and select the victim.
2. Choose Delete from the File menu, or press the Delete key.
3. When the alert box opens to confirm that you want to continue with the deletion, click on OK to continue or click on Cancel to abort the operation.

SAVING YOUR CHANGES

After you have made any changes, be sure to save them—otherwise they will only apply to your current Quick Access session and not be there the next time.

Select Save Configuration from the Configure menu if you are running Quick Access under the Desktop, or from the Options menu if you are running in stand-alone mode. This selection saves your Quick Access configuration, as well as the state of any open drive or group windows, including size, location, display size, and icon location.

There are other ways of saving your Desktop and Quick Access configurations, which we will look at in detail in the next chapter.

USING THE AUTOSTART GROUP

If you want to start particular applications running when you start up Quick Access, you can add these items to a special group called AutoStart. When Quick Access is launched, it examines the AutoStart group and launches any application programs it finds in it. The

AutoStart group is already defined for you, but is created as an empty group so that you can configure it to your own requirements.

You might want to add one of the Desktop calculators, your calendar, and your word processor to the AutoStart group so that you don't have to waste time starting these applications one at a time every day. If you drag a group or group item to the AutoStart group, Quick Access always copies the group or item. It never moves it.

NINE
Customizing the Desktop

IN WORKING WITH THE DESKTOP IN PREVIOUS chapters, we have used it pretty much as it was installed, without configuring or customizing it. The Desktop is a very flexible environment, however, and it offers many opportunities to tailor it exactly to your needs and work habits. If there are features of the Desktop that you use constantly, there may be ways that you can get even more performance out of your system. On the other hand, if there are Desktop options that you dislike or never use, there may be a way to turn them off so they don't get in the way.

In this chapter we will look at all of these configuration options and point out some of the pros and cons of using them on your system. The Configure menu, shown in Figure 9.1, lists the options you can use to configure your Desktop. I will go through each of the selections shown on this menu and describe ways that you can use them to get the most out of your system. I will also look at the different ways you can run the Desktop: as your Windows shell or as a regular Windows application.

CUSTOMIZING DESKTOP MENUS

■ If you are using the default short menus, the first selection in the Configure menu is always Full Menus; if you are already using full menus, this selection toggles to Short Menus.

The most obvious way to customize your Desktop menus is to select the first entry in the Configure menu. Desktop maintains two complete sets of menus, known as full menus and short menus. Short menus are used by default until you change to full menus. The short menu contains just the most commonly used commands you need for day-to-day use, whereas the full menu contains every Desktop command. You can customize and add your own items to the short menus (but not the full menus).

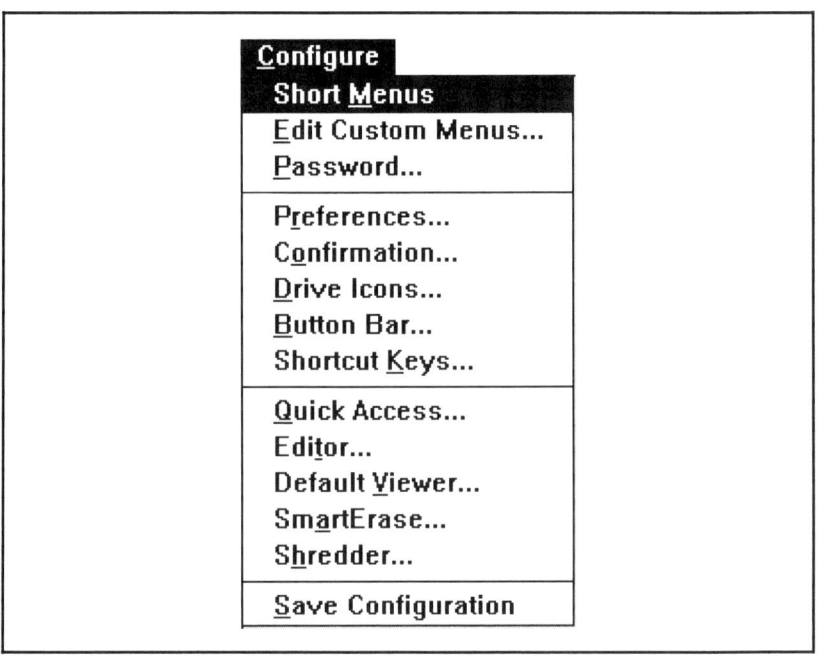

```
      Configure
      Short Menus
      Edit Custom Menus...
      Password...

      Preferences...
      Confirmation...
      Drive Icons...
      Button Bar...
      Shortcut Keys...

      Quick Access...
      Editor...
      Default Viewer...
      SmartErase...
      Shredder...

      Save Configuration
```

Figure 9.1: The Configure menu contains selections you can use to tailor the Desktop to your needs

Using the Edit Custom Menus selection from the Configure menu, you can customize your own Desktop even further. You can:

- change the menu bar text, or any text in a menu.
- remove a menu from the menu bar, or a command from a menu.
- add standard menu commands to your custom menu structure.
- change the sequence of menus on the menu bar.
- add your own applications programs or commands to the menu system.
- test your new menu system to make sure it does what you expect it to do.

The Edit Custom Menus command in the Configure menu opens the Menu Assignments dialog box shown in Figure 9.2. This dialog box looks a little complicated, so let's look at it piece by piece. The Commands list box on the left contains all the commands available in the full menus in the same order that they appear in each menu. This list starts with New, the first command in the File menu on the left of the Desktop menu bar, and ends with About, the last command in the Help menu on the right of the menu bar. At the top of the list is a menu item separator line, used to distinguish between different types of commands in the same menu. Below this list box is a small help box that contains a brief description of the currently highlighted command.

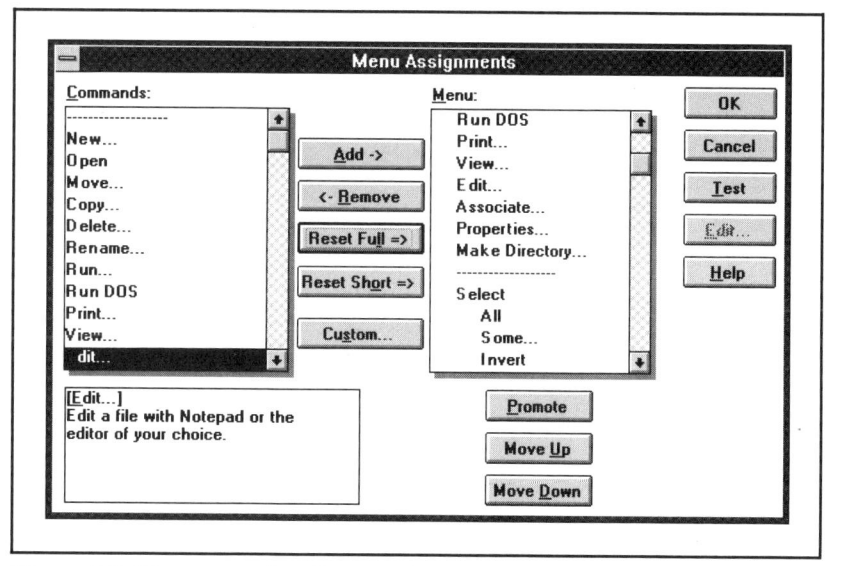

Figure 9.2: You can make all sorts of changes to the Desktop menu system using the Menu Assignments dialog box

The Menu list box on the right side of this dialog box lists the structure of your current custom menu. Items in the list that are left-justified in the list box are menu names—they appear on the Desktop menu bar (like the File menu). Items indented once are menu selections (like Make Directory in the File menu) or cascading menu titles (like Select in the File menu). Items indented twice are cascading menu selections (like All, Some, and Invert in the Select cascading menu in the File menu).

If you have not started work on your custom menu yet, your custom menu will be based on the full menu structure. This is because it is somewhat easier to take the full menu set and remove any items you don't want, rather than add items you *do* want to the short menu.

There are several command buttons between and below the Commands list box and the Menus list box, as follows:

Add adds a command to your custom menu. First highlight the item you want to add from the Commands list at left, then click on the place in the Menu list at right where you want to place this new command. Click on Add. The command is added immediately *above* the item you highlighted in the Menu list.

Remove removes the currently highlighted item from the Menu list. Remember that the Commands list always contains all the Desktop commands; you cannot add to or delete from this list, only from the Menu list. You will see the message **Menus cannot be left empty** if you try to remove all the items in a menu.

Reset Full resets your custom menu so that it contains all the selections initially available in the Desktop full menu. A warning dialog box opens to make sure you want to do this. When you use Reset Full, all your custom settings are lost. Use this button if you made changes to the custom menu and then decided later that you didn't like your changes. With this single selection, you can get rid of all your changes and start afresh with the full menu set.

Reset Short resets your custom menu so that it contains just the default selections in the short menu. Again, a warning dialog box opens to make sure that you want to do this. When you use Reset Short, all your custom menu selections are lost. Just like Reset Full, you can use Reset Short to override and replace any changes you made to your custom menu.

Custom adds a custom menu to the menu bar, or a custom menu item into a menu. I'll show you this function in a moment.

> There is no "Demote" button, but Move Up or Move Down will effectively demote an item for you.

Promote moves a highlighted item in the Menu list to the next highest "level" in the menu structure, essentially removing the item's indentation and moving it out of the group of other indented items. For instance, promoting the Move option in the File menu relocates it after the Exit option (the last option in the File menu) and before the Disk menu, where it becomes the "Move menu" (but without any indented options below it).

Move Up moves the highlighted item in the Menu list up in the menu order. If you move a menu title, all the indented menu options below it will move, too.

Move Down moves an entry in the Menu list down in the menu order.

Another way of changing the position of an item in the custom menu is to use the mouse to drag it up or down the menu system. As you drag the item, a small icon appears beside the mouse pointer. This icon looks like a small rectangle if you drag a command and looks like a small pull-down menu if you drag a menu title. When you drag a menu title, the items in that menu may be dimmed (depending on your monitor) to show that they are moving, too. When the highlight is immediately above the item's new location in the Menu list, release the mouse button.

In addition to the usual OK, Cancel, and Help command buttons on the right side of this dialog box, there are two more, Test and Edit:

> You cannot actually execute commands when you are in test mode; you can only look at the structure of your menus.

Test displays a replica of your custom menu in a long, narrow window, showing you what it will look like. It is used to confirm that your custom menu will actually behave as you think it should. To exit from test mode, close the Test window or select any menu "option."

Edit allows you to edit the text of an item in your custom menu or change the keyboard shortcut keys.

A couple of examples will make this clearer; in the next three sections we will add a standard Desktop command to the custom menu, create and add a custom command to the custom menu, and then look at how we can edit these additions.

ADDING STANDARD DESKTOP COMMANDS

In this first example, imagine you like using the short Desktop menu because it offers all the functions you need—except one, the Rename command in the File menu. To add this command, follow these steps:

1. Select Full Menus from the Configure menu if you don't already have full menus on, then select Edit Custom Menus.

2. Click the Reset Short button to make sure you are starting with the Short menu as the basis for your custom menu. (Click on Yes in the warning dialog box that opens next.)

3. Highlight the Rename Command in the Commands list box.

4. In the Menus list box, place the highlight on the separator bar above Print and below Delete. This is so that the Rename command will be added at the end of the first group of options in the File menu, below Delete.

5. Click on the Add button to add the Rename command where you specified.

6. Click on the Test command button to open a replica of your new menu structure. When the test menu bar opens, open the File menu and check that the Rename command is at the right place in the list. Close the test menu bar.

7. Click on OK to save these changes for now. See the section called "Saving Your Changes" at the end of the chapter for information on making these changes permanent.

Now when you use Short Menus in the Desktop, you'll have the Rename command available in the File menu.

In the next example, imagine that you use the Desktop calculator so often, that you want it to be available directly from the Desktop

Use this technique to add separator bars to delineate your own menus.

menu bar. Here are the steps:

1. Select Edit Custom Menus from the Configure menu.
2. Highlight the Calculator entry in the Commands list.
3. Highlight the View menu entry in the Menu list box (*not* the View... entry under File), because we want the Calculator to appear between the Disk and View menus on the menu bar.
4. Click on Add.
5. Click on the Test command button to look at the new menu bar and make sure that the Calculator entry is in the right place. Click on Calculator to close the test menu.
6. Click on OK in the dialog box.

Now when you use your custom menu in the Desktop, you will see that the Calculator has its own main menu bar selection.

ADDING YOUR OWN CUSTOM COMMANDS

Not only can you add selections from the Desktop to your custom menu, but you can add your own custom commands, programs that are not part of the standard Desktop menus. Here are the steps to follow:

1. Select Edit Custom Menus from the Configure menu.
2. Place the highlight in the Menu list box immediately below the place where you want to add this new item as either a menu bar selection or as an item in an existing menu.
3. Click on the Custom command button to open the dialog box shown in Figure 9.3.
4. In the Type of Item group box choose between the New Command and the New Menu option buttons, depending on the kind of item you are adding.
5. Type the menu or command title (capitalizing it as you wish) into the Text text box, and keep it short so that it will fit on

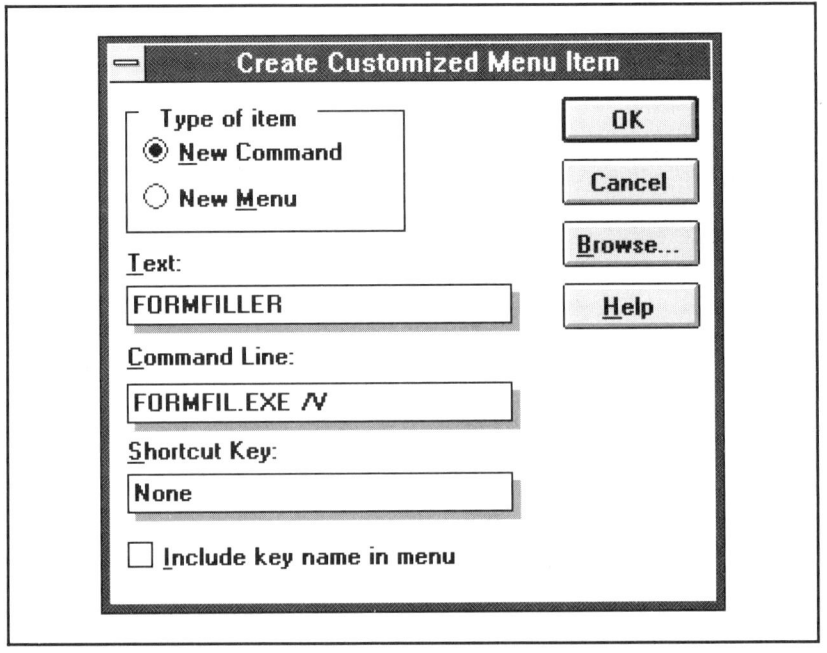

Figure 9.3: Add your own custom commands or application programs to your Desktop custom menu with the Create Customized Menu Item dialog box

the menu bar or in the menu you have chosen. Desktop displays text in a proportionally spaced font, so that different letters take up different amounts of room: the *m* is wider than the *l*, for instance. This means that there is no maximum number of characters you can use, just a maximum width available for the text. If you are only creating a menu, this is all you have to do, as the other items in the dialog box are dimmed and unavailable. Now you can add your commands to this new menu. If you are creating a new command, however, there is more work to be done.

6. In the Command Line text box, enter the file name of the application program you want to add, or use the Browse button to look for the exact file name. Include path information if the directory containing the program is not part of the path statement in the AUTOEXEC.BAT file.

7. The Shortcut Key text box is optional; enter any combination of Ctrl, Shift, and Alt, along with any letter or number. Illegal key combinations are not accepted. Leave this box blank if you don't want to use a shortcut. Be careful not to use a shortcut key that you have previously assigned to the Launch Manager.

8. Check the Include Key Name in Menu checkbox if you want to see the shortcut key on the menu beside the text title.

There are other ways of achieving this same result of making an application program easily available; you could use Quick Access groups as described in Chapter 8, for example.

EDITING YOUR COMMANDS

Once you have added a standard or custom menu item to your custom Desktop menu, you can edit or change the entry if it is not to your liking. Choose Edit Custom Menus in the Configure menu, and then either double-click on the item in the Menu list box that you want to edit or highlight the entry and click on Edit to bring up the Edit Menu Item Text dialog box, shown in Figure 9.4. If you are

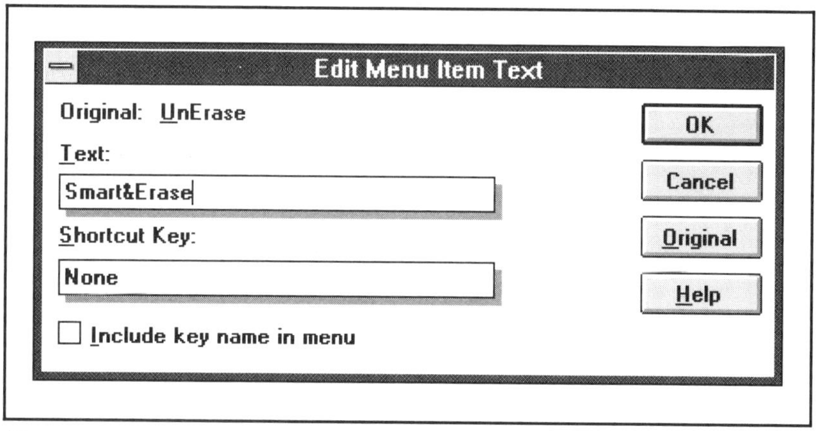

Figure 9.4: Alter an entry in your custom menu using the Edit Menu Item Text dialog box

editing a menu command, the original title and shortcut key (if available) are shown in their respective text boxes. If you are editing a menu title, the Shortcut Key text box, the Include Key Name in Menu checkbox, and the Original command button are dimmed and unavailable.

> Both SmartErase and Erase Protect are described in Chapter 11, and UnErase is described in Chapter 18.

The Tools menu on the Desktop includes an option called UnErase, which invokes the SmartErase program. UnErase is usually the name used in connection with the non-Windows file-recovery program located on the Emergency Disk, while SmartErase is the name for the Windows recovery program used with Erase Protect, and is the name associated with the icon on your Desktop. In this next example, you will change the name of the Tools menu item from UnErase to SmartErase:

1. Select Edit Custom Menus from the Configure menu.

2. Double-click the UnErase entry in the Menu list box.

> Click the Original command button to restore the command's original name and shortcut-key assignment.

3. Type the new name you want to use for this item into the Text box. Add an ampersand (&) immediately before the letter in the name that you want underlined. This is the letter you can use from the keyboard to choose the option. Sleeper already uses *S* in this menu, so our example will use *E* instead. Type **Smart&Erase** into this text box so that the *E* is underlined.

4. Add a shortcut key if you want to use one, and check the Include Key Name in Menu checkbox if you want to see this key when you open the menu.

5. Click on OK to close this dialog box, then click on OK again to close the Menu Assignments dialog box and return to the Desktop.

Now when you open the Tools menu, you will see that this entry is shown as Smart<u>E</u>rase, with the *E* available as the selection letter from the keyboard.

WORKING WITH PASSWORDS

Passwords restrict users to certain areas of the Desktop. To establish a password, choose Password from the Configure menu. Enter your choice of password into the text box and then enter it again into the next dialog box to confirm your password. As you type, only asterisks appear in these two text boxes, for security reasons.

To disable the password, choose Password from the Configure menu, enter your current password into the text box, and click on OK. When the Enter New Password dialog box opens, do not enter a password; leave the text box blank, but click on OK. The Confirm Disable Password dialog box opens; click on OK.

SELECTING PREFERENCES

Select Preferences in the Configure menu to open the Configure Preferences dialog box shown in Figure 9.5. By using selections from this dialog box, you can establish the following:

- which of the tools appear as individual icons on your Desktop.
- exactly when you will be prompted for a file name.
- which selections appear on the Control menu
- whether drive and tool icons have individual Control menus.

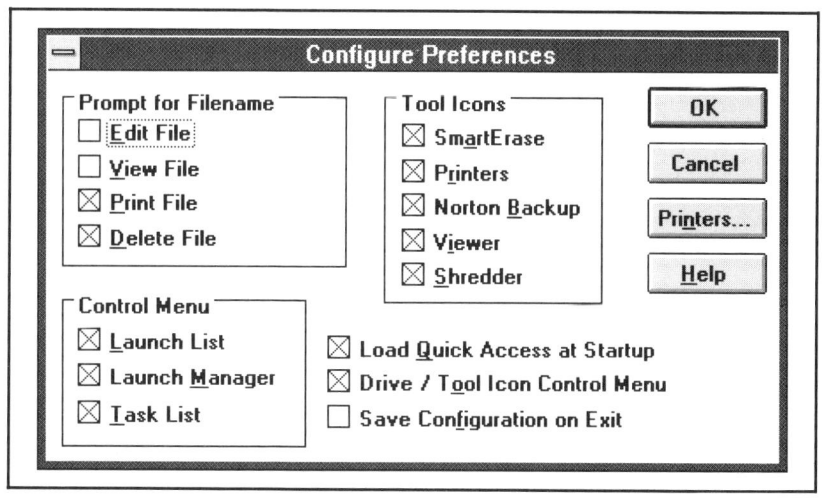

Figure 9.5: The Configure Preferences dialog box extends your control over several individual elements of the Desktop

- which configuration settings are saved automatically as you exit from the Desktop.
- whether Quick Access is launched when you start the Desktop.

CHOOSING THE PROMPT FOR A FILE NAME

When you invoke the Edit, View, Print, or Delete command from the File menu while a drive window is open, it acts on your files rather than on Quick Access groups. Each of these commands will open a prompt dialog box before performing the operation you requested. An example of this kind of dialog box is the Print dialog box shown in Figure 9.6.

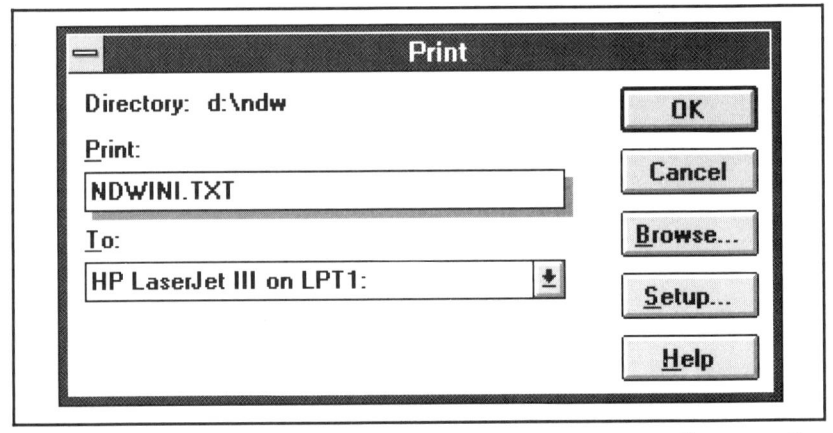

Figure 9.6: The Print command from the File menu opens a small prompt dialog box

The four prompt dialog boxes are slightly different, but they all include a text box for the currently selected file name and a Browse command button for choosing a different file name. If you select more than one file, the total number of files will be shown in this box, rather than the individual file names.

If you want a prompt dialog box to open when you use one of these four commands from the File menu, check the appropriate box in the Prompt for Filename group box (see Figure 9.5). If there is no × in the box, you will not see the prompt dialog box when you use the command. In that case, you'll have to select a file in the drive window *before* invoking the Print command.

This prompt dialog box is *not* the same as the "Are you sure you want to do this?" dialog box associated with potentially dangerous commands like Delete. You can configure those dialog boxes separately, as we will see in the next major section, "Setting Confirmation Options."

PICKING TOOL ICONS

The Tool Icons group box (see Figure 9.5) lists the five Desktop tools that you can place directly on your Desktop as icons. All of the icons except the Shredder are checked by default; if a tool icon box is checked, that icon will appear on your Desktop. You then invoke the tool by double-clicking on the icon or dragging a file and dropping it on the icon.

The Printers command button in this dialog box lets you select which of your printers to show as a Desktop tool icon. You can select up to four, but remember that you can also make a similar printer selection from the Print command in the File menu—so you don't have to have all your printers on the Desktop at the same time just in case you might want to use one of them. Just put the printer you use most often on your Desktop as a tool icon.

REFINING THE CONTROL MENU

Using the checkboxes in the Control Menu group, you can specify whether the Task List and/or the Launch List should appear in the Norton Desktop Control menu. If you select the Launch List you can also select the Launch Manager; otherwise the Launch Manager is dimmed out.

CHOOSING OTHER OPTIONS

There are also three other checkboxes in the Configure Preferences dialog box, as follows:

Load Quick Access at Startup controls whether or not Quick Access is launched automatically when you start Norton

Desktop. If you check the box, it is started automatically. This will take Desktop longer to load.

Drive/Tool Icon Control Menu specifies whether or not each drive window and tool icon has its Control menu available. Check the box to make these Control menus available. A drive window Control menu contains three selections: Open, Label, and Close; the Desktop tool icons contain four: Open, Label, Icon, and Close.

Save Configuration on Exit saves the current appearance of your Desktop so that when you next launch the Norton Desktop, it looks just the same as it does now. This option is described in more detail under the heading "Saving Your Changes."

SETTING CONFIRMATION OPTIONS

The Norton Desktop often asks you to confirm that you want to complete a potentially dangerous operation like deleting a file or removing part of your directory structure, just to be on the safe side. Some people find these messages annoying, so the Desktop provides a way to turn them off. Select Confirmation in the Configure menu to bring up the Configure Confirmation dialog box, shown in Figure 9.7. Each one of the five checkboxes in this dialog box controls a

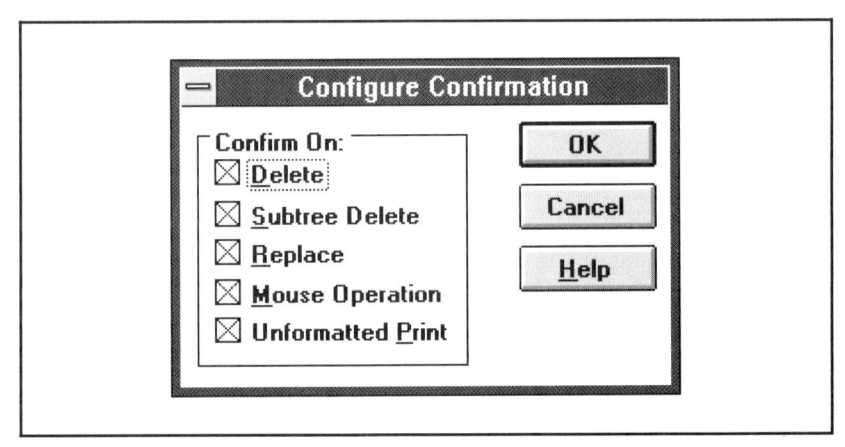

Figure 9.7: If you find the Desktop's confirmation messages annoying, you can turn them off in the Configure Confirmation dialog box

confirmation dialog box relating to the operation you are about to perform.

The checkboxes are as follows:

Delete. Check this box if you want to see a warning before deleting any files that are not protected by Erase Protect. If Erase Protect *is* installed, you can drag files and documents to the SmartErase icon without seeing this confirmation box. Erase Protect is described in Chapter 11.

Subtree Delete. Check this box if you want to see a warning before removing directories. This is independent of the Delete checkbox, which refers only to files.

Replace. Check this box if you want to see a warning before you write over an existing file. I suggest you always leave this option checked; overwriting operations can often introduce more problems (some of them subtle and complex) than just deleting a file. For instance, you wouldn't mistakenly want to overwrite an existing file that has the same name—but completely different content—without knowing about it!

Mouse Operation. Check this box if you want to see a warning before completing a mouse operation like copying, moving, or deleting a file, or launching an application.

Unformatted Print. Check this box to see a warning when you try to print a file but there is no established association for the document.

Click on OK to make these changes for your current Desktop session; see "Saving Your Changes" at the end of this chapter to make them permanent.

MANAGING YOUR DRIVE ICONS

When you start the Desktop, you will see different icons for your floppy drive(s) and hard drive(s) (both directly connected to your system and local-area-network hard drives)—as well as RAM drive(s) and CD-ROM(s), if you have any. These icons are shown down the left side of your Desktop by default. You can tell the Desktop which of these icons you want to have visible on your Desktop, and also where

The icon used for a 5¼-inch floppy disk drive looks different than the icon for a 3½-inch drive. Norton Desktop knows the difference.

CH. 9

> Log on to your network (with Connect Net Drive in the Disk menu) before opening this dialog box to show the network drive icon(s).

you want them to appear. You can even turn them off if you don't want them on your Desktop.

You make these selections by choosing Drive Icons in the Configure menu. This opens the Configure Drive Icons dialog box shown in Figure 9.8. All the drives that Desktop can find on your system are shown in the Drives list box. Highlight a specific drive if you want to see its icon on your Desktop; remove the highlight if you don't want to see it. In Figure 9.8 both floppy disk drives, all three hard disks, and the RAM drive appear on my Desktop.

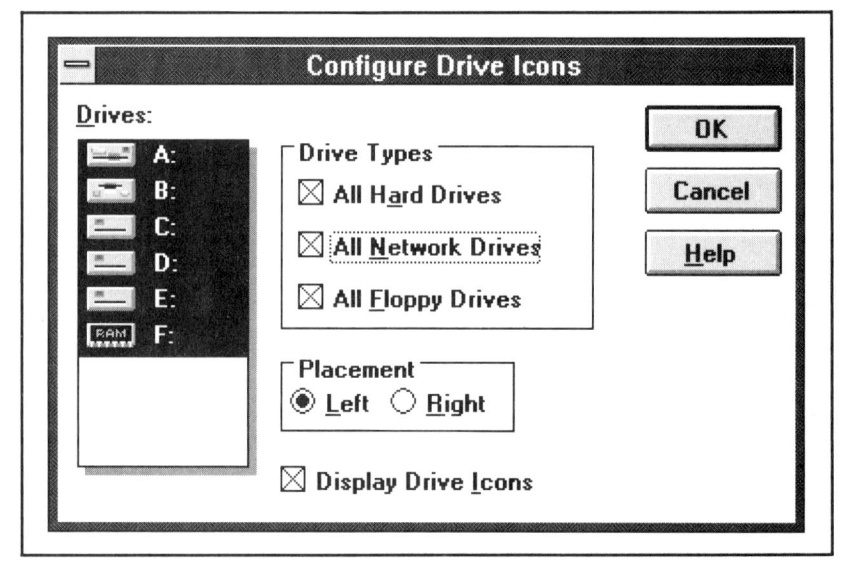

Figure 9.8: Specify which drive icons to show on your Desktop using the Configure Drive Icons dialog box

Use the checkboxes in the Drive Types group box to work with groups of drives rather than individual drives. To display all local hard disk drives (including RAM drives), check the All Hard Drives checkbox; to display all networked drives, check the All Network Drives checkbox; and to see icons for your floppy disks, be sure to check the All Floppy Drives checkbox.

When you first start the Desktop, these drive icons are aligned down the left side of the Desktop, but you can move them to the right side if you select the Right option button in the Placement group box.

Remember, too, that you can move your drive icons to any other location on your Desktop by dragging them with the mouse.

If you don't want to see any drive icons at all, remove the checkmark from the Display Drive Icons checkbox at the bottom of this dialog box. You will still be able to open a drive window by selecting the Open Drive Window command from the Window menu.

CUSTOMIZING THE BUTTON BAR

At the bottom of every drive window is a row of six buttons; Move, Copy, Delete, View Pane, Type Sort, and Name Sort are the initial default buttons. It should come as no surprise to you that you can change these functions and specify your own commands. You may assign any six Norton Desktop commands to your button bar. Because the button bar is so closely associated with the drive windows, however, it makes sense to choose commands associated with drives, directories, or disks for the button bar.

SuperFind is described in Chapter 13.

For example, if you find that you don't use the Move command button very often, you can replace it with one of the other Desktop commands, perhaps with Date Sort or Select All—or even with a Desktop tool like SuperFind. If you don't like the button bar at all, you can turn it off completely.

Choose the Button Bar selection from the Configure menu to open the Configure Button Bar dialog box. The Menu Item list box on the left side of this dialog box shows all the Desktop commands you can assign to a button. The current button assignments are shown along the bottom of the dialog box. To associate a different command with a button, follow these steps:

1. Highlight the command you want to add in the Menu Item list box; in our example, this is SuperFind. A short description of SuperFind appears in the box to the right of the Menu Item list box.

2. Click on the button you want to use with this command. The new command name appears on the button immediately, in exactly the same way as it appears in the Menu Items list box (see Figure 9.9). If you click on a button

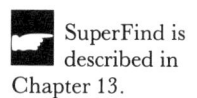

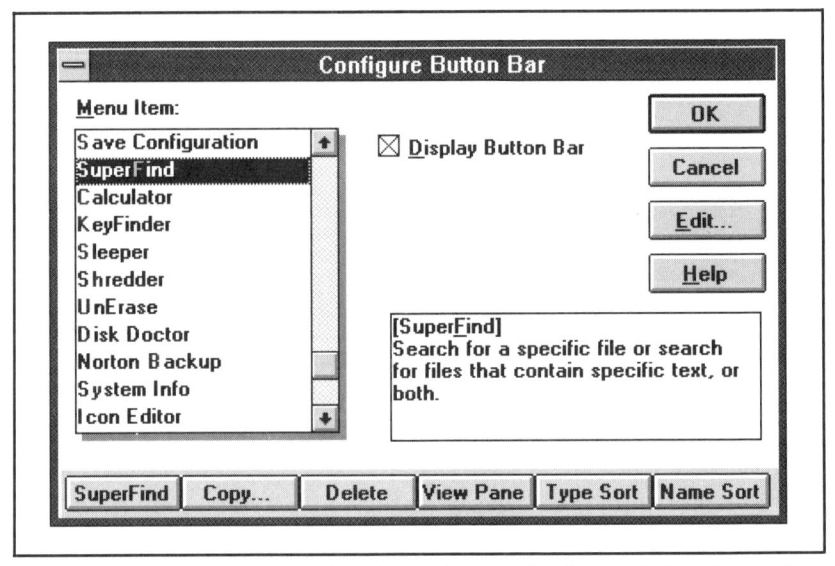

Figure 9.9: Add your own choice of functions to the drive window button bar using the Configure Button Bar dialog box

without making a selection from the Menu items list, or if you double-click on a button, the button will become blank and be no longer shown in a drive window.

3. Click on OK to accept this change.

> Put the functions you use most often on the buttons at the left side of button bar, because these buttons will be available even if you've resized the drive window so that not all the buttons are visible at the same time.

If the text on the button is too long to fit on the button, use the Edit command to open the dialog box shown in Figure 9.10. The labels appearing on all six buttons are shown in this dialog box, so you can change the text on as many buttons as you wish, all at the same time. A proportional spacing font is used, so it is difficult to say how many characters will fit on a button; it really depends on which characters they are. If you use any of the commands from a cascading menu, like the File Select or Deselect menu selections, change the command names to something more meaningful so that you are not confused. Both the Select and Deselect menus contain commands called All, Some, and Invert, and their precise meaning depends on the context. Click on OK to dismiss this dialog box, then click on OK again to return to the Desktop.

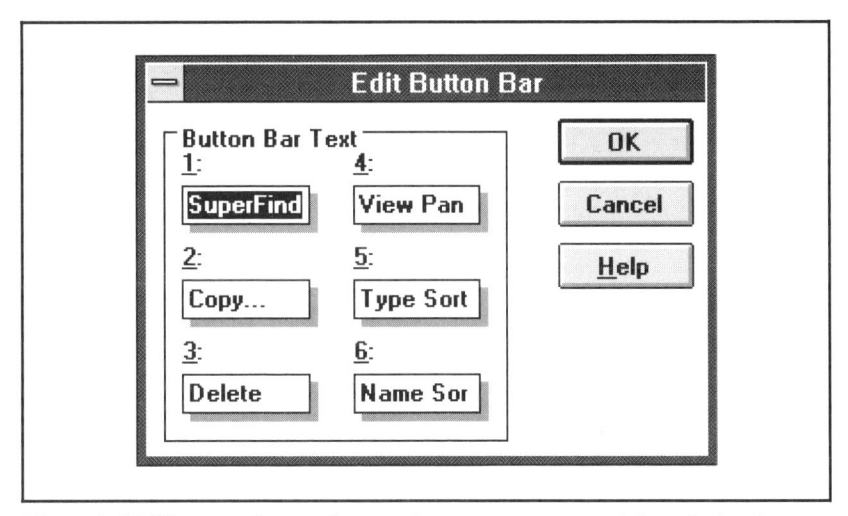

Figure 9.10: You can change the text that appears on any drive window button with the Edit Button Bar dialog box

If you don't want to see the button bar at all, remove the check mark from the Display Button Bar checkbox in the Configure Button Bar dialog box. When you click on OK, the button bar will not only be removed from any open drive windows, but it will not appear on any other drive windows you open subsequently. Just check the box again to restore the button bar.

ESTABLISHING SHORTCUT KEYS FOR COMMANDS

You can assign a shortcut key to any Norton Desktop command, so that you can invoke the command without first having to open its menu. Several menu items come with shortcut keys already assigned. For example, you can copy a file if you select a file in a drive window and then press F8; or press F5 if you want to refresh a file pane. You can change these key assignments—or add your own—in the Configure Shortcut Keys dialog box, as Figure 9.11 shows. You can also make these shortcut keys appear in the menus, if you wish.

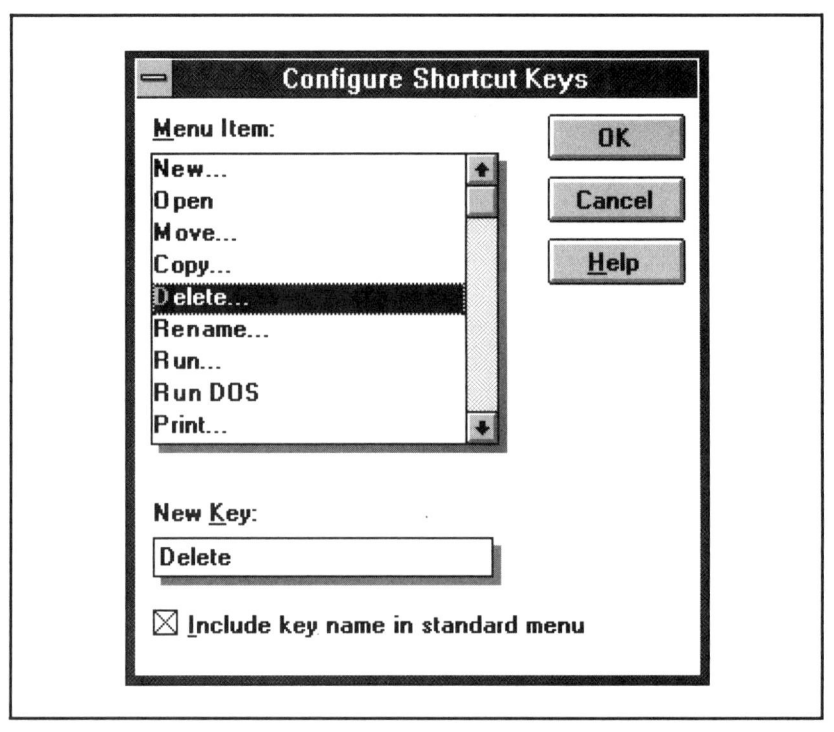

Figure 9.11: Assign new or edit existing shortcut keys using the Configure Shortcut Keys dialog box

> The Launch Manager also lets you assign shortcut keys to applications; if you use the same shortcut key in both places, the Launch Manager will take precedence over the menu command.

To look at or change any of the currently assigned shortcut keys, follow these steps:

1. Choose Shortcut Keys from the Configure menu. The Menu Item list box in the dialog box shows all the commands available on the Desktop.

2. Highlight the command you want to work with from this list. If it already has a shortcut key assigned, you will see the key in the New Key text box.

3. To add or change a shortcut key, just press the key(s). The New Key text box will show you what you pressed. If you try to enter an unacceptable key, nothing will be

displayed. You can use:

- any function key except F1.
- the Shift key with any function key except F1.
- the Ctrl key with any letter, number, or function key.
- the Ctrl and Shift keys together with any letter, number, or function key.
- a combination of the Alt key with either Ctrl, Shift, Tab, or the spacebar, along with any letter, number, or function key.

4. To include the key name in the menu alongside the command, check the Include Key Name in Standard Menu checkbox.
5. Click on OK.

If you want to remove a shortcut key, highlight the menu item in the Menu Item list box, click the New Key text box, and press the spacebar. The word **None** will appear in the New Key text box. Click on OK.

CONFIGURING THE DESKTOP TOOLS

You can configure three of the Desktop tools from entries in the lower part of the Configure menu: Quick Access, SmartErase, and the Shredder.

CONFIGURING QUICK ACCESS

Quick Access is described in detail in Chapter 8.

Select Quick Access from the Configure menu if you are running Quick Access as part of your Desktop, or from the Options menu if you are running Quick Access in stand-alone mode. In either case you will see the dialog box shown on Figure 9.12. Select the format for your new group windows from the Default Group View group box. You can select Icon View to see icons arranged in rows and columns, with names underneath, or choose List View to see your icons arranged in a single

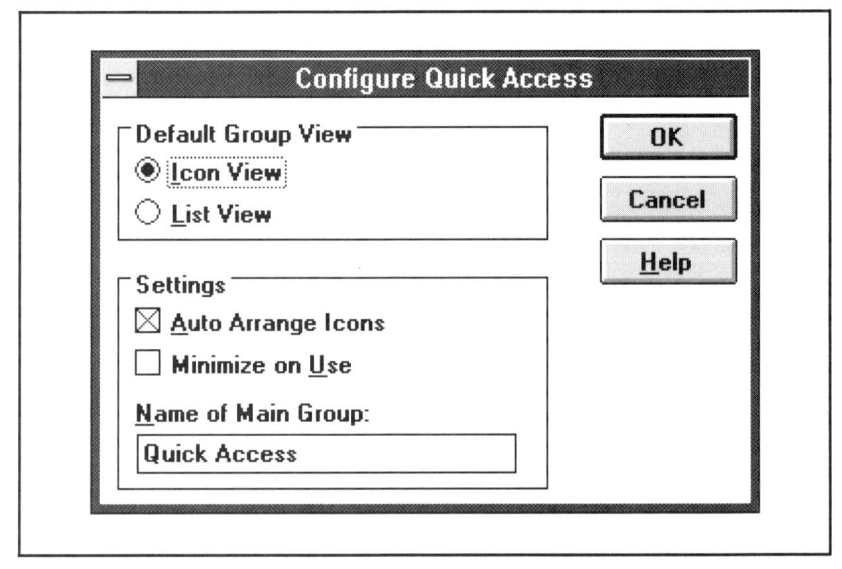

Figure 9.12: You can even change the name of the Quick Access main group window from the Configure Quick Access dialog box

long column down the window, with their names to the right, along with any descriptive text you have entered.

The two checkboxes are used as follows:

> **Auto Arrange Icons.** Check this box if you want all icons in group windows to be rearranged automatically each time you resize a group window or add a new item to the group. Icons are arranged so that they don't overlap. If you don't want to make a global decision here, leave this box unchecked, and use the Arrange Icons command from the Desktop Window menu to rearrange the icons in the currently active window.
>
> **Minimize on Use.** Check this box if you want Quick Access to minimize all open windows to icons on the Desktop each time you launch an application. If you don't check this box, the window will stay at its current size and location, even if that means that it is hidden from view by the application you launched.

The Name of Main Group text box contains the name used at the top of the Quick Access main window. Obviously, the default name for this window is Quick Access, although you can change this, if you wish, in this text box. Click on OK when your changes are complete.

See the last section in this chapter for information on making these changes permanent.

CONFIGURING SMARTERASE

> See Chapter 11 for a complete description of how to use SmartErase and Erase Protect.

SmartErase is available as a Desktop icon, as well as from the Desktop Tools menu. When you delete a file either using SmartErase or the Delete command from the File menu, the file you chose is not deleted immediately, but is copied to a special area of your disk known as the "Trashcan," where it is held for a period of time before being deleted. You can recover accidentally deleted files from the Trashcan quite easily using SmartErase.

You can specify several important options for SmartErase from the Configure menu if you choose the SmartErase option and open the dialog box shown in Figure 9.13. Check the Enable SmartErase Protection checkbox to activate Erase Protect; otherwise Erase Protect will not be active, even if it is loaded into memory. If Erase Protect is not loaded, this entry will be dimmed out.

Select an option from the Files to Protect group box, as follows:

> **All files.** This extends protection to all files on the chosen drives. This is the most extensive level of protection, and is the option you will probably use most of the time.

> To protect more than nine different extensions from deletion, just select All Files Except Those Listed, then specify the extensions that should *not* be protected.

> **Only the files listed.** Use this selection if you are sure that you only want to protect specific files. You can enter as many as nine file-name extensions into the File Extensions text box.

> **All files except those listed.** This option lets you reverse the sense of the previous choice. Enter the file-name extensions for those files that you do *not* want to protect.

> **Protect archived (backed up) files.** Erase Protect does not automatically save files that have already been backed up or

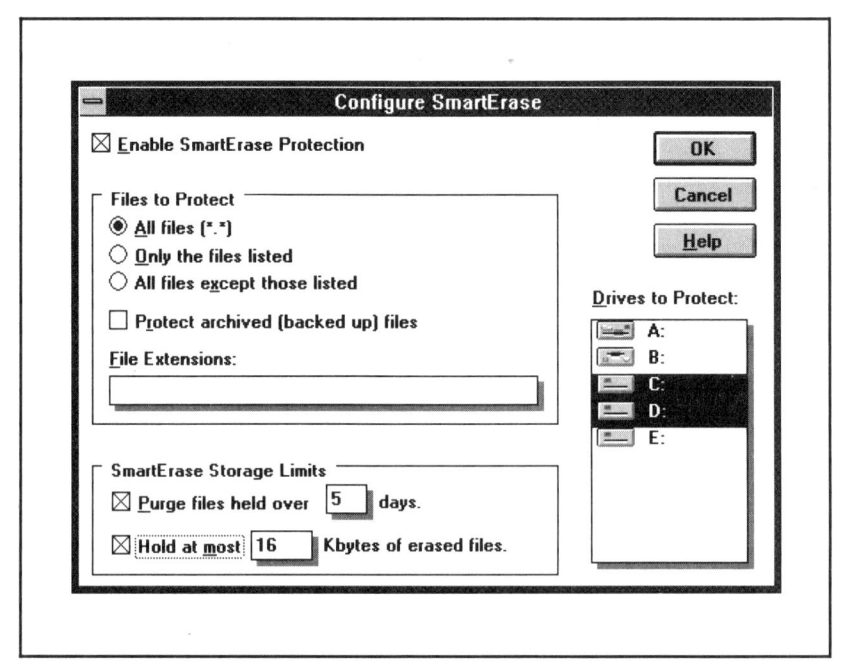

Figure 9.13: Set up SmartErase's operating parameters from the Configure SmartErase dialog box

archived—after all, you can always reload these files from your backup if you need them again. However, check this box if you want to make sure that Erase Protect includes archived files.

File Extensions. Enter the file extensions into this text box; either to protect or not to protect, depending on the option you picked above. You can enter up to nine different extensions if you separate each from the next by a single space or comma. You can mix upper- and lowercase letters, and you don't have to use the star and the dot before the extension (as in DOS): you can just enter **EXE** to specify all executable files, **WRI** for Write files, or **INI** for your Windows configuration files. If you selected All Files, this text box is dimmed.

With the next two entries you can also specify the storage limits for the SmartErase Trashcan:

Purge files held over XX days. Enter the number of days that you want to preserve files held in the Trashcan, before they are automatically deleted from your system, from 1 to 99 days; the default is 5 days. Enter 0 to specify no time limit.

Hold at most XX Kbytes of erased files. Enter the maximum amount of disk space you want to reserve for the Trashcan, in kilobytes, from 16 to 9,999. When the Trashcan fills up, the oldest files will be purged first to make room for later files. If you don't want to set an upper limit for the Trashcan, do not check this box; your deleted files will then be kept until you run out of disk space. Chapter 11 describes how to get around this. If you delete a file that is larger than the Trashcan, you will have to use the UnErase program on the Emergency Disk to recover the file.

Use the Drives to Protect list box to select as many of your drives for protection as you wish.

Unlike many of the other selections on the Configure menu, as soon as you click on OK in the Configure SmartErase dialog box, your changes are saved to disk. You do not have to use the Save Configuration command, or the Configure Preferences dialog box to make the changes permanent.

CONFIGURING THE SHREDDER

The Shredder is available from the Desktop as an icon, or from the Tools menu. The Shredder eradicates a file from your system so completely that it can never be recovered, even by the most advanced file-recovery programs. You can set some of the Shredder operating parameters using Shredder from the Configure menu. You will see the dialog box shown in Figure 9.14.

Check the U.S. Government Shredding check box if you want the Shredder to obliterate files according to the U.S. Department of Defense rules (DOD 5220.22M). Check the Use Special Over-Write

The U.S. Government method takes longer but is more secure.

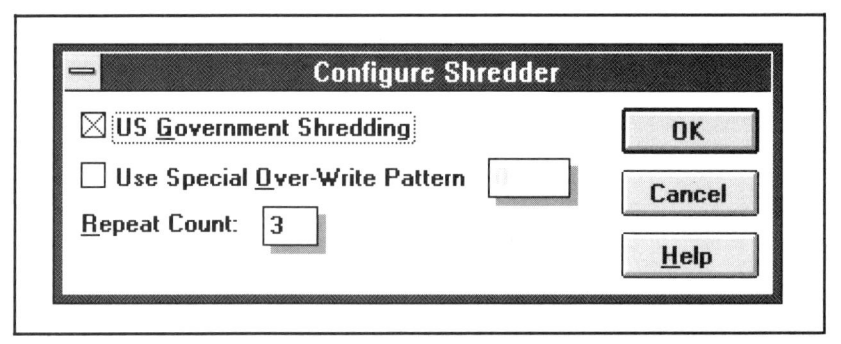

Figure 9.14: Set the Shredder operating options using the Configure Shredder dialog box

Pattern if you want to specify the character to use when shredding files. Enter the character you want to use for over-writing into the text box. You can enter any ASCII decimal value between 0 and 255 for overwriting. If you enter 69, your files will be shredded using the letter *E*; if you enter 48, your files will be shredded using the number 0. You must also specify the number of times you want the data in a shredded file to be overwritten, from 1 and 999.

If you select U.S. Government Shredding and leave the text box blank, the DOD rules require that ones and zeros be used for the initial passes over the file, then the number 246 for the last overwrite made on your file. If you select U.S. Government Shredding and *do* specify a character in this box, the character will be used for the last overwrite pass only. See Chapter 11 for more details.

The rules for U.S. Government Shredding call for three overwrite passes across the file, so if you check this box and then specify a repeat count of three, Shredded actually makes nine overwrite passes across your file.

See the last section in this chapter for information on saving your Shredder changes.

SPECIFYING THE DEFAULT EDITOR AND VIEWER

Your editor does not have to be a Windows application.

When you select a document on the Desktop, then choose the Edit command from the Desktop File menu, the Desktop opens the default editor on the file. When you first install the Desktop, Windows Notepad is configured as the default editor. If you have another editor that you would rather use instead, however, you can use the Editor command from the Configure menu to change this default.

When the Choose Editor dialog box opens, enter the program file name and extension of the editor you want to use into the Editor Program text box. If the editor's path is not specified in your path command in the AUTOEXEC.BAT file, you must include full path information in this text box. There is also a Browse button in this dialog box that you can use to search for the file name you want to use.

You can also select the default viewer from the Configure menu if you use Default Viewer. This command opens the dialog box shown in Figure 9.15. Norton Desktop uses the default viewer to display the contents of a file that has no established association with one of the other viewers. Unless you specify otherwise, the default is the Documents & Text viewer. This is a good general-purpose viewer for most people to use, although programmers might want to change it to the Hex Dump, as they spend so much time working with binary files.

To select the default Desktop viewer, highlight the name of the viewer you want to use in the Default Viewer list box and click on OK.

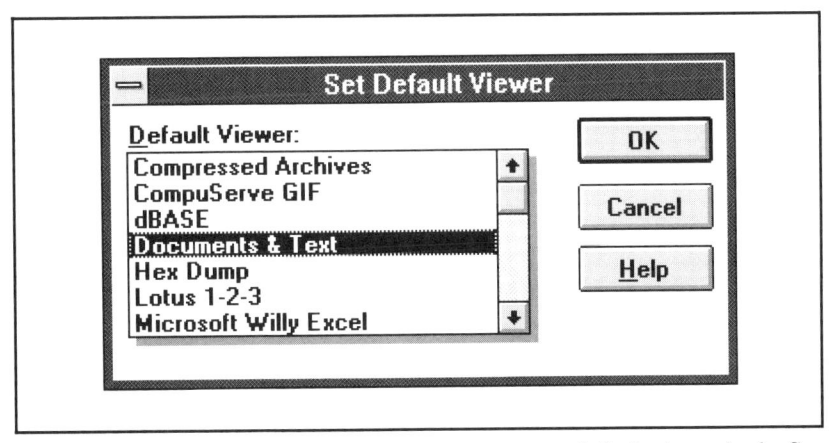

Figure 9.15: Select the viewer you want to use as your default viewer in the Set Default Viewer dialog box

USING THE DESKTOP AS YOUR WINDOWS SHELL

When you install the Norton Desktop on your system, the Desktop replaces the Windows Program Manager as your interface, or *shell,*

> To find out more about the contents of SYSTEM.INI, print the Windows file called SYSINI.TXT.

into the Windows operating environment. This means that every time you start Windows running you will see the Norton Desktop instead of the Windows Program Manager, and all the features of the Desktop will be immediately available for use. If you use the features of the Norton Desktop often, then this is the best way for you to run your system, the only drawback being that loading the Desktop takes some extra time. If you have a fast computer, you may not notice the small delay.

If you don't need all the features of the Desktop immediately at hand, but you still want access to all the functions and tools provided as part of the Desktop package, you can change a setting in your Windows SYSTEM.INI file to restore the Program Manager. This means that you can still access the Norton Desktop group window, and the Desktop will always be available as an icon from that group window; just click on the icon to open the Desktop.

If the Norton Desktop is loaded automatically when you start Windows, your SYSTEM.INI file contains an entry close to the top of the file that says:

SHELL = NDW.EXE

Use Notepad to change this to read:

SHELL = PROGMAN.EXE

Save the SYSTEM.INI file, exit Windows, and then restart Windows again to make sure that the SYSTEM.INI file is reloaded. After you make this change, you will see the Program Manager window open when you start Windows running.

If you chose not to install Norton Desktop as your shell when you first installed the package, and now you want to try using Desktop for a while, you have to reverse the process described above. Your SYSTEM.INI file contains an entry that reads:

SHELL = PROGMAN.EXE

Use Windows Notepad to open SYSTEM.INI and change this entry so that it reads:

SHELL = NDW.EXE

Save the SYSTEM.INI file, exit from Windows, and restart Windows. This time Norton Desktop will be loaded.

If you did not add details of the NDW directory to your path statement in your AUTOEXEC.BAT file, you may have to add that path information into SYSTEM.INI now. The entry now becomes

```
SHELL = C:\NDW\NDW.EXE
```

assuming you installed the Desktop files into a directory called NDW on drive C. If you used a different name or a different drive, then change this entry accordingly.

WHAT'S IN THE NDW.INI FILE?

Just like other parts of the Windows operating environment, the Norton Desktop maintains its own configuration file, saving your choices and preferences in a file called NDW.INI in the WINDOWS directory. Every time you launch the Desktop, it looks for this file and loads the contents.

The entries in NDW.INI have the following general format:

```
[Section Name]
keyname = value
```

just like the other Windows initialization files. NDW.INI contains the following sections:

[Calculators] This section contains entries for both the Tape and the Scientific Calculators.

[Configuration] This section contains entries that control the Norton Desktop configuration.

[Defaults] This section has entries that affect Norton Desktop history listings found in several Desktop dialog boxes, including Filter and Run.

[Disk Doctor] Here Desktop keeps information about the configuration of Norton Disk Doctor for Windows, including whether or not to run the partition table test, and whether you want to exclude any disk drives from testing.

[NBackup] This part of NDW.INI contains configuration information for Norton Backup for Windows, described in Chapter 10.

[Print Start] This part of the file contains settings that let you print documents with the Desktop Print icon using non-standard print commands. Some applications programs do not use the standard Windows File/Print/OK (!FP ~) sequence when printing documents. Informix Software's Wingz, for example, needs two OK's rather than just one, and so needs a special entry in Print Start that looks like this:

WINGZ.EXE = !FP ~ ~

Alphanumeric keys are used as they are, but special key equivalents are as follows:

Alt	!
Ctrl	^
Shift	...
Enter	~ *or* {Enter}
F1 *through* F16	{F1} *through* {F16}

[Print Stop] This part of the file contains instructions to the application program on how to close after printing is complete. For example, to close Microsoft Project after printing, add the following to NDW.INI:

WINPROJ.EXE = !FXN

In both [Print Start] and [Print Stop], be sure to match the program file name with the association name previously set up for the application program and the document. For example, if the association was established as C:\WINDOWS\WINPROJ.EXE, then

[Print Start] and [Print Stop] should be WINPROJ.EXE (be sure to include the file-name extension). If the association is C:\WINDOWS\WINPROJ, then just use WINPROJ (this time without the file-name extension).

[Quick Access] This section contains settings for Quick Access, including the title for the Quick Access main group window, as well as icon spacing information.

[Scheduler] This part of NDW.INI controls the Scheduler.

[SiCalc] Here you will find controls for the Scientific Calculator when used on a Hercules monochrome adapter. Remove the semi-colons at the start of each line to activate these statements, otherwise the calculator may be difficult to read.

[SmartErase] This section contains settings for SmartErase and Erase Protect. If you decide not to run Erase Protect on your system, you will see a warning message on the screen each time you start the Desktop. To stop this warning message from being displayed, use Windows Notepad to edit the following statement in NDW.INI:

    EPWARNING = 1

should be changed to read

    EPWARNING = 0

to avoid the Erase Protect warning message.

[TapeCalc] In this section of NDW.INI you will find settings for the Tape Calculator, including the current tax rate and the number of decimal digits to use.

[Viewer-Filemap] This section assigns a viewer to a document file-name extension. For example, the setting

    PCX = PCX.PRS HEX.PRS

tells the Desktop to use a viewer called PCX.PRS with any file that has a file-name extension of .PCX. If that viewer cannot view the file, the second viewer specified on the line, HEX.PRS, should be used instead.

[Viewer-Parsers] This last part of NDW.INI contains a series of settings that identify the viewers available in the Norton Desktop. Each viewer file is associated with a short editable description that appears in the Default View and Current View dialog boxes. For example, the entry

DOC.PRS = Documents & Text

associates the document viewer with its description.

Besides copying the NDW.INI file from the distribution disks onto your hard disk, the install program also copies a file called NDWINI.TXT into the directory on your hard disk where the Norton Directory system files are located (probably NDW). This file is a text file containing detailed information about NDW.INI and it describes how the file is used by Norton Desktop. If you want to see further information on NDW.INI, just load NDWINI.TXT into Notepad, or use the Printer icon on the Desktop to print a copy of the file.

SAVING YOUR CHANGES

There are two ways you can save your changes in the Norton Desktop:

- Click the Save Configuration on Exit checkbox in the Configure Preferences dialog box.
- Use the Save Configuration command in the Desktop Configure menu.

If you want your Desktop to start up looking just like it did when you *last closed it,* make sure that the Save Configuration on Exit checkbox is set. If you want your Desktop to start up looking the same *every time* you start it, use the Save Configuration command.

USING SAVE CONFIGURATION ON EXIT

Use Save Configuration on Exit if you want to be able to resume the Desktop at the same place that you left off in your last Desktop session. Select Preferences from the Configure menu and check the Save Configuration on Exit checkbox. This will save the following:

- the current location and size of all drive windows, Desktop tool icons, and Quick Access group windows.
- all changes made using selections in the Configure menu.
- options set in the View menu.
- any file associations made using the Associate command from the File menu.

If you prefer to have the Desktop layout appear the same way every time you launch Norton Desktop, make sure this checkbox is *not* checked, and use Save Configuration instead.

USING SAVE CONFIGURATION

Use this command if you like to start your Desktop looking the same every time you launch it. If you have made changes from the Configure menu, and you want to preserve these changes for future Desktop sessions, make sure the Desktop looks just how you like it, then select Save Configuration from the Configure menu. There is no dialog box associated with this command.

If you do not use this command, any changes you have made to the Desktop will only be available for the duration of your current session. When you exit from the Desktop, these changes will be lost, except changes made using the following Configure menu commands:

- Edit Custom Menus
- Shortcut Keys
- SmartErase

Changes made with these menu selections are always saved immediately.

PART THREE
The Windows Tools

Part III describes the extensive Windows tool set, including how to use Norton Backup for Windows to back up essential files and directories and to protect files from accidental deletion. You will also learn how to examine all the dark corners in your computer to reveal both hardware and software information, to locate lost files, and to use the calculators, KeyFinder, and Sleeper. The last chapter in Part III describes the advanced Windows tools: Batch Builder, Icon Editor, and Scheduler.

TEN
Backing Up Your System

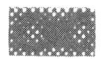

A *BACKUP* IS AN UP-TO-DATE COPY OF ALL YOUR files that you can use to reload your system in case of an accident. It is an insurance policy against anything happening to the hundreds or possibly thousands of files you might have on your hard disk. If the unthinkable were to occur—losing all your files due to a hard disk problem and not having any backup copies—it would take you weeks or even months to recreate all those files, if indeed they could be recreated. If you run your own business or work on your computer from home, it is crucial that you make regular, consistent backups—because no one will do it for you, and it is a sad fact that hard disks do fail occasionally, usually at the most inconvenient moment.

PLANNING YOUR BACKUPS

You should get into the habit of backing up your system regularly, so that you never have to do any extra work as a result of a damaged or missing file. How often you make a backup depends on how much you use your computer, and how often your files change. If you use your computer for entertainment on weekends, you don't have to back up very often. If your business depends on data in the computer, then you should back up at least every day. If you are a programmer, a writer, or the person in charge of the finance department, who is concerned with up-to-date and accurate accounts payable and receivable, then consider backing up your new data twice a day.

WHY SHOULD YOU MAKE A BACKUP?

There are several reasons for making a backup of the files on your hard disk:

- Protection against hard disk failure is the most common and important reason for backing up your hard disk. A hard disk can fail at almost any time, but it is always at the most inconvenient moment. You can install an up-to-date backup in a few minutes and be back in business very quickly. Your bank, utility company, and city, county, and state government agencies are constantly backing up their disk systems on all their computers to avoid having the down time and expense involved in recreating their data.

- Protection against accidental deletion is another prime reason for making a backup. SmartErase and Erase Protect (described in Chapter 11) can provide protection up to a point, but after the file has been purged from the Trashcan, you may not be able to recover it using Smart Erase; you will have to go to your backup set to find a copy of the file.

- Moving files from one computer to another can be done by means of a backup, particularly if you are working with files that are too large to fit onto a single floppy disk.

- You can use a backup as a way of freeing up valuable disk space on your computer. This is safer than just deleting the files; you can always recover and restore the files if you decide that you needed them after all.

- You can also use a backup to make a permanent archive at the end of a project, when a person leaves your company, or at the closing of the company's books at the end of the fiscal year.

- If you are going to use one of the hard disk optimizing programs like Speed Disk on the Emergency Disk (discussed in Chapter 17) to defragment your hard disk, it is a good idea to make a complete backup of all your important files before you use the program for the first time; your hard disk and the optimizing program may be incompatible. Power outages and brownouts can also occur at any time.

- You should make a precautionary backup of your files before you perform any maintenance work on your files and directories, like cleaning out old demonstration software that you have decided you don't need and removing games that you don't play anymore. No matter how careful you are, there is always the possibility that you will accidentally delete a file that really belongs to a different application program. If you find that this application program won't start after your housekeeping session, you can restore the missing file from your backup.

WHEN SHOULD YOU MAKE A BACKUP?

One of the most neglected topics in discussing backups is the emphasis on a consistent backup plan. Plan your strategy and—most important—stick to it! With no backup plan, you'll accumulate disks haphazardly, waste disks, and waste valuable time looking for that elusive file.

The first decision to make is how often you should make a backup. To arrive at a conclusion that fits the kind of work you do, ask yourself the following questions:

- How fast do the data in your files change: every minute, ten minutes, day, week, or month?

- How important to your day-to-day operations are these data? Can you work without them, and how long would it take to recreate the data?

- How much will it cost to recreate the data in terms of time spent and business lost?

> It all comes down to a very simple rule: back up all the files that you cannot afford to lose.

In our computerized world, it may take hours or days to create and maintain a file, but it can be lost or destroyed in just microseconds. A hard disk failure, a mistaken delete command, overwriting a long file with a short one with the same name—these can destroy a file just as completely as fire or flood. You just have to lose one file to become a convert to regular, planned backups.

WHAT KIND OF BACKUP SHOULD YOU MAKE?

A common backup strategy is to make a complete backup every Friday, and then make partial backups each day or even twice a day of all the files that have changed since that backup. This ensures that you have all your files on a backup disk somewhere. For example, if your hard disk crashed on Thursday, you could restore last Friday's full backup.

It is a very good idea to keep one full backup of your system in storage somewhere for at least six months; a year is even better. The file that you most want to recover may be the file you deleted three months ago, and your most recent backups won't show a trace of it.

If you use disks as your backup media, use 3½-inch disks if you can, rather than 5¼-inch disks, because the smaller disks are much more robust and less prone to mechanical damage. They also hold more data. Don't try to save money by using generic or secondhand disks for your backup; this will turn out to be a false economy. Use the best quality disks you can afford for your backups.

> You may reuse disks for future backups, but be sure to replace them regularly (e.g., every six months) with brand new disks.

HOW IS A BACKUP MADE?

When you create a new file or modify an existing file on your system, DOS uses one of the file's attributes, the archive attribute, to tell the rest of the world that the file has changed in some way. Norton Backup looks at this archive attribute and uses it to decide whether to back up the file or to leave it alone, depending on the backup method you have selected. When the backup is complete, Norton Backup resets this archive attribute so that it knows that the file has been backed up.

For some files this is a one-time operation; the file is created, the archive attribute tells Norton Backup to back up the file the next time you run it, and Norton Backup obliges. Other files that you or an application program change—like a company inventory database, a set of personnel records at your dentist, or a long report that you have been working on for weeks—change so often that they are backed up every time you run Norton Backup.

When you use Norton Backup to make a backup of the files and directories on your system, there is a definite sequence that you should follow in configuring the program to your specific hardware and then testing that the backup was successful. Here is a summary of the major steps involved in making a backup. These steps also provide the outline for the main part of this chapter:

1. Because of the many possible hardware configurations, you have to tell Norton Backup about the hardware you have

on your system. Norton Backup provides a function for this purpose called Configure, which performs a short series of tests to confirm that the chosen settings will work and produce a good backup.

2. Go ahead and back up the files and directories on your system. This you do with the Backup feature.

3. After the first backup, and again after you change any of the hardware on your computer, you should make a comparison between the files in the backup and the original files on your disk. This safety measure, called Compare, is designed to ensure that if and when you ever need to restore files from your backup, perhaps many months after you originally made the backup, your files will be usable.

4. In the event of an accident of some kind, you can make a claim on your backup insurance policy and use Restore to reload your files from the backup floppy disks onto your hard disk again.

ON-SITE OR OFF-SITE STORAGE?

If you use a computer as part of your business, consider rotating one of your backup sets to a safe, off-site storage location, just as you would for any other important company documents like financial records, photographs, drawings, and patent or trademark applications. People often back up their hard disk and put the backup disks right next to the computer. If the computer is damaged by an accident—be it fire, earthquake, flood, or vandalism—there is a good chance that the backups will be damaged, too.

If you *do* decide to keep your backups on location, remember that not all fireproof safes and strong boxes are rated for storing magnetic media. Most are meant for papers, but disks can become unusable at much lower temperatures than 451 °F, the temperature it takes to ignite paper. You should also protect your backup set against extremes of temperature, the presence of magnetic fields, and contaminants, such as dust and dirt, moisture, smoke, and chemicals. Very often the damage after a small fire does not come from smoke and flames but from the water used to fight the fire.

If you decide to use off-site storage, however, you will find that many companies specialize in the safe, secure storage of magnetic media; see if there is one in your area that will pick up and return your backups on a regular schedule. Look in the yellow pages under "Computer Data Storage" or "Business Records Storage."

The usual way that businesses rotate backups through an off-site storage location is to label all the disks for week one as Backup Set 1 and send them off to the storage company. Then during week two they make Backup Set 2 and send it out for storage, too. They start making Backup Set 3 and ask the courier company to return the disks that make up Set 1 so that they can be reused during week four. This way, as they are creating a new backup set, there is always one set in secure storage, and another, older set in the process of being returned to them for reuse.

CONFIGURING NORTON BACKUP

The first time you use Norton Backup, you must go through a series of steps that test your computer to make sure that you can take advantage of your hardware in making your backups. This process defines the types of floppy disk drives you have attached to your computer as well as the kind of disks you plan to use for your backups. Norton Backup also performs a backup compatibility test to check that your chosen configuration works. This information is stored in a file on your hard disk so that the next time you run Norton Backup, this file automatically loads your default settings.

It is not difficult to complete this configuration process; just follow the instructions given in the dialog boxes. Also, you must complete the configuration before you can actually make a backup.

Start Norton Backup by double-clicking on the Norton Backup icon on the Desktop, or the icon in the Norton Desktop group window. You can also start the program running if you select it in the Tools menu. An alert box opens to tell you that the compatibility test has not been performed on this computer yet. Click on OK to continue. Another alert box opens, as shown in Figure 10.1, to ask if you want to configure the program now. Do not skip this step; click on Yes.

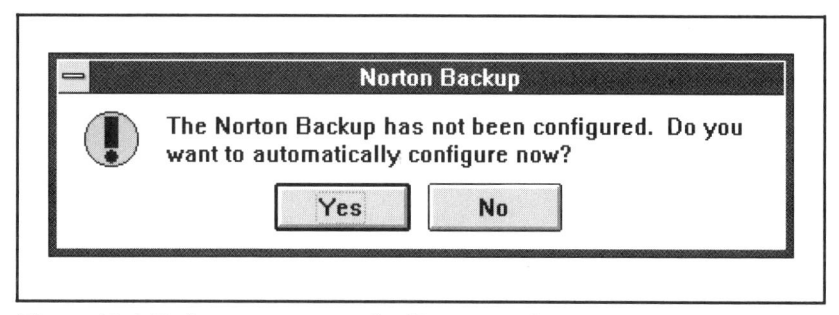

Figure 10.1: Before you can use the Norton Backup program you must first configure and test your computer system

DEFINING YOUR HARDWARE

Norton Backup checks your floppy disk drives and shows you what it recognizes in an alert box. Make sure that the disk drive capacities are correct, then click on OK. Next, Norton Backup performs two configuration tests on your hardware, a Direct Memory Access (DMA) test and a Disk Change test. DMA is a method of data transfer that does not involve the computer's microprocessor—and because of this the transfer is very fast. Unfortunately, some PC-compatibles may not support high speed DMA transfers due to hardware limitations. The DMA test is designed to find out whether or not your computer can do this. Click on the Start command button when you are ready to begin the tests. An alert box will ask you to remove all floppy disks from your floppy disk drives as the Disk Change test runs. If these tests fail, Norton Backup can compensate for them and still make reliable backups; if your computer passes these tests, no changes will be necessary.

Under certain circumstances it is possible that failing the DMA test will stop your computer running; if this happens just restart your computer and start Windows and the Norton Backup. You will find that Norton Backup has checked the Slow DMA checkbox to indicate the change from high-speed to low-speed DMA. Click on OK to close this dialog box.

Norton Backup is now configured. The next stage of this process is to run the compatibility test.

RUNNING THE BACKUP COMPATIBILITY TEST

Run another compatibility test if you change any of the hardware in your computer, especially hard disks or expansion boards. These additions can sometimes have subtle effects on the way the DMA works, and you should know about them before you realize that you cannot restore lost files from your backup. This step is described at the end of this section.

The backup compatibility test actually performs a short backup to a floppy disk, thus eliminating any doubts about Norton Backup's effectiveness or compatibility. It starts up automatically. Be sure to run and complete this test on your computer before you try to make a backup. You need to use two floppy disks during this test. They do not have to be formatted, but if they contain any files, Norton Backup will alert you before it overwrites and destroys them. It also needs full and exclusive access to the floppy disk during this test, so you will not be able to access your floppy drives with another program until this test is complete.

1. The Compatibility Test dialog box will open, as Figure 10.2 shows. Select the disk type you want to use from the Drive to Test drop-down list box. (This test checks your floppy disk controller using one disk and one floppy disk format. If you have had problems reading or writing data to your floppy disks, run this compatibility test on all the drives you want to use with Norton Backup.)

2. Click on the Start command button to start the test running.

3. The Backup Progress window opens to show the progress made so far. Follow the prompts that tell you when to insert the disks. If the disks were not formatted, Norton Backup formats them first, then makes a test backup.

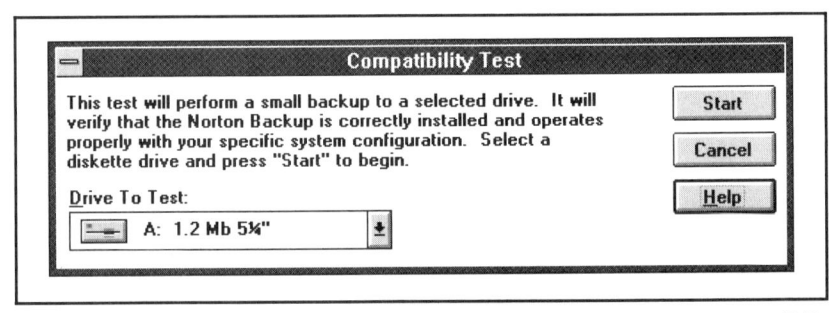

Figure 10.2: Norton Backup performs a test backup as part of the compatibility test

4. When the backup part of the test is complete, follow the prompt on the screen and insert the first disk once again for the compare part of the test, then click on OK.

5. The Compare Progress window opens, prompting for the second disk as necessary. At the end of this phase of the test you will see one of the following messages in an alert box on the screen:

    Compare phase of the compatibility test is complete. This message indicates that your computer will work with Norton Backup without any problems of any kind.

    Compatibility test interrupted. This message indicates that the tests were interrupted. You must complete the tests before you can be sure of making reliable backups on your system. Be sure to run the tests next time you start Norton backup.

    Compatibility test failed. This message indicates that your computer failed the test for some reason. Press F1 to display a Help screen that suggests some things you can try to solve the compatibility problem on your computer. A dialog box will open the next time you start Norton Backup to remind you that the compatibility test failed. You must correct any problems and pass the test before you can use Norton Backup.

6. Click on OK to open the main Norton Backup window. Your computer has passed all the tests and you are now ready to make your first real backup.

Norton Backup contains a Configure button that opens the Configure window in Figure 10.3. Once you have established your initial operating settings, you will probably never need to use Configure, except under the following circumstances:

- to change the program or user level.
- to store catalog files in a different directory.
- to check that newly installed disk drives or other hardware configuration changes do not affect Norton Backup.

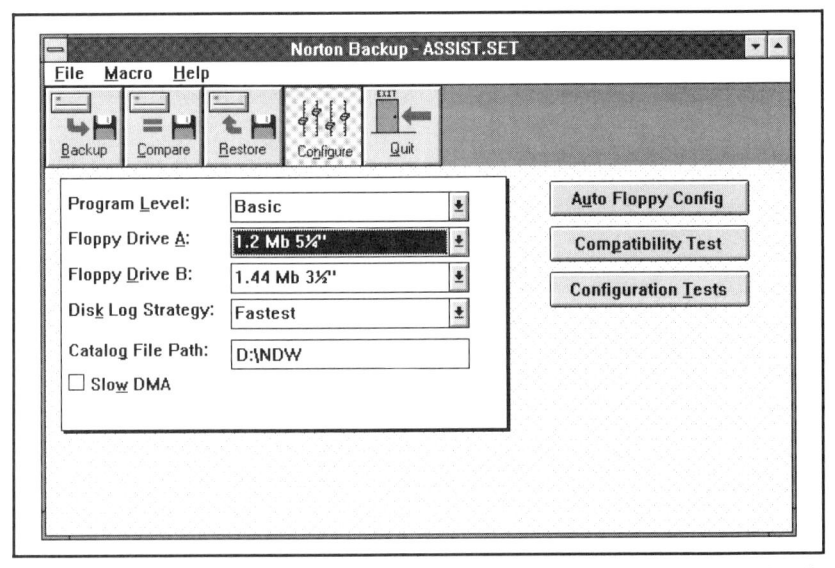

Figure 10.3: Use the Configure window to change the program or user level, and to rerun the Compatibility and Configuration tests if you change your disk hardware

If you need to rerun any of the tests you've already run, choose either the Compatibility Test or the Configuration Tests command buttons in the Configure window. The tests work in just the same way as I have already mentioned, so I will not describe them here again.

CHOOSING YOUR USER LEVEL

Norton Backup has three user levels: basic, advanced, and preset. When you first install Norton Backup, the program is configured at the basic level. When you change this user level, you change the number of options available to you in the Backup, Compare, and Restore windows. Norton Backup selects the safest settings and automatically configures them for you at the basic level. At the advanced level, you can choose how these same settings are made. The preset level is for non-technical people who want to see a simpler program interface, and who want to use a backup strategy set up by someone else. As you become more familiar with Norton Backup you will probably want to change your user level from basic or preset to advanced. The two sections in this chapter that describe making full and partial backups will be done at the basic level. The preset level is described under the heading "Using Setup Files" near the end of the chapter. The advanced options are described in the sections called "Choosing Backup Options" and "Choosing Restore Options" later in the chapter.

CHOOSING YOUR FLOPPY-DRIVE CONFIGURATION

Norton Backup supports all the usual disk drives and floppy disk formats, and—for most computers—can select the highest density floppy format that the disk drive can handle correctly. Select the Auto Floppy Config command button and you should see the highest capacity floppy disk format selected for each of your disk drives. If you don't, then follow these steps to configure your floppy drives manually:

1. Select a drive drop-down box.
2. Click on the floppy type in the drop-down list box. Choose Not Installed if you do not have a drive or you do not plan to use it.
3. Repeat this for your other drive, if you have one.

Be very careful to use the appropriate capacity disks for each of your drives. Do not use 360K disks in a 1.2MB disk drive, because you may not always be able to restore the files from your backup. Always use the appropriate capacity disks in 3½-inch drives, too: either 720K, 1.44MB, or 2.88MB.

SELECTING A DISK LOG METHOD

Before Norton Desktop starts to back up your disk, the program makes a list of all the files and directories on your hard disk. This is called a *log,* and there are two ways Norton Backup can make one:

Fastest. If you choose this setting, Norton Backup reads your hard disk directly. This works very quickly, but cannot work on substituted or network disk drives.

Most Compatible. This setting is somewhat slower, but will be able to read information from any kind of hard disk.

Select the method you want to use from the Disk Log Strategy drop-down list box.

SETTING THE CATALOG FILE PATH

When you make a backup, Norton Backup creates a *catalog file* that lists all the files and directories that you backed up this time round (called the *backup set*). This catalog is used when you come to restore files to your hard disk. By default, it writes the catalog file on your hard disk in the directory from which you ran Norton Backup and on the final floppy disk of the backup set. However, you can specify that Norton Backup write the catalog file into a different directory, using the Catalog File Path list box.

SAVING YOUR CONFIGURATION

When you make changes to your backup configuration, they will only apply to your current backup session. If you want to save them so that they are available for your next backup session, make sure that you check the Save Configuration checkbox in the dialog box that appears when you quit Norton Backup.

BACKING UP YOUR HARD DISK

Start Norton Backup by double-clicking on the Norton Backup icon on the Desktop, or the icon in the Norton Desktop group window. You can also start the program running if you select it in the Tools menu. There are three entries on the menu bar in Norton

BACKING UP YOUR SYSTEM   169

Backup, as Figure 10.4 shows. Not all these menu selections are available at all times:

File lets you work with setup files. Setup files are described later in this chapter.

> Macros can only record keypresses, not mouse selections.

Macro lets you create or run Norton Backup macros, which are described later in this chapter.

Help contains context-sensitive help appropriate to your user level. The menu also contains specific entries for the major components of Norton Backup: Backup, Compare, Restore, and Configure.

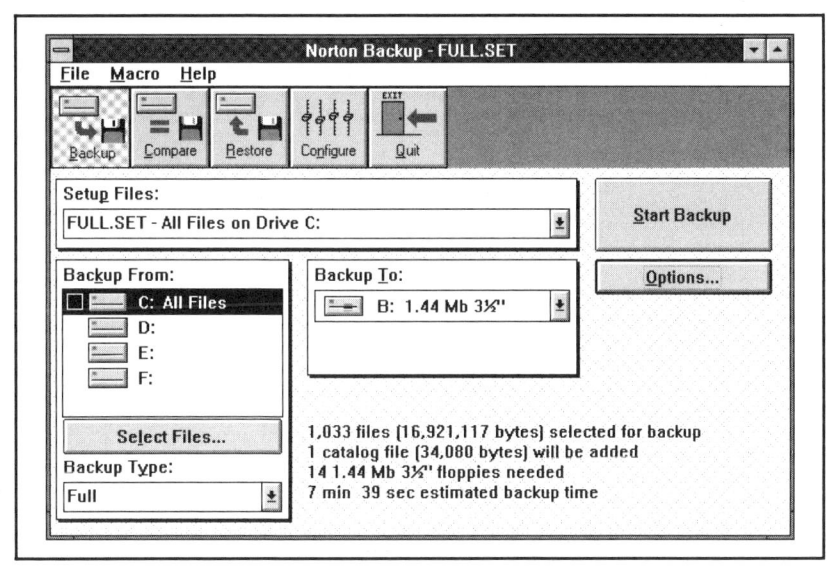

Figure 10.4: The Backup window manages all functions concerned with backing up files and directories

The major elements of the Backup window are as follows:

- The Setup Files drop-down list box lets you select the setup file you want to use for the backup; all the setup files on your system are listed in this box.
- The Backup From list box lets you select the hard disk drive to back up.

- The Select Files command button lets you choose the directories and files to back up.
- The Backup Type drop-down list box tells Norton Backup the type of backup to make.
- The Backup To drop-down list box lets you tell Norton Backup where to put the backup set. The information below this box shows the number of files selected for inclusion in this backup, and the amount of space these files occupy. When you back up to floppy disks, you will see an estimate of the number of disks needed to hold the backup, along with an estimate of how long the backup is expected to take.
- The Options command button lets you choose backup options, such as whether to use data compression or error correction, and whether Norton Backup should quit when the backup is finished.
- The Start Backup command button actually starts the backup process.

All of these options are described in more detail later in this chapter.

MAKING A COMPLETE BACKUP

The first thing you should do after configuring Norton Backup is make a full backup of all the directories and files on your hard disk. Here are the steps to follow:

1. Make sure you have enough floppy disks and labels for the backup set. You can find out how many to use by reading the estimate at the bottom of the main Backup window.

2. Launch Norton Backup. The Backup window opens automatically.

3. Select Configure if you want to change any of the disk drive capacity settings.

4. Change to the Backup window and select the FULL.SET setup file from the Setup Files drop-down list box.

5. Double-click on the drive you want to back up in the Backup From list box. A small square icon appears to the left of the drive you select.
6. Select Full in the Backup Type drop-down list box.
7. Choose the floppy disk drive you want to back up to from the list in the Backup To drop-down list box.
8. Click on the Start Backup command button to start the backup operation running. Follow the directions on the screen for changing disks.

If you insert a floppy disk that already contains files, Norton Backup will open a dialog box, informing you about the files and giving you the option of changing to an empty disk and clicking on the Retry command button or continuing with the same disk by using the Overwrite button. You can also use Cancel to abort this backup, or ask for Help.

Figure 10.5 shows the Backup Progress window. The main parts of this window are the following:

- The Now Backing Up entry displays the current drive, directory, and file being backed up.
- The upper-left panel in this window shows how the current floppy disk is filling up and how the whole backup is proceeding.
- The top-right panel shows the name of the setup file, the catalog file, and the session file.
- The center-left panel shows the estimated and actual number of disks, files, bytes, and time used for this backup.
- The center-right panel shows the time into the backup and the amount of time that Norton Backup has waited for you to respond to a request, usually to insert the next disk. This panel also shows you the current data-compression ratio.
- Click on the Settings command button to see a summary of your current Norton Backup options for error correction, data compression, data verification, and the overwrite warning. This appears at the bottom of this figure.

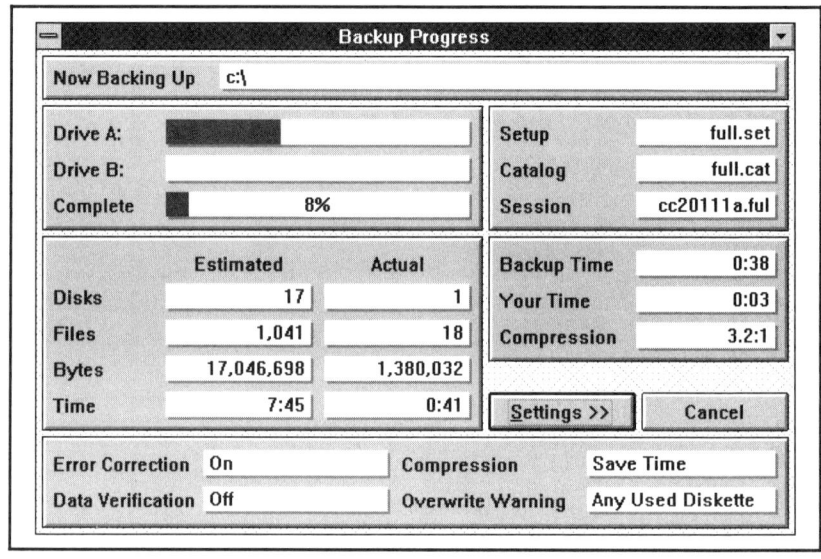

Figure 10.5: The Backup Progress window shows information about the current backup operation

> Be sure to label your disks in the proper order (e.g., "Disk 1 of 25"...).

If you wait more than approximately 15 seconds before inserting a floppy disk, a dialog box will open and prompt you to insert the next disk. As the backup proceeds, the bar graphs in the top-left panel of the window indicate the progress of the backup. You will find that the floppy disk drive light on your computer stays on during the backup; this is normal and is nothing to worry about. As you remove the disks, be sure to label them with the disk number and time and date of the backup, and note the fact that this is a full backup. If you have to restore this backup set at any time, you will have to use the disks in the same sequence that you used to make the backup.

When the backup is complete, the catalog for the entire backup set is written onto the last disk of the set, and a message indicates the number of files that were selected and backed up. Click on OK to return to the main Norton Backup window. Put the backup disks in a safe place.

Now is an excellent time to make a comparison between the files backed up to the floppy disks and the original files still on your hard disk. This ensures that the backup was complete. Use the Compare function for this. (Compare is described later in the chapter.)

MAKING A PARTIAL BACKUP

You may not always want to back up your whole disk. Often you will want to back up only the files that have changed, the files that changed after a certain date, or even only a certain type of file.

When DOS creates or modifies a file, the archive attribute is automatically turned on to indicate that the file should be backed up the next time a backup is made. This archive attribute may or may not be turned off by Norton Backup, depending on what kind of backup you make.

The steps you follow in making a partial backup are much the same as those described above for your first full backup, except that you have more choices to make and more flexibility in how you actually make the backup.

Deciding the Backup Type

> The backup files and copy files are written in a special format; you must use Norton Backup to restore them again.

You can select the following different types of backup in the Backup Type drop-down list box:

Full backs up all the selected files, ignoring the current setting of the archive attribute. When the backup is complete, Full resets the archive attribute for all files. Use this method to make your first backup.

Incremental backs up those selected files that are new or have changed in some way since the last backup. When the backup is complete, the archive attribute of all the backed up files is off. If you use this setting, use new disks for each incremental backup, otherwise you will write the changed files over the older versions on the backup disks.

Differential backs up all new files or all files that have changed since the last full or incremental backup. The status of the archive attribute is not changed.

Full Copy makes a copy of all the files you selected, whether the files have changed or not. Full Copy does not change the archive attribute, so it is useful for copying files from one system to another because it will not disturb your normal backup strategy. Remember, though, that this backup is not a copy of the files in the DOS or Windows sense of the word. You must use Restore to extract any data from (or open or view) a file; you cannot use DOS or Windows.

Incremental Copy is similar to the above selection, except that it copies just the files that have changed—again, without changing the status of the archive attribute.

The backup type you choose should depend on your individual circumstances and the goals that your backup strategy defines. You are not confined, however, to just these five methods; you can also choose which directories and files you want to back up.

Selecting Files to Back Up

Now that you have chosen the type of backup you want to make, you can further specify the directories and files that you want to include in the backup. If you are working at the basic level in Norton Backup, certain mechanisms are available to you; if you are working at the advanced level, you have more options.

Click on the Select Files command button in the Backup window (see Figure 10.4) to open the Select Backup Files window in Figure 10.6. This window has two panes just like a Desktop drive window—a tree pane on the left that lists directories and a file pane on the right that list files. The file pane lists the file name, extension, file size in bytes, date and time, and file attributes.

If the attribute is set for a particular file, you will see a letter representing that attribute in the right-most column in the file pane. Attributes are shown in the following order: read-only, hidden, system, and archive. You can use the drive icons at the top left of this window to change to another drive.

The menu bar contains two selections: File and Tree. The File menu contains options you can use to select or deselect all the files in the highlighted directory, and view or delete files. The Tree menu lets you alter the way that the tree display is shown in the window; you can use it to expand or contract the tree display. Below the drive icons you will see the volume label if the drive has one, and the current file

BACKING UP YOUR SYSTEM **175**

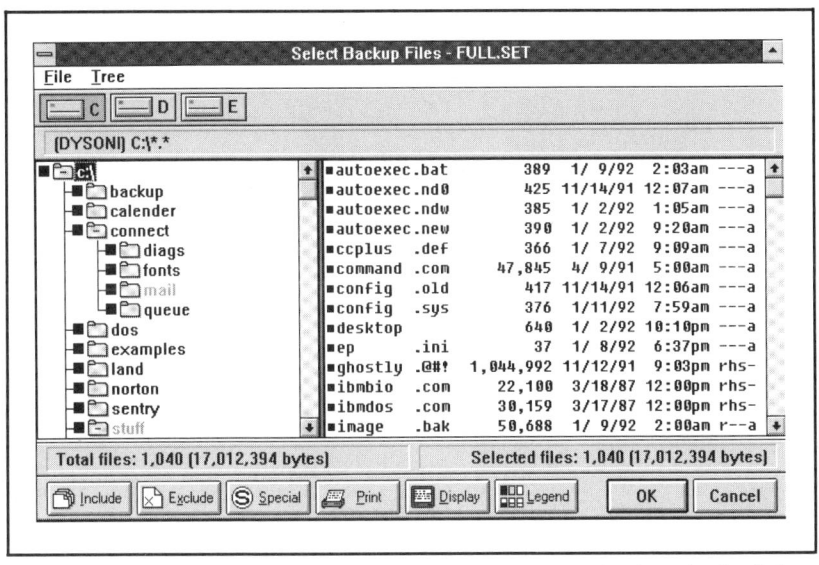

Figure 10.6: Choose the directories and files you want to back up in the Select Backup Files window

> If you are working at the advanced level, you will see three more command buttons: Include, Exclude, and Special. These buttons are described after the Legend command.

filter. This defaults to include all the files on the current drive, so it shows *.*.

At the bottom of the window you can see a summary line containing a count of the files on the current drive and the number of files selected for this backup, as well as three command buttons, Print, Display, and Legend:

Print This lets you make a listing of the files selected for this backup and opens the Print File List dialog box. You can send the report to your printer or to a file for printing later on, and you can select a text report or a graphics report. Be sure your printer can handle graphics printing before you select a graphics report. The Setup button in the Print File List dialog box connects to the Windows Print Manager so you can confirm your printer setup.

Display This lets you decide on the information that is shown in the Select Backup Files window. It opens the Display Options dialog box. In the Display group box you can choose to display the following in the file pane:

- file size
- file date
- file time
- file attributes

In the Sort Files By group box, you can choose to sort the files in the file pane by:

- file name
- file extension
- file size
- file date
- file attributes

And in the Other group box, you can choose the following:

Group Selected Files lets you collect all the selected files in each directory at the top of the file pane. This is particularly useful if you only want to back up a few files from each directory.

Show Directories Above Files lets you relocate the tree pane above the file pane, instead of both panes being shown side by side.

File Filter lets you select groups of files based on a wildcard specification in this text box. The default of *.* selects all files in the current directory. For example, to show just the initialization files in the current directory, enter *.INI into this text box. Files that you selected before applying this filter remain selected.

Legend This opens the dialog box shown in Figure 10.7, which explains the square symbols shown just to the left of a selected directory or file listed in the Select Backup Files window in Figure 10.6. These

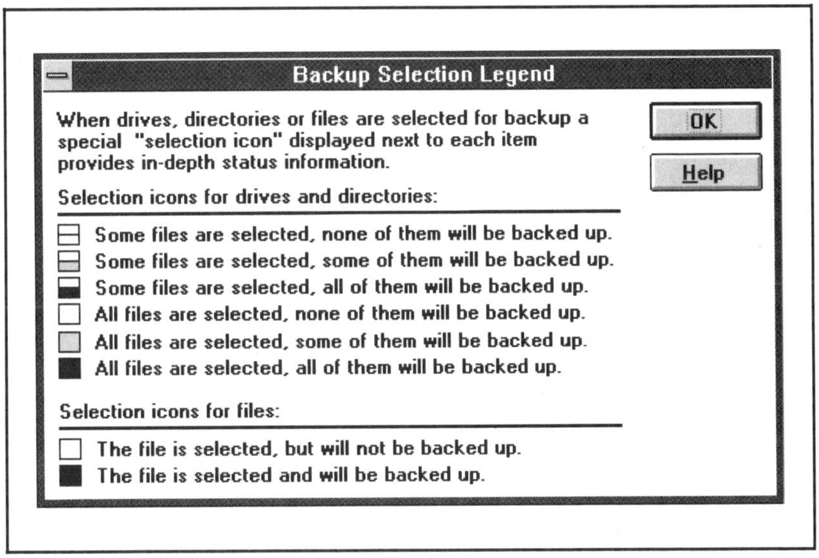

Figure 10.7: The backup selection icons are explained in the Backup Selection Legend dialog box

selection icons show which files and directories are selected and, of those files and directories selected, which ones will be backed up.

If you move the mouse cursor to one of these selection icons in either the tree or the file pane, it will turn into an information or i-cursor. If you click on the selection icon with the i-cursor, you can open a dialog box that gives specific information about the file. If you click on the selection icon of a directory in the tree pane, this dialog box will show the name of the dircctory, along with the directory creation time and date, number of files in the directory, number of files selected, and number of files to be backed up. If you click the i-cursor just to the left of a file in the file pane, this dialog box will show the file name and its status: whether it has been selected and whether it will be backed up.

> These options appear in advanced mode only.

Include/Exclude Select the correct drive in the Backup From list in the main Backup window *before* using Include/Exclude; otherwise your Include/Exclude list will be cleared. Click on either the Include or the Exclude command buttons in the Select Backup Files window to open the Include/Exclude Files dialog box shown in Figure 10.8. This dialog box includes the following:

Path contains the directory path of the files and/or directories you want to include or exclude. To use a different path, just type it into this text box.

File specifies the filter to use for including or excluding files; use the usual ? and * DOS wildcard characters.

Include/Exclude determine the operation to be performed.

Include All Subdirectories adds subdirectories to whatever is contained in the Path text box.

Include/Exclude List contains the actual statements that tell Norton Backup which files to include and exclude. These statements are executed in sequence, so if you want to back up all files in a directory except the .EXE files, for example, first specify that you want to include *all* files, then add another statement that excludes the files with an .EXE extension.

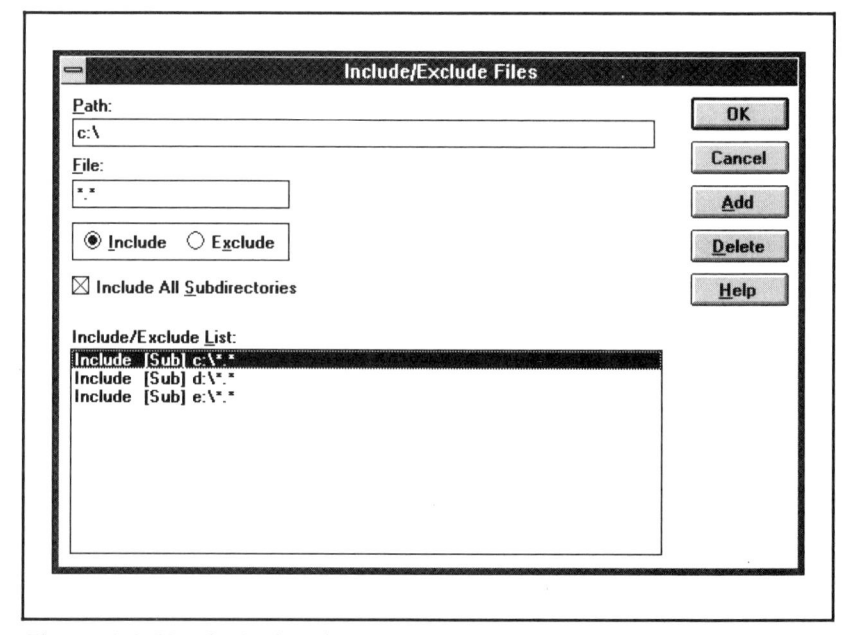

Figure 10.8: Use the Include/Exclude Files dialog box to refine your selection of files for backup

To add a line to the Include/Exclude list, follow these steps:

1. Choose the appropriate drive in the Backup From list box in the main Backup window (see Figure 10.4), make sure you are using the advanced level, then click on Select Files.

2. Click on either the Include or Exclude command buttons at the bottom of the Select Backup Files window to open the Include/Exclude Files dialog box. Enter any new directory path information into the Path text box, if necessary, and the new file filter you want to use into the File text box.

3. Choose the correct option button, either Include or Exclude.

4. Check the Include All Subdirectories checkbox if you want to include all the subdirectories.

5. Click on the Add command button when your entry is complete. This new entry will be added at the end of the list in the Include/Exclude List box.

To delete a line in the Include/Exclude box, highlight the entry and click on the Delete command button.

To edit a item, highlight the line to make the appropriate parts of the entry appear in the Path and File boxes at the top of the dialog box. Make the changes you need in these boxes and click on the Add command button. The new entry is added to the bottom of the list, so you can delete the original entry.

Once you have made an Include/Exclude filter, all the files selected will show a selection icon in the tree or file pane. You then can fine tune that selection manually, if you wish, before selecting more files or deselecting others.

> This option only appears at the advanced level.

Special This sets up separate conditions for including or excluding files in your backup. Click on this button to open the Special Selections dialog box shown in Figure 10.9. Here you can select all files that fall between a specific range of dates, as well as include or exclude copy-protected files, read-only files, system files, or hidden files. When you check the Exclude Copy Protected Files box, the five text boxes immediately to the right become active; type the name of

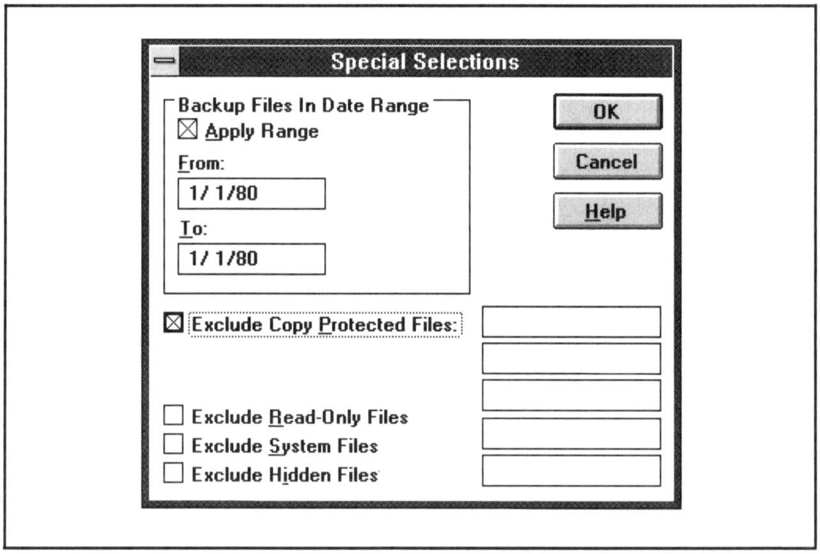

Figure 10.9: Set up criteria for including or excluding files in your backup using the Special Selections dialog box

one copy-protected file to exclude from the backup into each of these text boxes (wildcards are allowed).

Choosing the Drive to Backup To

> Your network system manager may not be too keen on you backing up your hard disk onto the network, particularly if server disk space is at a premium.

You use the Backup To drop-down box in the main Backup window (see Figure 10.4) to tell Norton Backup where to put the backup, either drive A or drive B—or any storage device that uses a DOS path, like another hard disk somewhere. If drives A and B are of the same type, there is an option in this drop-down list that allows you to use both drives during the same backup. You can be backing up to one drive while you are changing and labeling the other.

The DOS path option lets you specify your backup to be sent to any storage medium that has a DOS path, such as a network drive, a Bernoulli box (Iomega Corporation), or a tape drive if it can be configured as a DOS device.

CHOOSING BACKUP OPTIONS

Norton Backup lets you configure your backup settings. The number of settings changes as you change your user level from the basic to the advanced level. When you click on the Options button in the Backup window at the basic level, you open the Basic Backup Options dialog box; when you are at the advanced level you open the Advanced Backup Options dialog box, and this adds four more settings. We'll look at the basic level options first.

Basic Options

The Basic Backup Options dialog box is shown in Figure 10.10. You can make the following settings:

> **Verify Backup Data.** When you check this option, Norton Backup compares the original data in the files against the backup. This may slow down your backup slightly, but I recommend that you use it every time you make a backup, as protection against making an unusable backup.
>
> **Compress Backup Data.** Use this setting to invoke Norton Backup's data-compression option. Not all files can be compressed to the same extent; word-processor files and spreadsheets show the largest amount of compression, while .EXE files show less. If you check this box, you select the Save Time compression setting described next under "Advanced Options."

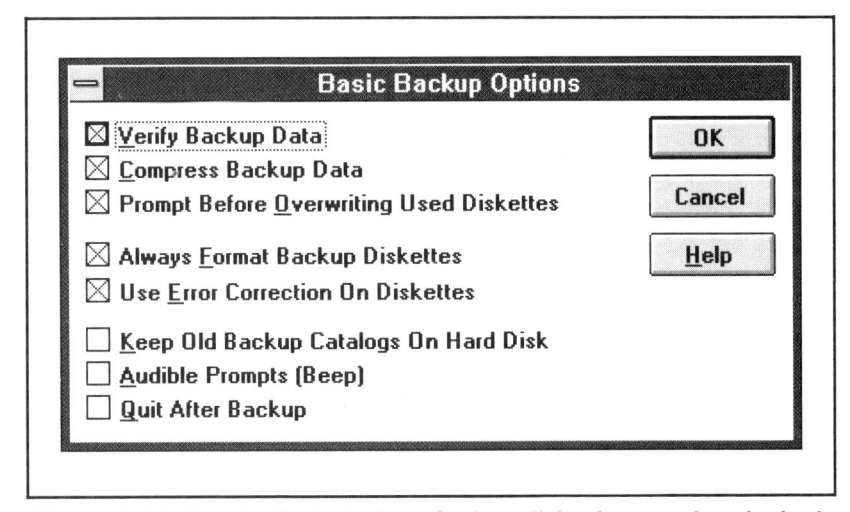

Figure 10.10: Use the Basic Backup Options dialog box to select the basic backup settings

Prompt Before Overwriting Used Diskette. Norton Backup opens an alert box if it finds you are trying to use a disk that already contains data. You can then choose to continue with this disk and overwrite these files or change to another disk.

Always Format Backup Diskettes. With this setting you can force Norton Backup to format every backup disk every time. This procedure will slow down the backup, but helps prevent problems associated with misaligned floppy disk read/write heads.

Use Error Correction On Diskettes. Norton Backup's error-correction code greatly increases your chance of making a successful backup and subsequent restoration. This setting is enabled by default and I recommend that you leave it turned on.

Keep Old Backup Catalogs On Hard Disk. Norton Backup writes the backup catalog onto the hard disk, as well as onto the final floppy disk in the backup set. The next time you make a full backup, Norton Backup usually deletes all the interim catalogs to conserve disk space. If you want to keep all these catalogs, check this box. Remember that you can always rebuild a catalog from the actual backup disks themselves. (Catalogs are described later in the section on comparing files.)

Audible Prompts (Beep). This setting allows Norton Backup to beep every time the program opens an alert box to tell you about an error or ask you to make a choice. You can turn this option off.

Quit After Backup. Use this setting if you want to exit Norton Backup when the backup is complete; otherwise you will return to the main Backup window. This option may save you several keystrokes at the end of a backup.

Most of the important settings in the Basic Backup Options dialog box are already set to their preferred settings by default, so there may be no need to change any of them. To change a setting, click on the checkbox of the appropriate option, then click on OK to return to the Backup window.

Advanced Options

The Options command button at the advanced level gives you control over a wider range of settings than at the basic level. This dialog box is shown in Figure 10.11. You have the following choices:

Data Verification. This increases the reliability of the backup, so you should use it. There are three possible settings for this option: Off, Sample Only, and Read and Compare. Off turns data verification off completely. Sample Only checks every eighth track written to the backup floppy disk. Read and Compare is the most comprehensive data-verification method in Norton Backup; all the files written to the backup disks are checked.

Data Compression. Using data compression does not affect the reliability of the backup but it can certainly affect the number of floppy disks needed or the length of time the backup takes. There are four settings available for data compression: Off, Save Time, Save Disks (Low), and Save Disks (High). Off turns data compression off completely, so no compression is performed. Save Time optimizes the backup speed to reduce the amount of time it takes to complete the backup. The faster your computer runs, the bigger time saving you will see. Save

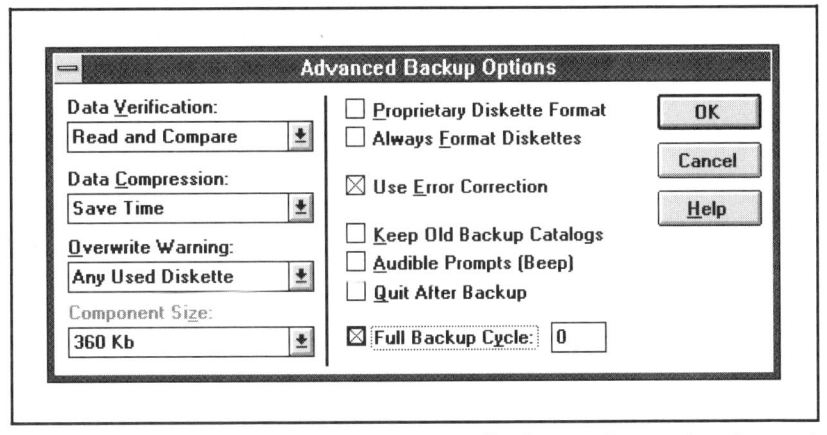

Figure 10.11: You can control a wide range of backup settings at the advanced level

Disks (Low) attempts to increase the amount of compression to minimize the number of disks needed for the backup. Save Disks (High) offers the maximum amount of compression and saves the largest amount of disk space, but usually increases the time that the backup takes.

Overwrite Warning. With this setting, you can tell Norton Backup how to react when it detects a disk that already contains files. Choose from Off, DOS Diskettes, Backup Diskettes, and Any Used Diskette. Off allows Norton Backup to overwrite any used disk automatically. If you select DOS Diskettes you will see an alert box open when you insert a disk that contains any DOS files. With Backup Diskettes you see the warning if you try to reuse old backup disks. If you insert a DOS disk there will be no warning prompt; the disk will be overwritten automatically. The safest option is Any Used Diskette. This opens a warning box when Norton Backup finds a disk containing any kind of file.

Component Size. This option is only available if you are backing up your system to a DOS path, rather than to floppy disks. You can use a DOS path to back up to another hard disk or to a Bernoulli box. Instead of backing up your hard disk as one huge file, you can choose to divide the file up into smaller pieces. Component Size lets you choose the size of these smaller files. Choose from Best Fit, 1.44MB, 1.2MB, 720K, or 360K. This setting can be very useful if you want to transfer files to another computer in backup form, and you know the size of the disk drive on the target computer. For example, if you select 1.44MB, each backup file will contain exactly the same data it would have contained had you backed up to real 1.44MB floppy disks.

Proprietary Diskette Format. This allows you to use a special disk format that is unique to Norton Backup. This format is not compatible with normal DOS and Windows files, so it cannot be read by them, but it does squeeze more information onto the disks. All disks will be reformatted when you first select this option, so you cannot change to this format in the middle of a backup set; the master catalog requires that the same disk format be used throughout the backup. If you want to use these disks with a regular DOS or Windows application, reformat the disk using the Desktop.

Full Backup Cycle. Use this setting as an alarm to tell you that it is time to make a full backup of your system, if your scheme calls for making incremental or differential backups between your full backups. Enter the number of days, between 0 and 999, that you want to pass before you make your next full backup. When the time has elapsed, Norton Backup will display a message telling you it is time to make a full backup. The program also temporarily switches the backup type to Full.

The other selections—Always Format Diskettes, Use Error Correction, Keep Old Backup Catalogs, Audible Prompts (Beep), and Quit After Backup—are the same as those described under "Basic Options." Click on the checkboxes corresponding to the options you want to use, then click on OK to return to the main Backup window.

COMPARING FILES

If you add a new expansion board to your computer, use the Compare command to be sure that the new board has not affected your backup in some subtle way.

After you have made a backup, you should compare the files contained in the backup against the original files on your hard disk. In this way, you can be sure that the files you backed up match the files on your hard disk, and that they can be restored successfully.

Start Norton Backup by double-clicking on the Norton Backup icon on the Desktop. You can also start the program if you select it in the Tools menu. When you choose the Compare button from the Norton Backup program, the Compare window opens, as Figure 10.12 shows. The major elements of the Compare window are summarized as follows:

- The Backup Set Catalog drop-down list box displays information for the catalogs created during previous backups. Select the catalog for the backup set that you want to compare.

- The Compare From drop-down list box contains the list of devices that can be used for backups on your system. Select the drive originally used to make the backup, usually one of your floppy disk drives.

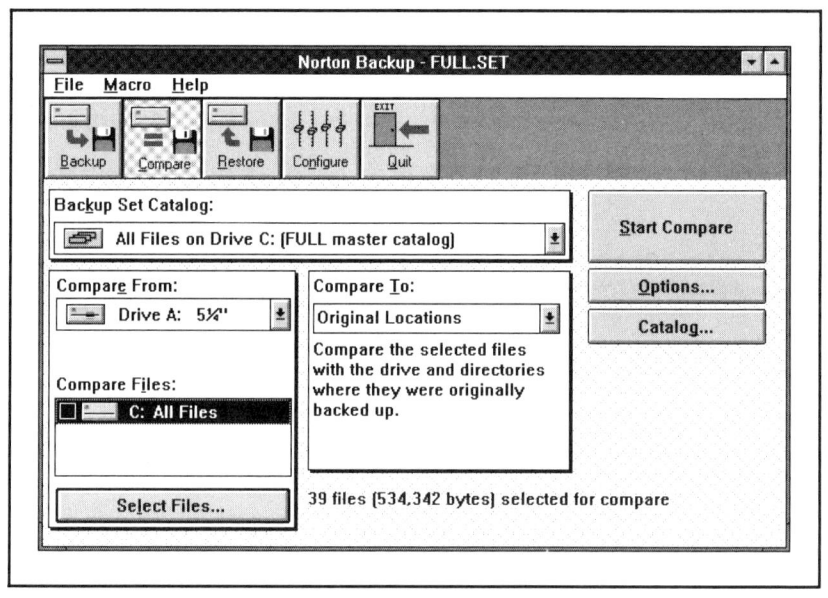

Figure 10.12: The Compare window checks your backup against the original files on your hard disk and looks for problems

- The Compare Files box contains disk icons for the drives that were fully or partially backed up. If you double-click on a drive icon, you select all the files on that drive.

- Use the Select Files button to compare only specific files.

- The Compare To drop-down list box specifies the location of the original files for this comparison. This is usually your hard disk.

- The Options button lets you specify whether a beep will sound when an alert box appears, and whether to quit Norton Backup when the comparison is complete.

- The Catalog button lets you find a catalog file in any directory, then load or delete it. You can also use this button to rebuild a catalog using the original backup disks in the event that the catalog is damaged, or to retrieve a catalog from a floppy disk.

- The Start Compare button starts the comparison process running.

MAKING A COMPLETE COMPARISON

To make a comparison between the files you have just backed up and the original files on your hard disk, using either the basic or the advanced level, follow these steps:

1. Collect all the floppy disks that comprise the backup set together in numerical order, then click the Compare button in the main Backup window (see Figure 10.4).
2. Select the appropriate catalog file from the Backup Set Catalog drop-down list box in the Compare window.
3. Choose the appropriate drive in the Compare From box. This is the drive you will use to load your backup disks for the comparison.
4. Use the Select Files command button if you want to compare specific parts of the backup.
5. Click on the Compare To list box to select the files on your hard disk you want the backup set compared against.
6. If you want to use a different catalog file in this comparison, click on Catalog to select another.
7. Click on Start Compare to begin the actual comparison process.

The Compare Progress window will open. This is very similar to the Backup Progress window mentioned before (see Figure 10.5). You will be prompted to load the next disk for the comparison in the top-left pane, and summary information is presented in the other panes. The horizontal bar graphs in the top-left pane indicate what percentage of the comparison is complete. At the end of the comparison, an information box opens to list the number of files selected and the number of files compared.

There are several Compare options and selections that it is important for you to know about. These are detailed below:

Backup Set Catalog The backup set catalog file contains an index to the backup and contains the information needed to compare or restore the files in the backup. Two catalogs are created for each backup, one stored on the last backup disk of a backup set and the other on your hard disk.

Use the Backup Set Catalog drop-down list box to look at all the catalogs on your hard disk; click on the one you want to use. Norton Backup gives each catalog file a unique name, based on the drive being backed up, the date, and a special sequence code. The filename extension reflects the backup type: .FUL for a full backup, .INC for incremental, .DIF for differential, and .CPY for a copy.

A master catalog is created or updated for each setup file when you make a full, incremental, or differential backup; it is not created for a full or incremental copy backup. The master catalog has the same name as the setup file and the file-name extension .CAT, and is used when you make a comparison of a full backup. Norton Backup automatically merges all the catalogs made during full, incremental, and differential backups for the same set.

Compare From Use the Compare From drop-down list box to tell Norton Backup where to look for the backup set used in the comparison. If you have two floppy disk drives of the same size, you can choose to use both of them. In this case, Norton Backup compares data in one, then in the other, speeding up the compare operation by quite some. You can also use a DOS path here for any device that uses one: a Bernoulli box, network drive, and so on.

Compare Files The Compare Files selection tells Norton Backup which drives contain the files against which you want to compare the backup set. When you select a drive, *all* the files on that drive are selected for the comparison, and a square icon appears to the left of the drive name. If you just want to compare a few files, use the Select Files command button described next.

Compare To You use the Compare To drop-down list box to tell Norton Backup where the original files are that you want to compare against the backup set. This is almost always the same drive and directory from which the files were originally backed up. You can choose from the following:

Original Location. Directories and files in the backup are compared against those from which they were backed up.

Alternate Drives. Use this selection to specify a directory of the same name as the original, but located on a different drive. A dialog box opens for the name of the drive.

Alternate Directories. With this selection you can specify that the comparison be made against files in a different directory. This can be a different drive as well as a different directory.

Single Directory. This last specification is used to compare the backup set against a specific directory, no matter what the original drive and directory. A dialog box appears for you to enter the name of the directory you want to use.

Options   There are two options you can elect to use during a comparison, both available at the basic and advanced level:

Audible Prompts beeps every time an alert box opens. Check this box to turn the beep off.

Quit After Compare lets you save your settings and exit to the Norton Desktop when the comparison is complete. If this box is not checked, you'll stay inside the backup program.

COMPARING SPECIFIC FILES OR DIRECTORIES

Click on the Select Files command button to open the Select Compare Files window. This window is very similar to the Select Backup Files window described earlier (see Figure 10.6) and works in much the same way. You select the directories and files for the comparison from the tree and file panes, close the window, then click the Start Compare command button.

You can also use the i-cursor to see information about a specific directory in the tree pane or file in the file pane.

There are several buttons available at the bottom of this window that you can use to select specific files for comparison, depending on the program level you are using. At the basic level you can use the following:

Version. When you load a master catalog, files from several backup sets will be available, and it is quite possible that the same file may be represented several times. By default, the latest version of a file will be compared, but if you use the Version command button, it is possible to compare a specific version of the file. If there is only one version of the file available, the Version button is dimmed and unavailable. But if there are several, choose the Version button to display a list of the available files. Highlight the version of the file you want to use for the comparison and click on OK.

Display. This button lets you decide on the information to show in the file pane. It opens the Display options dialog box. As well as the file name, you can choose to display the file size, date, time, or file attribute(s). You can also sort the files in this window by name, extension, size, date, or attribute(s). Besides being able to apply a file filter so that only certain files are shown in the window, you can also opt to group all the selected files together at the top of the file pane, irrespective of where they are actually located in the directory. Finally, you may move the tree pane to the top of the Select Compare Files window, above the file pane.

Print. When you have chosen the files for the comparison, you can print the list now or send the list to a file using the Print command button.

Legend. This command button contains an explanation of the small compare icons shown to the left of each selected drive, directory, or file name in the Select Compare Files window.

At the advanced level, you have access to another command button:

Special. Use this to exclude files from any comparison. Clicking on Special opens the Special Selections dialog box. Here you can exclude files that fall into a specific range of dates, as well as files based on their copy-protection status and status of their read-only, hidden, or system attributes.

By using these Select Files options carefully, you can proceed to compare all files in your backup, or just compare those specific files that you are most interested in.

WORKING WITH CATALOGS

A catalog contains all the information about a particular backup, including a copy of the directory structure of the backed up hard disk, the names of all the files included in the backup, the total number of files backed up, and the name of the setup file used to make the backup. The catalog is saved in two places for safety reasons: on your hard disk and on the last floppy disk in a set of floppy-disk backups. Before you can do a backup comparison or restoration, you must select the appropriate catalog to use. If the correct catalog is not already shown in the Backup Set Catalog drop-down list box, you can click the Catalog command button to find or recreate it. The Catalog button is available at both the basic and advanced levels; when you click on it, you'll see the Select Catalog dialog box shown in Figure 10.13.

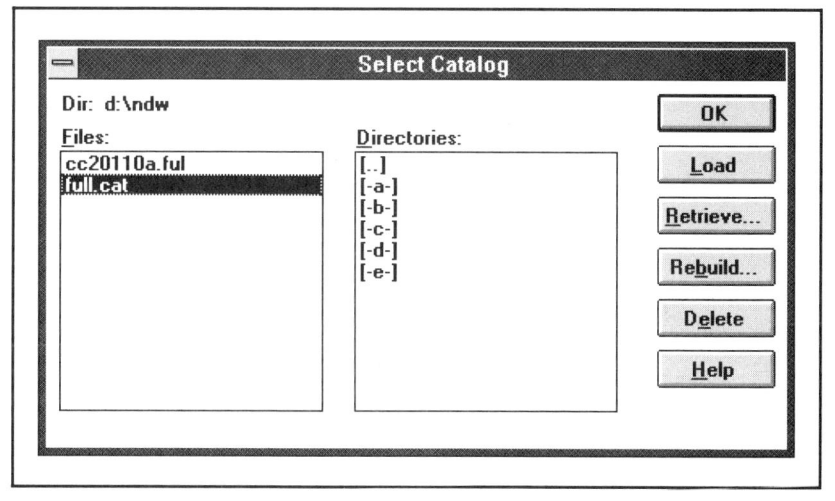

Figure 10.13: You can load, rebuild, or delete a catalog file in the Select Catalog dialog box

All the catalog files in the current directory are shown in the Files list box and all your drives and directories are shown in the Directories list box. Find the correct catalog here. Highlight it and then click on one of the command buttons on the right side of this dialog box:

> **Load.** This selection loads the highlighted catalog and returns to the main Compare window.
>
> **Retrieve.** If the catalog file you want to use is no longer available on your hard disk through accidental deletion or other

mishap, you can reload it from the last floppy disk of the backup set using this command. Norton Backup prompts you to load the last floppy disk in the backup set.

Rebuild. If the catalog file is missing from both your hard disk and the last floppy disk, you can use the Rebuild command to reconstruct as much as possible of the catalog file. Norton Backup reads the directory structure and file name information from the backup floppy disks and adds it to a new catalog file, one disk at a time. If a disk is missing from the middle of the backup set, you will have to create two new catalogs, one that describes the files up to the missing disk and one that describes the files after the missing disk.

Delete. You can remove obsolete catalogs from your hard disk with the Delete command. Highlight the catalog you want to delete, then click on the Delete command button. You will be asked to confirm that you want to delete the catalog before it is actually removed from your hard disk.

RESTORING FILES

> You must use the same speed for the restoration that you used when you made the original backup.

Start Norton Backup by double-clicking on the Norton Backup icon on the Desktop, or the icon in the Norton Desktop group window. You can also start the program running if you select it in the Tools menu. Select the Restore button from the main Backup window (see Figure 10.4) when you are ready to restore files to your hard disk or load them to another disk somewhere. You will see the Restore window shown in Figure 10.14. This window shares much in common with the main Backup window; just remember, however, that you are doing things the other way around when you restore files to your system. The main elements of the window are as follows:

- The Backup Set Catalog drop-down box shows the names and descriptions of existing catalogs corresponding to existing backup sets. Select the catalog that corresponds to the backup set that you want to restore.

- The Restore From drop-down list box shows the drives you can use to restore the backup.

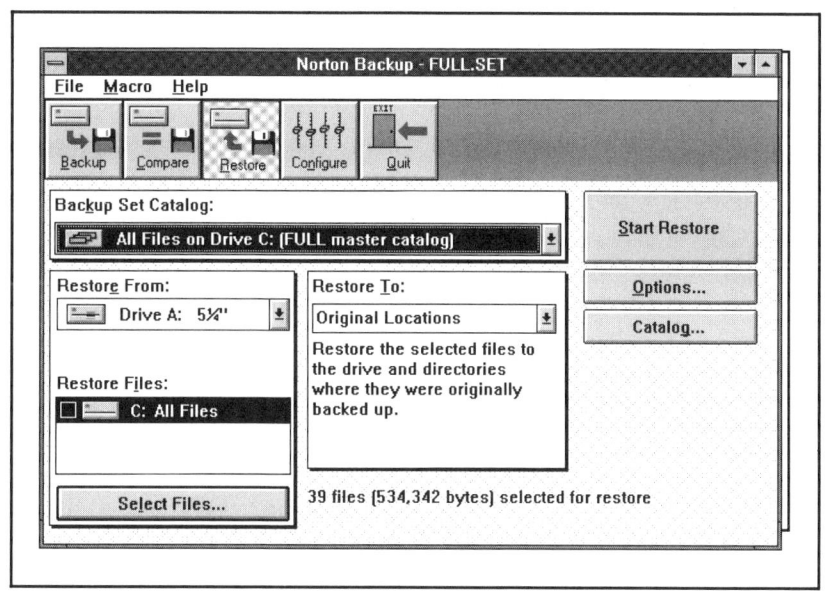

Figure 10.14: Control the restoration of files to your system using the Restore window

- The Restore Files box contains icons for the drives that were fully or partially backed up. Double-click on the icon to select *all* the files on that drive.

- Use the Select Files command button to restore only specific files. This is discussed in the next section.

- The Restore To drop-down list box lets you select where you want to put the restored files.

- The Options command button lets you specify several restoration settings, depending on your user level. These settings are described later in this section under "Choosing Restore Options."

- The Catalog command button lets you load, retrieve, rebuild, or delete a catalog, as I described previously under "Working with Catalogs."

- Use the Start Restore button when everything is set to your liking and you are ready to start the restoration.

If you are planning to restore your hard disk to the same state it was in after your last backup, you must restore the backups in the following order:

- If you made a full backup, restore the latest full backup set.
- If you made a full backup followed by several incremental backups, restore the full backup first, followed by each of the incremental backups in order, starting with the oldest set.
- If you made a full backup, followed by differential backups, restore the full backup first, followed by the most recent differential backup.

To restore previously backed up files to your hard disk:

1. Collect all the disks that are included in the backup set.
2. Select the catalog for the backup set that you want to restore.
3. Choose a floppy disk drive in the Restore From drop-down list box, or specify a DOS path.
4. Select the disk drive you want to restore these files to in the Restore Files list box. This selects all files.
5. Click on the Start Restore button to begin the process of restoring your files; the Restore Progress window also opens.

The Restore Progress Window is similar to the other two progress windows in Norton Backup, and shows how the restoration is progressing with horizontal bar graphs. You are prompted to insert disks as necessary. Click on the Settings button to see information on the settings for Data Verification, the Overwrite Warning, and the Archive Flag. At the end of the restoration, a message box opens, showing the number of files selected and the number restored.

RESTORING SPECIFIC FILES OR DIRECTORIES

Often a partial restoration may be all you need to recover, for example, a file or directory deleted by accident. Follow the steps given above for a complete restore, but use the Select Files command button to choose the files you want to restore. This button opens the Select Restore Files window containing several file-selection command buttons. At the basic level you can use the following:

> **Version.** Files from several different backup sets may be available for you to restore, and it is quite possible that the same file may be represented several times. By default, the latest version of a file will be restored, but if you use the Version command button, it is possible to restore a specific version of the file. If there is only one version available, the Version button is dimmed and unavailable. But if there are several, choose the Version button to display a list of the available files. Highlight the version of the file you want to restore and click on OK.
>
> **Display.** This button lets you decide on the information to show in the Select Restore Files window, and opens the Display options dialog box. As well as the file name, you can display the file size, date, time, or file attribute(s). You can also sort the files in this window by name, extension, size, date, or attribute(s). Besides being able to apply a file filter so that only certain files are shown in the window, you can also opt to group all the selected files together at the top of the file pane, irrespective of where they are actually located in the directory. Finally, you may choose to move the tree pane to the top of the Select Restore Files window, above the file pane.
>
> **Print.** When you have chosen the files you want to restore, you can print the list now or send the list to a file using the Print command button.
>
> **Legend.** This command button contains an explanation of the small restore icons shown to the left of each selected drive, directory, or file name in the Select Restore Files window.

If you are at the advanced level, you can also use the following command button:

> **Special.** Use this button to exclude certain files from the restoration. Click on Special to open the Special Selections dialog

box if you want to restore files that fall between two specific dates. This does not restore files from within this range, so you must still select the individual files to restore. This selection just excludes files that are outside the range of dates from being restored. You can also exclude files based on their copy-protection status, as well as on the status of their read-only, hidden, or system attributes.

You can also use the i-cursor to see information about a specific directory or file.

RESTORING FILES AFTER A HARD DISK FAILURE

One of the prime reasons for backing up your files is so that you can reload them again after an accident, such as a hard disk problem. There are a few steps you must go through first, however, before you can get to that point. You have to get to the point were your computer can run a program before you can think about restoring your data, and that may mean repartitioning your hard disk, reinstalling your DOS files, installing all the Windows files, and then installing the Norton Desktop before you can even load Norton Backup. Once Norton Backup is loaded, proceed as you would for a complete restoration of your hard disk.

CHOOSING RESTORE OPTIONS

Norton Backup lets you configure your restore settings in the Restore Options dialog box. The number of settings depends on your user level. When you click on the Options button in the Restore window at the basic level, you open the Basic Restore Options window; when you are at the advanced level you open the Advanced Restore Options dialog box, and this adds three more settings.

Basic Options

When you choose the Options command button at the basic level in the Restore window, the Basic Restore Options dialog box opens, as shown in Figure 10.15. Choose from the following settings:

Verify Restored Files. When you check this option, Norton Backup compares the files restored onto your hard disk with the files in the backup set to make sure the files are restored properly. This may slow down your backup slightly, but I recommend that you use this setting every time you make a backup, as a protection against serious disk problems.

Prompt Before Creating Directories. Turn this option on to see a message before the restore creates any new directories on your hard disk.

Prompt Before Creating Files. Turn this option on if you want to be prompted before any new files not on the target disk are created from the backup.

Prompt Before Overwriting Existing Files. Select this to see a prompt before overwriting a file of the same name.

Restore Empty Directories. This setting lets Norton Backup restore empty directories, even if they do not contain any files.

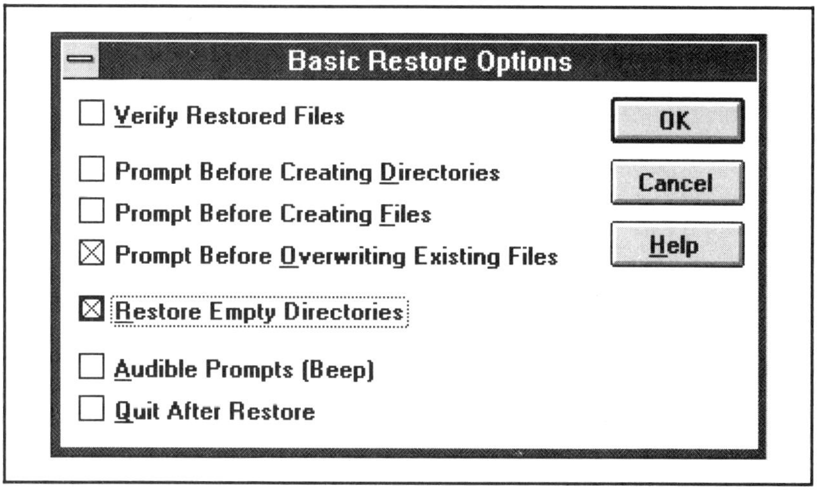

Figure 10.15: Select the Restore options you want to use in the Basic Restore Options dialog box

Audible Prompts (Beep). Turn the beep off with this option.

Quit After Restore. You can also make Norton Backup return to the Desktop at the end of the restoration, if you wish.

Click on the options you want to use, then click on OK to return to the main Restore window.

Advanced Options

At the advanced level, the Restore options contain three additional selections besides those described at the basic level:

Data Verification. Data restored to your hard disk can be compared against the data in the backup to ensure that there were no problems. You can choose one of three settings: Off, Sample Only, or Read and Compare. Off turns data verification off. Sample Only reads every eighth track on the hard disk and compares it to the floppy-disk backup. Read and Compare is the most rigorous method because it compares all the data written to your hard disk against the data in the backup set.

Overwrite Files. Files that you are restoring may overwrite files with the same names already on your disk. You have three choices: Never Overwrite, Older Files Only, and Always Overwrite. Never Overwrite tells Norton Backup not to restore a file if it already exists on your hard disk. Older Files Only makes Norton Backup restore the backup file only if it is more recent than the file already on your hard disk. Always Overwrite restores all files to your hard disk, irrespective of the file's creation date.

Archive Flag. This selection tells Norton Backup how to treat the archive attribute on each file. The choices are: Leave Alone, Mark As Backed Up, and Mark As Not Backed Up. Leave Alone does not alter the archive attribute; Mark As Backed Up sets the archive attribute to indicate that the file has been backed up. Mark As Not Backed Up sets the archive attribute to indicate that the file has not been backed up. These settings obviously have an effect on subsequent backups you make. Files whose archive attribute indicates that they have been backed up will only now be backed up by the Full and Full Copy backup types. Files whose archive attribute indicates that they have not been backed up will always be backed up.

Select the options of your choice and click on OK to return to the main Restore window.

AUTOMATING YOUR BACKUPS

There are several ways you can automate and streamline your backup operations. You can use setup files, invoke macros, use command-line switches in the Run dialog box, and use the built-in Norton Desktop Scheduler. We will look at each method in turn, starting with setup files.

USING SETUP FILES

Any time you use Norton Backup you are actually using a *setup file*. Setup files contain Backup program settings and file selections, and are a fast way of loading a preset configuration, so that you don't have to reconfigure Norton Backup every time you want to use it. When you change something in one of the main windows—Backup, Compare, or Restore—or make different selections using Select Files, you are changing information in the setup file. These changes will only apply to the current backup session unless you explicitly save them back into a setup file. You can either save them in the current setup file to modify that file, or save them in a different file to create a new setup file. If you want to perform different types of backup, you can have a different setup file for each type of backup.

Use the commands in the File menu to work with setup files when you are at the basic or advanced levels. At the preset level, you can load a setup file using the Preset Backups list box, but the selections in the File menu are dimmed out and unavailable. When you select the File menu, the most recently used setup file name appears at the end of this menu; you may see a maximum of five such entries. You can load a setup file from this menu, or you can use Open Setup and choose a file from any drive or directory on your system. Use any Norton Backup commands to change this setup file, then save it using Save Setup. Or if you want to change the name of the setup to something different, use Save Setup As. Use the Print command to make a hard copy the contents of a setup file.

Using a setup file is one of the easiest ways that you can configure a backup strategy for someone else who is perhaps less technical than you are. Then that person can use the preset level with the setup file, rather than the basic or advanced levels, to make his or her backup. In this way, you can reduce a complex operation to just a few choices, and the backup can be run with a minimum of interaction with the program.

Norton Backup comes with several useful setup files already configured:

> These preconfigured setup files all perform attended backups.

FULL.SET	Runs a full backup when launched, backing up all files on the first drive to a high-capacity floppy disk in drive A, and quits when the backup is complete. FULL.SET has its own icon called Full Backup in the Desktop group window.
ASSIST.SET	Another setup file with its own icon in the Desktop group window, ASSIST.SET makes a full backup when first run, and then every seven days thereafter. Makes incremental backups in between the full backups.
DBASE.SET	Makes a full backup of all dBASE and Q&A files it can find.
SPRDSHT.SET	Makes a full backup of Lotus 1-2-3 and Microsoft Excel files.
WORDPROC.SET	Makes a full backup of files made by Microsoft Word (for Windows and for DOS), Ami and Ami Pro, WordPerfect, and JustWrite—as well as plain text files.

If you find that your requirements are very close to one of these preconfigured files, open the setup file and modify it to your own needs by making the necessary changes, then save the file to a new name using Save Setup As from the File menu. This way you don't have to create the setup file from scratch.

MAKING AND USING MACROS

Another way you can speed up your backups is by using a *macro*, which is a series of keystrokes stored in a file that you play back at a later date to automate the backup, compare, or restore procedure. Norton Backup stores a macro with the setup file in effect when you created the macro, and you can only use one macro with each setup file.

You must be in the Backup window when you start recording your macro because this is the reference point that Norton Backup uses as its starting point for running the macro.

You must also use the keyboard to generate the keystrokes needed for the macro; you cannot use mouse clicks. If a letter in a menu name or a command button is underlined, you can press the Alt key and the underlined letter together to select the item directly from the keyboard. Most of these underlined letters are easy to associate with their corresponding functions, like *B* for Backup, *C* for Compare, and *R* for Restore. Others, however, are less than intuitive, like *N* for Configure and *K* for Backup Set Catalog. Use the Insert key to select a file or to turn an option on in your macro; use the Delete key to deselect a file or to turn an option off; and use the Ctrl and Enter keys together to represent pressing the Start Backup or Start Restore buttons. Do not use the spacebar to toggle check boxes or option buttons on or off while you are recording your macro, because the toggle will reverse every time you run the macro; use the Insert or Delete keys to turn options on or off. This way it does not matter what the setting is when the macro is run.

To record a macro:

1. Open Norton Backup and load the setup file you want to use.
2. Select the program level you (or someone else) will use when running the macro.

> Run the procedure you plan to automate with the macro a few times in manual mode first, so that you are familiar with the required steps—and to make sure the program is going to do what you expect it to do.

3. Click the Backup button and choose Record (or press F7) from the Macro menu. If a macro already exists for this setup file, Backup will ask if you want to overwrite it. The macro recording starts, waiting for your keystrokes. You will see the message **Norton Backup Macro Recorder—Press F7 to end** on the bottom line of the Backup window to remind you that the macro recorder is running.

4. Press the keystrokes needed to run the procedure. You cannot record mouse selections.

5. Press F7 to stop the recording, then use Save Setup or Save Setup As from the File menu to save your macro.

When you have finished making the macro, run it a few times to make sure it does what you think it should. This is particularly important if you are going to give the macro to someone else!

To play a macro:

You cannot play a macro if Norton Backup is minimized.

1. Launch Norton Backup and select the setup file that contains the macro you want to use.

2. Click on the Backup button if you are not in the Backup window.

3. Choose the Run command from the Macro menu (or press F8).

Norton Backup turns the mouse and keyboard off when it runs a macro, so make sure you are familiar with a procedure before you turn it into a macro.

USING COMMAND-LINE SWITCHES

See Chapter 8 for more information on Quick Access.

There are several important command-line options you can use with Norton Backup. You can use these switches with the Windows Program Manager, or with Quick Access and the Norton Desktop. The switches are:

@   Runs a macro associated with a setup file. For example, to play a macro associated with

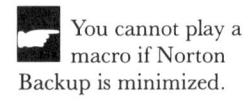

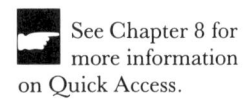

DAILY.SET, enter the following in the Run command in the File menu: **NBWIN.EXE @DAILY**.

/a   Launches a backup immediately, just as though you had clicked on the Start Backup command button. The /a and @ options are mutually exclusive; you can specify one or the other on the command line, but you cannot use them together. To start Norton Backup using the setup file called DAILY.SET, for example, enter **NBWIN.EXE DAILY.SET /a** in the Run dialog box. The SET file-name extension is optional here.

/tc   Specifies a Full Copy backup.

/td   Specifies a Differential backup.

/tf   Specifies a Full backup.

/ti   Specifies an Incremental backup

/to   Specifies an Incremental Copy backup

You can combine macros with command-line switches to make Norton Backup a very powerful program that is very easy for the inexperienced user to work with.

USING THE SCHEDULER

The Scheduler is described in detail in Chapter 14.

You can use the Norton Desktop Scheduler to post a message on your screen at a certain time—reminding you that it is time to make a backup, or to launch an unattended backup at a preset time—even if you are nowhere near your computer. You must remember, however, that if Norton Backup encounters an error, or enters a state that requires your intervention, the program will stop and wait for your input just as if you were making a regular attended backup. Try to anticipate those conditions and use Norton Backup options to configure the program so that these stops don't occur. Also make sure that the files you want to back up will fit on one floppy disk (or two if you have two identical floppy disk drives). Here are several things to

> A successfully completed, unattended backup can return to the Desktop if you select the Quit After Backup checkbox in any of the basic or advanced options dialog boxes.

watch out for when making an unattended backup:

- Make sure the system time and date are correct in your computer. If they are not correct, the Scheduler will not start your backup when you expect it to.

- Ensure that your backup files will fit onto the backup medium. This is especially important if you back up to floppy disks; it is less important if you back up to a DOS path, using a local or networked hard disk.

- Turn off the overwrite warnings, so that Norton Backup will not stop if it encounters existing files on your backup disks.

- Make sure that the backup floppy disks are formatted to the correct capacity, or turn on Always Format Backup Diskettes.

RUNNING NORTON BACKUP IN THE BACKGROUND

Windows brings *multitasking* to the PC, the ability to run more than one program at a time. The program you are working with now is said to be the "foreground application," while all the other programs are said to be "running in the background." Making a backup is one of those tasks ideally suited to running in the background, because it is always a chore to make and is not very interesting to watch—but is also absolutely vital.

Norton Backup has been designed to run in either foreground or background mode. It obviously runs faster in foreground mode, but if you don't really care how long it takes to make a backup, then run it in the background. Any alert boxes Norton Backup generates will come to the foreground automatically when you need to change floppy disks. There are also a few precautions that you should take:

- Do not open, close, alter, or move any files selected for backup.

- Do not allow another application to access any floppy disks on your system. If you have two floppy disks installed in your computer and you are backing up to one of them, don't allow another program to access the other disk, even though Norton Backup is not using it.

ELEVEN

Protecting Your Files

THIS CHAPTER LOOKS AT TWO OF THE WAYS THAT you can use the Norton Desktop to protect your files. You can protect your files against accidental deletion with SmartErase and protect them from prying eyes using the Shredder. SmartErase saves deleted files in a special area of your hard disk, making recovery of accidentally deleted files fast and easy. The Shredder completely obliterates files so that they can never be recovered—ever.

USING SMARTERASE TO RECOVER DELETED FILES

Have you ever worried about deleting a file or document in case you might need it again? SmartErase lets you delete that file with confidence, because it actually delays the deletion. When SmartErase and its companion program, Erase Protect, are installed on your system, they intercept the erase command—even if you erase a file from within another application program and don't use the Desktop. Rather than completing the delete operation, the file(s) or directory are moved into another directory on your hard disk, called the Trashcan. This procedure has the added benefit of protecting the files from being overwritten, which in turn makes them easier to recover if you change your mind and decide that you wanted to keep them after all.

The files are held in the Trashcan for the period of time that you specify; then they are automatically deleted. You can also specify the amount of disk space you want to reserve for the Trashcan.

SmartErase offers five very handy and important features:

- You can delete files by dragging them to the SmartErase icon on your Desktop.

- You can open the SmartErase icon and look at the deleted files held in the Trashcan, and also see how full the Trashcan is.

- You can easily recover the deleted files as long as they are still held in the Trashcan, even if they were deleted by another application program.

- You control when and how the Trashcan is emptied.

- You can specify the drives and file types you want to be protected by SmartErase.

All these features will do a great deal for your piece of mind, especially when combined with a regular hard disk backup made by Norton Backup, described in Chapter 10. If the file is still in the Trashcan, you can recover it using SmartErase. If the file is no longer in the Trashcan, restore the file from your backup.

HOW SMARTERASE AND ERASE PROTECT WORK TOGETHER

See Chapter 18 for a more detailed explanation of what happens on your disk when you delete or add a file.

When you delete a file from your system, the data in the file are not actually removed. What happens is that the disk bookkeeping information is updated to reflect the file's deletion, and the name is removed from its directory. The data in the file and the file name (minus its first letter) stay on your disk until they are overwritten by another file at some time in the future.

SmartErase works with another separate program, a memory-resident program called Erase Protect, to intercept the delete commands on your system and copy the files to the Trashcan directory. As long as the disk space set aside for the Trashcan is not needed for new files that you add to your system, you will be able to recover deleted files every time, even from networked hard drives.

The Norton Desktop installation program adds a command into your AUTOEXEC.BAT file that loads Erase Protect automatically each time you boot up your computer, as follows:

```
EP /ON
```

> If Erase Protect is not running when you start Norton Desktop, you will see a message reminding you that file protection is not available on your system.

If this statement is not present in your AUTOEXEC.BAT file, open Windows Notepad and AUTOEXEC.BAT and add the command.

When you start your computer up, you will see a set of short messages as Erase Protect starts working. These messages are shown in Figure 11.1. You may also see other messages from other memory resident programs, like whether your mouse driver is loaded, each time you start your computer.

```
Erase Protect, Norton Utilities 6.0, Copyright 1991 by Symantec Corporation

Erase Protect status:   Enabled
Drives Protected:       C: (Trashcan contains 1808K in 148 files)
                        D: (Trashcan is empty)
Files Protected:        All files
Archive Files:          Not Protected
Files Deleted After:    5 days
Image, Norton Utilities 6.0, Copyright 1991 by Symantec Corporation

Finished updating IMAGE for drive C:
Finished updating IMAGE for drive D:
C:\>
```

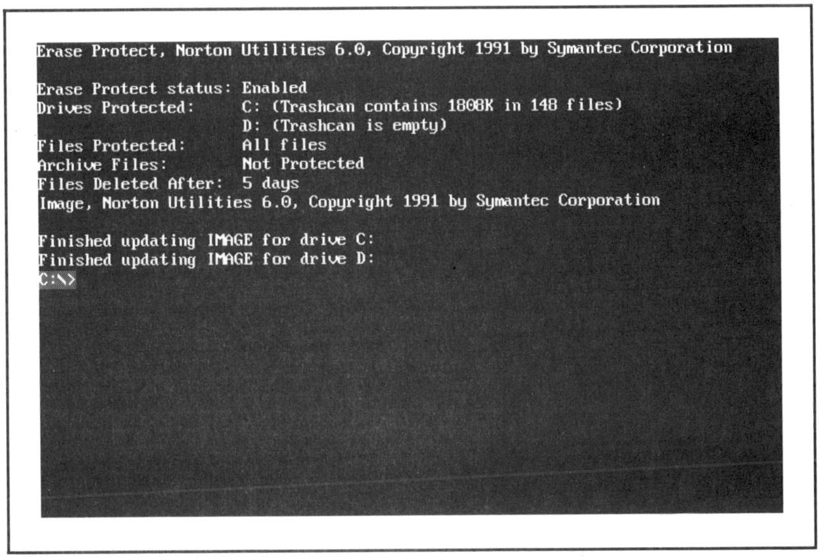

Figure 11.1: Erase Protect checks the Trashcan every time you start your computer

The Desktop installation program also adds a command for the Image program into your AUTOEXEC.BAT file. Image saves a copy of the information from your hard disk system area for use in the event of an accident. The system area contains the hard disk boot record, the file allocation tables, and the root directory, and Image saves information on all these areas. If you have more than one hard disk, use Notepad to make sure they are all referenced in your AUTOEXEC.BAT file. For example, my hard disk is divided into two parts, drive C and drive D, so the Image statement in my AUTOEXEC.BAT file looks like this:

    IMAGE C: D:

It is not usually necessary to save Image information for floppy disks.

Once Erase Protect is loaded, you have to decide how to control the Trashcan, and which of your files you want protected against accidental erasure. Select the Configure menu in the Desktop and then select SmartErase to open the Configure SmartErase dialog box. I already described how to use this dialog box in Chapter 9, so this will just be a quick refresher.

Use the Enable SmartErase Protection checkbox to enable or disable Erase Protect. It will be selected by default if you have just installed the Norton Desktop, and you should leave it this way. If Erase Protect was not installed on your system when you started it running, this entry will be dimmed and unavailable. You cannot load Erase Protect once you have started Windows running.

In the Files to Protect group box, indicate the kind of files you want to preserve in the Trashcan when they are deleted from the Desktop. Choose from All Files, Only the Files Listed, and All the Files Except Those Listed. Type your entries into the File Extension text box; you can enter up to nine different extensions, separated by a space or comma. Erase Protect can protect your files if they are deleted singly, as a group, or as part of a directory deletion. Do not protect any of the Windows temporary files because they do not usually have much meaning outside of your current Windows session, and there are so many of them that you will fill up the Trashcan in a hurry. These files have .TMP or .SWP file-name extensions.

By default, Erase Protect protects your files for five days, then it automatically purges your files—that is, it *really* deletes them from your system. You can change this five day default to any time period you like, and you can specify the amount of hard disk space you want to reserve for the Trashcan on your system in the Configure Smart-Erase dialog box. Finally, don't forget to specify the drives you want to protect.

> If you are not using the Desktop as your Windows shell, click on the SmartErase icon in the Norton Desktop group window to start Smart-Erase. Then choose the Configure entry from the SmartErase menu bar to open the Configure Smart-Erase dialog box.

DELETING FILES WITH SMARTERASE

SmartErase is available as a tool icon on your Desktop and also as a selection from the Desktop Tools menu, where it is called UnErase.

If you are not using the Norton Desktop as your Windows interface, you can click on the SmartErase icon in the Desktop group window and start SmartErase as a stand-alone program.

In stand-alone mode, SmartErase has a File menu for selecting and deselecting files, a View menu so that you can manage the SmartErase drive window and sort and filter files, a Configure selection, and a Help menu. When you run SmartErase from inside the Desktop, all the usual Desktop menus are available.

> Files that have read-only or system attributes always require your confirmation before they are deleted.

The easiest way to delete a file using SmartErase is to drag it from a drive window to the SmartErase icon on the Desktop. Just be sure that you are dragging only the file(s) you want to delete. A dialog box opens, asking you to confirm the deletion. If Erase Protect is not turned on, the confirmation message will tell you **Erase Protection is not available.**

You can also drag a directory to the SmartErase desktop icon to delete the directory and all its files. If the directory contains other subdirectories, they must either be selected for deletion, or be empty. Another way of deleting subdirectories is to use the Delete command from the File menu and check the Include Subdirectories checkbox.

Files and directories will not be protected when:

- Erase Protect is not loaded on your system, or is not turned on.

- the file does not match the protection criteria established when you configured SmartErase.

- the file is too large to fit into the Trashcan.

- you deleted the file using the Shredder, described later.

RECOVERING ERASED FILES

To recover an erased file, double-click on the SmartErase Desktop icon, start SmartErase in stand-alone mode, or use the Run command with the file name SMTERASE.EXE, and you will see the SmartErase window in Figure 11.2.

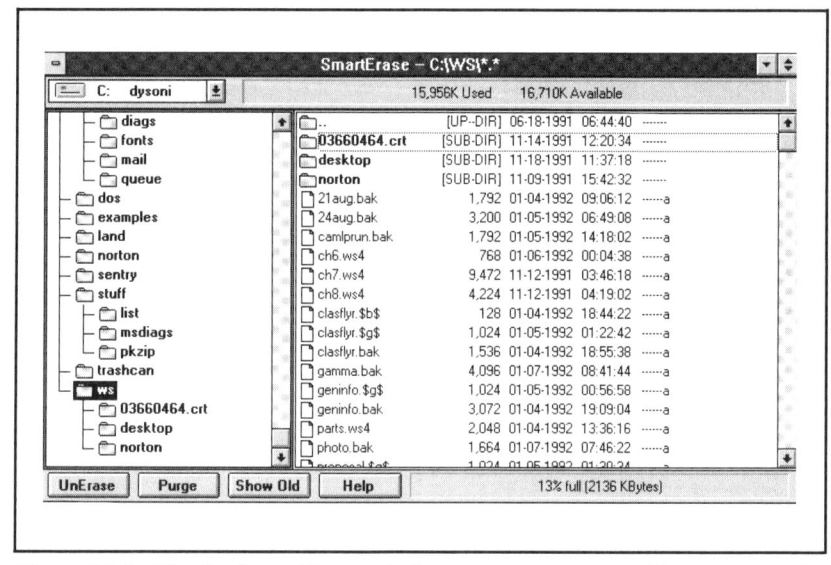

Figure 11.2: Use the SmartErase window to recover erased files or purge the Trashcan

The SmartErase window works in exactly the same way that the Desktop drive windows work, and they share many common elements, including the tree pane, the file pane, and a set of command buttons below these two panes. The area to the right of these buttons shows the current status of the Trashcan, both the percent-full level and the number of bytes occupied. You can control the major elements of the SmartErase window using commands from the View menu, just as you do with drive windows.

The SmartErase file pane lists the erased files found in the directory that is selected in the tree pane, along with any subdirectories of the current directory. Sometimes you will see the message **No Files Found** in the file pane. This does not mean that there are no files in the selected directory; it just means that SmartErase was unable to find any *deleted* files belonging to this directory.

Any files that were deleted without the benefit of SmartErase protection are listed in the SmartErase window with a question mark as the first character of their file name, because this first character was overwritten by DOS when the file was deleted.

> Maximize the SmartErase window if you are planning to work with a large number of deleted files, or use the Show Entire Drive command in the View menu.

To recover a deleted file:

1. Locate the directory in the SmartErase tree pane that originally contained the deleted file(s).
2. Select the file(s) you want to recover.
3. Select View Pane from the View menu, if necessary, to look at the contents of a file before you recover it.
4. Click on the UnErase command button below the tree pane. When the file is recovered, it disappears from the SmartErase file pane and reappears in the normal drive window file pane.
5. Open the original application program that created the file to make sure that the file can still be read.

Do not try to recover deleted files that have existing copies currently in use by Windows or by the Desktop. For example, if you are using SmartErase, you are obviously using Windows and there is a good chance that Windows has created a swap file for use during this Windows session. Do not try to recover an old swap file from a previous Windows session, because Windows will get confused very quickly if it finds that there are now *two* swap files on your system. Be careful when recovering any files that have .SWP, .MAP, .QAG, .DAT or .BIN file-name extensions.

If the deleted file was not protected by SmartErase, you will be asked to provide the missing first letter. Enter the original letter if you can remember it; if you can't, just type in any letter and use the Rename command to restore the correct name to the file when you remember it again. Recovering unprotected files is much more difficult than recovering protected files. Sometimes a part of the deleted file will have been overwritten by another file. It may not even be possible to recover the whole file.

The UnErase program can also recover files from the Trashcan very quickly.

If a SmartErase recovery is not complete, try the non-Windows UnErase program on the Norton Desktop Emergency Disk. This program is described in detail in Chapter 18. In the unlikely event that this is also unsuccessful, restore the missing file or files from your backup set.

LISTING OLD FILES

If SmartErase finds that there are several version of the same deleted file in the Trashcan, it only shows you the most recent version, assuming that this is the one you will want to recover. SmartErase also does not usually show entries for deleted files that it knows are incomplete and have been overwritten. If you want to see files in either of these categories, click on the Show Old command button in the SmartErase window. The Show Old command button name now changes to Hide Old.

If you are working on a Novell network, you will only be able to see files that *you* have deleted, unless, of course, you have network supervisor privileges.

PURGING DELETED FILES

> In this context, *purging* means that protection is removed from the file and it is finally deleted from your system.

Every time you start up your computer with Erase Protect loaded, it checks the Trashcan and purges any files that have been preserved for longer then the time limit. Erase Protect also purges files from the Trashcan to stay within any size constraints you may have specified, and to make room for more data.

But you can also purge the Trashcan yourself. You might consider doing this if you know that there are several very large files clogging up the Trashcan and you are sure that you have no further use for them. Purging is probably best left to Erase Protect, but if you are planning to do it yourself, be sure to click on Show Old first, so that you know exactly which files will be purged from your Trashcan. Once a file has been purged from the Trashcan, your chances of recovering it later become much less certain.

Using Purge is the only safe way of removing files from the Trashcan. If you use regular delete commands to remove them, Erase Protect will carefully make another copy and put them back into the Trashcan as long as they meet the Files to Protect criteria.

SMARTERASE AND DOS 5

SmartErase is completely compatible with Microsoft's DOS 5 Mirror and Delete Tracking features. The DOS 5 Mirror program is very similar to the Image program described before: it also saves a copy of important system information for use in the event of an emergency. SmartErase will always use the most recent information that it can find, from whatever source. It can use:

- the MIRROR.FIL data file made by DOS 5's Mirror program.

- the IMAGE.DAT data file made by Norton Desktop or by the Norton Utilities (for DOS), Version 5 and later.

- the FRECOVER.DAT data file made by the Norton Utilities (for DOS), Version 4.5 or earlier.

So you can see that you have the best of all possible worlds when you use SmartErase.

USING ERASE PROTECT ON A NETWORK

You can use Erase Protect on a Novell network, as long as you are running up-to-date versions of certain network files; VIPX.386, VNETWARE.386, and NWPOPUP.EXE must be dated later than 9/20/90.

Don't install Erase Protect by yourself; ask your network supervisor to do it for you. The first time Erase Protect is run on a network, it creates the Trashcan directory one level below the root directory. This is because networks are very fussy about files in the root directory; it is easier for many reasons to do it this way. For Erase Protect to work correctly, all users should have full rights except search rights for the Trashcan directory.

If you have Erase Protect installed and you are having problems printing on the network printer, open Notepad on your Windows WIN.INI file and make the following change. For each occurrence in the [ports] section of the file of **LPT***x***:** = , where *x* is either 1, 2, or 3, add **.PRN** before the colon, making the statement read **LPT***x***.PRN:** = . Just make this change for network printers. You do not have to make the change for your local printer.

OBLITERATING FILES WITH THE SHREDDER

Now that you know how to recover deleted files from your system, what's to stop someone recovering confidential files that you think you have deleted? Let's say you have just finished working on the documentation for a confidential project. You make backup copies of your files in a secure location, but you want to be sure that all traces of the original files are removed from your hard disk. Deleted files can be recovered. Even formatting the disk may not remove all of the data.

The answer is the Shredder. Using this Norton Desktop tool ensures that the files are removed permanently. Not even the UnErase program on the Emergency Disk can recover files that have been overwritten by the Shredder.

EXAMINING SHREDDING METHODS

As you saw in the section in Chapter 9 on configuring the Shredder, there are two ways to overwrite files. The normal method just writes a value of zero into every part of the file, including any unused portions or *slack space* in the file. You can specify the value used and the number of times the original data are overwritten by checking the Use Special Over-Write Pattern box, and by specifying the number of times that the data should be overwritten in the Repeat Count text box.

If you want to conform to the Department of Defense (DOD 5220.22M) standard for media protection, choose Use Government Shredding. The pattern used is:

1. The original file is overwritten first using zero, then again using one, for a total of six passes over the file.

2. The data are overwritten again, this time using a different character, ASCII decimal 246. You can also specify that a special overwrite pattern be used instead.

3. The last write is verified.

Certain disk-cache programs perform delayed writes to speed up disk operations by queuing up several disk-write "requests" and then doing them all at once. If they are told to write the same thing several times to the same place on the same disk, they may just write the information once in an attempt to save time. If you use such a caching program, and you need to use the U.S. Government method, you must disable your cache before you start shredding.

As you prepare to obliterate a confidential file, pause for a moment to think of the other places where there might be a copy of the same or a very similar file. You will want to shred these files, too:

- Did you copy this file from another directory on your disk, and does this original still exist, perhaps under a different name?
- Does your application program make automatic copies of the main file? If so, where on your disk are these backup files?
- Does your application program create temporary files as you update the original? If so, where on your disk are those temporary files?
- Is there a copy of this file in the Trashcan?
- Is there a copy of this file on the network?

SHREDDING FILES AND DIRECTORIES

The Shredder eradicates files from a disk completely; it does not just erase them. The Shredder writes new information into every part of the file on your disk, overwriting the original data. Shredder even removes the original directory entry for the file so that no trace whatsoever remains of your confidential file.

Let me reiterate what I have said about the Shredder before I go further: once you shred a file, *there is no way to recover it—ever.* So be careful!

The easiest way to shred a file is to open a drive window for the disk that contains the file you are working with and drag the file to the Shredder Desktop icon. You can also drag groups of files and even whole directories to the Shredder in this way. The files are shredded first, then, as long as the directory is empty, it too is destroyed. Be careful if you use file filters to display only certain kinds of files in the file pane; you may think that the directory is empty, when in fact you can't see some of the

The Shredder represents a powerful and irreversible process, so proceed slowly and carefully.

files because they have been filtered out. If the Shredder is not iconized on your Desktop, you can choose Shredder from the Tools menu.

In any case, the Shredder dialog box in Figure 11.3 opens. If you selected files or directories in a drive window before invoking the Shredder, they will be shown in this dialog box. If not, then enter a file name now. There is a Browse button you can use to locate the file, too. You can also use wildcard characters in the Shred text box, but—quite frankly—I do not recommend anything that makes the shredding operation any broader than it needs to be. Unanticipated results may occur unless you have thought through the operation very carefully!

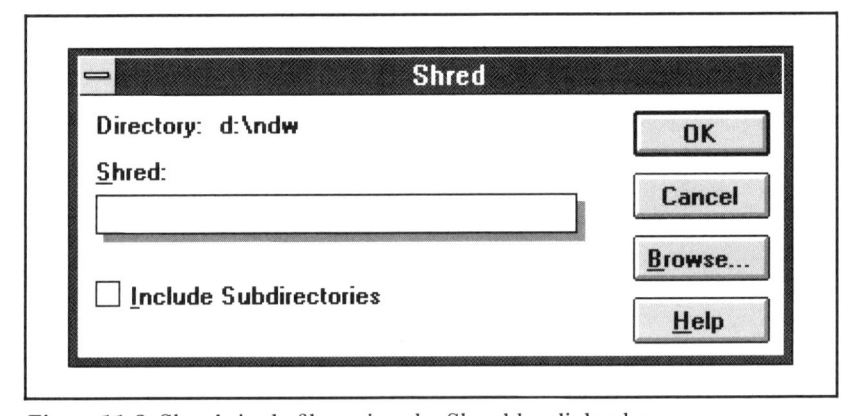

Figure 11.3: Shred single files using the Shredder dialog box

The Shredder dialog box also includes a checkbox to include all subdirectories. Be careful to make the right selection here.

Click on OK when you are ready to start shredding. The Shredder always asks you twice to confirm that you want to shred the file before the file is obliterated, so you can always change your mind.

USING THE SHREDDER IN STAND-ALONE MODE

You can also start the Shredder in stand-alone mode by double-clicking on the Shredder icon in the Desktop group item in Windows or by using the Run command and entering **SHRED.EXE**. Now that you know how to use the SmartErase window, the Shredder window shown in Figure 11.4 will present no problems at all.

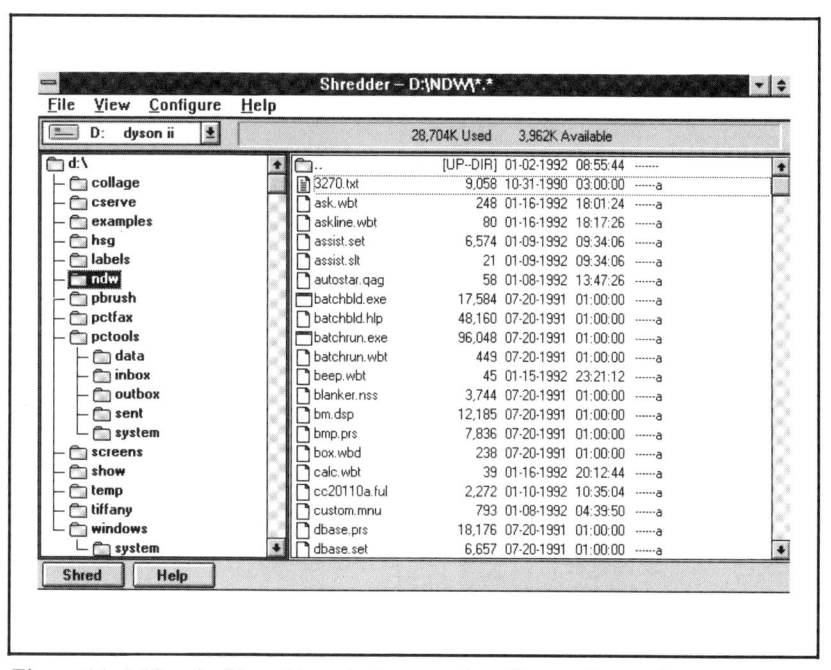

Figure 11.4: Use the Shredder window to select files or directories you want to shred

> The View menu also works just like the View menu on the Norton Desktop, containing entries to control the drive panes and apply file filters.

You can select files and directories for shredding by clicking on them in the file or tree panes in the main Shredder window, or using the Select cascading menu selections in the File menu: All, Some, or Invert. These selections, along with the corresponding entries in the Deselect cascading menu, work just like their counterparts in the Desktop File menu.

When you have selected the file(s) you want to shred, click on the Shred command button at the bottom of the window. The Shredder will ask you twice to confirm that you want to continue with the destruction before obliterating the file.

TWELVE
Examining Your System

IN THIS CHAPTER WE WILL LOOK AT YOUR COMPUTER hardware in two different ways. First, we'll look at your disks using Norton Disk Doctor for Windows, then we'll look into all the dark corners of your computer using System Information. You don't have to be a computer expert to use either of these programs; they are both easy to use. The Norton Disk Doctor is completely automatic once you have chosen a disk to work with, and System Information uses icons to locate the part of your computer system that you want to look at.

USING NORTON DISK DOCTOR FOR WINDOWS

> Norton Disk Doctor for Windows can *find* disk problems, but it cannot fix them. Use NDD on the Emergency Disk to *fix* the problems.

Norton Disk Doctor for Windows examines your disk, looking for problems in several different areas. When it finds something, the program explains the nature of the problem, and you should run the version of Norton Disk Doctor (NDD) on the Emergency Disk to fix it. If your disk is so badly damaged that you cannot even start Windows or Norton Disk Doctor, then you should go directly to NDD on the Emergency Disk. Chapter 16 explains how to use it.

To start Norton Disk Doctor for Windows from the Desktop, double-click on the Disk Doctor icon or select Disk Doctor from the Tools menu. Either way, the Norton Disk Doctor for Windows program starts and opens a dialog box so you can choose the disk drive you want to test. Click on the drive icon for the drive you want to work with, and you will see the window shown in Figure 12.1.

Norton Disk Doctor checks six different areas of your disk, each one represented by a different icon in the main window. As each test is performed, the doctor graphic visits each of the test icons in sequence and the border of the icon darkens to indicate that the test is in progress. A

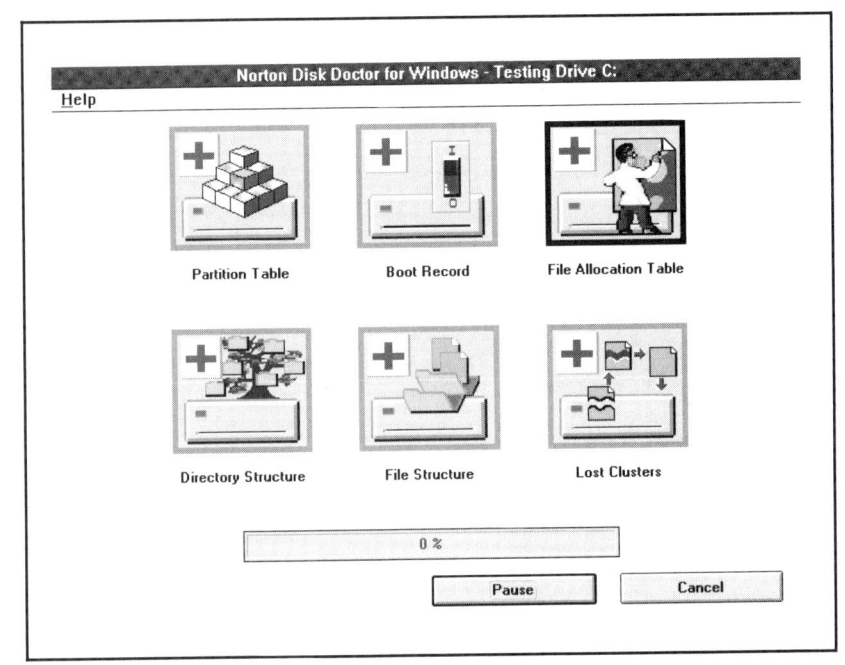

Figure 12.1: The main Norton Disk Doctor window contains six icons representing the different tests that the program will perform on your disk

horizontal bar graph at the bottom of the window also indicates the progress of the test as it runs. The Select Drives command button changes into the Pause button in case you want to pause the test.

The six Norton Disk Doctor tests are as follows:

Partition Table. The partition table tells DOS where to find information on your hard disk. If the partition table is damaged, DOS may not be able to access the hard disk. Floppy disks do not have partition tables, so this test will not run on floppy disks.

Boot Record. The boot record is the first part of the disk that DOS reads. It contains information on disk characteristics, including size, number of sectors, and clusters. If the boot record is damaged, DOS may not be able to access the hard disk properly.

File Allocation Table. The file allocation table (FAT) contains a list of all the files and directories on your disk. If the FAT is

> If you are working with a floppy disk, the first icon for the Partition Table test will be dimmed out and unavailable, because floppy disks do not have partition tables to test.

missing or damaged in some way, you may not be able to access one or more files on your system.

Directory Structure. Norton Disk Doctor reads every directory on the disk, checking for illegal file names and file allocation table errors. You will see the names of all your directories below this test icon as the test runs.

File Structure. Norton Disk Doctor also checks the file structure against the information contained in the FAT.

Lost Clusters. Lost clusters are file fragments marked as "in use" in the FAT, but they are not allocated to any specific file.

If the Disk Doctor finds an error, it opens a dialog box that describes the problem. Remember that Norton Disk Doctor for Windows is a diagnostic tool: it can find errors, but it cannot fix them. Figure 12.2 shows the kind of dialog box you may see when Norton Disk Doctor locates a disk problem.

> Help is always available from the menu bar inside Norton Disk Doctor.

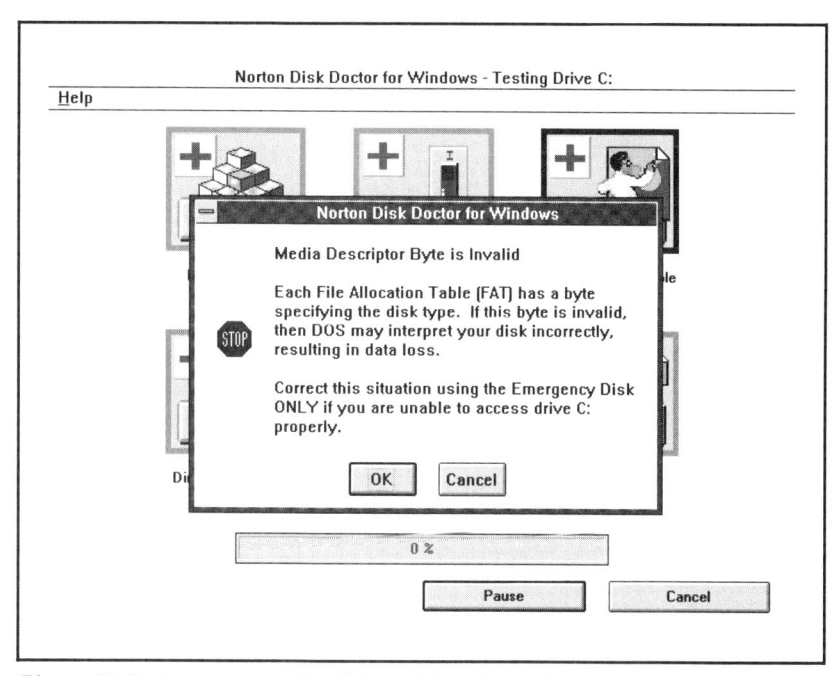

Figure 12.2: An example of a disk problem found by Norton Disk Doctor

At the end of the analysis, a summary dialog box opens, listing the six tests and showing a pass (✓) or fail (×) opposite each of the tests. If any of the tests fail, be prepared to run NDD from the Emergency Disk to fix the problems. Click on OK to close this dialog box—or, if you want to see a more detailed report on your disk, click on Info to open the Report on Drive window. In this window you can use the Save command button to save a copy of Norton Disk Doctor report to a file. Save opens a Browse box so you can choose where to put the report file; if you are having trouble with a disk, don't save the report to the same disk, because you may never be able to read it. Click on Print if you want to make a hard copy of the report instead. At the end of the tests, the Pause command button changes back into the Select Drives command button. Either select another drive to test or click the Exit command button to return to the Norton Desktop.

USING SYSTEM INFORMATION

System Information provides a wealth of information about your computer's hardware, including disk specifications, memory layout, and usage. It calculates performance indices and can even print a detailed report of its findings. If your job entails installing, demonstrating, or troubleshooting hardware or software products on unfamiliar computers, this is the program for you. System Information can also save the average computer user a lot of time and frustration. Many applications programs require users to supply hardware information during installation. However, most people do not know the details of their computer's hardware, particularly if they did not actually install it themselves. Also, some hardware can be used in different modes, which can further confuse the issue. Running System Information is a quick, efficient way to gather this information.

Double-click on the SysInfo icon on the Desktop or select System Info from the Tools menu to start the program running. Initially there are three menu items on the menu bar in System Information: File, Summary, and the usual Help selection. The File menu contains commands for saving and printing reports; we will look at these selections towards the end of this chapter. When you open more than one window in System Information, another menu item appears on the menu bar, called Window, to help you tile or cascade the windows you are using.

I will describe all of the options in System Information in the same sequence used in the Summary menu, starting with the System Summary screen. You can also click on one of the 11 buttons arranged across the window just below the menu bar to open the same window. If you use Help from System Information, you can click on replicas of these same buttons inside the Help system to see the appropriate information.

SYSTEM SUMMARY

The System Summary screen, shown in Figure 12.3, details the basic configuration of your computer: it lists information about your disks, memory, and other hardware systems. Several of the other display screens in System Information expand on the basic information shown in this window.

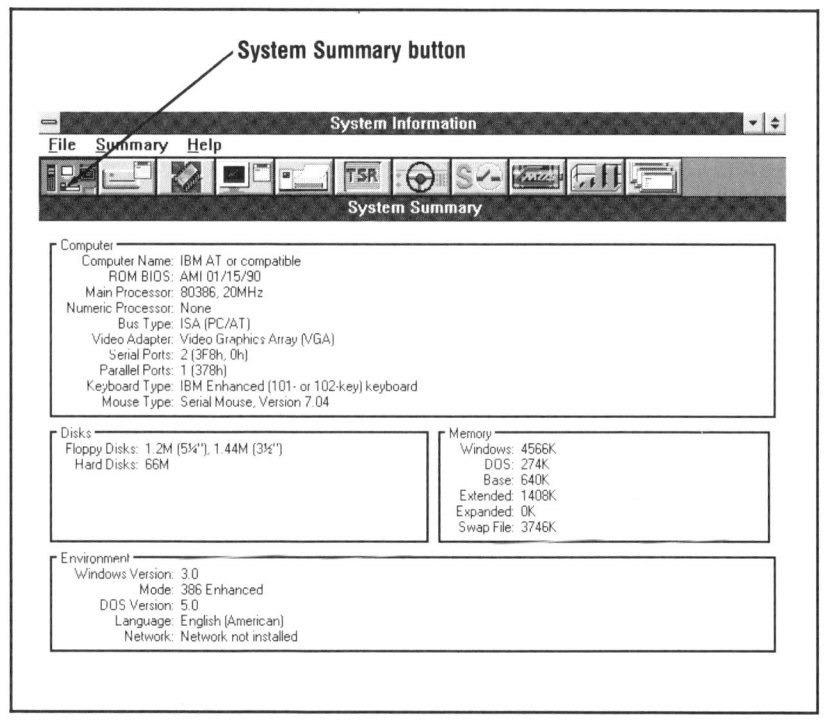

Figure 12.3: The System Summary window

This window contains important information that is useful to all computer users; therefore, I will describe each of the elements in detail. In the Computer area of the window, you will see:

- Computer Name: System Information retrieves the name of the computer from the system's read-only memory (ROM). For many IBM compatibles, System Information displays only a copyright notice or a general computer type rather than the actual computer name.

- ROM BIOS: This is the name of the read-only memory basic input/output system (ROM BIOS) and the date it was made. The BIOS is a layer of software that lets DOS communicate with the computer's hardware. It handles the basic input and output functions in the computer.

- Main Processor: This is the name of the microprocessor used in your computer. The microprocessor is the computer's engine. It translates information from RAM, ROM, or the files on a disk into instructions that it can execute, and it executes them very quickly. The IBM PC, IBM PC/XT, and most compatibles use the Intel 8086 or 8088 microprocessor. The PC/AT computer and compatibles use the Intel 80286 chip. More recent machines use the Intel 80386 or the 80486 chip. The clock speed in megahertz (MHz) is also shown on the same line.

- Numeric Co-Processor: The Intel microprocessors used in PCs are designed so that other chips can be linked to them, thus increasing their power. One such additional chip is a math, or *numeric,* coprocessor, and the IBM PC and most compatibles include a socket on the main motherboard for it. Each Intel chip has a matching math coprocessor.

Certain Intel 80486 chips have an on-chip floating point unit as part of its circuitry. Software written for the 80387 math coprocessor will run on the 80486 on-chip numeric processor without any modifications.

For example, the 8087 is used with the 8086, the 80287 is used with the 80286, and the 80387 is used with the 80386. These '87s perform some of the number-crunching operations that the main microprocessor normally executes; in doing so, the coprocessors greatly increase the speed and accuracy of numeric calculations. In addition to simple add/subtract/multiply/divide operations, math coprocessors can do trigonometric calculations such as sine, cosine, and tangent. Computer-aided design applications and scientific or statistical programs usually benefit from the use of a coprocessor, whereas word processors generally do not.

The speed gained by using a math coprocessor varies widely from application to application, but generally a math coprocessor performs calculations five to fifty times faster than a regular processor. (These coprocessors are not the same as the add-in accelerator boards that occupy a slot in the computer chassis and actually take over the original microprocessor's work by replacing it with a faster processor.)

- Bus Type: This describes the type of data bus that your computer uses. ISA (Industry Standard Architecture) is found in PC/XT and PC/AT computers, EISA (Extended Industry Standard Architecture) is a newer type of bus that supports 32-bit operations but retains compatibility with the original ISA, and MCA (Micro Channel Architecture) is IBM's proprietary bus mostly used in PS/2 computers.

- Video Adapter: This is the name of the current video display adapter. Five types of video adapter boards are available: the monochrome display adapter (MDA); the color graphics adapter (CGA); the Hercules graphics adapter, which is also known as the monochrome graphics display adapter (MGDA); the enhanced graphics adapter (EGA); and the video graphics array (VGA).

- Serial Ports and Parallel Ports: These entries report the number of installed parallel and serial interface ports. DOS 3.2 and earlier supported only two serial ports, but beginning with DOS 3.3, the number increased to four. The parallel port is normally used to connect the system printer; serial ports can connect to a variety of serial devices, including a modem, mouse, serial printer, or digitizer. As their names imply, the serial port handles data serially— one bit at a time—and the parallel port handles several data bits at once—in this case, eight. Consequently, the data-transfer rate of a parallel port is usually higher than that of a serial port. The serial port, however, is more flexible.

- Keyboard Type: This lists either a standard 84-key or an extended 101- or 102-key keyboard.

- Mouse Type: This is the name of the mouse (if one is in use) that is connected to your computer. In Figure 12.3, the system includes a serial mouse.

In the Disks portion of the window, you will see:

- Floppy Disks: This entry provides details about your floppy disks.

- Hard Disks: This entry lists the size of your hard disks in megabytes (MB).

In the Memory portion of the window, you will see:

> All memory in this part of the window is described in terms of kilobytes, where 1K equals 1,024 bytes.

- Windows: This is the total amount of memory available to Windows, both to the Windows system and to Windows applications programs. See the Windows Memory section later in this chapter for more information.

- DOS: This is the amount of memory that DOS occupies before you invoke Windows.

- Base: This is the amount of conventional memory present in your computer, usually 640K.

- Extended Memory. Extended memory is system memory above 1MB, available in 286 or later computers, based on the Extended Memory Specification (XMS) developed by Lotus, Microsoft, Intel, and AST Research. This memory is not managed by DOS but by an installable device driver called HIMEM.SYS when provided by Microsoft, QEMM386.SYS when provided by Quarterdeck Office Systems, or 386MAX.SYS when supplied by Qualitas.

- Expanded Memory: Expanded memory is system memory above 1MB based on the Expanded Memory Specification developed by Lotus, Intel, and Microsoft (LIM EMS). There are two major versions of the specification, 3.2 or 4.0, and they determine how programs interact with this memory. An installable device driver called the Expanded Memory Manager organizes this memory.

- Swap File: This is the current size of your permanent Windows swap file. If you don't have one, there will be no number after the label Swap File.

In the Environment part of the window, you will see:

- Windows Version: This is the version number of the Windows system you are running on your computer.

- Mode: This is the mode in which Windows is running on your computer.

- DOS Version: This is the version of DOS being run on your computer.

- Language: This is the language you selected in the International settings part of the Windows Control Panel.

- Network: This is the name of the system software running on your network, if one is installed.

DISK SUMMARY

Select Disk from the Summary menu or click on the Disk Summary button to see a single-screen listing of all the hard disks on your computer. An example is shown in Figure 12.4.

Here drives C, D, and E are three partitions on a 65MB drive. Drive F is a RAM disk of 128K; notice that it has a special icon in the Drive column. In the Volume/Default Directory column you can see the volume label listed (if the disk has a volume label) along with the name of the current default directory for all the drives on your system. The other columns detail the total amount of disk space on each drive, the amount used, and the amount still free. The last column contains a percent-used graph for each disk drive.

Click on one of the disk icons in this window to open the Drive Summary window, which shows more details about a particular disk drive.

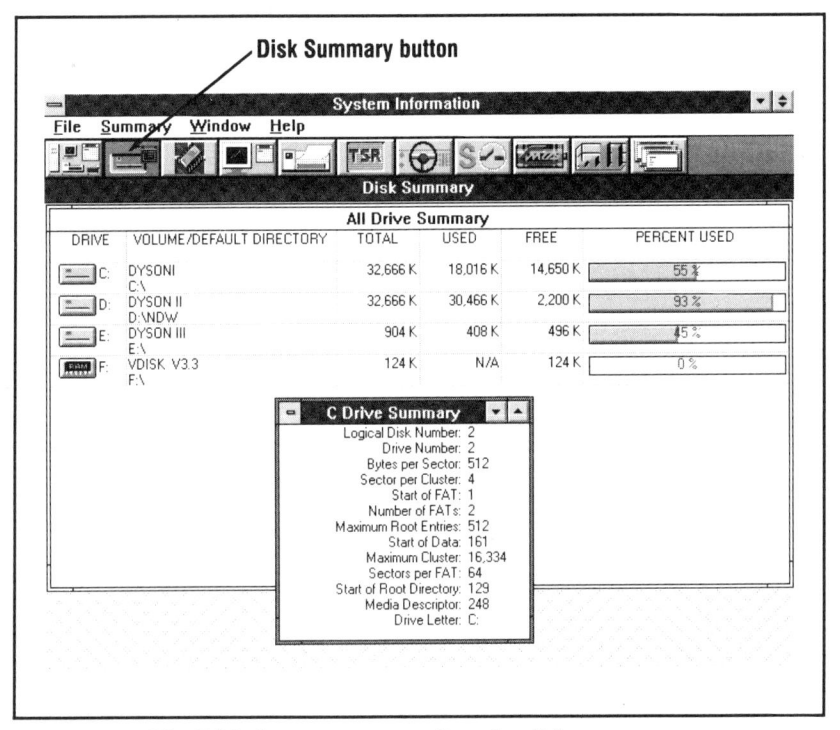

Figure 12.4: The Disk Summary screen lists the disks on your computer

This window contains information about the layout of the disk from the system's viewpoint, including the number of bytes per sector, the number of sectors per cluster, the total number of clusters, the number and type of the FAT, and the media descriptor byte. It also includes details of the starting location and size of the FAT, the root directory, and the data area. If you are using a RAM disk, notice that it contains only one copy of the FAT.

WINDOWS MEMORY

Select Windows Memory from the Summary menu or click on the Windows Memory button to open the screen in Figure 12.5. This window summarizes the amount of memory that Windows is using and shows how Windows is using that space. A bar graph is shown

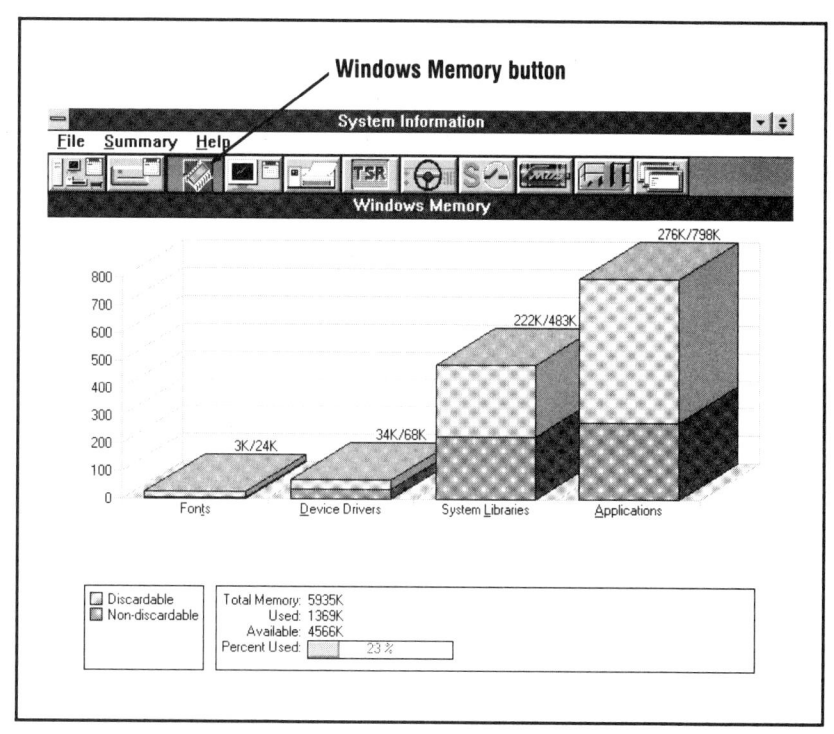

Figure 12.5: The Windows Memory screen summarizes the amount of memory Windows is using on your computer, as well as shows how that memory is being used

across the screen, with one bar each for Fonts, Device Drivers, System Libraries, and Applications:

>**Fonts** details the amount of memory used for screen and printer fonts.
>
>**Device Drivers** shows how much memory is used by device drivers on your system.
>
>**System Libraries** shows the amount of memory space used for program code libraries, used by both the Windows system and by your applications programs.
>
>**Applications** shows the amount of memory space being used by the current applications running on your system.

Each bar is divided into two parts, the upper part labeled Discardable and the lower portion labeled Non-discardable:

Discardable means that this information can be read from the disk again if you run out of Windows memory space.

Non-discardable means that this information must remain in memory at all times.

At the bottom of this window you can see summary information that lists the total amount of memory available to Windows, the amount currently in use, and the amount of memory space still available for use.

Click on one of the bars to open a small window, listing all the individual components that go into making up the larger bars. Figure 12.6 shows the Windows Device Drivers summary for my system after I clicked on the Device Drivers bar. You may recognize some of the names shown in these summaries; others are more cryptic. If

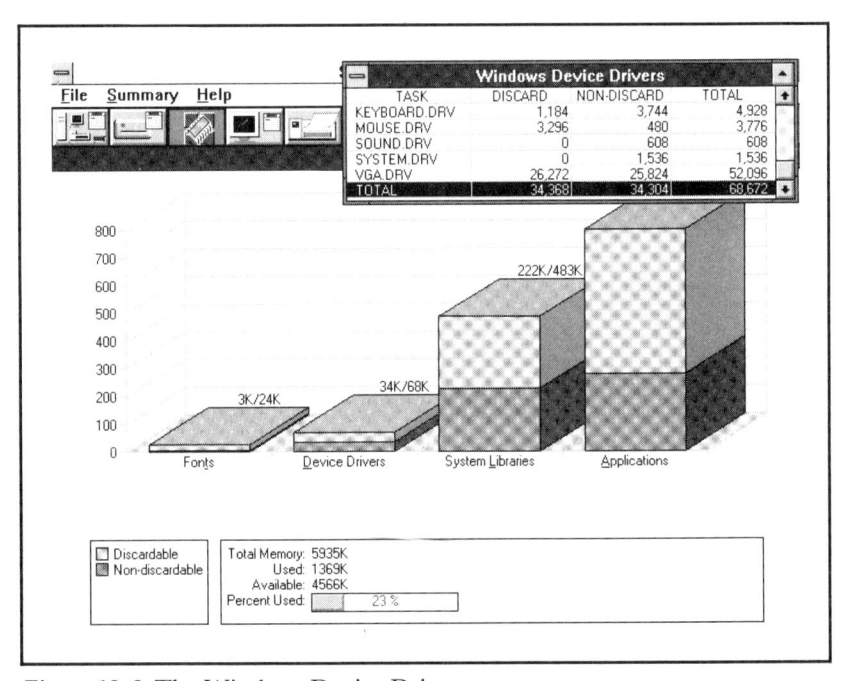

Figure 12.6: The Windows Device Drivers summary

there are too many entries in the summary window for all of them to be shown at the same time, use the scroll bars to see the other entries in the list.

DISPLAY SUMMARY

Choose Display from the Summary menu or click the Display Summary button to display the screen shown in Figure 12.7. All video systems except the MDA can be programmed with different parameters. This enables you to select from several video modes. Each video mode is characterized by the *resolution* (the number of pixels displayed horizontally and vertically) and by the number of colors that can be displayed at the same time. CGA video modes include 80-column-by-25-line mode and 40-column-by-25-line mode. The EGA can support as many as 43 lines of text; the VGA can support as many as 50 lines of text. The

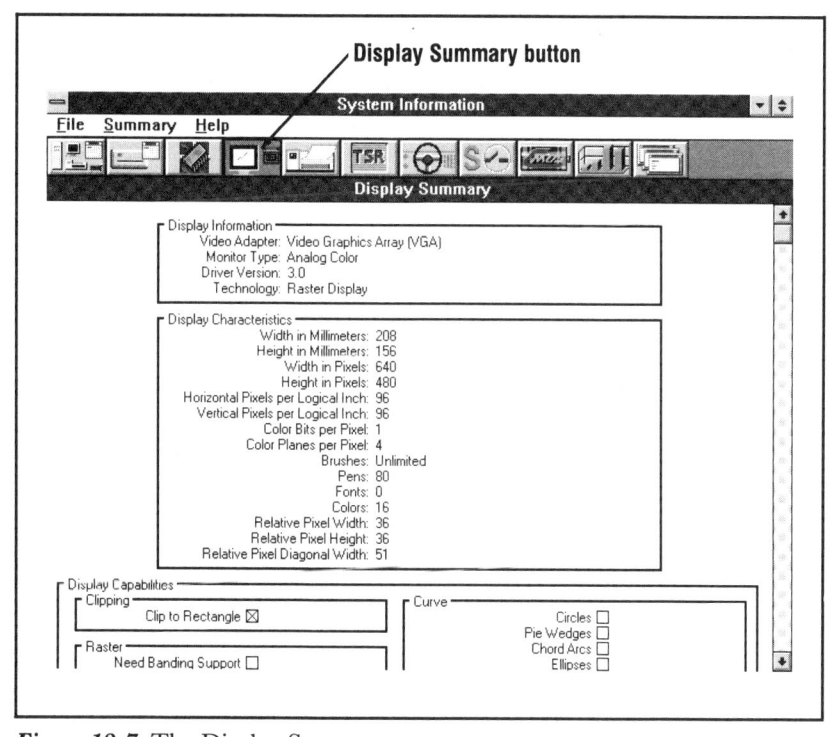

Figure 12.7: The Display Summary screen

amount of video memory needed to support these different display adapters varies in each case.

The Display Information portion of this window lists the basic attributes of your video or display system, including your adapter type, and the version of the Windows device driver that works with your display hardware.

The Display Characteristics and Display Capabilities parts of this window list all the physical attributes of your video system, along with the different types of video operations that your device driver supports on your system. Some of this information is of little interest to the general Windows user and is aimed at the programmer. You may need to use the scroll bars to read all the information.

PRINTER SUMMARY

Choose Printer from the Summary menu or click on the Printer Summary button to open the window shown in Figure 12.8. This is essentially the same as the Display Summary window seen previously, but biased towards your printer. Some of the information in this window will change if you change your Windows printer configuration.

TSR SUMMARY

One of the main limitations of DOS is that it cannot support more than one program running at one time. DOS is a single-user, single-tasking operating system. The terminate-and-stay-resident (TSR) or memory-resident program is an ingenious method that partially overcomes this limitation.

After you load a TSR program into memory, it returns control to DOS, but waits in the background. When you press a certain key combination (the *hotkey*), the TSR interrupts the application program you were running and executes its own services. When you finish using the TSR program and exit, control returns to your application program again.

Other memory-resident programs work in a slightly different way: they attach themselves to the operating system and remain in memory, working constantly in the background. The DOS PRINT utility

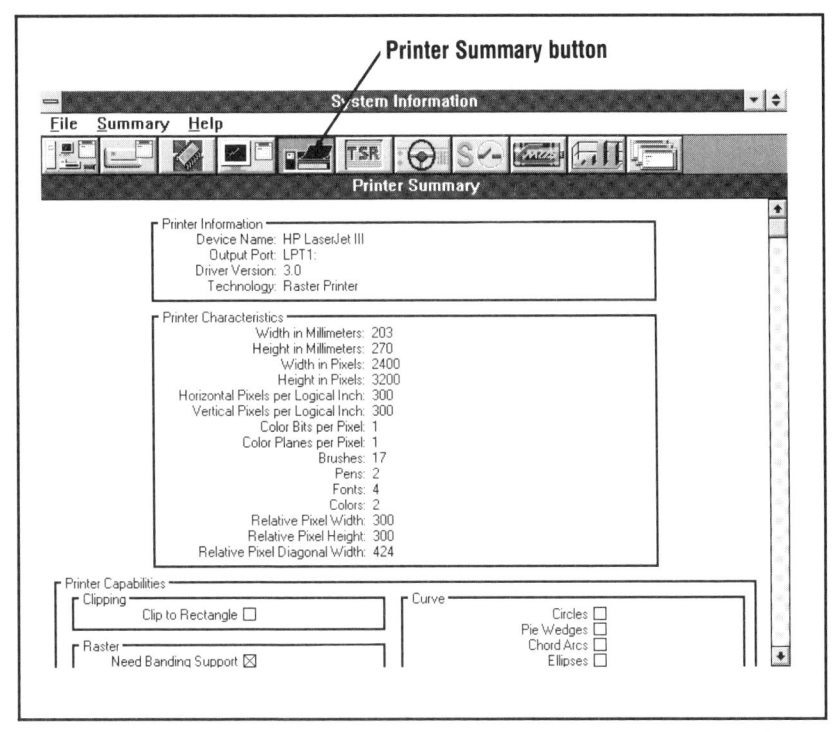

Figure 12.8: The Printer Summary window lists the characteristics of your printer in the Windows environment

is an example of this; indeed, PRINT is often called the first real memory-resident program. The Norton Desktop Erase Protect program also falls into this category.

Because DOS interrupts are always channeled through the same interrupt vector table (described in a moment), it is relatively easy for a TSR program to alter these vectors to change the way the interrupts work. For example, virtually all programs read the keyboard through interrupt 16H, which normally points to a service routine in the BIOS. It is a simple matter for a program to change the response of the system to keyboard-read requests by rerouting this vector through an alternative procedure. These replaced vectors are called *hooked* vectors. If you choose TSR from the Summary menu or click on the TSR button, you can list all of the TSR programs installed in your computer. You can see several of these hooked vectors listed in Figure 12.9.

236 UNDERSTANDING NORTON DESKTOP FOR WINDOWS

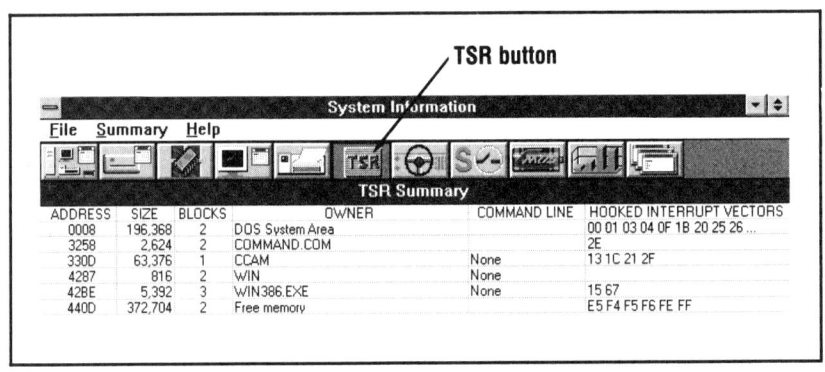

CH. 12

ADDRESS	SIZE	BLOCKS	OWNER	COMMAND LINE	HOOKED INTERRUPT VECTORS
0008	196,368	2	DOS System Area		00 01 03 04 0F 1B 20 25 26 ...
3258	2,624	2	COMMAND.COM		2E
330D	63,376	1	CCAM	None	13 1C 21 2F
4287	816	2	WIN	None	
42BE	5,392	3	WIN386.EXE	None	15 67
440D	372,704	2	Free memory		E5 F4 F5 F6 FE FF

Figure 12.9: System Information's TSR window lists program names and hooked interrupt vectors

The display shown in Figure 12.9 has the following columns:

Address shows the hexadecimal address where the terminate-and-stay-resident program is loaded on your system.

Size shows you the amount of memory used by this program, in bytes. This is a decimal number, not a hexadecimal number.

Blocks shows you the number of blocks allocated to the program.

Owner shows the name of the resident program, if it is known.

Command Line lists any command-line switches used to start the program.

Hooked Interrupt Vectors shows all the interrupt vectors that the program reroutes. These numbers are all hexadecimal numbers.

Selecting System Info twice from the Tools menu opens *two* System Information windows on the Desktop.

You can switch between the Memory part of the System Summary window and the TSR Summary window (or view both at once) to evaluate the effect of loading additional TSR programs. The amount of memory in your computer is fixed, so as you add TSR programs, the amount of memory space available for your application programs decreases. At some point you may find that you cannot open a large database or use a large application program because there is no longer sufficient room. You must then decide if the utility of your TSRs is worth the memory space that they occupy; try to strike the right balance for the way you work.

DOS DEVICE DRIVERS

A *device driver* is a special program that manipulates one specific piece of hardware. DOS uses device drivers as extensions to the operating system. Some device drivers are actually part of DOS; these are called *built-in device drivers.* Others exist as separate files and are called *loadable device drivers.* These drivers free DOS from having to include code for every single piece of hardware that can be attached to your computer. As long as there is a device driver supplied with the hardware, you can use it on your computer. When you want to use a new piece of hardware, merely connect it to your system, copy the device driver into a directory on your boot disk, and add a statement to your CONFIG.SYS or AUTOEXEC.BAT file to load the device driver at boot-up time. For example, if you plug a mouse into one of your serial ports, DOS does not know about the device until you add the device driver, often called MOUSE.SYS, into your configuration file. Loadable device drivers also reduce memory requirements; you only have to load the device drivers that you need for your specific hardware configuration.

Select DOS Device Drivers from the Summary menu or click the DOS Device Drivers button to display a list of the device drivers in use on your system. Your screen will look similar to the one shown in Figure 12.10.

This window has the following columns:

> **Address** shows the hexadecimal address of the device driver in the standard Intel *segment:offset* form.
>
> **Name** contains the name of the device driver.
>
> **Description** describes the device. If the name is not one of the standard names, this entry will read **Unrecognized Device**.

In Figure 12.10, you can see the loadable device driver called MS$MOUSE as the second entry. Notice also the built-in drivers for the keyboard, screen, and serial and parallel ports.

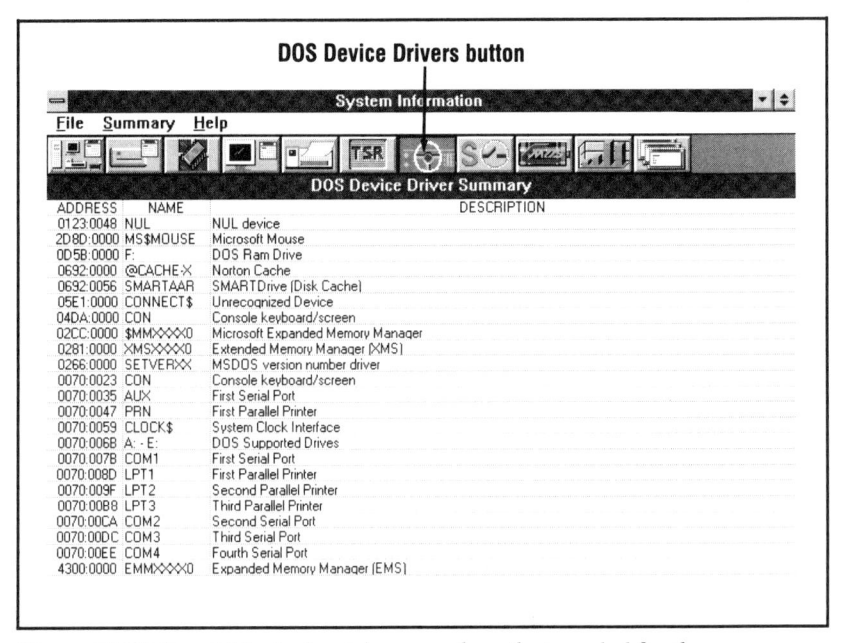

```
                    DOS Device Drivers button
┌─────────────────────────────────────────────────────────────┐
│                    System Information                       │
│  File  Summary  Help                                         │
│  [icons...]  TSR  [icon]  SC  [icons...]                     │
│                  DOS Device Driver Summary                   │
│  ADDRESS    NAME        DESCRIPTION                          │
│  0123:0048  NUL         NUL device                           │
│  2D8D:0000  MS$MOUSE    Microsoft Mouse                      │
│  0D5B:0000  F:          DOS Ram Drive                        │
│  0692:0000  @CACHE-X    Norton Cache                         │
│  0692:0056  SMARTAAR    SMARTDrive (Disk Cache)              │
│  05E1:0000  CONNECT$    Unrecognized Device                  │
│  04DA:0000  CON         Console keyboard/screen              │
│  02CC:0000  $MMXXXX0    Microsoft Expanded Memory Manager    │
│  0281:0000  XMSXXXX0    Extended Memory Manager (XMS)        │
│  0266:0000  SETVERXX    MSDOS version number driver          │
│  0070:0023  CON         Console keyboard/screen              │
│  0070:0035  AUX         First Serial Port                    │
│  0070:0047  PRN         First Parallel Printer               │
│  0070:0059  CLOCK$      System Clock Interface               │
│  0070:006B  A: - E:     DOS Supported Drives                 │
│  0070:007B  COM1        First Serial Port                    │
│  0070:008D  LPT1        First Parallel Printer               │
│  0070:009F  LPT2        Second Parallel Printer              │
│  0070:00B8  LPT3        Third Parallel Printer               │
│  0070:00CA  COM2        Second Serial Port                   │
│  0070:00DC  COM3        Third Serial Port                    │
│  0070:00EE  COM4        Fourth Serial Port                   │
│  4300:0000  EMMXXXX0    Expanded Memory Manager (EMS)        │
└─────────────────────────────────────────────────────────────┘
```

Figure 12.10: Loadable device drivers, such as that needed for the mouse, are shown in this display

SOFTWARE INTERRUPTS

Before I discuss the information shown in the Software Interrupts screen, let's briefly examine what interrupts are and how they work.

Often, after you have given the computer a task to perform, you will need it to respond quickly to a new request—for example, to begin a new task at the press of a key or the click of a mouse. The mechanism that accomplishes this is known as an *interrupt,* an "event" that causes the processor to suspend its current activity, save its place, and look up an *interrupt vector* in the *interrupt vector table.* The interrupt vector tells the processor the address of the *interrupt handler,* or service routine, that it should branch to. After the service routine performs its task, control is returned to the suspended process. DOS interrupts are often divided into three types: internal hardware, external hardware, and software interrupts. The Intel 80*x*86 family of processors supports 256 prioritized interrupts, of which the first 64 are reserved for use by the system hardware or by DOS itself.

In the IBM PC, the main processor does not accept interrupts from hardware devices directly; instead, interrupts are routed to an Intel 8259A Programmable Interrupt Controller (PIC) chip. This chip responds to each hardware interrupt, assigns a priority, and forwards it to the main processor. Each hardware device is hardwired, or "jumpered," into inputs known as IRQs or *interrupt requests,* and this is why you see an IRQ assigned to an interrupt. A hardware interrupt is generated by a device such as the keyboard, the computer clock, or one of the parallel or serial ports on the computer.

Select Software Interrupts from the Summary menu or click the Software Interrupts button to see a list of all the entries in the interrupt vector table on your computer when it is running in real mode (as distinct from protected mode). Real mode is the only mode in which DOS can operate on Intel 286 and higher microprocessors; unlike the more versatile protected mode, real mode does not offer features for memory management and memory protection. Figure 12.11 shows a sample display for an 80386 computer.

The Real Mode Software Interrupts screen has the following columns:

> \# contains the hexadecimal interrupt number.
>
> **Interrupt Name** contains the common name used with this interrupt.
>
> **Address** lists the address of each interrupt handler in hexadecimal.
>
> **Owner** lists the name of the program that installed the interrupt handler, if the name is known. Most of the interrupt handlers are established at boot-up time, but several of them can be intercepted or "hooked" by TSR programs or even by Windows itself.

Many of the software interrupts perform more than one single service. For example, interrupt 21H is the main entry point for DOS services and offers the programmer more than 100 different *function calls,* including character input and output, file creation, file reading and writing, and file deletion.

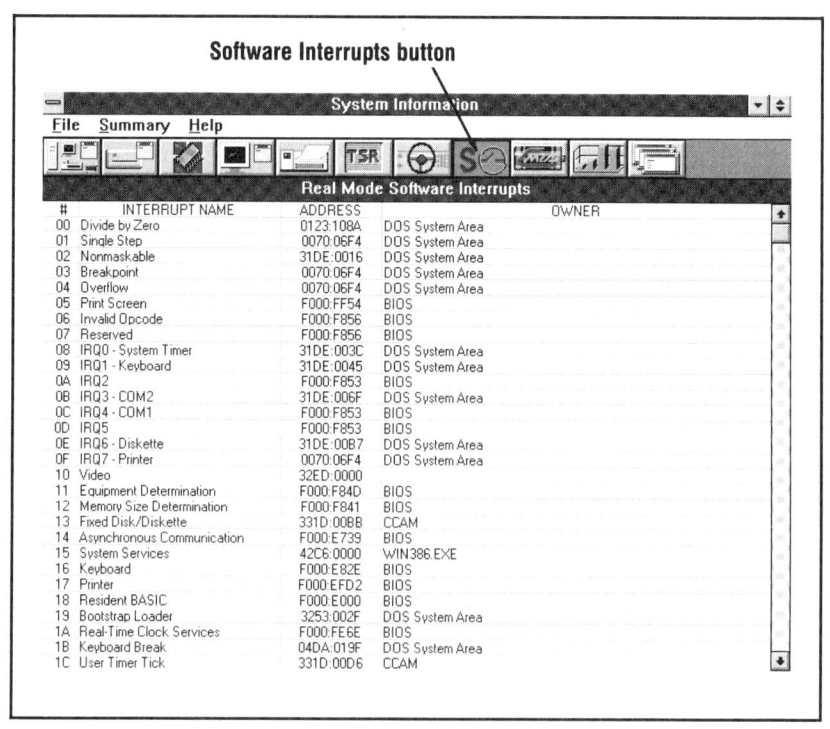

Figure 12.11: The Real Mode Software Interrupts screen lists the entries in the interrupt vector table

CMOS SUMMARY

> Print out the CMOS values; then, if your computer battery fails and loses the current settings, you can simply reenter the values.

Computers made after the PC/AT use a portion of Complementary Metal Oxide Semiconductor memory, abbreviated as CMOS and pronounced "sea moss," to hold basic configuration information for the computer. CMOS memory requires such low-power levels that it can be maintained by a small battery; therefore, your computer's information is not lost when you turn off the power at the end of your session. To examine the information held in CMOS on your computer, select CMOS from the Summary menu or click the CMOS button. Figure 12.12 shows a typical example from an 80386 computer.

One of the most crucial pieces of information on this screen is the hard disk type number shown in the Hard Disks box on the left side of this window. In Figure 12.12 the disk-type number for the first, or primary, hard disk drive is 1. The BIOS in your computer can read

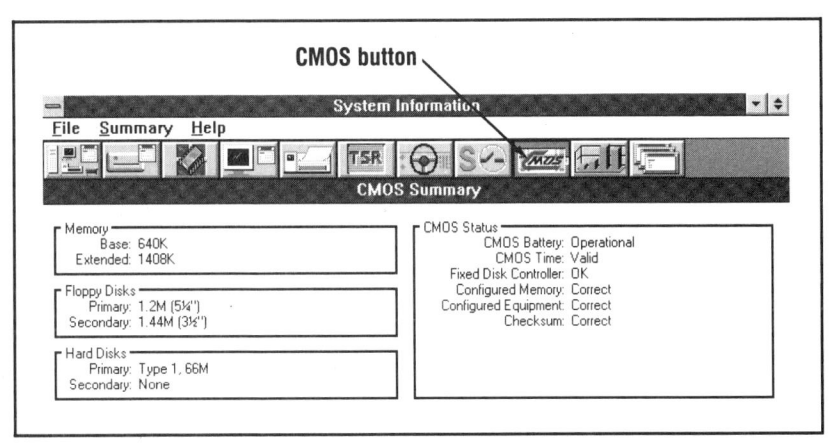

Figure 12.12: Typical CMOS values from an 80386 computer

many hard disk types from different manufacturers. This hard disk type number is the code that tells the BIOS how many heads and cylinders your specific disk drive has. If your computer's battery loses power, the contents of CMOS memory will be lost, and you will not be able to boot up your computer from the hard disk until you replace the battery and reset this number. With some computers you must use the "setup" disk that came with your computer to reset the number; other computers have the setup routines built into the ROM BIOS itself.

The rest of this screen displays details about your floppy disk types and installed memory, and includes additional information contained in CMOS.

PROCESSOR BENCHMARK

Select Processor Benchmark from the Summary menu or click the Processor Benchmark button to display a window similar to the one shown in Figure 12.13. The bar graph compares the *computing index*—a measurement of a computer's CPU or disk-independent computing power—of your computer with that of industry standard computers. A basic IBM PC/XT running an 8088 at 4.77 megahertz has a computing index equal to 1, an IBM PC/AT running an 80286 at 8 MHz has a computing index of 4.4, and a Compaq 386 running an 80386 at 33 MHz has a computing index of 34.7. In other words, the Compaq 386

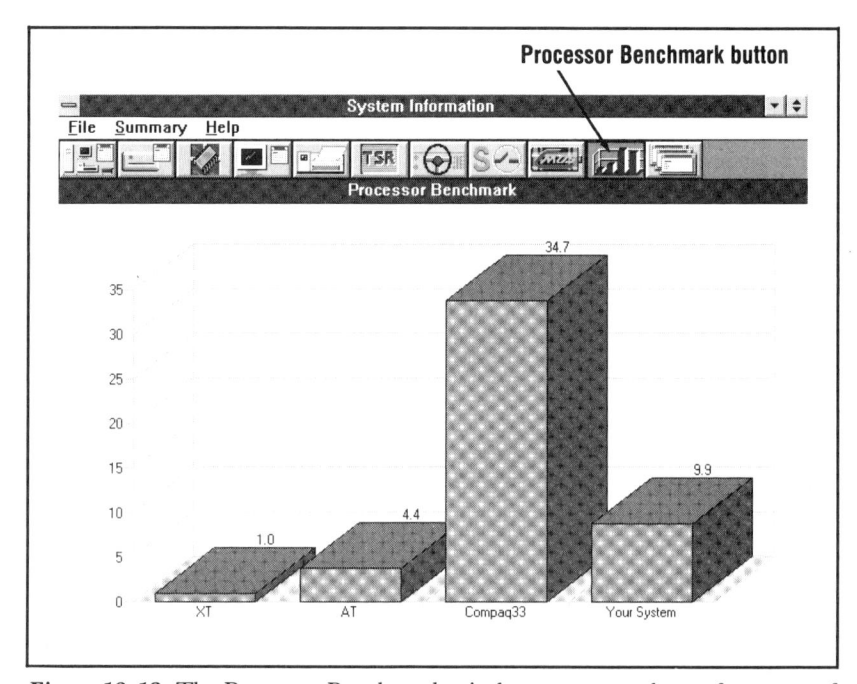

Figure 12.13: The Processor Benchmark window compares the performance of your computer with that of three industry standard computers

runs the System Information processor benchmark tests 34.7 times faster than the original IBM PC/XT. If your computer has a "turbo" button, press it and select Processor Benchmark again to see what effect changing the speed has on your computing index.

STARTUP FILES

To see a listing of your DOS and Windows configuration and initialization files, choose Startup Files from the Summary menu or click the Startup Files button. The contents of several files are displayed on the screen: CONFIG.SYS and AUTOEXEC.BAT—the DOS configuration files—and WIN.INI, SYSTEM.INI, and NDW INI—the Windows and Norton Desktop initialization files. Each file is displayed in its own document window, so you can use the Tile or Cascade commands from the Window menu to arrange these windows on your screen. In Figure 12.14 these document windows are

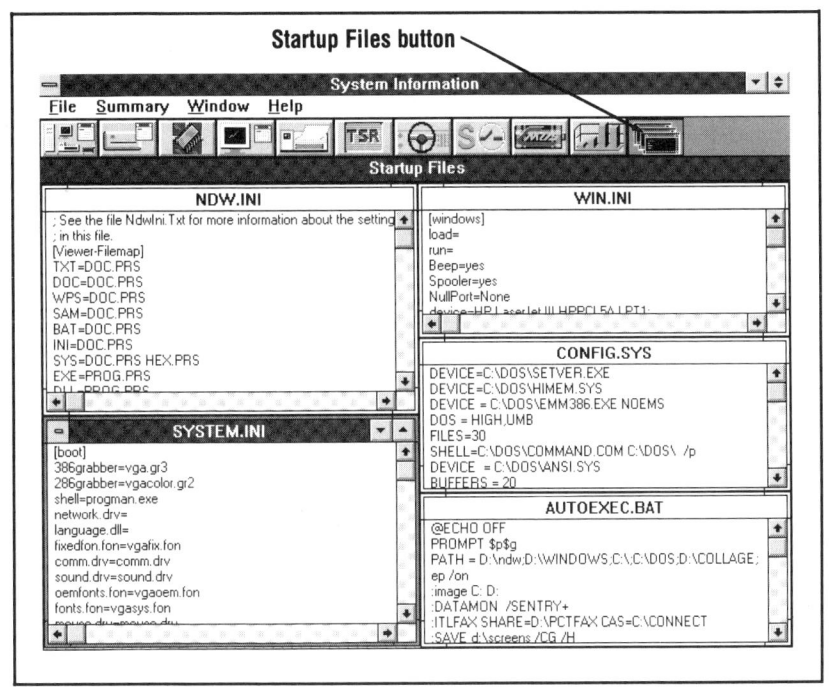

Figure 12.14: You can choose to tile or cascade the windows containing your startup files

shown tiled. Use the cursor control keys to scroll through the listings, or click on the scroll bars with the mouse.

PRINTING AND SAVING THE SYSTEM INFORMATION REPORT

Choosing Report Options from the File menu displays the screen shown in Figure 12.15. This dialog box lets you configure the System Information report so you can print only the information you are interested in. Check the boxes for the element(s) you want to include in your report, then click on OK to return to the main System Information screen. Choose Print Report from the File menu to make a hard copy of the System Information report, or choose Save Report to open a Browse box so you can decide where to store the System Information report as a file.

> The report made by System Information can take a long time to print, and can be very long if you select all of the print options. The report is not always divided up into neat pages. Send the output to a disk file first; then use your word processor to edit and arrange the information in the file so that the output is neat and orderly.

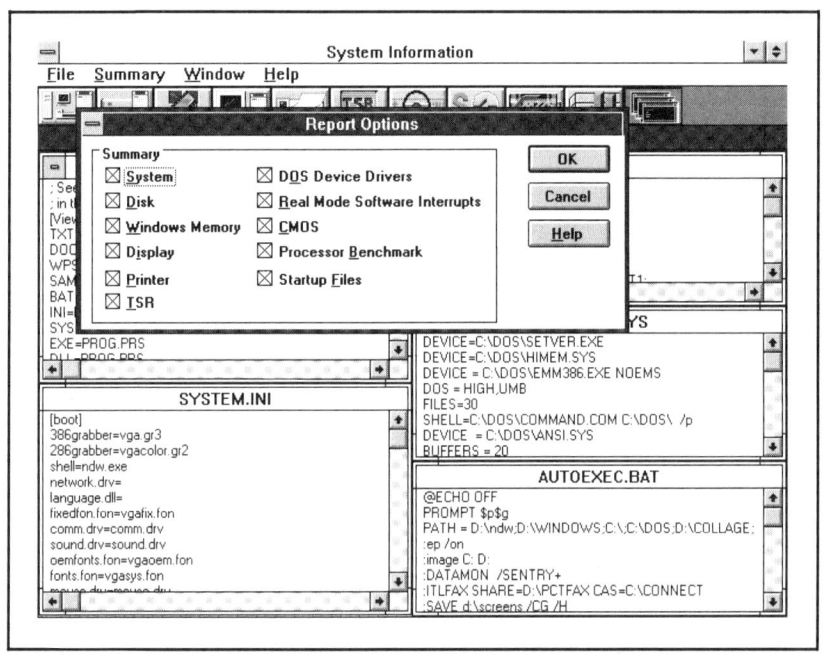

Figure 12.15: The Report Options dialog box lets you select the System Information elements you want to print in your report

THIRTEEN
Enhancing Windows

IN THIS CHAPTER I WILL EXAMINE THE NORTON
Desktop tools that enhance the Windows environment: SuperFind,
the two Desktop calculators, the screen-saver program called Sleeper,
and KeyFinder, the program that displays all the characters in any
particular font. I will begin by looking at SuperFind.

USING SUPERFIND

Sometimes you know the name of the file that you want to work with, but you can't remember where it is or which directory it's in. On other occasions you may not be able to remember the complete name of the file, but you can remember a few words or a phrase that the file containes. Unfortunately, the Windows File Manager is of little use in this situation. SuperFind, however, can find a lost or misplaced file anywhere in your directory structure on any drive, and can locate specific occurrences of text inside that file. SuperFind contains predefined search groups of files called *file sets* and predefined groups of drives and directories called *location sets*. For example, one of the predefined file sets automatically selects all files, while one of the predefined location sets automatically chooses all drives except floppies. These are convenient shorthand ways of defining the search. I'll look at both kinds of sets later on in this chapter.

There are several steps to follow in using SuperFind to locate a file:

1. Tell SuperFind *what* to look for in the Find Files text box. Several useful file sets are provided to help define the search.

2. Tell SuperFind *where* to look using the Where text box. Several useful location sets are provided to help speed up the selection process.

3. Tell SuperFind about any text you are looking for.

4. Select any of the advanced search criteria you want to use.
5. Start the search.

When SuperFind locates files matching these settings, a drive window opens, listing these files. You can then use the normal file-management buttons at the bottom of the drive window, like Move or Copy, to work with the files you have just located.

LOCATING FILES WITH SUPERFIND

To launch SuperFind, choose it from the Desktop Tools menu or double-click on the SuperFind icon in the Norton Desktop group window. You can also run SuperFind as a stand-alone program independent from the Desktop if you use the Run command in the Windows Program Manager and enter **SFIND.EXE** into the Command Line text box. However you start the program, you'll see the SuperFind dialog box shown in Figure 13.1.

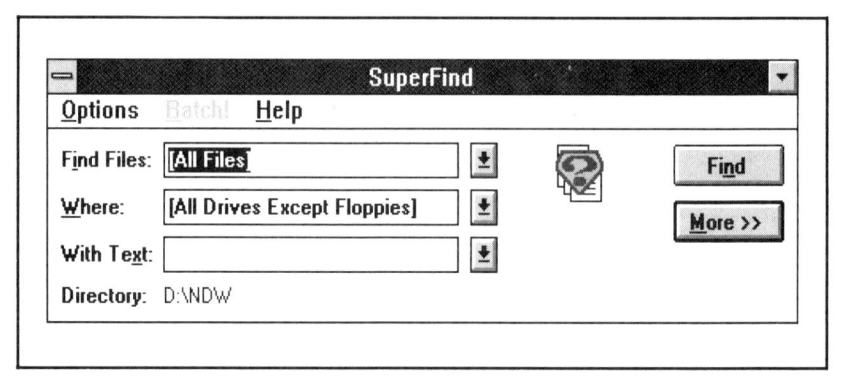

Figure 13.1: Use the SuperFind dialog box to enter your file-search criteria

> When you run SuperFind in stand-alone mode, the menu bar also contains the standard File and View menus, in addition to Options and Help.

There are three entries on the SuperFind menu bar: Options, Batch, and Help. However, you can use SuperFind in its simplest mode—to locate one or more files on your disks—without using any of the menu items. Enter as much of the file name as you can remember into the Find Files text box, using the wildcard characters * and ? to represent the part of the name you cannot remember. You can also choose one of the predefined file sets in the Find Files drop-down list box:

All Files is equivalent to the wildcard statement *.* and finds all files of all types.

All Files Except Programs finds all files except files that have .EXE, .COM, or .BAT file-name extensions.

Programs finds all files that have file-name extensions of .EXE, .COM, or .BAT, excluding all others.

Database Files finds all files made by dBASE or other programs that use dBASE file-name extensions, and all files made by Symantec's Q&A database program.

Documents finds all document files with file-name extensions of .DOC, .TXT, and .WRI.

Spreadsheet Files locates all files that use Lotus 1-2-3 and Microsoft Excel compatible file-name extensions, .WK?, .WQ?, and .XLS.

For the next step, choose where you want SuperFind to look for the lost file and enter it into the Where text box. You can also choose from several predefined location sets:

All Drives includes *all* drives (A–Z) including floppy disks, network file servers, and CD-ROMs—whether they exist on your system or not. This kind of search can take a long time.

All Drives Except Floppies just excludes floppy disk drives from the search.

Current Drive Only includes just the current drive. This is the setting you will probably use most often.

Current Directory and Subdirectories restricts the search even more, just searching the current directory—and subdirectories if there are any.

Current Directory Only restricts the search to just the current directory. This is another set you will use quite frequently.

> Searching large disks like network file servers can take a long time. Be sure that you want to use this option before you start the search.

Floppy Drives Only searches only floppy disk drives. Make sure you have inserted the appropriate disks before you start to use this location set, otherwise you will see a warning message when you click on Start to begin the search.

Local Hard Drives Only excludes all network drives from the search area.

Network Drives Only includes all network drives but excludes your local drives.

Path searches all the drives and directories specified in your path statement.

Now that you have told SuperFind which files to look for, and how to look for them, you can click on Find to start the search running. The Find command button becomes the Stop command button during a search. The bottom row of this dialog box shows the Directory entry. When you first start SuperFind, it displays the current directory, but as a search proceeds, it changes to show the directory being searched. A count of the number of files found is shown just below the SuperFind icon. When the search is complete, you will see the words **Search Done** appear here—unless you stop the search, in which case you will see the words **Search Aborted**. If files are found that match the search criteria, a drive window will open that lists all the files and their locations.

> The SuperFind drive windows are individually numbered, in sequence, so you can easily tell them apart.

SuperFind opens a new drive window for each search you make, but you can reuse the same window for all searches if you check the Reuse Drive Window selection in the SuperFind Options menu. A check mark appears to the left of this menu selection to indicate that it is on; if there is no check mark, this selection is off.

As a search proceeds, you will see SuperFind shuffle the document icons in the SuperFind dialog box. This is controlled by the Animation entry in the Options menu. The search will actually run faster with this selection turned off.

If you know you are about to start a long search, you can run SuperFind minimized by choosing Minimized Search in the Options menu. Turn off the Exclusive Search setting in the Options menu, as well, since this lets you switch to another task as you wait for SuperFind to complete the search. Select the search criteria as normal. Then when you click on the Find command button, SuperFind shrinks down to an icon on the screen. You will also see another icon representing the SuperFind drive window. If you turn on the Animation option in SuperFind, you will be able to tell when the search is complete because the icon animation will stop.

SEARCHING FOR TEXT

> You cannot use the wildcard characters * and ? in a search string, because SuperFind will look for those specific characters instead.

If you want to find a specific piece of text that you think is in one of your files, enter that string into the With Text text box. SuperFind now searches through your files for the text you entered as the search text or *search string*. Any files found that match the Find Files specifications and contain the With Text search string will be displayed in the drive window at the bottom of the screen. The default setting for SuperFind text searches is not case-sensitive, so *NORTON, Norton,* and *norton* will all match. If you want to make the text search more specific, turn on Match Upper/Lowercase in the Options menu to make the search case-sensitive.

ADVANCED FILE SEARCHES

There are several advanced search options you can access if you click on the More command button to open the lower portion of the SuperFind dialog box. Figure 13.2 shows this SuperFind dialog box. After you have expanded the SuperFind dialog box, the More command button is now labeled Less. (Use it to shrink the SuperFind dialog box back to its original size.)

SuperFind lets you select criteria to focus the search even further by selecting one or more of the following:

- Date
- Time
- Size
- Owner (network only)
- Attributes

Let's look at each of these selections in turn.

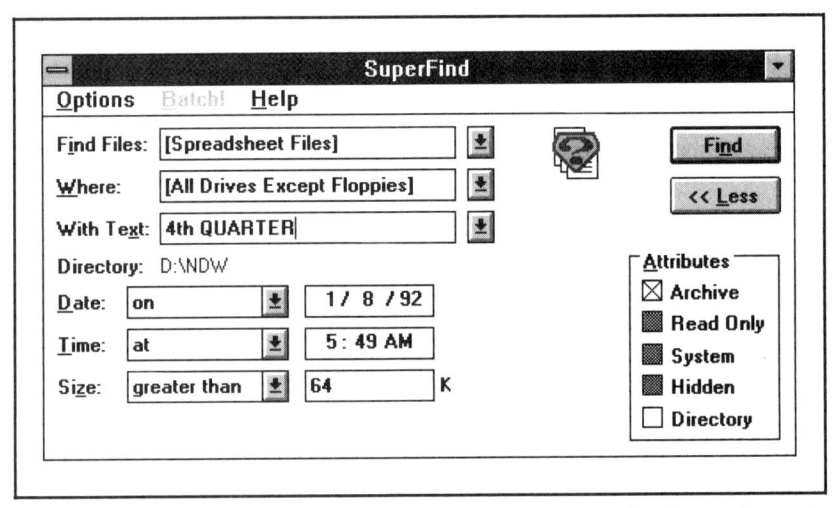

Figure 13.2: The SuperFind dialog box contains several advanced search options

Searching by File Date

You have the following options in the Date drop-down list box:

- Ignore
- On
- Not On
- Before
- Before or On
- After
- After or On
- Between
- Not Between

> The format you use to enter the date or time must be the same as that specified in the Windows Control Panel's International Date Format dialog box.

The default setting is Ignore, but you can choose any of these settings. One of two dialog boxes appears when you make a selection. You are asked to enter either a single date or a pair of dates. The current system date is displayed in this dialog box, but you can change it to another date if you wish. The Between selection is inclusive of the dates you enter, while Not Between does not include the two dates you enter.

Searching by File Time

You have a similar set of selections in the Time drop-down list box:

- Ignore
- At
- Not At
- Before
- Before or At
- After
- After or At
- Between
- Not Between

The default setting for Time is Ignore, but you can choose any setting. The Between and Not Between time options work just like their counterparts under the Date heading described above.

Searching by File Size

The Size options include:

- Ignore
- Less Than
- Greater Than
- Between
- Not Between

The default setting for Size is Ignore. The acceptable range of file sizes goes from 0 to 65MB.

Searching by File Owner

If you are currently logged on to your network, you will see an entry for Owner at the bottom of the SuperFind dialog box. (Otherwise this combination box does not appear.) The default setting is Ignore and the drop-down list box contains a list of user names that are specific to your network. You can search for files belonging to just one user at a time.

Searching by File Attributes

You can also search for files using the setting of specific file attributes as search criteria. Each file can have different settings for each of the four attributes: archive, read-only, hidden, and system. The Attributes check boxes can have one of three possible states:

Checked. A check mark appears in the box and SuperFind searches for files with this attribute *set*.

Blank. There is nothing in the checkbox and SuperFind searches for files with this attribute *cleared* or *not set*.

Gray. The checkbox is grayed out. SuperFind ignores this attribute during the search.

TIPS FOR OPTIMIZING A SEARCH

Using advanced options can make a search extremely specific, and that is a good way to make the search run as fast as possible, or to *optimize* it. There are several other things you can do to optimize a search:

- Don't use animation, as the extra overhead slows down the search.
- Don't minimize the search; make the search in the foreground.
- Turn on Match Upper/Lowercase in the Options menu to make the text search as specific as possible.
- Use as many of the advanced file options as you can.

- Use wildcards carefully in the Find Files text box to limit the search as much as possible.

- Select the smallest and most restricted choice in the Where text box.

- Turn on the Exclusive Search setting in the Options menu. This suspends all other tasks and concentrates on SuperFind.

- Turn on the Reuse Drive Window setting so that you don't waste time managing different drive windows.

CREATING FILE AND LOCATION SETS

> You can have up to 16 file sets and 16 location sets active at one time.

If you find yourself using particular file specifications in the Find Files or Where text boxes over and over again, you can create your own file sets or location sets to automate this part of the search process. Click on Search Sets in the Options menu to open the dialog box shown in Figure 13.3.

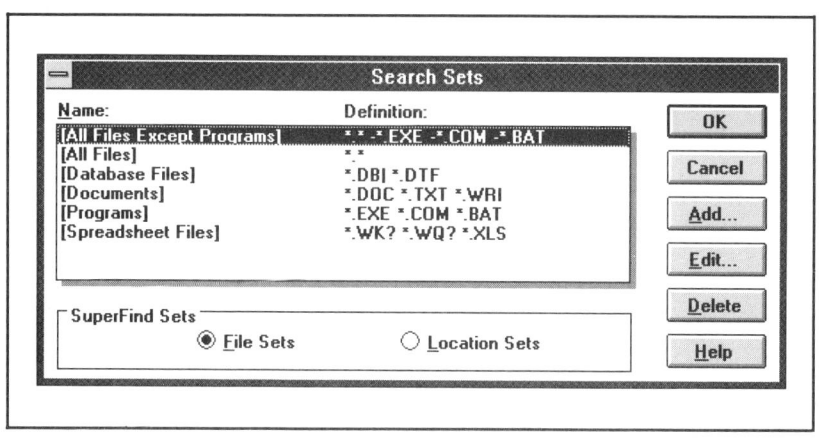

Figure 13.3: Use the Search Sets dialog box to customize your own file or location sets

> To delete a file or location set, highlight the victim and click on the Delete command button.

The process of creating a file set or location set is essentially the same. In the dialog box click the File Sets option button to add or edit a file set, or click the Location Sets option button to add or edit a location set.

Adding or Editing a File Set

Figure 13.4 shows the dialog box that opens when you click on Add for a file set; the Edit dialog box is very similar. Enter the name you want to use for the file set into the Name text box (the brackets are added automatically). This is the name you will see in the Find Files drop-down list box in the main SuperFind dialog box.

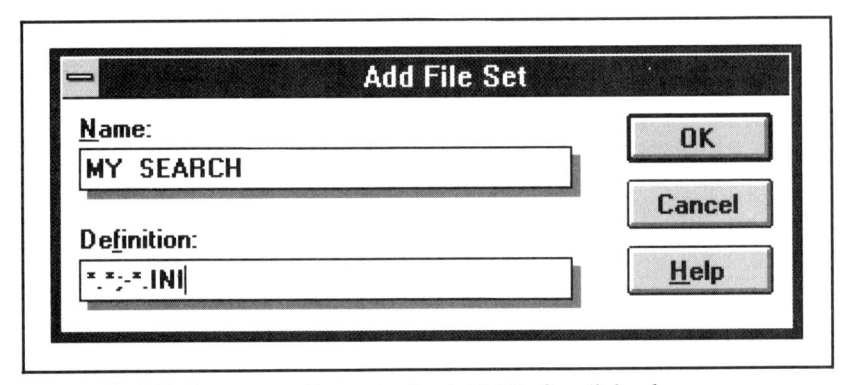

Figure 13.4: Define a new file set in the Add File Set dialog box

Enter one or more file specifications into the Definition text box. You can enter several file specifications into this text box if you want to search for different types of files at the same time, or you can just enter one specific entry. If you use more than one, separate them with a space, comma, plus sign, or semicolon. If you want to exclude a file specification from the search, place a minus sign before the entry. For example, if you want to include all possible file types except Windows .INI files, type:

.; − *.INI

The *.* wildcard statement includes all file types, while the − *.INI specifically excludes files with the .INI extension. You can use the single character wildcard symbol, ?, the multiple wildcard character, *, or the wildcard character, |, which represents one or fewer characters. An example might make this clearer. In SuperFind, ????.EXE finds all executable files with exactly four characters in their file names, whereas | | | |.EXE finds all executable files with four or fewer characters in their names. (To get the | on-screen, press the ¦ key).

Click on OK to add your new file set to the list available in SuperFind.

Adding or Editing a Location Set

When you click on Add for a location set, you will see the dialog box shown in Figure 13.5. The Edit dialog box is very similar to the Add dialog box.

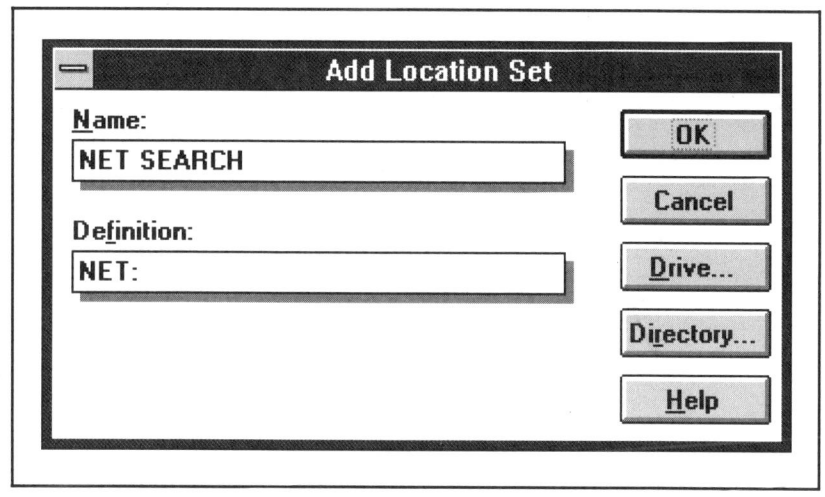

Figure 13.5: Create a new location set in the Add Location Set dialog box

Enter the name you want to associate with this new location set into the Name text box. This is the name you will see in the Where drop-down list box in the main SuperFind dialog box. In the Definition box, specify the disk drives and directories to use in this new location set; you cannot specify files in this definition box. SuperFind supports the following shorthand disk-drive specifiers:

Floppy:	All floppy disk drives
Hard:	All local non-network hard disks
Net:	All network hard disks
*:	All drives
d:	Drive d

d1: – dn: All disk drives from *d1* to *dn*, inclusive

d1:,d2:   Two or more disk drives, separated by commas

as well as the following shorthand directory specifiers:

.	The current directory
..	The parent directory of the current directory
d:\path	A specific directory
d:\path +	A specific directory including all subdirectories
path1, path2	Two or more directories, separated by commas
%name%	All the directories included in the DOS environment variable specified by *name*. This is of special interest to programmers using SuperFind

You can also use the Drive command button to open a dialog box containing icons for all the drives on your system, as well as checkboxes for the following groups: all floppy disks, all hard disks, and all network drives. Make your selections, then click on OK to return to the Add Location Set dialog box.

There is a command button called Directory that you can use to open the Select Directory to Search dialog box. Here you can select a drive and directory to add to the location set. Check the Include Subdirectories box if you want to include the subdirectories of the selected directory. Click on OK to return to the Add Location Set dialog box.

Now you should have a name for the location set, as well as path and directory entries, each separated by commas in the Definition text box. Click on OK to add this new location set to the list in SuperFind.

Now you can use your own file and location sets next time you want to use SuperFind to search for that elusive file.

CREATING BATCH FILES FROM A FILE LIST

The Batch menu entry creates a DOS batch file that runs on each of the files that SuperFind locates. (See Chapter 14 for more information on batch files.) Select Batch to see the dialog box shown in Figure 13.6.

> You can also use Batch to save a list of files that SuperFind has located to another file for later printing.

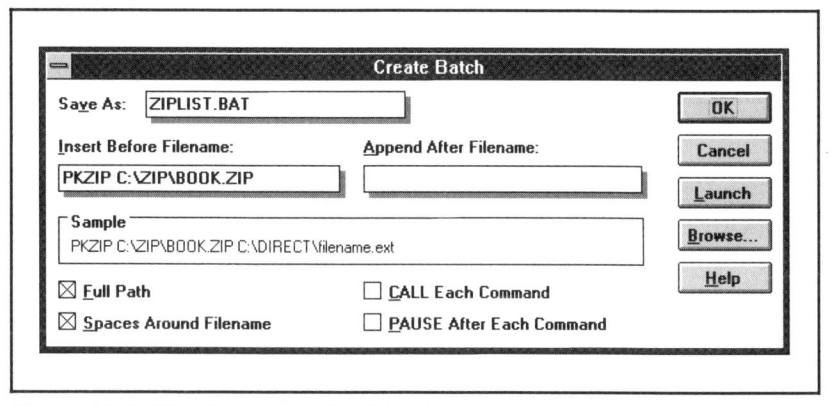

Figure 13.6: The Create Batch dialog box lets you create a DOS batch file using the results of a SuperFind search

The batch file contains one line for each file in the SuperFind drive window, and you can use this dialog box to add commands before and after each file name. First enter the file name you want to use with the batch file; then enter any commands you want to use before or after all the file names that SuperFind locates. If you just want to create a simple ASCII list of the files that SuperFind locates, leave both of these text boxes blank. Several of the steps involved in converting the list of files into a useful batch file can be automated by clicking the following:

Full Path. Check this box if you want to use the full DOS path before each file name. Leave this box unchecked if you want to use just the file name and extension without the path information.

Spaces Around Filename. Check this box to add a space before and after each file name. This can make the batch file easier to read. However, there may be times when you want a character like a quote mark to be placed right against the file name. If this is the case, leave this box unchecked.

CALL Each Command. In DOS 3.3 and later, there is a batch command called Call that you can use to invoke other batch files from inside a batch file. If you want to insert Call at the beginning of every line in your batch file, check this box.

PAUSE After Each Command. When you check this box, the DOS Pause command is inserted between every line in your batch file. This means that you can stop the batch file running if you press Ctrl-C when you see the **Press any key to continue...** prompt.

To create and test your batch file, click on the Launch command button. This runs the batch file in a DOS window. If there are errors in the batch file, it will be aborted. When you are happy that you have everything in place, click on OK to save the batch file and return to the SuperFind dialog box. This does not have to be the end of the road for your batch file. You can use Edit from the Desktop File menu to open the default editor on your batch file to continue development. Alternatively, you can go directly to Windows Notepad and open the batch file there.

WORKING WITH THE TWO CALCULATORS

How often do you reach for your pocket calculator to make a quick (or complex) calculation for a report that you are writing on your word processor, when the computer should be able to do it for you? With the Norton Desktop, those days are gone.

> Both Desktop Calculators use Windows Helvetica font, so don't delete this font from your WIN.INI file. Otherwise you may see unexpected vertical stripes on your screen.

The Norton Desktop includes two different calculators: the 10-Key Tape Calculator for your financial calculations and the Scientific Calculator for more complex scientific or engineering calculations. Both are present as icons in the Desktop group window. If you use the calculators very often, however, you might find them easier to use if you drag them to your Desktop and leave them there.

THE 10-KEY TAPE CALCULATOR

> Clicking on the minimize button iconizes the calculator so that it is always available for calculations.

To start the 10-Key Tape Calculator, double-click on the Tape Calculator icon in the Norton Desktop group window or select Calculator from the Tools menu. In the latter case, the last calculator you used opens on the Desktop; if necessary, open the Calculator menu to change to the Tape Calculator. When you start the Tape Calculator, you will see the image shown in Figure 13.7 on your screen.

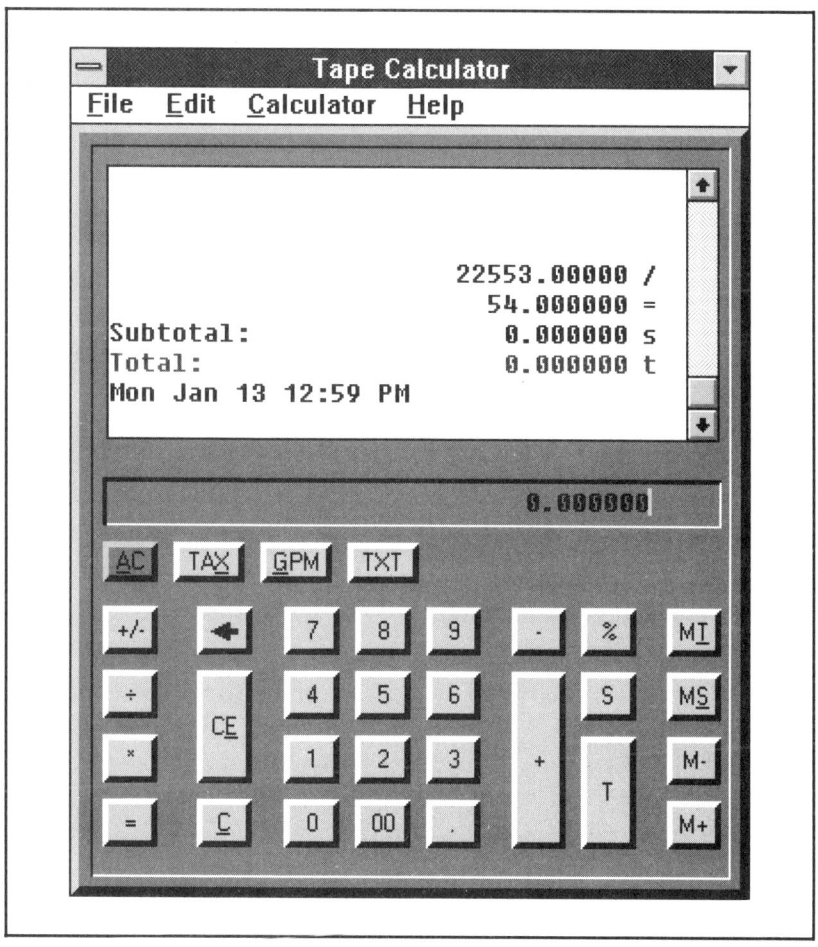

Figure 13.7: The 10-Key Tape Calculator, for basic calculations

> Before you use the numbers on your ten-key pad, make sure the Num Lock key is toggled on.

There are four entries on the menu bar: File, Edit, Calculator, and Help. Using the 10-Key Tape Calculator is like using an adding machine with a paper tape printout. If you like to use the mouse, just click on the numbers and operators you want to use. To enter numbers from the keyboard, use the keys on the ten-key pad or the keys along the top of your keyboard. Press the keyboard keys to represent addition (+), subtraction (−), multiplication (*), and division (/). As you make your calculations, the numbers, the operations, and the results are shown on the tape. The current operation is shown in the single-line display below the tape display.

> Selecting Index from the Help menu shows a replica of the calculator keyboard on the screen. Click on any key here to see a short description of its function.

This calculator works just like the large noisy ten-key calculators you are used to using for your financial calculations, except that this calculator is silent and very convenient. For example, to multiply 20 by 21, enter:

20*21 =

To add numbers together, enter each number followed by the plus sign. When you are ready to see a total, click on T or press the Enter key from the keyboard. For example, to add 50 to 75, display the answer as a subtotal, then subtract 20 and display the answer as a total, enter **50 + 75 +** , press Shift-Enter or click on the S key, enter **20 −** , and press Enter or click on the T key. To divide 256 by 64, type **256/64 =** . (Note that Enter is not the same as = .)

You probably think of percentages in terms of whole numbers rather than decimal fractions—"6 percent" rather than "0.06," for instance. You can use whole number percentages with this calculator if you follow them with the % symbol. For example, to calculate 15 percent of a $75 restaurant bill, enter **75*15%**. The result is **11.25** or a tip of $11.25.

The calculator has several other important functions, including built-in tax and gross profit margin calculators. Table 13.1 summarizes all the functions available in the Desktop 10-Key Tape Calculator.

Numeric entries can be up to ten digits long, the decimal point and any sign character counting as one digit each. Anything you enter after the tenth digit is ignored. If you don't explicitly enter a decimal point, the calculator places it after the rightmost digit in any number.

Using the Two Displays

> The TXT button stays pressed when the calculator is in memo mode to remind you that memo mode is still active.

The single display line, just above the calculator keys, is used for entering data and showing running totals. It is made up of two separate parts, the number field on the right side and the memo field on the left. The number field is where you enter data to be used in calculations—and, if you want to, you can annotate those entries using the TXT key on the calculator with the memo field. This can be very useful if you want to annotate a set of calculations with notes to help you make sense of them later on. You can enter up to 30 alphanumeric characters into the memo field, except for

Table 13.1: The 10-Key Tape Calculator Functions

FUNCTION	KEYBOARD	MOUSE
Add	+	+
Subtract	–	–
Multiply	*	*
Divide	/	/
Equals	=	=
Subtotal	Shift-Enter	S
Total	Enter	T
All Clear	Ctrl-A	AC
Clear Transaction	Ctrl-C	C
Clear Entry	Ctrl-E	CE
Change Sign	\	+/–
Calculate percentage	%	%
Tax	Ctrl-X	TAX
Gross Profit Margin	Ctrl-G	GPM
Text Mode	Ctrl-"	TXT
Memory Total/Clear	Ctrl-T	MT
Memory Subtotal	Ctrl-S	MS
Subtract from Memory Register	Ctrl- –	M –
Add to Memory Register	Ctrl- +	M +

" % * + – / = and the period. Click on the TXT key to place the calculator into memo mode, enter your annotation, and click on TXT again to toggle to numeric mode.

The multi-line display, equivalent to the tape on old adding machines, shows the last nine lines of calculations. When you click on an operator or function key following a number in the single-line display, the item becomes the newest entry at the bottom of the multi-line display. The operator for each number is shown to the right of the number (using standard abbreviations) and any memo text you entered is shown to the left. When you have more than nine entries in this display, you can use the scroll bars to look at entries that have rolled off the top of your "tape." The total number of entries in this part of the display is restricted only by the amount of free memory available on your system. The Tape Calculator posts a warning message when you near your limit. If you continue, it treats the multi-line display as a first-in-first-out list by abandoning early entries to make room for more recent entries. Your calculations and your running totals are not affected, however.

Setting Up the Tape Calculator

Choose Setup from the calculator's File menu to open the dialog box shown in Figure 13.8. You can use this dialog box to set certain options in the 10-Key Tape Calculator, as follows:

> Regardless of the Notation setting you use, the Tape Calculator always uses high-precision arithmetic internally.

Notation. Click an option button inside this group box to set the calculator's display mode. You can display numbers in floating format to show results with the maximum amount of precision, or you can choose any number of decimal places from none to four. Leave this setting at two decimals for normal financial calculations.

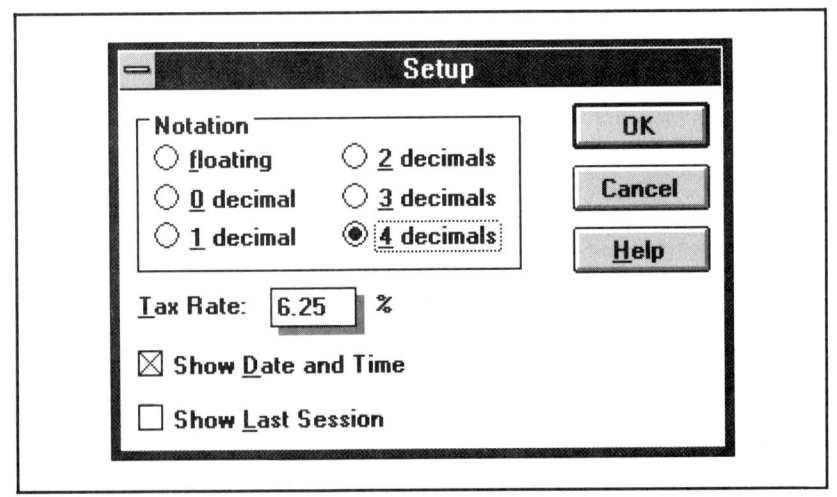

Figure 13.8: Use the Setup dialog box to choose various calculator options

Tax Rate. Specify the percentage rate you want to use in calculations involving the Tax function.

Show Date and Time. Check this box if you want to display the current computer date and time with each new calculation. This can be a time saver later, when you are trying to decide which of two tapes is newer.

Show Last Session. Check this box if you want the calculator to save the tape for use in the next session. This way you can pick up from where you left off without delay.

Choose OK when you are happy with your settings so that they can be retained for your next session with the calculator.

Using and Reusing the Tape

One of the main problems in making running total calculations is entering an incorrect number and not realizing you have done so for several steps. With a conventional calculator, you must reenter all those steps to rerun the calculations. Not so with the Tape Calculator. Here you can edit the incorrect number and then recalculate all subsequent calculations. All editing is done in the single-line display; entries from the multi-line display are recalled into the single-line display first, where numbers, operators, or memo text are edited. To edit a number from the multi-line display:

1. Highlight the entry you want to edit by double-clicking it or by moving the highlight with the arrow keys on the keyboard. This recalls the number to the single-line display.

2. Edit the number or enter a new number in the single-line display.

3. Click on the operator associated with the new number to recalculate everything with this new number.

If you decide not to change the number, just press the ↓ key or move the scroll box down to move the highlight to the bottom of the multi-line display. The display will not change.

If you are performing a particularly important set of calculations, you can save the tape as a file on disk, so that you can refer to the calculations in the future. To save the current tape as a file, choose Save Tape from the calculator's File menu; subsequent changes can be saved with Save Tape or Save Tape As.

If you want to open a tape already saved on disk, just select Open Tape in the calculator's File menu and choose the tape you want to open from the Browse dialog box. Often you will need a printed copy of the tape. You can use Print Tape in the File menu for this task.

Using the Memory Functions

The 10-Key Tape Calculator has one memory register you can use to collect totals from a series of calculations when you only care about the combined total. If you use the memory register, an M appears to the right of the numeric field in the single-line display. There are four memory functions:

> Use MT before starting to use the memory register, just to make sure it is zero when you start.

M +	Adds a number to the total in memory
M −	Subtracts a number from the memory register
MS	Displays a subtotal of the memory register
MT	Displays a total of the memory register, then clears the memory register when used again

Cutting and Pasting to the Clipboard

You can transfer information from the 10-Key Tape Calculator to other Windows applications quickly and easily using the Windows Clipboard:

1. Perform the calculation and leave the result in the single-line display.

2. Select the Copy command from the calculator's Edit menu (or press Ctrl-Insert) to copy the result into the Windows Clipboard.

3. Switch to the other application program using Ctrl-Escape or Alt-Tab.

4. Select the Paste command from the Edit menu of your application program to paste the result into your document.

You can also copy calculations from the Windows Clipboard into the Calculator using the Paste command in the calculator's Edit menu.

THE SCIENTIFIC CALCULATOR

The Scientific Calculator can perform the normal arithmetic operations you might expect from an advanced calculator, but it can also handle transcendental functions, convert decimal numbers to hexadecimal or octal, convert degrees to radians and vice versa, and transform polar coordinates to rectangular coordinates and vice versa. The Scientific Calculator is shown in Figure 13.9.

This calculator does not use infix notation like the 10-Key Tape Calculator, but uses reverse Polish notation (often abbreviated RPN). This logic, used in advanced calculators from Hewlett-Packard and other manufacturers, requires the operator to be entered *after* the variables. Some examples will make this clear. In a two-number calculation, enter the numbers for the calculation first, followed by the operator last. To add 50 to 75, for instance, type **50**, press Enter, type **75**, then press the + key. You will see the answer **125** in the calculator's display.

When making a one-number calculation, like finding the square root of a number, enter the number followed by the square-root operator. To find the square root of 81, for instance, type **81** and press Enter. Then click on the square-root key, or press Q on the keyboard (because Q is the underlined letter on the square-root key) to see the result **9** in the display.

Using Primary and Secondary Functions

Most of the keys on this calculator have two functions, a primary function printed on the key and a secondary function printed above it. To access these alternative functions, you must first press the Alt key on the calculator or the keyboard. You will see the annotation **ALT** above the calculator display when you are in this mode.

It's time for another example. Let's use the mouse first. We will divide 10 by 3.33, then derive the fractional portion of this result using

Selecting Index from the Help menu shows a replica of the calculator keyboard. Click on any key here to see a short description of its function.

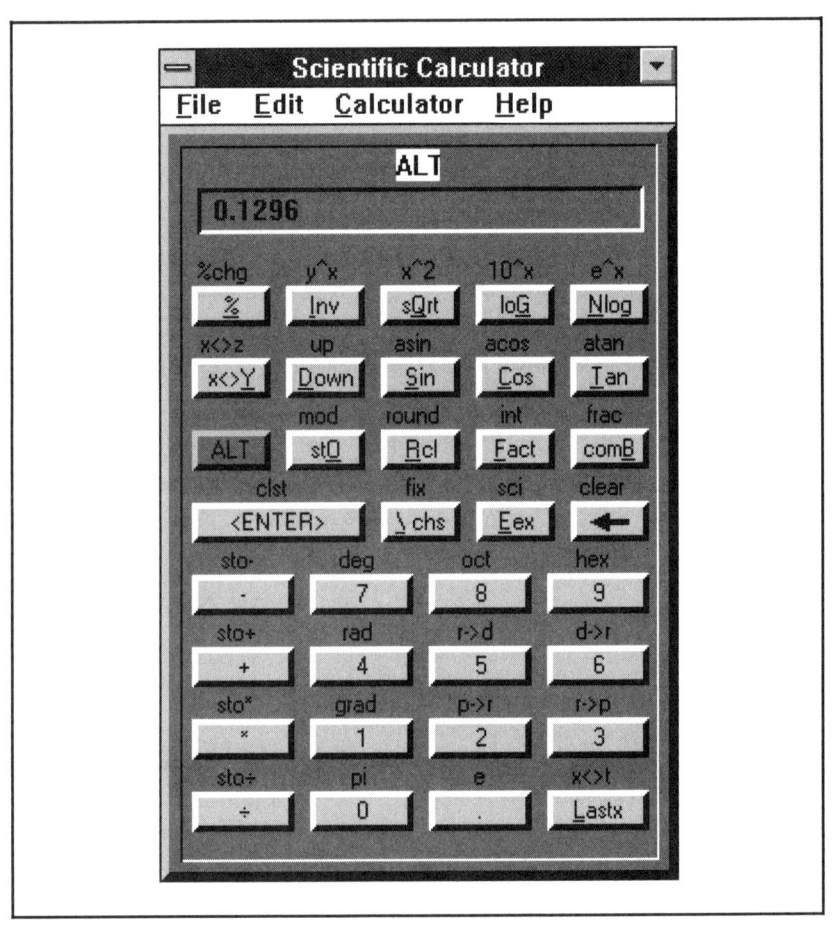

Figure 13.9: The Scientific Calculator, for complex calculations

Frac. Click on 1, 0, Enter, 3, ., 3, 3, and ÷ (in that order). You will see the result **3.0030** in the display. To derive the fractional portion of this number, click on Alt and then click on the key labeled Comb with Frac above it, and you will see the result **0.0030** in the display. To do the same thing using the keyboard is straightforward. Type **10**, press the Enter key, type **3.33**, and press /. You will see the same answer in the display. Now press the Alt key, followed by B, because *B* is the underlined letter on the Comb/Frac key. The answer, once again, is **0.0030**.

Table 13.2 lists all the math and transcendental functions found on the Scientific Calculator.

Table 13.2: Mathematical Functions Included in the Scientific Calculator

Key	Function
%	Computes x percent of the value in the Y register
%Chg	Computes the percentage difference between the contents of the Y register and the contents of the X register
10^x	Computes the common antilogarithm: raises 10 to the power of the number in the display
Acos	Calculates the arccosine of an angle
Asin	Calculates the arcsine of an angle
Atan	Calculates the arctangent of an angle
Chs	Reverses the sign of the displayed number
Comb	Computes the number of combinations of y taken x at a time, without repetition; must be a positive integer
Cos	Calculates the cosine of an angle
e	Enters Euler's constant, the base number of the natural logarithm system, to five places: 2.71828
Eex	Allows entry of numbers in exponential notation, by indicating that the next number to be entered should be treated as the base-10 exponent
e^x	Computes the natural antilogarithm. Raises e to the power of the number in the display
Fact	Computes the factorial of a positive integer
Frac	Displays the fractional part of a number
Int	Displays the integer portion of a number
Inv	Computes the reciprocal or multiplicative inverse of a number
Log	Computes the common logarithm (base 10) of a positive number
Mod	Computes the integer division, x divided by y, and displays the remainder

Table 13.2: Mathematical Functions Included in the Scientific Calculator (continued)

Key	Function
Nln	Computes the natural logarithm of a number, the logarithm to the base *e*
Pi	Enters the constant π to 15 places: 3.1415926543589793
Round	Rounds the displayed number up or down to the nearest integer
Sin	Calculates the sine of an angle
Sqrt	Computes the square root of the number in the X register
Tan	Calculates the tangent of an angle
x^2	Squares the number in the X register
y^x	Raises the number in the Y register to the power of the number in the display

Performing Display and Unit Conversions

The Scientific Calculator can display results in fixed and scientific (exponential) notation:

- In *fixed* format, numbers in the display are always shown with the same number of digits after the decimal point. You can set the number of decimal places from zero to nine; the default is four. Calculations are always performed to the highest internal accuracy that the calculator can achieve.

- In *scientific* notation, you can display a very large or very small number easily with a minimum of digits. Numbers are shown followed by an *E* and a positive or negative integer less than or equal to 17, where this integer indicates a power of ten. For example, 45,678 is displayed as **4.5678 E+004**.

Table 13.3 lists all the display and unit conversion functions found in the Scientific Calculator.

Table 13.3: Display and Conversion Functions Available in the Scientific Calculator

Key	Function
Fix n	Fixes the number of decimals for the display, where n is a number between 0 and 9
Sci n	Sets the display to scientific notation and specifies the number of decimals, where n is a number between 0 and 9
Deg	Sets the display mode to decimal degrees. This is the default mode for all trigonometric functions
Grad	Sets the display mode to gradients. A **GRAD** indicator appears above the calculator display
Rad	Sets the display mode to radians. A **RAD** indicator appears over the calculator display
r→d	Converts the displayed value from radians to decimal degrees
d→r	Converts the displayed value from decimal degrees to radians
p→r	Converts the polar coordinates in the X and Y registers (magnitude r, angle ϕ) to rectangular coordinates (x,y)
r→p	Converts the rectangular coordinates in the X and Y registers (x,y) to polar coordinates (magnitude r, angle ϕ)
Hex	Converts the integer portion of a positive number in the display into hexadecimal format (base 16)
Oct	Converts the integer portion of a positive number in the display into octal format (base 8)

Using Storage Registers

There are two kinds of storage registers you can use on the Scientific Calculator. The calculator automatically maintains four registers called the *automatic memory stack*. This stack holds numbers being used in your current calculation, as well as intermediate answers you can use later in your calculations. These four registers are known as X, Y, Z, and T. The calculator display always shows the contents of the X register. As you work with the calculator and perform a calculation, the contents of the X register is moved to the Y register, and anything in the Y register is pushed up to the Z register. Entries pushed out of the T register are lost. There are several keys on the Scientific Calculator that you can use to look at or manage these stack registers:

X<>Z	Exchanges the contents of the X and Z registers
X<>Y	Exchanges the contents of the X and Y registers
X<>T	Exchanges the contents of the X and T registers
Enter	Terminates data entry and copies the contents of the X register into the Y register
Up	Rolls the register stack up, so that the contents of the X register are moved to the Y register, Y to Z, Z to T, and the contents of the T register are moved into X, the display register (the ↑ key on the keyboard also works)
Down	Rolls the register stack down, moving X to T, T to Z, Z to Y, and Y to X; the ↓ key achieves the same function
LastX	Contains the number that was in the X register before you performed the last calculation; you can recall this number so that you don't have to reenter the number for the next calculation, or if you have made a mistake in the current calculation
Clst	Clears all four registers in the automatic memory stack
Clear	Clears any error message from the display and clears the contents of the X register

> The contents of these storage register will be lost if you leave Windows.

In addition to these stack registers, the Scientific Calculator provides 100 general-purpose data storage registers you can use for your own purposes. Each register has its own unique address, from 0 to 99, for quick access. A number stored in one of these data storage registers will stay there until you replace the number with another number or clear it by storing 0 in the register. There are several keys on the Scientific Calculator that you can use to look at or manage these storage registers:

Sto	Stores the displayed value in a storage register
Rcl	Recalls and displays the contents of a storage register
Sto +	Adds the displayed value to a specified storage register
Sto −	Subtracts the displayed value from a specified storage register
Sto *	Multiplies the displayed value by the contents of a specified storage register, storing the result back into the same register
Sto ÷	Divides the displayed value by the contents of a specified storage register, storing the result back to the same register

Cutting and Pasting with the Clipboard

You can use the Windows Clipboard as a transfer mechanism with the Scientific Calculator just as you can with the 10-Key Tape Calculator. Use the Copy or Paste commands in the calculator's Edit menu to move information to or from the Clipboard.

Getting Error Messages

The Scientific Calculator can show you several different error messages, depending on the conditions. There are the usual messages designed for operations like dividing by zero, attempting the square root of a negative number, or using a noninteger argument when the calculator is expecting one. If you see one of these error messages, press the backspace key from the keyboard, or click on the Backspace key on the calculator to clear the message. Then continue with your calculations.

USING THE SCREEN SAVER

When an image is displayed on your computer screen for a long period of time, there is a danger that it may be "burned in" on the

> Only use one screen saver program at a time. If you have another such program, make sure it is turned off before you use Sleeper.

screen and become permanently visible as a ghost image. You can often see this kind of ghost image on screens used by automatic teller machines outside banks. Windows and other applications programs always leave a title bar and a menu bar visible at the top of most of their windows, so there is the chance that these windows elements could become burned in on the screen.

Sleeper is meant to prevent burn-in. It blanks your screen when you are not using your computer and displays a constantly moving graphic image rather than a static display.

There is also a more serious side to Sleeper. You can use it to hide confidential information that is appearing on your screen, in case someone not privy to this information unexpectedly comes into your office, or in case you have to move away from your computer for a few moments and don't want anybody to look over and see your screen. Using Sleeper is much faster than closing your application program and then reopening the same file and finding your place when your visitor has left. You can also use a password with Sleeper, so that you are the only person who can turn Sleeper off before returning to your application program.

CHOOSING THE RIGHT SLEEPER IMAGE

When you first use Sleeper, the default image is called Starless Night. This is a completely blank screen that makes your monitor look as though it is turned off. If you want a more animated image, choose one from the following list:

> Not all of these screen savers are suitable for hiding confidential information from prying eyes, but they are all lighthearted and entertaining.

Bouncing Lines Example. This image shows one or two bouncing horizontal lines. If you choose to display two lines, they are out of phase, so that one line is at the top of the screen when the other line is at the bottom.

Staring Eyes. Pairs of eyes wander around the screen. You can choose the number of pairs of eyes and control the speed that they move.

Fading Away. This screen saver slowly eats away at your screen image. If you choose Vertical scanning, the screen starts disappearing from the left side; if you choose Horizontal, it disappears from the top down; and if you choose

Random Pixel Fading, it slowly fades away. If you check the Restore After Blanking checkbox, this screen saver can rebuild your original screen image again, using the same method it used to remove it in the first place. There is also a scroll bar so you can also control the speed.

Message. You can specify the text of a message you want to see moving around the screen, as well as its color, font, point size, and text attributes. You can also choose to have your message displayed on a hot-air balloon, towed behind an airplane, and so on.

Micro Fish. This screen saver converts your computer into an aquarium by displaying fish moving across the screen. Choose the number of fish you want to see and the speed that they move.

Rotation. Three-dimensional shapes move across the screen. Choose from Larger Shapes or Compound Shapes, and specify the number of shapes and their speed.

Triquetrous Lights. Triangular shaped fireworks move across your screen. You can control their speed and specify Jumbo Fragments or Shaded Fragments.

Clock. The current time moves around your screen. Choose between analog or digital and specify the speed, color, and size of the display.

Space Voyage. This screen saver shows you the view from a spaceship. You can change the speed from impulse power to Warp Factor 9.

Screen Shuffle. This screen saver moves pieces of your original display around, block by block. Choose the block size and the speed.

Spotlight. This screen saver "illuminates" your original display with a bouncing spotlight. You can specify the number of lights, the size of the image, and the speed.

Tornadoes. Animated twisters float about the screen. You can specify the number of tornadoes and the speed at which they twist.

To start Sleeper, double-click on its Desktop icon or choose Sleeper from the Tools menu. The window shown in Figure 13.10 opens so that you can choose the screen saver you want to use. On the left side of this window is a list box containing all the different screen savers, listed by name. In the center of the window is the control box for the selected screen saver. The controls shown in this part of the window will change as you select different screen savers. To choose a screen saver, just highlight your choice in the list box and watch the central portion of the window change to reflect the controls available for that screen saver. Click the spin buttons to change the various settings and use the scroll bar to change the speed, if one is available. To demonstrate a screen saver, click on the Sample command button. Your whole screen, except for this central area, will display the screen saver image. Click on the Restore command button when you are ready to return to the Sleeper window.

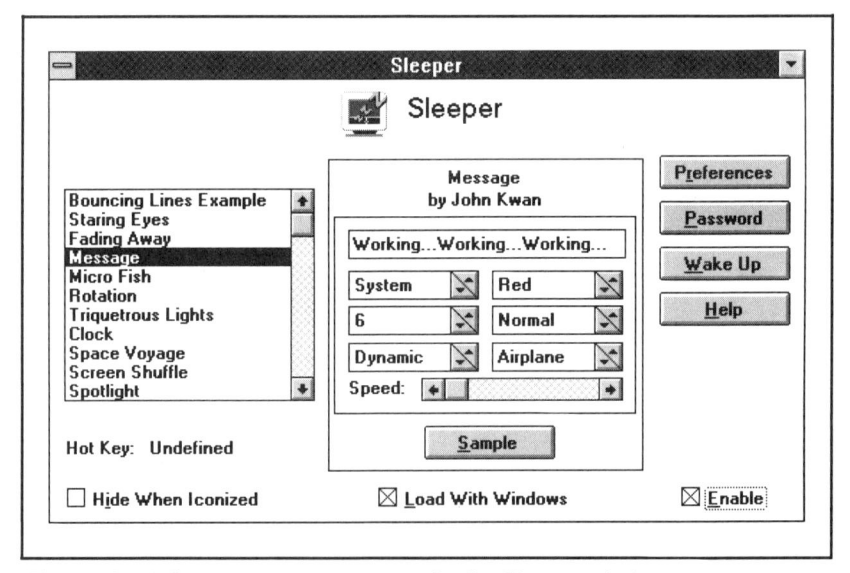

Figure 13.10: Set up your screen saver in the Sleeper window

You can also control how Sleeper is launched on your system. Check the Load with Windows checkbox if you want Sleeper to start every time you run Windows on your system. This choice actually adds an entry to the Windows initialization file, WIN.INI, to tell Windows to load Sleeper when it starts. To hide the Sleeper icon when the window is minimized, check the Hide When Iconized box. Check Enable to activate Sleeper, then click the minimize button in the upper-right corner of the window. After the specified period of time has elapsed or the mouse has been moved to a sleep corner (described next), you will see the screen saver you selected appear on your screen.

SETTING PREFERENCES

Click on the Preferences command button to see the dialog box shown in Figure 13.11. Here you can enter the time you want Sleeper to wait after the last keystroke or mouse movement before clearing your

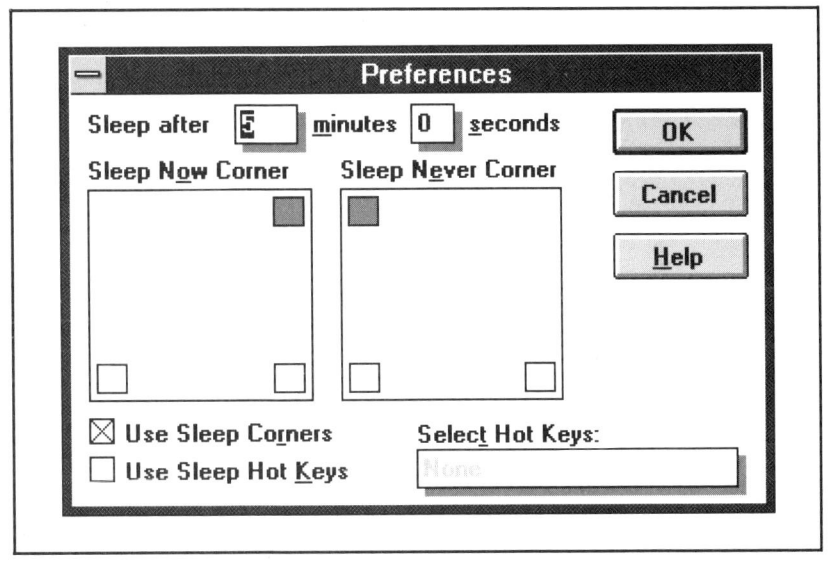

Figure 13.11: Select the way that Sleeper is triggered in the Preferences dialog box

screen and displaying the screen saver—any time period from 10 seconds to 999 minutes and 59 seconds. Usually a minute or two is sufficient, unless you are working with confidential information, in which case 30 seconds might be more appropriate.

The Sleep Now Corner lets you select one corner of your screen so that when you move the mouse into this corner, Sleeper will blank your screen immediately. The Sleep Never Corner turns all the other triggers off, so if you park your mouse in this corner, Sleeper will *not* invoke the screen saver. Click on an available box to make it the active corner. To use either of these options, the Use Sleep Corners box must be checked.

You can also use a hotkey to trigger Sleeper if you prefer; just check the Use Sleep Hot Keys box and press the key combination you want to use into the Select Hot Keys text box.

USING A PASSWORD

You can prevent unauthorized people from looking at the screen that Sleeper is hiding by using a password. Select the Password command button from the Sleeper window to see the dialog box shown in Figure 13.12. If you don't want to use a password, select the No Password option. You can use your network password if you have one, or you can enter a custom password of your own. If you *do* specify a password, you must enter the password before you can regain use of your screen.

> The Sleeper password does not protect your files and directories, it just prevents people from looking at the current document displayed on your screen.

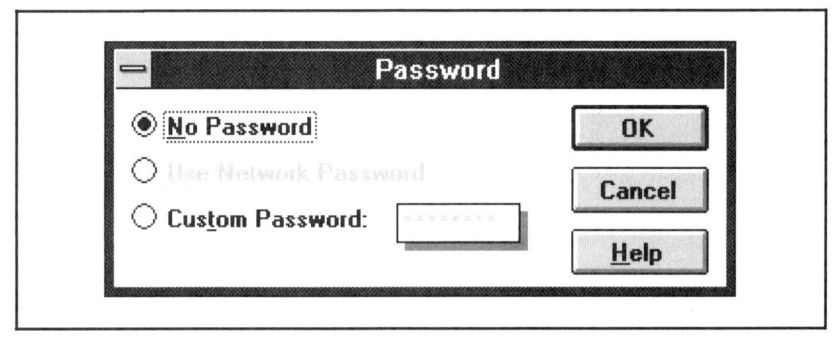

Figure 13.12: Enter your password using the Password dialog box

If you don't work on sensitive or confidential information, I do not recommend using a password with Sleeper. If you forget the password, the only way to turn Sleeper off and get back to work will be to reboot your computer—and this means that you will lose all your unsaved work in any currently open documents.

SELECTING WAKE UP SETTINGS

There are three ways to wake up your computer once Sleeper has taken over. Click on Wake Up in the Sleeper window and you will see the Wake Up Settings dialog box shown in Figure 13.13. Click on Wake on Key Strokes to make Sleeper relinquish your screen to you when you press a key on the keyboard, Wake on Mouse Clicks when you click your mouse, and Wake on Mouse Movement when you move your mouse. You may use any combination of these settings, but you must use at least one of them. If you turn them all off, you will see an alert message telling you that you cannot set all the wake up settings to off. Since you'll want to turn Sleeper off in some way, this makes sense. Click on OK to confirm you choice.

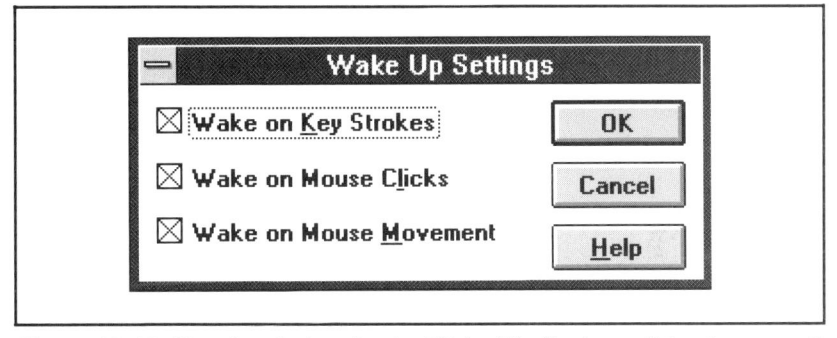

Figure 13.13: Use the choices in the Wake Up Settings dialog box to tell Sleeper how to wake up again

USING KEYFINDER

KeyFinder is a Desktop tool you can use to display all the characters available in a specific font on the screen at the same time. If you have ever wondered how to generate a foreign language symbol like the English £ symbol to represent pounds sterling or the German ß symbol to represent *ss,* KeyFinder will show you which keystrokes generate these symbols. If you are a programmer, you can use KeyFinder to show you the decimal or hexadecimal ASCII equivalents of a character.

Windows supports two very different kinds of fonts, GDI (Graphics Device Interface) based fonts and device-based fonts. GDI-based fonts are very common and are contained in .FON files in your Windows directory. Device-based fonts are internal fonts usually reserved for printers, although they are becoming more common, especially with the popularity of products like Adobe System's Type Manager, Bitstream's FaceLift for Microsoft Windows, and other third-party font managers. Because most device-based fonts are internal to their specific device, you won't see them listed in KeyFinder's Available Fonts list.

GDI-based fonts can be of two types: *raster* (or bit-mapped) fonts, and *vector* (or stroke) fonts. Raster fonts are stored as bit maps, and it is these bit maps that give raster fonts that jagged look when they are enlarged on the screen. The default Windows font, System, is a GDI-based raster font. Vector fonts, on the other hand, are stored as a series of line fragments, which allows them to be scaled to almost any size without noticeable deterioration. The Roman and Modern fonts are both vector fonts.

KeyFinder can display any Windows font, as well as fonts from other third-party sources. If you or an application program add or remove fonts when Keyfinder is running, KeyFinder will automatically rebuild the font list.

FINDING AND USING SPECIAL CHARACTERS

Select KeyFinder from the Desktop Tools menu or double-click on the KeyFinder icon in the Desktop group window and you will see the window shown in Figure 13.14.

A 16-by-16–character matrix is shown on the left side of the window. This matrix displays all the characters available in a particular font. Blank cells indicate nondisplayable characters like the first few ASCII characters (carriage return, line feed, and so on). Cells containing a vertical bar do not have a character assigned in that particular font, and so no character is displayed. This depends on the font, because not all fonts contain a character for each of the possible 256 locations.

To find the keystrokes that generate a specific character:

1. Select the font you want to use by clicking on the font name in the scrollable list.

It is not possible to enter ASCII character codes directly into this display to generate a character; selecting a cell or typing a key is the only way to interact with KeyFinder.

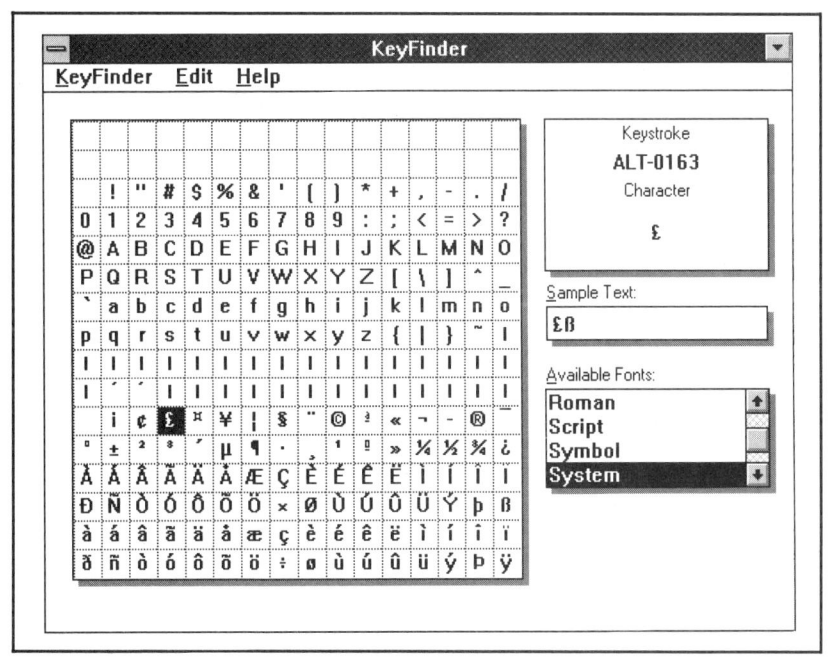

Figure 13.14: The KeyFinder window shows all the characters available in a specific font

2. Find the character you are curious about in the 16-by-16 matrix and click on it with the mouse. The keystrokes that generate the character in this font are shown in the box at the top right.

Below this box is a list of all the fonts available in Windows. Use the scroll bars to move through this list. As you select other fonts, the characters in the 16-by-16–cell matrix will change to reflect the new font. Select the Roman font to see the changes in the matrix.

To check that a particular keystroke sequence generates the character you want, just type the keystrokes from the keyboard. The highlight will move to the new location in the matrix, no matter where the cursor was originally located.

Keys that must be used in combination to generate a character are shown hyphenated in the Keystroke box. For example, to access *e,* you just type **e** from the keyboard; to access *E* you have to hold down the Shift key as you type **e**. In Windows, to access special codes greater than

127 in the ASCII table, you must use the Alt key in conjunction with the numeric keypad on your keyboard. The keypad must be in Num Lock mode and you must always use a leading zero in the number. For example, if you are using the default System font to generate the English £ character, hold down the Alt key as you type **0163** from the numeric keypad, then release the Alt key. For the German ß character, use the Alt key as you type **0223**, then release the Alt key.

USING THE KEYFINDER MENU

There are several selections in the KeyFinder menu to help you work with KeyFinder, as follows:

Swap Orientation. The cells in the KeyFinder display are usually oriented from top left to bottom right in horizontal rows of increasing ASCII character code numbers. Use Swap Orientation to change these rows to vertical columns.

Real Font Size. The character shown in the box at the top right of the KeyFinder window is enlarged so that you can see the character in detail. Use Real Font Size to see the character in an actual point size selected from the Font Sizes list box in the lower-right corner of the window.

Show ASCII. The low-order ASCII characters, up to ASCII 32, usually do not have a displayable character associated with them. They are usually shown in the matrix as rectangles or open cells. If you turn on Show ASCII, a two or three-letter abbreviation will be shown in the Keystroke box, instead of a Ctrl-key combination. For example, carriage return or ASCII 13 is labeled **CR** instead of Ctrl-M, and the bell or ASCII 7 is labeled **BEL** instead of Ctrl-G.

Programmer Mode. This adds hexadecimal guides to the top and left sides of the cell matrix, so that you can locate a specific ASCII character and determine its hexadecimal equivalent quickly and easily. (More on this later.)

Sample Text. This opens a box between the Keystroke/ Character box and the scrollable list of fonts. Double-click on any character in the matrix to copy it to the Sample Text box.

ENHANCING WINDOWS   283

If you wish, you can enter a string of characters into this box, rather than just one character, and copy them all to the Clipboard.

Exit. This closes KeyFinder and returns you to the Norton Desktop.

With the cell table ordered in horizontal rows, select Programmer Mode and Show ASCII from the KeyFinder menu. This makes the low-order ASCII characters visible in the Keystroke box and adds the hexadecimal guides around the edges of the matrix. If you select the System font, you will see that the KeyFinder window looks like Figure 13.15.

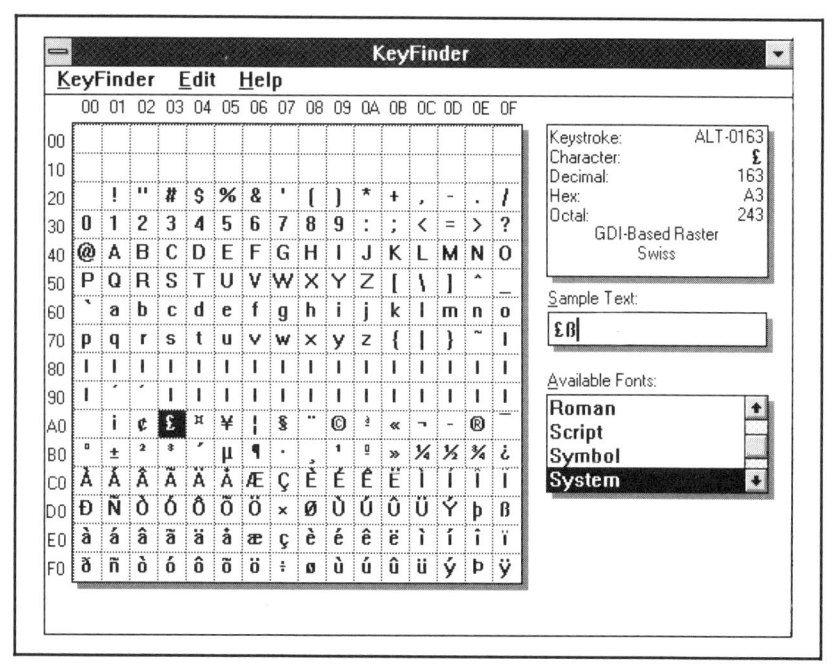

Figure 13.15: KeyFinder Programmer Mode

Click on a character in the matrix. Then note the hexadecimal guide number from the left margin and add it to the guide number from the top margin to determine the hex equivalent of the character. For example, carriage return, or CR, is 0 + D or D in hex; the number 1 is 30 + 1 or 31 in hex; and so on.

The box at the top right of the window shows information about the ASCII character, including the keystrokes that generate the character, its appearance, and the ASCII equivalent in decimal, hexadecimal, and octal. For example, in System font, £ is generated when you press Alt-0163. This character is equivalent to A3 in hex and 243 in octal.

USING THE EDIT MENU WITH THE CLIPBOARD

Once you have found a particular ASCII character in KeyFinder, you can transfer it to another application program via the Clipboard. Sample Text must be selected before you can cut text to the Clipboard. The main selections from the Edit menu used to move text onto the Clipboard are as follows:

> The Clipboard can only hold one item at a time. Any text will stay on the Clipboard until it is replaced by something else.

Cut moves text to the Clipboard. Collect the characters you want to cut to the Clipboard in the Sample Text box and then highlight the characters by dragging the mouse over them. After using Cut, the original characters in the Sample Text box will disappear as they are cut to the Clipboard. When you paste the characters into your application program, remember that you are moving the ASCII characters only, not the symbol, so the results you see will depend on the font you have chosen in the applications program.

Copy works just like the Cut command, except that the text is not removed from the Sample Text window.

Paste moves characters from the Clipboard into KeyFinder. Sample Text must be enabled to do this. To see the keystrokes that generate a character brought in via the Clipboard, click somewhere in the text box and move the cursor to the left of the character with the arrow keys. (Clicking to the left of the character will not do.) The keystrokes will be shown above. To see what the imported ASCII characters look like in another font, highlight the characters in the text box and select the font you want from the scrollable font list. The Sample Text box will show the characters in the new font.

There are several other commands in this menu that you can use to manage the characters in the Sample Text text box:

Undo undoes the last operation performed on the characters in the Sample Text box.

Delete deletes the highlighted characters from the Sample Text box.

Uppercase changes the text in the Sample Text box into uppercase characters in the same font.

Lowercase changes the text to lowercase.

Copy Cell copies a highlighted character from the 16-by-16 matrix into the Sample Text box. This has the same effect as double-clicking on a cell in the matrix.

FOURTEEN

Advanced Desktop Utilities

THIS CHAPTER DEALS WITH THE ADVANCED UTILITIES in Norton Desktop: the Batch Builder, the Icon Editor, and the Scheduler. The Batch Builder is a complex application and requires some prior knowledge of programming techniques to gain a full understanding of its capabilities. I describe how to use the Batch Builder in this chapter, and include examples of some of the things you can use it for. See the appendix, however, for a complete list of all the commands and functions available in the Batch Builder language, as well as a list of the predefined constants and a description of error handling. In contrast to this utility, the Icon Editor and the Scheduler are relatively straightforward programs. I'll start this chapter with the Icon Editor, move on to describe the Scheduler, and discuss the Batch Builder last.

EDITING DESKTOP ICONS

One of the most attractive elements of the Windows environment is its use of icons to represent programs, documents, or groups of programs. The Norton Desktop takes the concept further, allowing groups within groups—so icons become important very quickly. It is not surprising to find, therefore, that the Norton Desktop includes a powerful icon editor you can use to create new or edit and change existing icons.

In Windows, icons can be stored in several different ways in different kinds of files. There are three major types of icon files:

- Individual icons are stored in separate files with the .ICO or .ICN file-name extension.

- The icons that represent minimized applications usually shown at the bottom of the screen are contained in the appropriate .EXE file for that program. They are extracted by Windows when needed.

> The Icon Editor cannot work with Windows 2.X icons. Some Windows 3 applications like Aldus PageMaker 3.01 and Microsoft Word for Windows 1.1 actually contain Windows 2.X icons.

> You can buy packages of icons like Silly Little Icons from Dunn Enterprises or Icons 300+ from Vitesse, Inc. You can also download icons free from many bulletin boards.

- Icons can also be contained in icon library files. NDW.NIL is an example of an icon library file that is installed as part of Norton Desktop for Windows; it is one I shall look at later in this chapter.

> The Icon Editor can edit all 16-color, 32-by-32 pixel Windows 3 EGA and VGA icons; it cannot edit Windows 2 icons, icons intended for monochrome VGAs, or any CGA icons.

The Icon Editor can work with all three types of icons, as you will see in a moment. It does not matter what type they are, because the Icon Editor tools you use are always the same. If you have used any of the popular paint programs, then working with the Icon Editor should be a breeze. Even if you haven't, it won't take you long to get the hang of it.

USING THE ICON EDITOR WORKSPACE

> You cannot use the Icon Editor on a monochrome VGA or Hercules monitor.

To start the Icon Editor, double-click on the Icon Editor icon in the Norton Desktop group window or choose Icon Edit from the Tools menu. The Icon Editor main window opens, as in Figure 14.1.

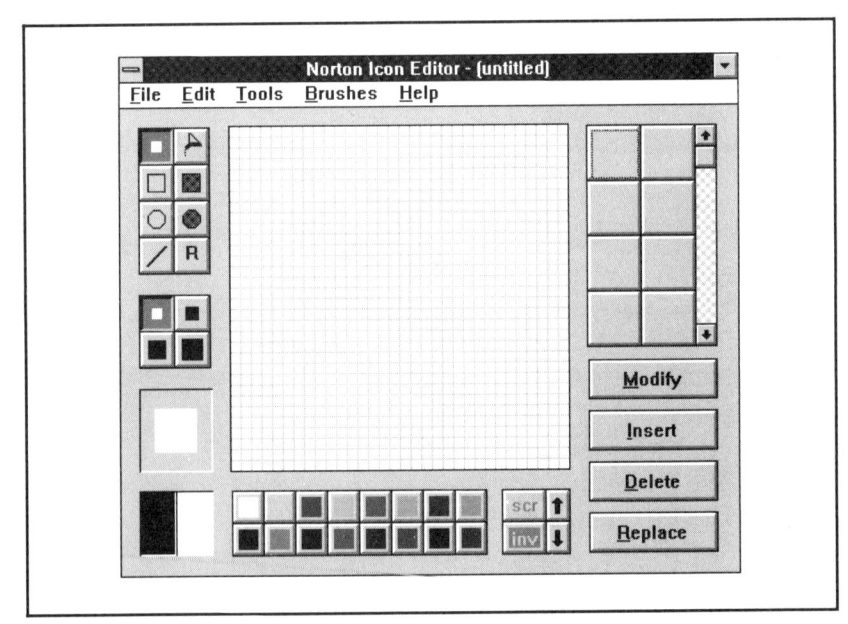

Figure 14.1: The main Icon Editor window gives you access to all the Icon Editor functions

In the center of the window is the Icon Editor workspace, a 32-by-32 grid that helps you create or edit your icons. Each icon is defined as a square element, 32 pixels (picture elements) wide by 32 pixels high. Each square on the Icon Editor grid is equivalent to one spot of color in an icon. Of course, this is the maximum space that is available for an icon; you don't have to use all of it.

Below the Icon Editor title bar, you can see that there are four menu entries on the menu bar: File, Edit, Tools, and Brushes, as well as the usual Help menu. The selections from the Tools and Brushes menus are also available as buttons around the workspace. Down the left side of the workspace, for instance, are several groups of buttons. The first, consisting of eight buttons, is the tool group. Then come the four brush-size buttons. The next area down the left is an actual-size representation of the icon. As you create or edit your icon, you can evaluate the changes here. Along the bottom of the window are the mouse-button assignment color boxes, the complete Icon Editor palette, and two buttons to manipulate the screen colors. Down the right side of the workspace is an area used for loading icons and four command buttons to manage them: Modify, Insert, Delete, and Replace.

I will look at all these individual Icon Editor window elements in turn, starting with the tool icons.

Icon Editing Tools

The editing tools are laid out to the left of the main workspace. The first set of boxes below the File and Edit menus represents the editing tools. Each of these eight small icons is equivalent to an entry in the Icon Editor Tools menu, from top left (Brush) to bottom right (Replacer), as follows:

> **Brush** changes the color of the squares on the grid. You can assign a different color to both the left and right mouse buttons. The size of the brush you use is determined by the choice you make in the Brushes menu, or using the brush-size buttons described in a moment. When you select a brush tool, the mouse cursor changes to a square the same size as the brush size.

Filler fills or floods an area of the workspace with whatever color is currently assigned. When you choose this tool, the mouse cursor changes to the shape of a funnel. Click on a pixel in the region you want to fill and all contiguous grid squares with the same original color will be changed to the new color. Any areas of the same original color that are not contiguous, but which are separated by a band of pixels of another color, will not be filled until you click on a pixel in this particular region. If you don't like the effect, either choose another color and use the filler tool a second time, or choose Undo (Alt-Backspace) from the Edit menu.

Square and Filled Square draw rectangles, either empty or filled. When you select either of these tools, the mouse cursor turns into a set of cross-hairs. Click the mouse where you want to anchor the upper-left corner of the square, then hold down the mouse button as you drag the mouse to the lower-right corner of your rectangle. When you release the mouse button, the rectangle will appear. The square tool draws only the rectangle border in the current color, but the filled square fills both the border and inside of the square with the current color. The current brush size determines the thickness of the border.

Circle and Filled Circle work just like the square and filled square tools mentioned above, except that they create a close approximation of an ellipse or oval in the workspace.

Line draws straight horizontal or vertical lines. Diagonal lines are as straight as they can be, but will show some degree of stairstepping (jaggedness) due to the scale of the workspace (they will look better in the finished icon than they do here). To draw a line, position the mouse cursor at one end and drag it to the other end. When you release the mouse button, the line will appear in the current color; its width is determined by the current brush size.

Replacer replaces pixels of one color with pixels of another color in any area of the workspace you select.

The next four buttons represent differently sized brushes, equivalent to the entries in the Brushes menu, from top left to bottom right:

1*1 is the smallest brush, equivalent to one pixel in the workspace.

2*2 fills an area two pixels by two pixels when you use it.

3*3 fills a block three pixels wide by three pixels high.

4*4 fills 16 pixels in an area of four pixels by four pixels.

You can either click on these small icons to change the brush size or use the corresponding selections from the Brushes menu.

Below these buttons is the icon viewer. This is an actual-size representation of the icon you are currently creating or editing in the workspace. This viewer gives you an idea of how your icon will look when it is finished.

Choosing and Applying Colors

The palette area across the bottom of the window contains two mouse color-assignment indicators, 16 colored buttons, two buttons that select the screen and inverse colors, and two spin buttons that cycle through the screen and inverse colors.

The two colored areas at the bottom left are for assigning a color to each of the two mouse buttons. Click on the left area, then click on a color in the palette. You will see that the left area changes to the color you clicked. Do the same for the right button, but choose a different color. Now when you choose a tool, you can have two colors selected at the same time; just click the left or right mouse button, depending on how you want to color your icon.

Now that you know how to assign colors to the mouse buttons and choose different brush sizes, let's try an example. Create the international dive symbol, a red diagonal on a white background:

1. Start with a blank workspace. If you already have doodles in your workspace, select Clear Workspace from the Edit menu and click on OK to throw away the current image in the workspace.

2. Choose the line tool, choose the widest brush size, and assign red to the left mouse button.

3. Draw a single red line from the lower-left corner to the upper-right corner of the workspace.

Now let's play with this image. Assign yellow to the right mouse button and choose the replacer tool. Now when you click the left (red) mouse button on a blank area of the workspace, nothing happens. When you click the right (yellow) mouse button in an empty area, nothing happens either. But when you click the right mouse button over a red area of the workspace, the area under the cursor turns yellow, and vice versa: any yellow areas turn red when you click on them with the left mouse button. So, when you use the replacer tool, a mouse button color can only replace the color assigned to the other mouse button.

Creating Screen and Inverse Colors

The color shown as the background color behind your icon in the icon viewer is called the *screen color.* Pixels painted in this color change when displayed in Windows or by an application as the background changes, thus giving the illusion that you can see through part of the icon to the background. The *inverse color* is a predefined color that contrasts well with the screen color and is easily seen against the Windows background color. The inverse color changes whenever you change the screen color. To assign the screen or inverse color to a mouse button, click the left or right mouse button on either the Scr or Inv button. The color-selection area changes to show the current screen or inverse color, with an *s* or *i* in the center, so you know that one of these colors is in effect—not the palette color.

When you paint with one of the palette colors, your icon stays that color. If you use either the screen color or the inverse color, your icon will change color whenever the Windows background changes. Use the spin buttons next to the Scr and Inv buttons to cycle through all possible screen and inverse colors. The only difference between these buttons is that one shows colors in the reverse order from the other.

Undoing Changes and Clearing the Workspace

There are two selections in the Edit menu, one to undo the last change to the icon and one to clear the workspace. When you select Undo or press Alt-Backspace, you can restore the workspace to the condition it was in at the last undo point, i.e. when you last clicked a button in the Icon Editor window. Undo may therefore undo several operations at once. For example, if you choose the circle tool and make several circles without changing your color selection or the brush size, then selecting Undo will remove all these circles from the workspace, not just the last one you made.

To clear the workspace completely, select Clear Workspace from the Edit menu. The Icon Editor opens an information box, telling you how to save your work. Click on Cancel and use Replace or Insert in the main window to save your work, or click on OK to clear the workspace.

WORKING WITH ICON LIBRARIES

When the Icon Editor first starts, it is always in library mode. You can use the Icon Editor to create a new icon library, open an existing icon library, and import icons into and export icons from an existing library.

Opening an Existing Icon Library

To open an existing library file:

> If you are concerned about preserving the contents of the NDW.NIL file, make a copy of it using a different name and do all your work on the copy.

1. Select Open from the File menu. If you currently have work in the workspace, a message appears warning you to save it before proceeding.

2. Use the Open dialog box, shown in Figure 14.2, to choose the NDW.NIL file, and be sure to select the Library option button at the bottom.

3. Click on OK to load the library into the Icon Editor.

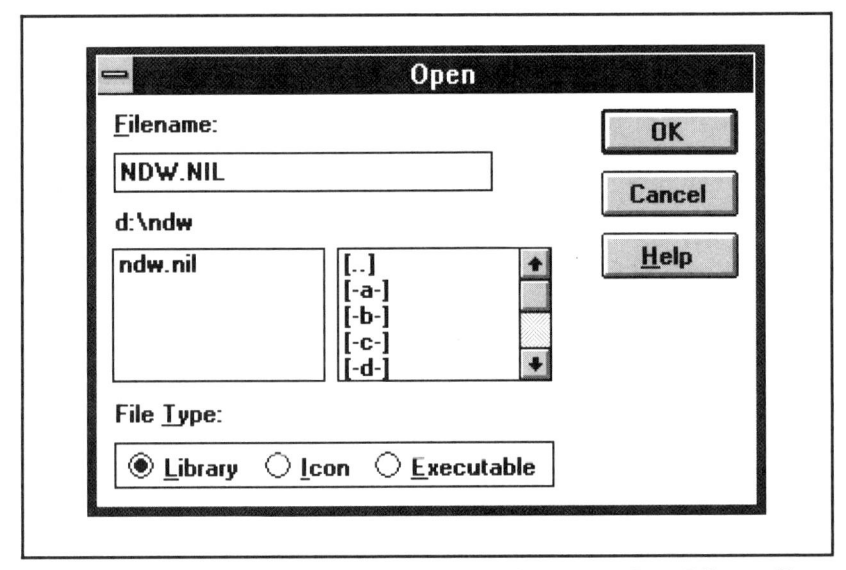

Figure 14.2: Use the Open dialog box to load the Norton Icon Library file

The main Icon Editor window reappears with the icon library loaded. The icon selector at the top right of the window now contains the first eight icons in the library; if there are more than eight icons in the library, as there are in NDW.NIL, use the scroll bars to see the rest of them. Note that the first icon is selected by default.

Now that the library is open, you can edit existing icons, replace icons you don't like with new ones, and import and export icons to and from this library. In the next few sections I'll look at all these operations.

Modifying, Inserting, and Deleting Icons

To modify an existing icon, you have to select it and load it into the workspace:

1. Use the scroll bars to find the icon you want to work with. At the very end of the NDW.NIL file, you will find several icons that bear more than a passing resemblance to Peter Norton, originator of the Norton Desktop. These icons show his characteristic folded arms, and these are interesting icons to play with.

ADVANCED DESKTOP UTILITIES   **295**

2. Click on the Modify command button to load a copy of one of these icons into the Icon Editor workspace, replacing whatever image was there before.

3. Choose the color you want to work with from the palette, choose a tool, and go to work on the icon you chose. I decided to give Peter Norton a beard (see Figure 14.3).

> The Modify, Insert, Delete, and Replace command buttons only act on the *copy* of the icon library loaded into the Icon Editor; they have no effect whatsoever on the original file on your hard disk.

4. When you have finished modifying the icon to your satisfaction or amusement, click on the Replace command button to copy the contents of the workspace back into the icon selector. Make sure the original icon is still selected in the icon selector, otherwise you may find yourself replacing the wrong icon. Notice that the original, unmodified icon shown in the icon selector has been replaced by your edited icon.

To insert a new icon into the library:

1. Click in the icon selector where you want to position the new icon.

Figure 14.3: The NDW.NIL icon library file contains many useful icons—like one of Peter Norton, whom you can make hirsute

2. Click on the Insert command button. The existing icons are shuffled down in the icon selector and repositioned to make room for this new icon.

To delete an existing icon:

1. Click on the icon you want to delete in the icon selector.

2. Click on the Delete command button. The chosen icon disappears from the icon selector immediately and the other icons are repositioned to fill the gap.

Importing and Exporting Icons

The Icon Editor allows you to import an icon into the workspace from one of several different sources: as an .ICO file, an .EXE file, or as an .NIL library file. To import an icon into the current library:

1. Select Import Icon from the File menu.

2. In the Import Icon dialog box, shown in Figure 14.4, select the appropriate option button for the correct icon file type, either Library, individual Icon, or Executable.

3. Select the appropriate drive, directory, and file name or type the path information into the Filename text box.

4. Click on OK. Any icons found in the file you selected will be displayed in the scrollable icon area. If the file does not contain any icons, an information box will open containing the message **No icons found in this file**.

5. Double-click on the icon you want to import, or select the icon and click on OK.

The chosen icon is imported into the Icon Editor workspace, replacing whatever was there originally. You can now edit or modify the icon. When you are ready to place the imported icon into your library, select the location and click on the Insert command button.

To export the current contents of the Icon Editor workspace into an .ICO file, follow these steps:

1. Place the correct icon in the workspace.

2. Choose Export Icon from the File menu.

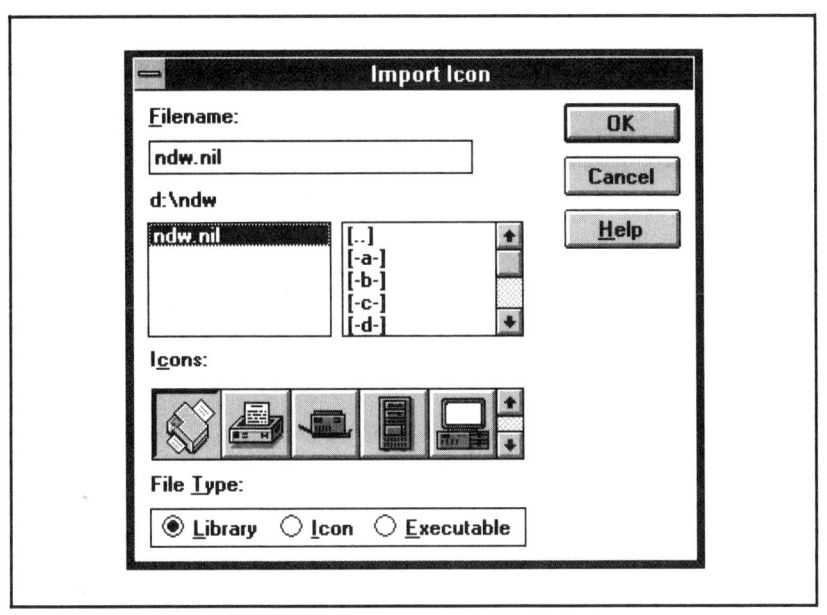

Figure 14.4: Select the correct icon file type in the Import Icon dialog box

3. Enter the file name you want to use into the Filename box, and be sure to use the .ICO file-name extension. The Icon Editor will warn you if the .ICO file already exists on your system.

You now have two copies of this icon, one in the icon library and another contained in the .ICO file you just exported.

Saving Your Changes

When you have finished making all modifications, insertions, and deletions to your icon library, it is time to save your changes:

1. Select Save or Save As from the File menu, depending on whether a library file is already open.

2. In the Save or the Save As dialog box, enter the drive, directory, and file name you want to use for the library.

3. Click on OK.

> If you use Save when no icon library file is currently open, the Icon Editor will open the Save As dialog box instead.

If you try to open a new library file while the current one still has unsaved changes, you will see a message telling you about it. If you try to exit the Icon Editor without saving changes, you will see a similar message.

Creating a New Icon Library

You can also use the Icon Editor to create a brand new icon library file from scratch:

1. Select New from the File menu.
2. Select the Icon Library option button in the New dialog box.
3. Click on OK.
4. Create or import each new icon and use the Insert command button to place it in your new library.
5. Because creating a new icon library can take some time, use the Save As selection from the File menu from time to time so that you don't lose any work due to accidents or power failures.

You can also create a new icon library by modifying or adapting an existing library, or by merging two libraries together, choosing the best icons out of each one.

WORKING WITH ICONS IN EXECUTABLE FILES

Working with icons in executable (.EXE) files is very much like working with icon libraries. There are often several icons in each file, one for an EGA monitor and another for a VGA monitor. Very often the first icon found in an .EXE file is used as the minimized icon. Using the Icon Editor, you can open existing icons, edit and replace them, and save the changes back into the original .EXE file.

To open an icon from an executable file:

1. Choose Open from the File menu.
2. Select the Executable option button.

3. Click on the file you want to work with. Any icons found in the file will be loaded into the icon selector area.

4. Load the icon you want to work on into the work area.

5. Make your changes, then use the Save command from the File menu to save your changes.

Several of the files that make up the Windows accessories have icons contained in their executable files, like

- Calendar (CALENDAR.EXE)
- Clock (CLOCK.EXE)
- Paintbrush (PBRUSH.EXE).

If there are no icons in the file, you will see the message **No icons found in the file**.

CREATING INDIVIDUAL ICON FILES

You can also create and edit icons stored as individual icons in .ICO files. As I said earlier, when the Icon Editor starts running it starts in library mode, so you must put it into icon mode. To do this:

1. Use the New command in the File menu to open the New dialog box.

2. Select the Icon option button.

3. Click on OK.

If you forgot to use New and you have spent a lot of time creating an icon that the Icon Editor won't let you save as an .ICO file, you can always *export* it as an individual .ICO file.

Using New from the File menu gets you ready to work on an .ICO file, but it hasn't created one yet. To assign the file a name, first create your icon, then use Save As from the File menu. The Icon Editor knows you are working with an .ICO file and won't let you save your work as an .EXE or icon library file. However, you can save the file as an .ICO file now, and then import it later into a library file, if you wish.

One thing you cannot do with the Icon Editor is insert a new icon into or delete an icon from an .EXE or .ICO file. There is no mechanism in the Windows world that you can use to tell an executable file that a change has taken place that it should react to, like the addition or removal of an icon. In the case of .ICO files, they are defined as containing a single icon, so adding more icons or deleting the existing icon would completely violate the accepted definition of an .ICO file.

MAKING APPOINTMENTS WITH THE SCHEDULER

> ⊙ Make sure the system time is correct on your computer before you rely on the Scheduler!

The Norton Desktop Scheduler is a program you can use to send yourself reminders about important events or to schedule programs to run at a specific time, even when you are away from your computer. You tell the Scheduler what the event is, when the event takes place, and how frequently you want to repeat the event, and it takes care of the rest. If you tell it to launch a program, the Scheduler will start the program as soon as the designated time has come. If some other event prevents the Scheduler from starting the application program—perhaps your printer is busy—the Scheduler will launch the program as soon as possible after the system resource becomes free. You can even use the Scheduler to launch several applications at the same moment, but be careful about the sequence you use in case these programs communicate with each other and the launch sequence is important.

To start the Scheduler, double-click on the Scheduler icon in the Norton Desktop group window or select it from the Tools menu. The Scheduler window opens on the Desktop, as Figure 14.5 shows.

All the events you currently have scheduled are shown in the list box in the center of the window, with the event name on the left, its frequency in the center, and the time and date the event is scheduled for on the right. If you just want to review the events scheduled on your system, you don't have to go any further. If there are too many events scheduled, use the scroll bars at the side of this list box to bring the other events into view.

In order for the Scheduler to post reminder messages and run programs unattended, the Scheduler must be active and running on your system. At the bottom of the Scheduler window are two checkboxes to

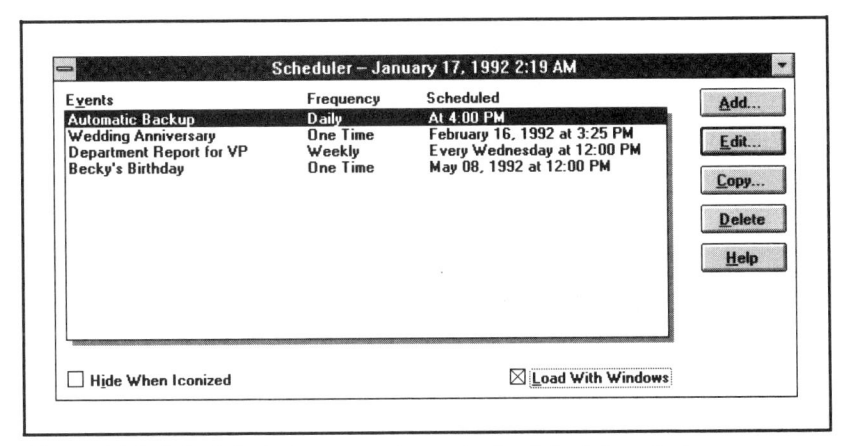

Figure 14.5: Scheduled events are shown in the Scheduler window

help you configure the Scheduler to run the way you want it to:

> **Hide When Iconized.** When you iconize the Scheduler, it stays active without taking over your whole screen. If you think you already have too many icons on your Desktop, click this checkbox to hide the Scheduler icon from view. Once the Scheduler is hidden, you can select Scheduler in the Tools menu to reopen the Scheduler window.
>
> **Load with Windows.** Check this box to load the Scheduler every time you start Windows on your computer. This is a good way to make sure that the Scheduler is running on your computer all the time. When you check this box, your Windows initialization file, WIN.INI, is modified so that the Scheduler is loaded automatically and is iconized at the bottom of the Desktop every time you start Windows on your system.

If you check both of these boxes, the Scheduler will load every time you start Windows on your computer, and then be iconized and hidden from view.

There are several command buttons down the right side of the Scheduler window that you use to work with the Scheduler. Before you can use one of these buttons, however, you must first select an event from the central scrollable list box. The command buttons are as follows:

Add When you want to add a new entry to the Scheduler list of events, click on Add to open the Add Event dialog box shown in Figure 14.6. This dialog box is very similar to the dialog boxes used for Editing or Copying events, described later. There are several important group boxes in the Add Event dialog box:

Description. The description you enter into this text box is shown under the event heading in the main Scheduler window. Make the description as self-explanatory as possible.

Type of Action. Select one of the two option buttons, either the default Run Program, used for scheduling program launches, or Display Message if you want to use the Scheduler to post a reminder message.

Command Line to Run. If you chose the Run Program option button, you can enter the name of the program you want to run into this text box, along with the file-name extension and data file name if necessary. You can also enter any command-line switches here. Cilck the Browse button to help locate the file name to run.

> If you want to schedule a Batch Runner file, be sure to include the .WBT file-name extension here.

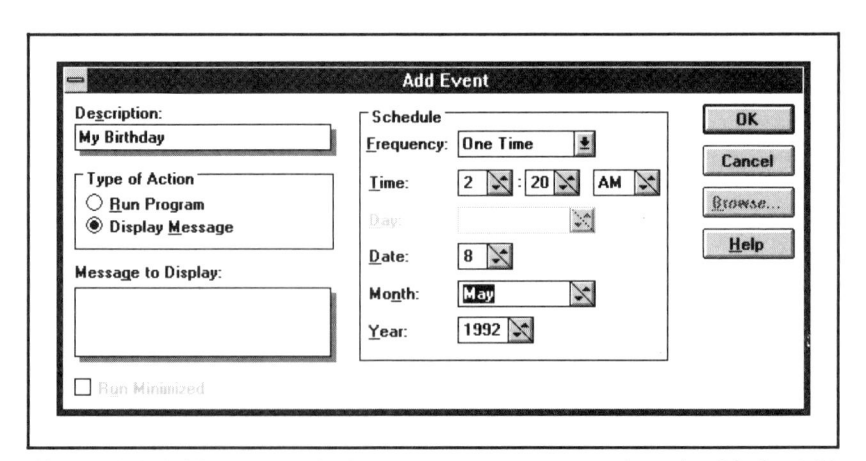

Figure 14.6: Add a new reminder message or program to launch with the Add Event dialog box

Run Minimized. If you chose the Run Program option button, this checkbox becomes enabled. You can choose to start your program as a minimized desktop icon rather than a normal sized window if you check this box.

Display Message. If you chose the Display Message option button, the Command Line to Run box changes into the Message to Display box. Enter the text of your message into this box. If your message is longer than one line, you can let the line wrap to the next line by itself, or you can force a new line if you press Ctrl-Enter.

Schedule. Use the controls in the Schedule group box to specify when you want the event to take place. You have lots of flexibility here. Start by selecting Frequency to specify how often you want the event to take place. Choose from One Time, Hourly, Daily, Week Days, Weekly, and Monthly. If you choose One Time, the event will be deleted automatically by the Scheduler as soon as the event has been processed. If you choose one of the other settings, and want to have two events in the same time period, like two events in one hour or two events in the same day, just give the second event a different time. Depending on your selection here, you can use the appropriate spin buttons to select the Time, Day, Date, Month, or Year for your event. Some of these controls may be dimmed, depending on your choice for Frequency.

> The time and date format used by the Scheduler is determined by the setting in the Windows Control Panel.

Edit If you want to modify or edit an existing event, highlight the event in the Scheduler scrollable list, then click on Edit to open the Edit Event dialog box to make the changes. Click on OK when your changes are complete.

Copy Copy duplicates the scheduled event and opens the Copy Event dialog box. This is a good way to use an existing event as the base and then modify it to represent another event. Click on OK after you have made the necessary modifications and you will see the copied event in the Scheduler scrollable list.

Delete If you want to delete an event, highlight it in the Scheduler scrollable list, then click on the Delete command button. There is no need to delete events that just occur once because the Scheduler will delete these events automatically as soon as they have been processed. A message box opens, indicating that the expired event is about to be dropped from your list of events. When you click on OK, the event is removed from your event list.

CREATING A REMINDER MESSAGE

Now that you are familiar with the components of the Scheduler window, let's look at the steps needed to create a reminder message. Start Scheduler and open the main Scheduler window, then:

1. Click on the Add command button to open the Add Event dialog box.

2. Enter a description of your event, birthday, wedding anniversary, or dinner appointment. This description will appear in the scrollable list in the main Scheduler window, so make it as obvious as you can in the space provided. The description text box beeps when it is full and can accept no more characters.

3. Choose the Display Message option button and enter your message, up to 128 characters in length, into the Message to Display text box.

4. Specify how often you want this event to occur from the choices in the Frequency list box and complete the time, day, and date information by using the spin buttons.

5. Click on OK to return to the main Scheduler window. You should see your new event displayed in the scrollable list in this window.

When the time and date arrive for your event, the Scheduler will open a message box on the screen, displaying the message text you entered. A beep will also sound to attract your attention. The message box will stay open until you click on OK to indicate that you have received the message.

SCHEDULING A PROGRAM

The steps involved in scheduling a particular program are very similar to those just described for a reminder message. Start the Scheduler from the Tools menu. When the main Scheduler window opens:

1. Click on the Add command button to open the Add Event dialog box.

2. Enter a description of the program you plan to launch. Make this description as obvious as possible so that you won't forget which program you are scheduling.

3. Choose the Run program option button and enter the name of the program (Windows or non-Windows application) you want to run into the Command Line to Run text box. Your command-line entry can be up to 128 characters in length so you can also specify any command-line switches you like to use with this application program or batch file.

4. If you want the program to be minimized as soon as it starts, check the Run Minimized check box.

5. Specify the frequency and the time that you want the program launched.

6. Click on OK to return to the main Scheduler window. You should see your new event displayed in the scrollable list in this window.

When the designated time arrives, your application program will start.

SCHEDULING A BACKUP

Combining the power of the Norton Backup program and the Scheduler is an excellent way to back up your hard disk. You can have the Scheduler post a reminder message, indicating it is time to run the Backup program, or—better still—you can make the Scheduler run the program for you at the appointed time. You can use one of the setup files, described in Chapter 10, to make configuring Norton Backup fast and easy and then use the Scheduler to launch Norton Backup automatically. That way you don't have to remember to configure or launch anything; Scheduler will do it all for you.

Follow the steps outlined above under the heading "Scheduling a Program," but bear in mind the following points if you want the backup to be performed while unattended:

- The system time and date on your computer must be correct and must be relatively accurate. Be especially careful if you work with networks, as the network software can sometimes reset the local workstation time to be the same as the network time.

- The files you want to back up must fit on a single floppy disk, because you may not be by your computer to change disks. This is less of a problem if you back up to a DOS path using another hard disk.

- Make sure you turn off all the settings in Norton Backup that might stop the backup to wait for a response from you, the user, such as overwrite warnings.

- Use a Norton Backup setup file in the Command Line to Run box in Scheduler. Your entry might look like this:

    NBWIN.EXE ASSIST.SET

    or you might add some of the other Norton Backup command-line switches to preconfigure the program. These switches are described in detail at the end of Chapter 10 under the heading "Using Command-Line Switches."

- Check the Run Minimized box, so that Norton Backup runs minimized.

- Choose a sensible time to schedule the backup. If you eat lunch every day at 12:00, try scheduling the backup for noon. If you schedule the backup to take place after you have left work, remember to insert the backup floppy disk before you leave, or schedule a message timed to appear just before you leave to remind you to insert the floppy disk.

Of course, you can schedule different kinds of backups to take place on different days, too, perhaps a full backup on Fridays and an incremental backup Monday through Thursday.

CREATING BATCH PROGRAMS

Before Norton Desktop, there was no easy way of running batch files in Windows. Now there is, with the Batch Builder. To take full advantage of the Batch Builder you must have some knowledge of programming and programming concepts. Unfortunately, there is not enough room in this chapter to describe the Batch Builder *and* teach you how to write a program. So by way of a compromise, I will describe here the Batch Builder and include examples of how you can use it, along with some Batch Builder code fragments. But for a definitive command and function reference, I refer you to the appendix.

WHAT IS A BATCH FILE?

A *batch,* a term that originated with mainframe computers, signifies a series of commands contained in a file that is invoked by running the file. In a DOS batch file, you can include any of the DOS internal and external commands, exactly as you would if you were typing them at the DOS command prompt. Batch files are ASCII text files, with a carriage return and line feed at the end of each line. You cannot include any word-processor formatting commands in batch files.

BATCH BUILDER AND BATCH RUNNER

Working with batch files involves two quite separate processes. First there is the editor or programming environment used to create the batch file. The editor takes care of opening and saving the file and provides basic text-editing facilities. In the Desktop, this is called the Batch Builder, which is much more powerful than a standard text editor as we'll see in the next section.

The second part is the batch processor or interpreter that actually runs the batch file. In the Desktop, this program is called the Batch

Runner. Batch Runner does not have a Desktop icon and it is not selectable from the Tools menu, because you don't need to select it. It is invoked by the Desktop automatically whenever it is needed to process a batch file. You will see a minimized Batch Runner icon on the Desktop, however, when Batch Runner is running your batch file, along with the batch file name.

In the next two sections I will look at the Batch Builder and describe how you can use it. Then I'll take a look at the major components of the Batch Builder language.

EXAMINING THE BATCH BUILDER WINDOW

When you click on the Batch Builder icon in the Norton Desktop group window or select Batch Builder from the Tools menu, you open the main Batch Builder window shown in Figure 14.7. You use the commands in the Batch Builder File menu to open and save files in the usual way: use New to create a file, Open to load an existing file, and Save or Save As to save your work from time to time and when you have finished work on the batch file. The Print and Printer

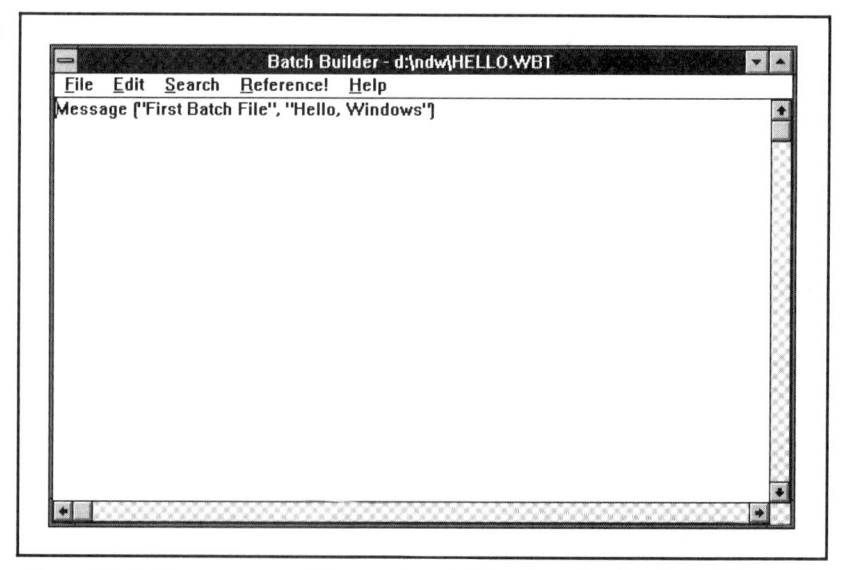

Figure 14.7: Create or modify your batch file using the Batch Builder main window

Setup commands in the File menu work just as you would expect them to: Print sends a copy of your batch file to your printer and Printer Setup opens the standard Windows Printer Setup dialog box.

The Edit menu contains several commands that work with the Windows Clipboard, as follows:

> **Undo** (Alt-Backspace) returns the text in the Batch Builder to its previous state, undoing the last operation.
>
> **Cut** (Shift-Del) places the selected text into the Windows Clipboard and deletes it from the Batch Builder.
>
> **Copy** (Ctrl-Ins) copies the selected text to the Clipboard without deleting it from the Batch Builder.
>
> **Paste** (Shift-Ins) copies the contents of the Clipboard into the main Batch Builder window.
>
> **Delete** (Del) deletes the selected text from the Batch Builder window.
>
> **Select All** selects all the text in the Batch Builder.

Using these commands, you can move text to and from the Windows Clipboard as you edit your batch file.

The Search menu contains entries to help you find specific occurrences of text in your batch files:

> **Find** opens the Find dialog box shown in Figure 14.8. In this dialog box you enter the text you want to search for, select the search direction, either Forward or Backward, and specify whether you want the search to be case-sensitive or not. Click on OK to start the search. If Batch Builder finds a match, it will highlight the first occurrence of the search string. You will see a message on the screen if no match is found.
>
> **Find Next** continues the search to look for more occurrences of the search string. Find Next always searches forwards.
>
> **Previous** searches backwards from the current location in the batch file.

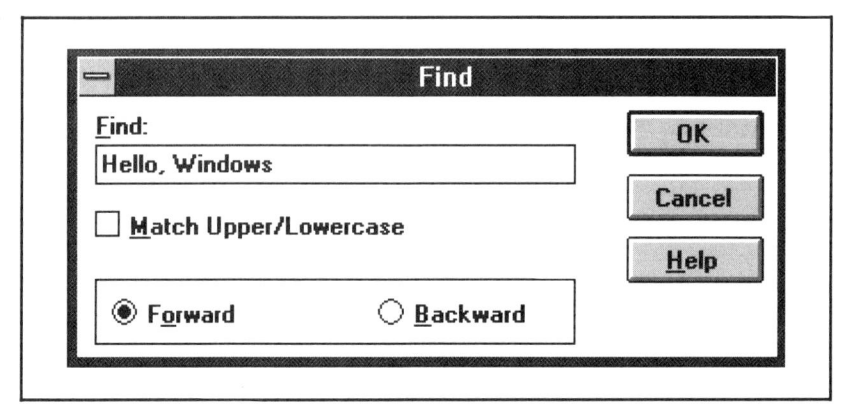

Figure 14.8: Enter the text you want to search for in the Find dialog box

The Find Next and Previous selections in the Search menu remain dimmed until you enter a search string in the Find dialog box.

Your first clue that the Batch Builder is no ordinary text editor comes when you click on the Reference entry in the Batch Builder menu bar and open the Reference dialog box, shown in Figure 14.9. When you are working with your batch file, either creating one from scratch or editing an existing file, you can see a complete list of all Batch Runner commands and functions here. This list is displayed at left, in alphabetical order. Either use the scroll bars to bring a function into view or type a letter to go straight to the first function in the list that begins with that letter. For instance, type a *y* to go to Yield or a *v* to go to Version. Beside this list box you can see a short description

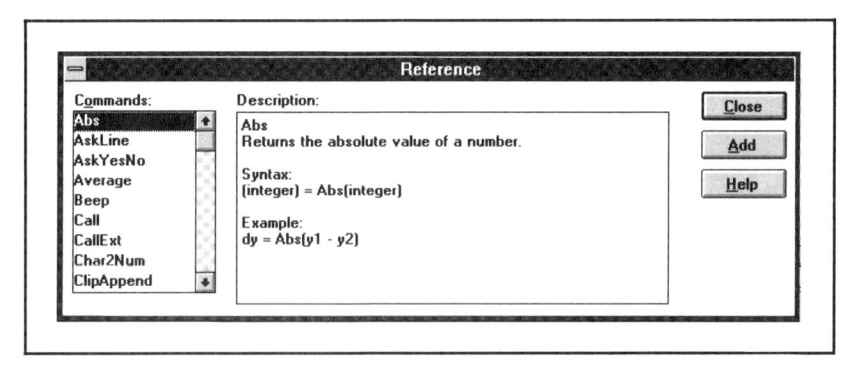

Figure 14.9: The Reference dialog box lists all the available Batch Runner commands

of what the command or function does, its syntax, and an example of how you might use the command.

Entering Commands and Functions into a Batch File

The real power of the Reference window is that you can use it to add commands and functions directly into your batch file or use it to replace existing commands. To add a command:

1. Position the cursor at the place in your batch file where you want to insert a command.

2. Find the command or function you want to use in the list box and either double-click the command or highlight it and click on the Add command button.

The item will appear at the insertion point in your batch file. If it's a function, you can complete the entry by adding any variables or strings you need for the function. If you've added a command, you won't have to complete the entry.

To replace an existing entry in a batch file:

1. Highlight the entry you want to replace in the batch file.

2. Find the command or function you want to use in the list box and either double-click on the function or highlight it and click on the Add command button.

The new command will replace the highlighted one in your batch file.

Of course, this is not the only way to add to your batch file. You can also type each of the commands in full—and this is how you must complete an entry, adding variable names, other functions, or strings as needed.

Starting a Batch File

You can start a batch file running in one of several different ways:

- by using the Run command in the File menu and entering the name of the batch file into the text box.

> When you install Batch Runner on your system, the .WBT file-name extension is automatically associated with the executable file BATCHRUN.EXE.

- by opening a drive window and double-clicking on the batch file name.

- by adding the batch file to a group window and selecting it from there.

- by adding the batch file to your Launch List and running it from there.

When you run a batch file, the following command line is actually executed:

BATCHRUN *filename.WBT*

A Batch File Example

Before we move into the section on the Batch Builder language, it's time for an example that will put all that I have said so far about batch files into sharp focus. Let's look at a very simple, one-line batch file that uses only one function, the Message function. Message opens a dialog box on your screen that contains a message you specify and an OK button. The message box stays open on your Desktop until you click on OK, then it closes. You can also specify the text in the message box title bar. To create this example, follow these steps:

1. Launch the Batch Builder and click on the Reference entry on the menu bar to open the Reference dialog box.

2. Type an *M* from the keyboard or use the scroll bars until the Message function is shown in the Commands list box. Double-click on Message or select it and click the Add command button to copy the function into the Batch Builder window.

3. Complete the function by adding this line to the Message function:

    ("First Batch File", "Hello, Windows")

   The first text string enclosed in quotation marks it for the dialog box title bar and the second string is the actual

> If you type a file name without an extension, Batch Builder will add the extension .WBT.

message. The entry in the Batch Builder window should now read:

Message ("First Batch File", "Hello, Windows")

4. Select Save As from the File menu and save the file with the name HELLO.WBT, then click on OK.
5. Close the Reference window and close or minimize the Batch Builder.
6. Select the Run command from the Desktop File menu, enter the file name **HELLO.WBT** into the Command Line text box, and click on OK.

An icon appears on the Desktop, representing the Batch Runner, and then a dialog box opens in the middle of the Desktop containing the message **Hello, Windows**, as Figure 14.10 shows. This is a real Windows dialog box. All I did was use the Message function and specify the text for the title bar and message; Batch Runner took care of the rest. Try clicking on the title bar to see if you can drag the box to a new location on the screen; it works. When you have finished with this batch file marvel, click on the OK button to close the dialog box.

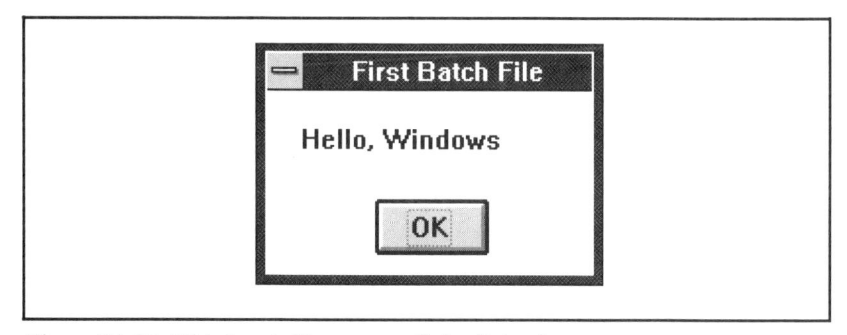

Figure 14.10: This batch file opens a little dialog box

Using Batch Builder is that simple; all the hard work is done by the Batch Runner. Batch files written using the Norton Desktop are infinitely more powerful than regular DOS batch files and the Batch Builder language itself is much richer, with many more functions, than the DOS batch language.

THE BATCH BUILDER LANGUAGE

There are well over 100 different functions and commands you can use in the Batch Builder for your batch programming. Because the Windows environment is potentially quite complex for a programmer, the Batch Builder language provides many powerful functions to help you open, manage, and close your own windows, and use dialog boxes, list boxes, and most of the other elements of the Windows setting. Basic math facilities are also available, along with bitwise operators for use with some of the more complex system-related Batch Builder functions. In the next few sections I'll look at the different components of the Batch Builder language.

Comments

You can include comments in a Batch Builder file if you start the line with a semicolon. Anything that follows the semicolon is ignored by the Batch Runner when the file is running. Use comments generously throughout your batch files to explain what the batch file is doing. Although this may be obvious to you now as you are writing the batch file, you may forget some or all of the details in a year's time, especially if the batch file executes complicated procedures.

Constants

The Batch Builder language includes three kinds of constants: integers, strings, and predefined constants:

- An *integer* is any whole number, positive or negative, including zero. In the Batch Builder you can use integers in the range of approximately minus two billion to plus two billion; integers outside this range may produce unexpected results.

- A *string* is one or more displayable characters, enclosed in quotes. You can use single, back, or double quotes to define a string, as long as you use the same type at both ends of the string. In the examples that follow in this chapter and in the appendix, all strings are enclosed by double quotes. In the example of using the Message function, I used two strings, "First Batch File" and "Hello, Windows."

- Batch Runner provides several *predefined constants* you can use. They all start with the @ symbol and are case-insensitive; you can use uppercase letters, lowercase letters, or any combination of the two. You will find a full list of all the predefined constants listed in the appendix.

Commands

The Batch Runner language provides seven commands for performing system management:

- Beep
- Execute
- Exit
- Goto
- If...Then
- Return
- Yield

Commands stand alone and do not accept parameters.

Functions

All Batch Runner functions include parentheses after the identifier. Any parameters you want to pass to the function should be contained inside them. For example, as we have seen, the Message function accepts two parameters, both strings. The first string contains the text for the dialog box title bar and the second string contains the text of the message itself. If the function does not have any parameters, you must use a set of empty parentheses.

Function parameters can be one of three types:

- Integers
- Strings
- Variable names

Variables

A variable can contain an integer, a string, or a string representing an integer. During execution, Batch Runner converts integers to strings and vice versa, as needed.

Identifiers

Identifiers are the names you use for variables, functions, parameters, and commands in your batch files. An identifier can be as small as a single letter, and can be as large as 30 characters. All identifiers are case-insensitive, and can contain any combination of upper-and lowercase letters. The only specific exception to this is that a labels used with the Goto statement must start with a colon, as in:

```
:label
```

Operators

The operators in the Batch Builder language are of two types:

- Unary Operators take just one operand, like Logical Not (!) and Bitwise Not (~).
- Binary arithmetic operators take two operands, like division (/), modulo (mod), or left shift (<<).

The single equal sign (=) is used as the assignment operator, as in:

```
A = 20
```

where the variable *A* is set to an initial value of 20. The double equal sign (= =) is used to decide if two variables are equal or to determine their equivalence, as in:

```
If A = = 20 Then Beep
```

See the section in the appendix called "Mathematical, Relational, and Bitwise Operators" for more details on operators, and see the section called "Precedence and Order of Evaluation" for information on the hierarchy you should use with different operators. The appendix also contains a short treatment of Batch Runner error handling.

BATCH BUILDER COMMANDS AND FUNCTIONS

Now that I have described the building blocks that make up the Batch Builder language, let's look at how we can use some of them in batch programs. In the following sections, you will see that I have grouped the commands and functions in the Batch Builder language together according to the job that they do. For a full list of all the commands and functions in the language, see the appendix.

Running Programs

The Batch Builder language provides four different functions for running applications programs. You can start a program in a normal window with Run, in a hidden window with RunHide, as an icon with RunIcon, and in a maximized window using RunZoom.

All these forms of the Run command can take two parameters, the name of the application program you want to start and the data file to open with the application. Using the RunZoom function, this might look like the following:

```
RunZoom ("NOTEPAD.EXE", "TESTFILE.TXT")
```

This opens a Windows notepad on the file TESTFILE.TXT. You can abbreviate this Run statement in several ways. If the application program is an .EXE file, you can leave the extension out of the first string and just use:

```
Run ("NOTEPAD", "TESTFILE.TXT")
```

If the file-name extension of the data file has an association already established with Desktop, the statement can be cut down even further:

```
Run ("TESTFILE.TXT", " ")
```

When you specify a file, the Batch Runner first looks in the current directory. If it doesn't find the file there, it looks in all the directories in your DOS path. If you wish, you an include path information with the program name parameter in a Run statement. Now our Run function might look something like this:

```
Run ("C:\WINDOWS\TESTFILE.TXT", " ")
```

Asking for Input

There are four functions in the Batch Builder language you can use to secure information from the user. All four open a dialog box of some sort on the screen and include OK and Cancel buttons. You don't have to program anything special to get these additional windows elements; they are built into each of the functions AskYesNo, AskLine, ItemSelect, and TextBox.

> As a courtesy to your users, add a question mark after the text in the dialog box to show them that you are really asking a question.

AskYesNo Very often, you have to ask the user a question that requires a Yes or No answer to decide what the program should do next. You can use AskYesNo for this task. Enter and run the following batch file fragment to explore AskYesNo:

```
answer = AskYesNo ("Intelligent Life", "Is there intelligent life on this planet?")
If answer = = @NO Then Goto No
Message ("Yes Answer", "See? I told you, Bones.")
Goto Out
:No
Message ("No Answer", "Nothing doing here, Captain. Let's go.")
:Out
```

Run this a couple of times and try answering with a Yes the first time and a No the second.

AskLine This is slightly different; it opens a dialog box containing a prompt and a text box for input, as well as OK and Cancel buttons. You can also specify a default entry that AskLine will place in the text box for you. Type in (all on one line) and run the following example:

```
vessel = AskLine ("Vessel Name", "Enter the name of your ship", "USS Enterprise")
```

ItemSelect This creates a list box containing all the items specified in a "list" parameter. This function is most powerful when you use it with other functions like FileItemize or DirItemize. These functions return lists of file or directories, where each entry in the list is separated from the next by a space. For example, the function

```
FileItemize ("*.TXT")
```

makes a list of all the text files in the current directory. Once you have built the list using one of these functions, you can use ItemSelect to open the list box and help the user choose one of the files in the list. Then, once the user has chosen a file, you can use the Run command to open Windows Notepad on the file. Here is the example:

```
Names = FileItemize ("*.TXT")
Selectfile = ItemSelect("Select a file to edit", Names, " ")
Run ("NOTEPAD.EXE", Selectfile)
```

Figure 14.11 shows the resulting dialog box.

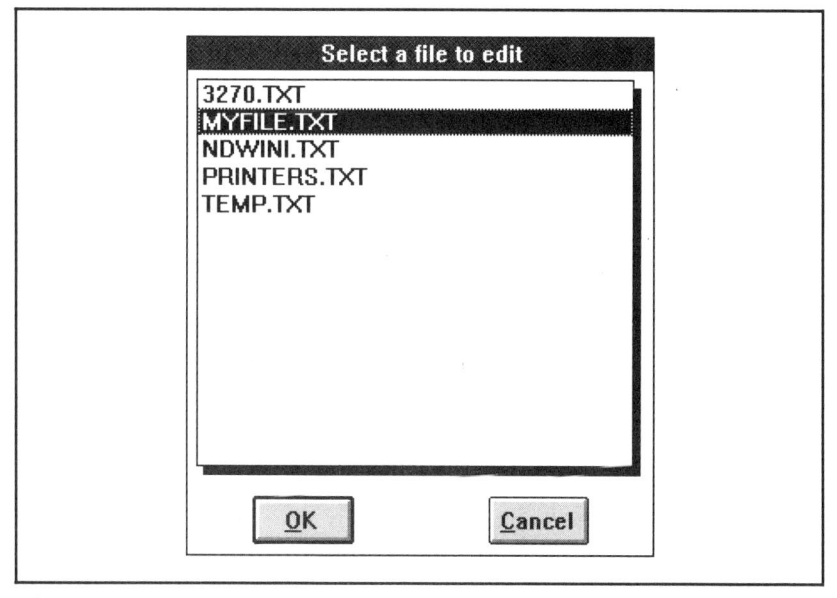

Figure 14.11: FileItemize prepares a list of file names; choose one using ItemSelect

TextBox This also displays a list box and lets the user choose an item. The list box contains the contents of a text file and each item is a line in the file. Try the following example (the resulting dialog box is shown in Figure 14.12):

```
; display the windows file WIN.INI
Line = TextBox ("Please Select a Line", "D:\Windows\WIN.INI")
Display (5, "The line you chose is:", Line)
```

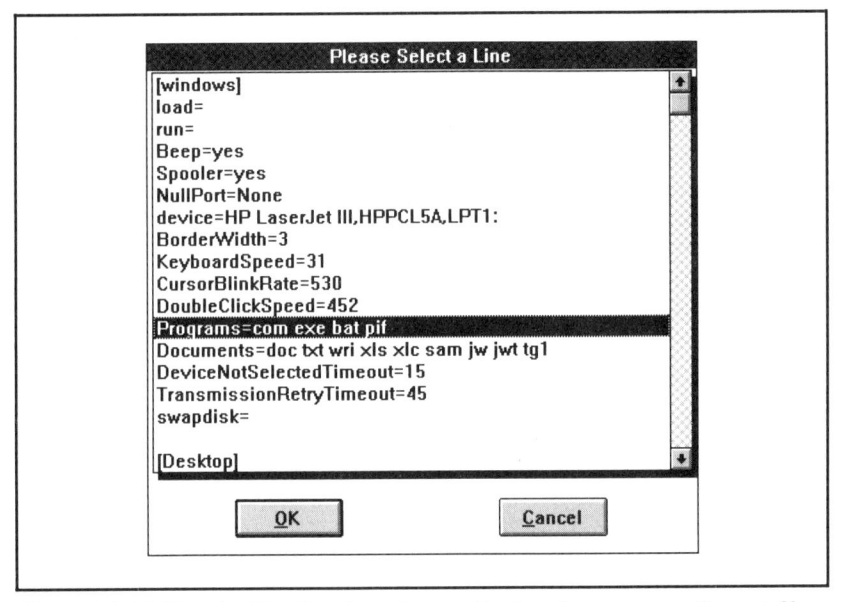

Figure 14.12: Use the TextBox function to display the contents of a text file

Use the scroll bars to convince yourself that they do actually work, then click on a line in the list box and choose OK. Another box opens, containing a replica of the line you chose in the list box. The first parameter in the Display statement above specifies the number of seconds to leave the second box open. If you used 5, the box will stay open for five seconds, then close automatically. If you want to have an OK and a Cancel button on this second dialog box, use the Message function here instead of Display.

Managing Information

We have already looked at a couple of the functions in this group, Display and Message. Most of the others are just as straightforward. Beep makes a noise on the computer speaker and Pause displays a message until the user clicks on OK or Cancel. Three of the functions are somewhat more complex, however: DialogBox opens a dialog box specified in a .WBD file, ItemCount counts the number of items in a list, and ItemExtract finds and returns an item from a list.

Let's take a longer look at DialogBox because it is a rather complex function. DialogBox lets you specify and use all sorts of familiar Windows and Norton Desktop elements, like option buttons, checkboxes, and so on. It does this by loading a separate template file containing a definition of all these elements.

> The DialogBox dialog box can be up to 20 by 60 text characters in size, but no larger. You will see a fatal error message if your DialogBox text is too long.

The syntax is deceptively simple:

DialogBox ("*box title*", "*FILENAME.WBD*")

and the complexity is provided as the file runs and is interpreted by Batch Runner. The .WBD file is an ordinary ASCII text file and can be no larger than 15 lines containing 60 characters each. The file can contain spaces but *must not* contain tab spaces because they may affect the text spacing calculations. Each statement inside the .WBD file is contained inside square brackets. The first DialogBox example uses option buttons, representing four different selections, one of which we want the user to select. The DialogBox function looks like this:

DialogBox ("Choose One", "OPTION.WBD")

Save it in a file called DBOX.WBT. The OPTION.WBD template file layout looks exactly like this (watch your spacing):

[choose^1Option One]   [choose^2Option Two]
[choose^3Option Three]   [choose^4Option Four]

Save it in a file of the same name as the DialogBox parameter, OPTION.WBD. Run the DBOX.WBT file and you will see the dialog box shown in Figure 14.13. The purpose of this example is to provide input to the variable "choose": when the user selects Option

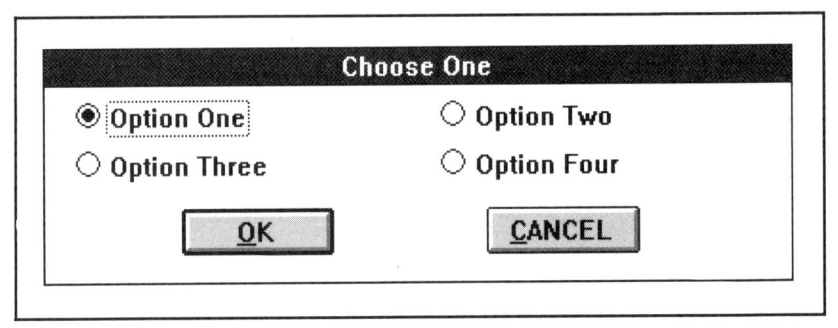

Figure 14.13: Option buttons created by a DialogBox .WBD template file

Four from the dialog box, "choose" is assigned a value of 4. You can assign "choose" a value before you use the DialogBox function if you want to use an option other than Option One as the default when the dialog box first opens. If the user selects Option One, then "choose" will be assigned a value of 1. The rest of your batch file decides how to react to the user's choice.

There are many other characters you can use in a .WBD template file to indicate the other Windows and Desktop elements, checkboxes, text boxes, file list boxes, and so on. These are summarized in the appendix under the DialogBox function heading.

Managing Files

The Batch Builder not only provides several functions you can use to perform file-management tasks like finding, copying, deleting, and renaming files, but also provides functions for opening, reading, writing, and closing text files. There are four very specialized commands you can use to read entries from or write entries into .INI initialization files: IniRead, IniReadPvt, IniWrite, and IniWritePvt. This is considered to be a rather advanced operation because of the potential dangers of writing into files like WIN.INI. If you make a bad mistake, well, just be glad you used the Norton Backup program when you did.

Managing Directories

Functions for managing directories are as follows: DirChange changes to another directory, DirGet tells you the current directory path, DirMake makes a new directory, DirRename changes a directory name, and DirRemove deletes a directory.

Managing Disk Drives

There are two main functions you can use with disk drives: DiskFree returns the amount of free space remaining on a disk and LogDisk makes another drive the current drive.

Managing Windows

As you might imagine, the Batch Builder language includes many functions for organizing your windows. There are 15 in total, but I will look at the four most often used: WinZoom, WinIconize, WinShow, and WinWaitClose. All these functions take a window title as a parameter. The match with the title can be truncated, but whatever you provide must match exactly, including case and any punctuation. This is to allow you to manipulate a window when you don't know the complete title—indeed the window title may change if you load a different data or document file into your application program.

WinZoom maximizes the selected window, WinIconize has the same effect as selecting the minimize button, and WinShow is the same as selecting Restore. The WinWaitClose function pauses your batch file until the user closes the specified window or icon. During the time that the batch file is in suspended animation, the Batch Runner icon stays on the Desktop. You can cancel the batch file at any time if you choose Close from the icon's control menu.

The other window-related functions let you arrange windows on the Desktop, either by tiling or cascading them, test for the existence of a window, hide a window, and so on.

Managing Strings

Strings are very important in the Batch Runner language. There are functions you can use to build up a string from several substrings and there are functions that do the opposite, i.e. break a string down into substrings. You can search strings for specific substrings, perform search-and-replace operations, compare strings, and even change the case of all the letters in a string.

Arithmetic Functions

If there is a single weakness in the Batch Builder language, you could argue that it is the lack of support for arithmetic operations. On the other hand, you can also argue that most people using the Batch Runner will want to manipulate objects rather than perform calculations, so perhaps it isn't really a weakness.

Handling System Control

Sometimes you will want to pass control from one batch file to another. The function you use to do this is the Call function if you want to treat the other file as a subroutine, or CallExt to treat it as a subprogram. The difference between these two functions is that variables are global and are shared between the original caller and the called .WBT file if you use Call, but are local and not shared if you use CallExt.

Three version commands, DOSVersion, Version, and WinVersion, obtain the version number of DOS running on your system, the version number of the Batch Runner, and the version number of Windows running on your system, respectively.

You can also turn the Batch Runner Debug mode on or off using the Debug function. When Debug mode is on you can step through your batch file a line at a time, with a dialog box showing you the current state of your variables. This is often the only way to can debug and find problems in a batch file. An example of the Debug dialog box is shown in Figure 14.14. The Debug dialog box has four command buttons:

> **Next** advances the batch file to the next statement, while staying in debug mode (unless the next statement in the batch file is Debug(@OFF)).
>
> **Run** cancels debug mode and processes the rest of the batch file normally.
>
> **Cancel** terminates batch processing and stops the Batch Runner.
>
> **Show Var** displays the contents of any variable name you type into the text box.

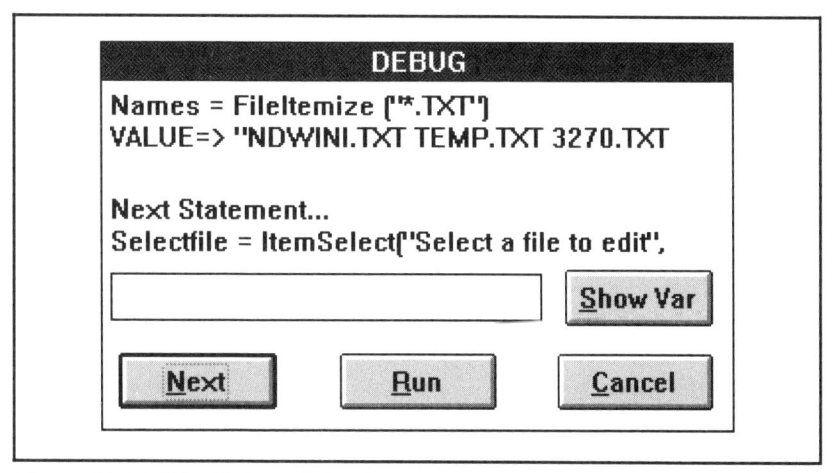

```
                            DEBUG
    Names = FileItemize ["*.TXT"]
    VALUE=> "NDWINI.TXT TEMP.TXT 3270.TXT

    Next Statement...
    Selectfile = ItemSelect["Select a file to edit",

    [                                      ]   [ Show Var ]

         [ Next ]      [ Run ]      [ Cancel ]
```

Figure 14.14: The Debug dialog box provides information on your variables that you can use to troubleshoot your batch file

Using the Windows Clipboard

There are three Batch Builder functions you can use with the Windows Clipboard: ClipAppend adds the contents of a string to the contents of the Clipboard, ClipGet copies the contents of the Clipboard into a Batch Builder string, and ClipPut replaces the contents of the Clipboard with the contents of the specified string.

Be creative with the Batch Runner language. You can use it to help with almost all common tasks you will need to perform in Windows. If you find that you can't do it using the Batch Runner, you are probably trying to perform a task outside of its scope, and you will have to use a fully-featured computer language like Pascal or C to get the job done.

PART FOUR

The DOS Tools

Part IV describes the programs you use to diagnose and fix problems with files or disks. You will learn how to rescue deleted files, how to improve the performance of your hard disk system by reducing or eliminating file fragmentation, and even how to recover the contents of your hard disk after it has been accidentally formatted.

FIFTEEN
Using the Emergency Disk

THE EMERGENCY DISK INCLUDED WITH THE NORTON Desktop package contains four very important programs that can diagnose and fix problems associated with your hard or floppy disks, increase the performance of your hard disk system, recover deleted files, and fix an accidentally reformatted hard disk.

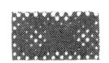

> Do not copy the Emergency Disk programs onto your hard disk until *after* you have rescued data or recovered files.

These programs are on this separate Emergency Disk for two important reasons: to ensure that the programs are available if you cannot boot up your computer or access the hard disk for some reason, and to separate them from the rest of the Norton Desktop package. These programs are the following:

Norton Disk Doctor (NDD) finds and fixes hard and floppy disk problems, moves any information that is in danger due to read errors, and tests your hard disk to ensure maximum data integrity. Use *this* version of NDD when Norton Disk Doctor for Windows reports a disk problem.

Speed Disk analyses the degree of file fragmentation on your disk and offers several different methods for reducing or eliminating that fragmentation.

UnErase helps you recover erased files automatically, or by using advanced manual recovery techniques.

UnFormat recovers the information on your hard disk after an accidental reformat.

WINDOWS INCOMPATIBILITIES WITH THE EMERGENCY DISK PROGRAMS

Windows brings *multitasking* capabilities to DOS, which means running several different applications programs at the same time and switching from one to another without quitting any of them. Many

DOS utility programs cannot run under Windows, as it is very difficult for them to observe all the conventions necessary for the multitasking environment. The Norton programs on the Emergency Disk contain extensive error-checking routines to avoid anything unpleasant happening if you do try to run them from Windows. In general, programs that have the capability of modifying the file-allocation table can pose potential problems. The following programs on the Emergency Disk will politely refuse to run in a Windows setting: the Norton Disk Doctor, UnErase, UnFormat, and Speed Disk. If you try to start one of these programs under Windows, you will see a message similar to the one shown in Figure 15.1—in this case from Speed Disk. This doesn't mean you can't use these programs on your system. It just means that you must run them from the DOS command line.

WHEN AND HOW TO USE THE EMERGENCY DISK

You should use the programs on the Emergency Disk when you are having problems booting up your system or accessing your hard disk drive, when you want to recover an erased file or optimize your hard disk, or when you want to recover the contents of a hard disk that has just been accidentally reformatted with the DOS FORMAT command.

Do not copy the programs from the Emergency Disk to your hard disk until *after* you have corrected the problem, particularly if you wish to recover an erased file. If you were to copy the programs *before* completing the recovery operation, you might inadvertently overwrite the very file you are trying to recover, rendering a complete recovery impossible.

Only after the problem has been fixed is it safe to copy the programs from the Emergency Disk to a directory on your hard disk. This operation is simple from the Desktop:

1. Create a subdirectory called EDISK in the NDW directory on the hard disk, using the Make Directory option from the File menu.

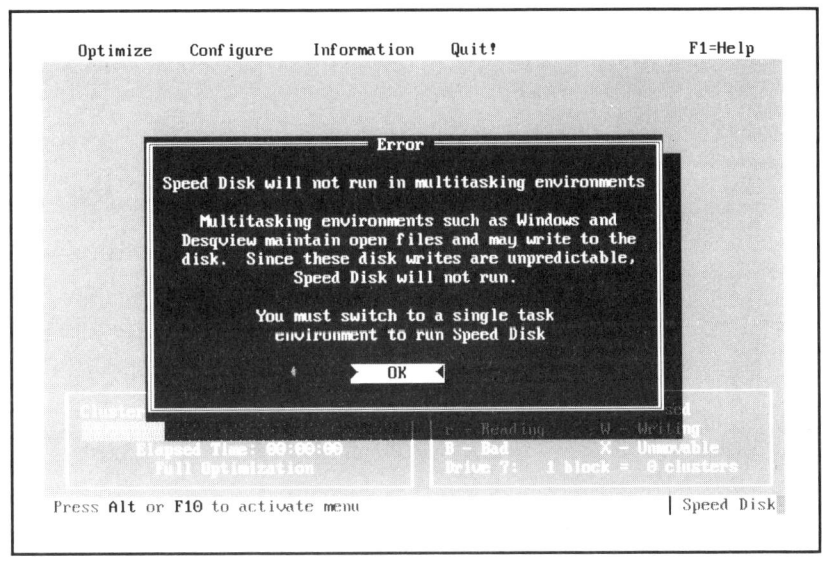

Figure 15.1: You will see this dialog box if you try to run Speed Disk from Windows

2. Place the Emergency Disk in drive A.

3. Open the drive window for drive A—and C if it is not already open.

4. Select the .EXE files to copy from drive A and drag them to the EDISK directory.

5. Add details of this new directory to your path statement. Your path might look something like this:

   PATH = C:\;C:\DOS;C:\WINDOWS;C:\NDW;C:\NDW\EDISK.

If you cannot run Norton Desktop for some reason, copy the files using commands from the DOS prompt, as follows:

1. Create a subdirectory called EDISK in the NDW directory.

2. Place the Emergency Disk in drive A and make that drive current by typing **A:** at the DOS prompt.

3. Copy the files into the new directory with the command:

   COPY *.EXE C:\NDW\EDISK

4. Add details of this new directory to your path statement.

The next sections detail the circumstances under which you should consider running these programs.

RUNNING THE EMERGENCY DISK PROGRAMS

All the programs on the Emergency Disk use a full-screen display designed to make them easy to use. If you are familiar with menus, help screens, dialog boxes, and so on, you will have no trouble using these programs.

EXAMINING THE SCREEN LAYOUT

I'll use the UnErase program to illustrate this user interface. The UnErase screen shown in Figure 15.2 has the following components:

- The horizontal *menu bar* that runs across the top of the screen contains the names of the pull-down menus. In UnErase, this menu bar contains the entries File, Search, Options, and Quit.

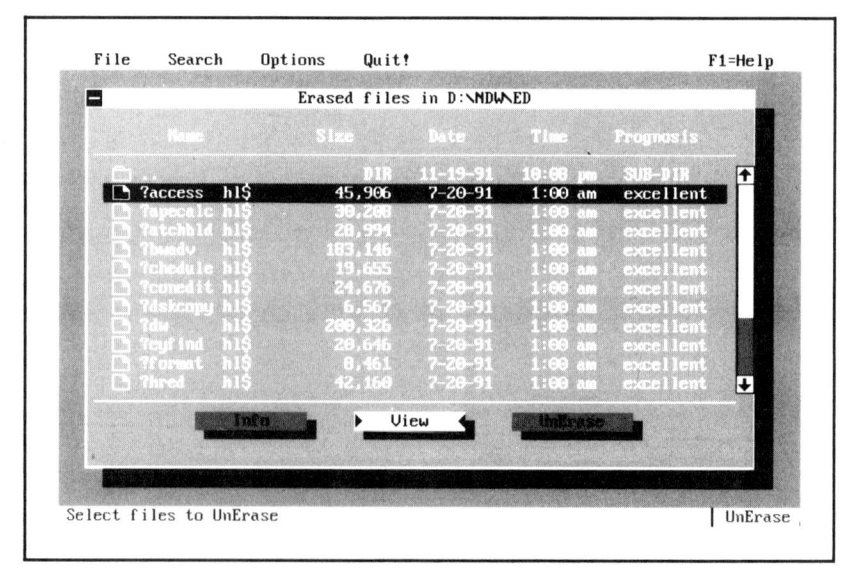

Figure 15.2: The main UnErase window

- The center of the screen lists the deleted file(s) in the current directory and shows the name, size, date, time, and recovery prognosisof each file.
- Near the bottom of the window, the program displays three boxes that offer you additional choices and options.
- The bottom line of the screen displays help text that reminds you of the operation in progress; the right side of this line shows the current program name.

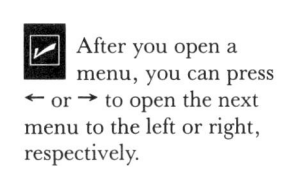

USING THE KEYBOARD TO SELECT ITEMS

> After you open a menu, you can press ← or → to open the next menu to the left or right, respectively.

To open a pull-down menu, hold down the Alt key and type the menu's initial letter. For example, to open the File menu, hold down the Alt key and type **F**; to open the Search menu, hold down the Alt key and type **S**.

Similarly, to select an item from a menu, type the highlighted (or capitalized) letter. For example, in the File menu, type **C** to choose View the Current Directory, or type **A** to choose View All Directories. Because each letter can represent only one option in each menu, the choices are sometimes less than intuitive. You can also move the highlight in a menu with the up and down arrow keys and then press Enter to select your menu item. To close a menu, press the Escape key.

Some of the most frequently used menu selections have keyboard shortcuts, so you don't have to bother with opening menus. For example, to choose View the Current Directory, just hold down the Alt key and press **C**; to choose View All Directories, hold down Alt and press **A**.

To move through the list of files in the main window, press ↑ or ↓ to move one line at a time, or press the PgUp or PgDn keys to move an entire window at a time. The Home key moves to the start of the file list displayed in the window; the End key moves to the end of the list.

Press the Tab key to highlight one of the three buttons at the bottom of the screen, and then use the left or right arrow keys to choose the correct one. Press Enter to confirm your choice. To close a window, press the Escape key.

If a window contains radio buttons or check boxes, press the spacebar to toggle the button or check mark on or off.

USING THE MOUSE TO SELECT ITEMS

The Emergency Disk programs are optimized for the mouse user, and navigating your way through the pull-down menus with a mouse is fast and easy. To open a menu, click on the name in the menu bar at the top of the screen. To select an option from the menu, simply click on the item you want. To close a menu, click the mouse in the display area outside the menu.

To scroll through the list of files shown on the screen, hold down the right mouse button and drag the mouse. As the mouse moves, the highlighted bar moves. You can also move through a list by using the scroll bars at the right side of the window. Clicking on the scroll arrow moves the highlight in the direction of the arrow. Click on the scroll bar and hold down the mouse button to scroll continuously.

You can also use the scroll bar to move to a specific point in the display. For example, if you move the scroll box to the middle of the scroll bar, the screen displays items from the middle of the list.

Move the mouse pointer from the main window to the boxes at the bottom of the screen, and then simply click on the appropriate box to select it. To select a radio button or check box, click the mouse on that field to toggle the bullet or check mark on or off.

Press both mouse buttons at the same time to close a window or menu.

HOW TO GET HELP

At the DOS prompt, you can get helpful information about any of the programs by typing the program's name followed by a question mark. For example, to display the help text for the Norton Disk Doctor, at the DOS prompt type

NDD ?

and you will see a display like the one shown in Figure 15.3.

When you are using one of the Emergency Disk programs, press F1 to open a help window at any time, or—if you are using a

```
D:\NDW\EDISK>NDD /?
NDD, Norton Utilities 6.0, Copyright 1991 by Symantec Corporation

Automatically diagnose and repair damaged disks.

NDD [d:][d:]... [/C!/Q] [/R[A]:pathname] [/X:drives] [/SKIPHIGH]
NDD [d:][d:]... /REBUILD [/SKIPHIGH]
NDD [d:][d:]... /UNDELETE [/SKIPHIGH]

   /C              Complete test, including surface test.
   /Q              All tests excepts surface test.
   /R[A]:pathname  Write (or Append) report to pathname.
   /X:drives       Exclude drives from testing.
   /REBUILD        Rebuild an entire disk that has been destroyed.
   /UNDELETE       Undelete a partition that was previously skipped.
   /SKIPHIGH       Skip using high memory.

D:\NDW\EDISK>
```

Figure 15.3: A display of NDD's command-line help

mouse—click on the **F1 = Help** entry in the menu bar at the top right of the display. The window that opens displays context-sensitive help text. Use the ↑ and ↓, PgUp and PgDn, or Home and End keys to move through the text. With the mouse, click on the scroll bars to move through the text. The help text is arranged under a series of headings or topics. You can either access a specific part of the program and ask for help about it, or you can choose help directly from a general list of program topics. The bottom of each help screen usually lists four selections:

> **Next** displays the first help screen of the next help topic.
>
> **Previous** displays the first help screen of the previous help topic.
>
> **Topics** displays the list of help topics for this particular program. Use the mouse or arrow keys to select a topic and display its help screen.
>
> **Cancel** ends the help module and returns control to the utility program.

USING THE NORTON DISK DOCTOR

> For detailed information on running these programs, see Chapter 16 for the Norton Disk Doctor, Chapter 17 for Speed Disk, and Chapter 18 for UnErase and UnFormat.

Use the Norton Disk Doctor

- when Windows or DOS reports disk errors.
- when the Norton Disk Doctor for Windows indicates that there is a disk-related problem.
- if your computer will not boot up and you suspect a problem with the boot record.
- if your computer will not boot up and you suspect a problem with the partition table.
- if files or directories behave strangely, or appear to be missing but were never deleted.
- when you want to perform an analysis of the disk itself and test your disk for physical defects.

To run the Norton Disk Doctor, follow these steps:

> You can use whichever floppy-disk drive you like.

1. Place the Emergency Disk in drive A.
2. Type **A:NDD** at the DOS prompt to start the program.
3. Select the Diagnose Disk command.
4. Choose the drive(s) you want to work with and press Enter to continue.
5. Norton Disk Doctor guides you through the analysis and repair procedure, explaining your choices at each stage. If errors are detected, prepare an Undo file so that the repair process can be reversed in the future, if necessary.

USING SPEED DISK

Use Speed Disk

- when you want to restore the performance of your hard disk by optimizing your disk or unfragmenting your files.

- when you want to create a permanent Windows *swap file*. You will see the best performance from your system with a permanent swap file for two reasons. First, the swap file must consist of a single large area of disk space; second, Windows does not have to create the file anew for every Windows session. By reserving disk space for the permanent swap file, you also guarantee that Windows never runs out of swap file space. For more information about swap files see your Windows documentation.

To run Speed Disk, follow these steps:

1. Place the Emergency Disk in drive A.
2. At the DOS prompt, type **A:SPEEDISK** to start the program.
3. Speed Disk performs an analysis of the degree of fragmentation of the files on your disk system and recommends an optimization method. Either use the recommended method or choose one of the other methods.

USING UNERASE

Run UnErase when you want to recover a deleted file. To run UnErase, follow these steps:

1. Place the Emergency Disk in drive A.
2. At the DOS prompt, type **A:UNERASE** to start the program.
3. Select the file or directory you want to recover and click on the UnErase button.
4. Enter the first letter of the file name if it is not provided for you by UnErase.

USING UNFORMAT

Use UnFormat

- if you accidentally reformat your hard disk using the DOS FORMAT command.

- if your hard disk has been damaged by a virus.
- to recover a floppy disk after it has been reformatted using the Safe format option of the Format Diskette command in the Disk menu.

To run UnFormat, follow these steps:

1. Reboot your computer from a floppy disk containing the same version of DOS used to format your hard disk.
2. Place the Emergency Disk in drive A.
3. At the DOS prompt, type **A:UNFORMAT** to start the program.
4. Read the information contained in the opening window, then press the Enter key to proceed.
5. Select the disk drive you want to recover and press Enter.
6. Follow the prompts on the screen to complete the recovery operation.

SIXTEEN

Diagnosing and Fixing Disk Problems

WHAT DO YOU DO IF YOUR DISK CONTAINS FILES that you cannot read? You can use the Norton Disk Doctor (NDD) on the Emergency Disk to diagnose and fix the unreadable files.

If Windows or the Norton Desktop reports disk errors, or if you have run the Norton Disk Doctor for Windows and the program indicates that there are problems, you should run the Norton Disk Doctor from the Emergency Disk. NDD finds and fixes any logical or high-level physical errors on your floppy or hard disk. The program is very easy to use: in most cases it is completely automatic, and it certainly does not require large amounts of arcane knowledge on your part about sectors, clusters, and the internal workings of disk drives to get it to work. I do not go into great depth about the cause and nature of disk errors in this chapter. Suffice it to say, you should run the NDD as soon as Windows or the Desktop reports disk errors.

To start the program you must first exit the Desktop; then to run the Norton Disk Doctor from the DOS prompt, type **NDD.** The opening screen is shown in Figure 16.1. Unlike the Norton Desktop, the Norton Disk Doctor does not feature pull-down menus; it uses command buttons instead. You can select four options from the main Disk Doctor screen: Diagnose Disk, Undo Changes, Options, and Quit Disk Doctor.

FINDING DISK PROBLEMS WITH DIAGNOSE DISK

NDD will not work on disks that have more than 1,024 cylinders.

Diagnose Disk is the most important part of the Norton Disk Doctor. After choosing this selection, you are asked to select a disk drive from the list of active drives, as shown in Figure 16.2. This inserts a small check mark next to the drive letter. Press Enter to start the analysis.

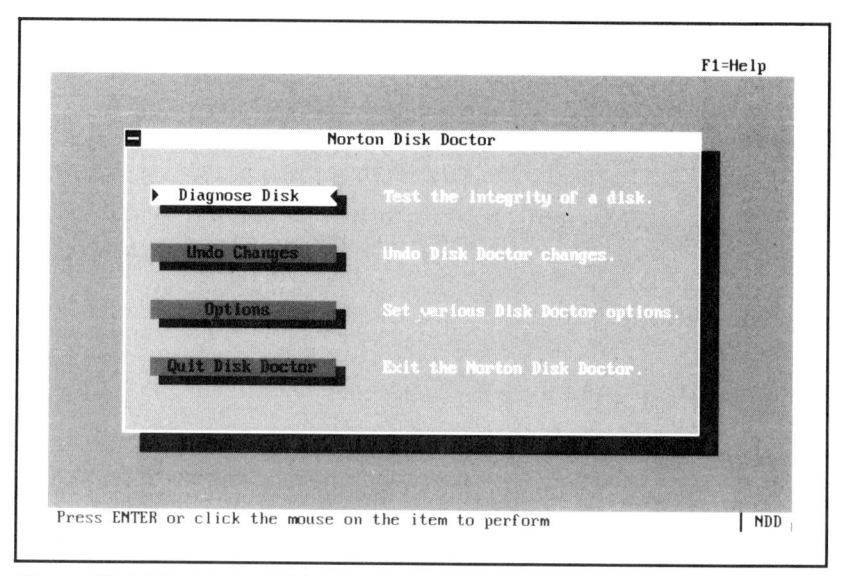

Figure 16.1: The Norton Disk Doctor opening screen

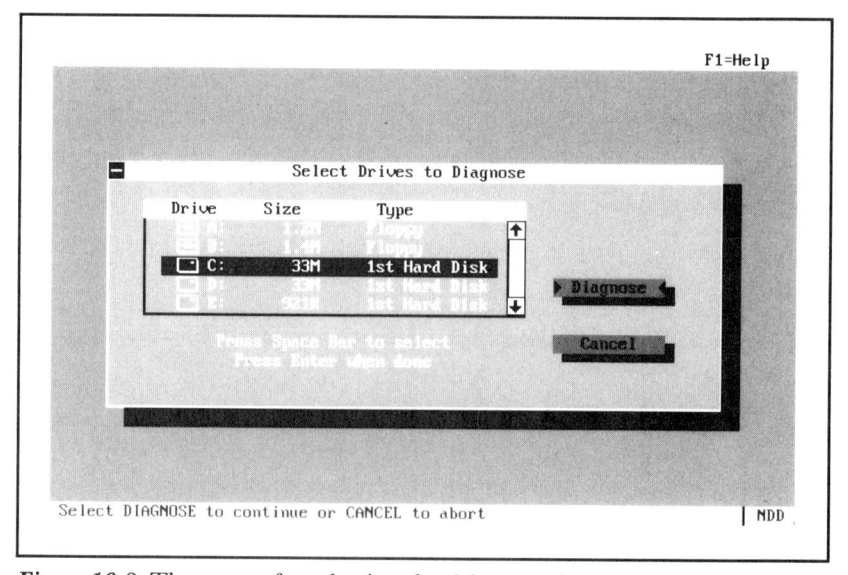

Figure 16.2: The screen for selecting the drives to diagnose

Norton Disk Doctor analyzes the following areas of your disks:

- Partition Table. If the disk you specified is a hard disk, NDD checks the partition table.
- DOS Boot Record. NDD examines the boot record to ensure that it is not damaged. The BIOS Parameter Block is also checked to verify that the media descriptor byte is correct for the type of disk being checked.
- File Allocation Table. The file allocation table (FAT) is a list of the addresses of all the files and directories on a disk. Because this indexes *all* your program and data files, DOS keeps two copies of the FAT on each disk. NDD checks for read errors in both copies of the FAT. If it finds a read error, it copies the good FAT over the FAT containing the read error. Next, both tables are checked to ensure that they are identical and that they contain only legal DOS entries.
- Directory Structure. NDD reads every directory on the disk, searching for illegal file names and file sizes, FAT errors, and cross-linked files.
- File Structure. NDD checks the file structure in the same way as it checks the directories.
- Lost Clusters. These are clusters on the disk marked as "in use" by the FAT, but they are not actually allocated to a specific file. NDD converts lost clusters into files and writes them into the root directory.

If the Norton Disk Doctor finds an error, it describes the problem and asks whether you want to fix it. For example, Figure 16.3 shows the screen you'll see when it finds an error in the FAT. Select Yes to fix the problem or No to move to the next set of tests. Choose Cancel to return to the main Disk Doctor menu.

EXAMINING YOUR DISK WITH SURFACE TEST

Surface Test runs a complete sector-by-sector test of the entire disk. If you have a large hard disk, this test can take some time to

```
                          ┌─────────────────────────────────────┐
                          │                           F1=Help   │
                          │   ┌─────────────────────────────┐   │
                          │   │     Error on Drive B:       │   │
                          │   │  Error reading a sector in the FAT │
                          │   │ ─────── Description ───────  │   │
                          │   │  The File Allocation Table (FAT) has a │
                          │   │  physical error. There are 2 copies of │
                          │   │  the FAT, therefore you have a spare, BUT │
                          │   │  if both go bad, you could lose files.  │
                          │   │           BACKUP OFTEN!     │   │
                          │   │ ─────── Recommendation ───  │   │
                          │   │  Correct this situation ONLY if you are │
                          │   │  unable to access drive B: properly. │
                          │   │                             │   │
                          │   │  Do you wish to correct this problem? │
                          │   │  ▶ Yes ◀    No     Cancel   │   │
                          │   └─────────────────────────────┘   │
                          │ Press ESC or click a mouse button to abort │  NDD │
                          └─────────────────────────────────────┘
```

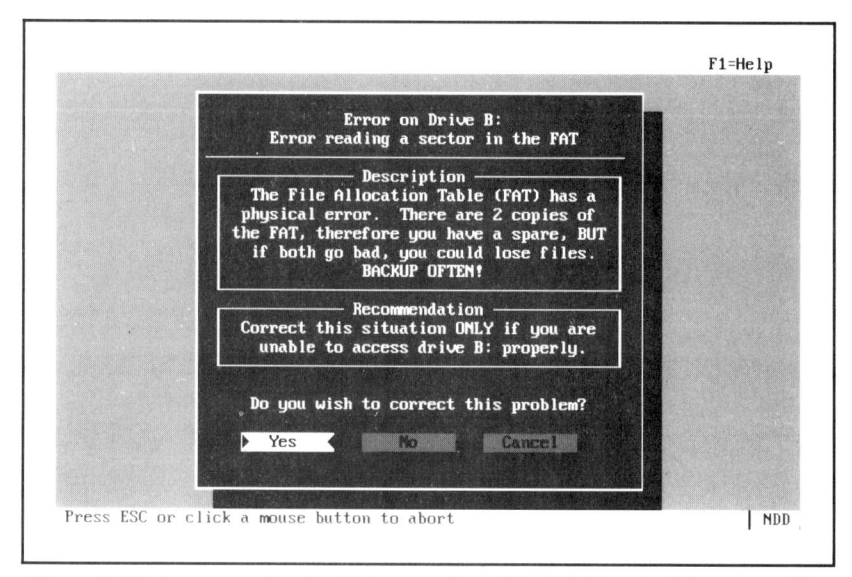

Figure 16.3: An example of a disk error found by NDD—in this case, a FAT error

run. NDD can check a 65MB hard disk in less than ten minutes if it doesn't find any bad clusters. It will take longer if it does.

Disk errors occur for a variety of reasons, usually at the most inconvenient moment. They can also take on a variety of forms. But Surface Test is especially helpful at isolating—and in some cases curing—problems associated with *read errors*. When a read error occurs, you can see a variety of messages on your screen, ranging from the typical **Abort, Retry, Ignore, Fail?** in DOS to the Windows message **System Error, Cannot read from drive B:**. Because Surface Test actually reads or attempts to read the data from each cluster on a disk, it differs from the DOS CHKDSK command, which tests only for logical errors in the data contained in the FAT and the directories.

The Surface Test selection screen is shown in Figure 16.4. Set up the appropriate Surface Test parameters by making selections from this screen. The test criteria you can specify include the following:

Test   Choose from Disk Test or File Test:

Disk Test reads every part of the disk, including both the system area and the data area. Because it is so thorough

DIAGNOSING AND FIXING DISK PROBLEMS   345

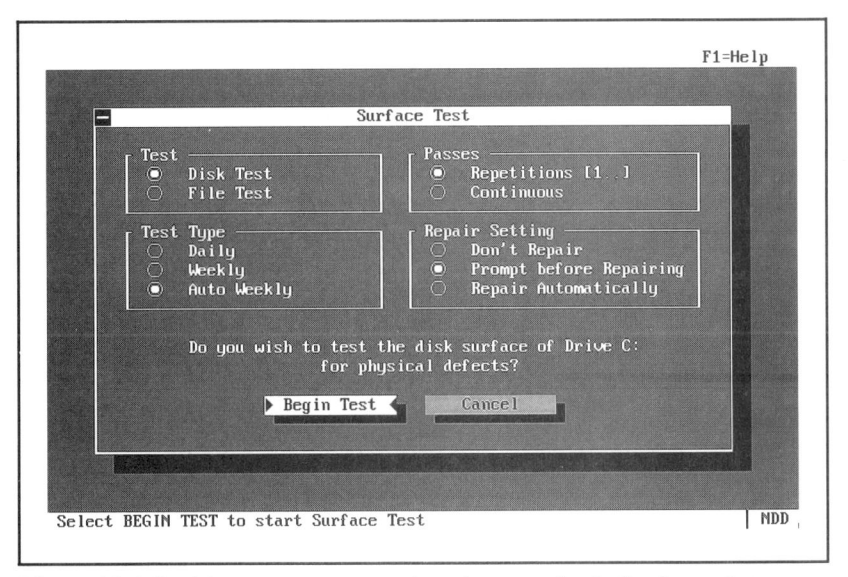

Figure 16.4: In this screen you can select the test criteria for the surface test

(it checks the entire disk), the disk-read test can take a long time to run.

File Test checks all current data and program files and directories for errors. However, it does not check the erased file space, the unused file space, or the system area, which is why it usually takes less time to run than Disk Test.

Passes   Enter the number of times you want the test repeated, from 1 to 999 times, or select Continuous to run the test until you press the Escape key.

Test Type   Choose the type of test you want to run:

Daily runs a fast check of the disk.

Weekly runs a comprehensive disk test that takes at least twice as long to run as the daily selection. It also detects errors that the daily test might miss.

Auto Weekly (the default setting for Norton Disk Doctor) runs the Weekly test if it is run on any Friday; otherwise it runs the Daily test.

Repair Setting This option lets you choose how you want NDD to respond when it finds an error:

> **Don't Repair** tells NDD to ignore any read errors. You are not likely to use this setting.
>
> **Prompt Before Repairing** tells NDD to inform you of the error and ask whether you want to move the file to a safe area on the disk. This is the setting you will use most often.
>
> **Repair Automatically** makes the repair process as automatic as possible; bad sectors are moved without delay. Use it when you want to run NDD unattended.

An actual test screen is shown in Figure 16.5. Sectors in use by files are shown as a light box with a dark center, and unused sectors are shown as darker boxes. Bad sectors are marked with a **B**, and the actual area under examination is shown by a special character.

While the disk test is being made, an analog display shows the progress of the test (in percentage completed) at the bottom left of the screen (see Figure 16.5). The program updates this display as the test proceeds. The number of the sector currently being tested and the

> You can run NDD from a network drive, but you cannot use it to test a network file server.

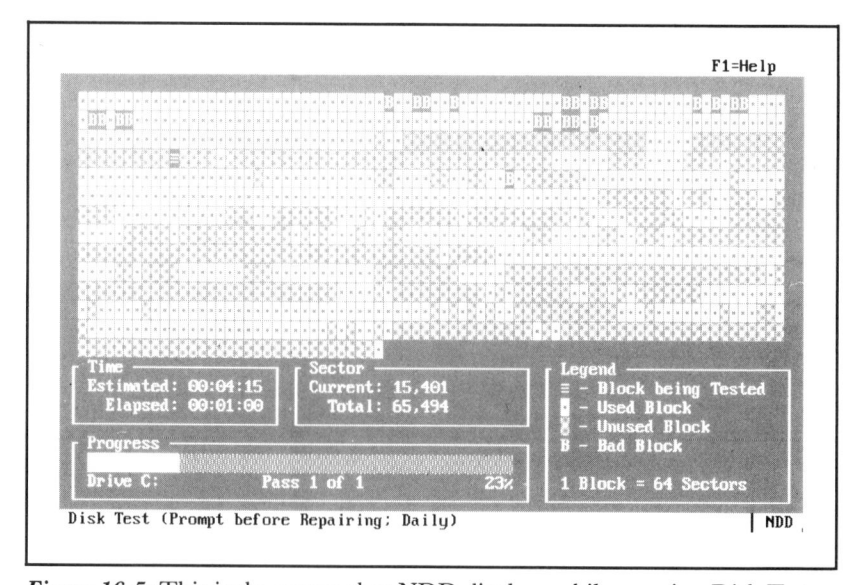

Figure 16.5: This is the screen that NDD displays while running Disk Test

DIAGNOSING AND FIXING DISK PROBLEMS 347

total number of sectors on the disk are shown on the screen. The estimated and elapsed times are also shown to give you an idea of how long this test will take. The disk test first checks the system area of the disk; then it checks the data area where your files and directories are located. Any errors encountered are displayed on the screen.

The names of any files found to contain unreadable clusters are displayed on the screen, along with an error message. If a data sector is found to be bad, but is not in use by a file, NDD marks it as bad so that it will not be available for use in the future. If a data sector is bad and is being used by a file, the program copies the file to a safe location on the disk, and the sector is marked as bad. Norton Disk Doctor displays the names of any files that it moves. You must check the list afterward to ensure that all your files are safe.

When the test is done, NDD lists the areas of the disk that were tested, along with the status of the test (see Figure 16.6). The test status codes include the following:

> A cluster already marked as bad is not usually an indication of a deteriorating disk; most hard disks have a small number of clusters containing sectors that are marked as bad by the low-level formatting program.

OK. No problems were found.

Fixed. A problem was found and fixed.

Not Fixed. A problem was found, but it was not fixed.

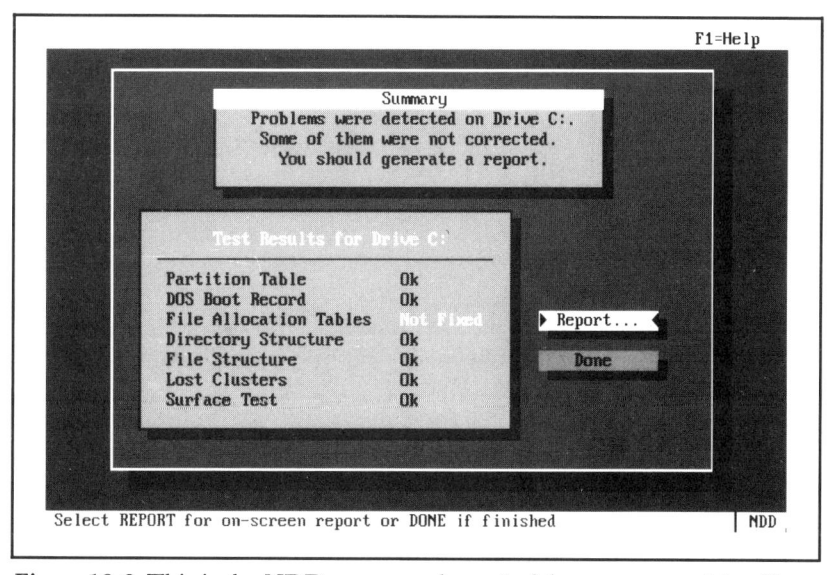

Figure 16.6: This is the NDD screen at the end of the test run on drive C

Skipped. The test was not performed.

Canceled. The test was interrupted and did not run to completion.

NDD also generates a tabulated report suitable for printing or capturing as a file, as shown in Figure 16.7. You can examine the report on the screen; just press the PgUp or PgDn keys to move through the report, or click on the scroll bars with the mouse. To print the report, select the Print box. If you don't have time to look at the report now, click the Save As box to save the report as a file. When the Save Report window opens, enter the name you want to save the report under. After the file is saved, another window opens to confirm that the report was written to the specified file name.

> Don't save the report to the same disk that you are testing: if the disk is in bad shape, you may never be able to load the report to read it.

REVERSING THE REPAIR WITH UNDO CHANGES

The Norton Disk Doctor contains a major advance in disk testing capability. Unlike other disk-repair programs, Norton Disk Doctor can actually *reverse* the repair process and remove the changes made during the repair cycle. Details of any changes made to a disk by NDD are saved in a file called NDDUNDO.DAT, located in the root directory. To restore the disk to its original condition, select Undo Changes from the main menu. When the disk selection window appears, choose the drive letter of the disk that contains NDDUNDO.DAT. Norton Disk Doctor uses its information to reverse the changes and return the disk to its original condition.

CUSTOMIZING THE NORTON DISK DOCTOR

The Options selection from the main Norton Disk Doctor window, shown in Figure 16.8, configures the program to your own requirements. Three selections are available: Surface Test, Custom Message, and Tests to Skip.

DIAGNOSING AND FIXING DISK PROBLEMS   349

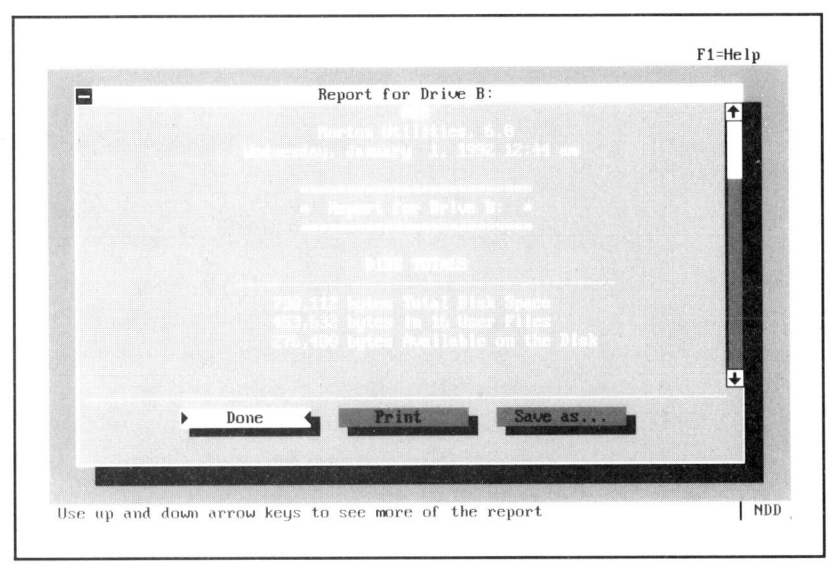

Figure 16.7: NDD's report for a 720K floppy disk

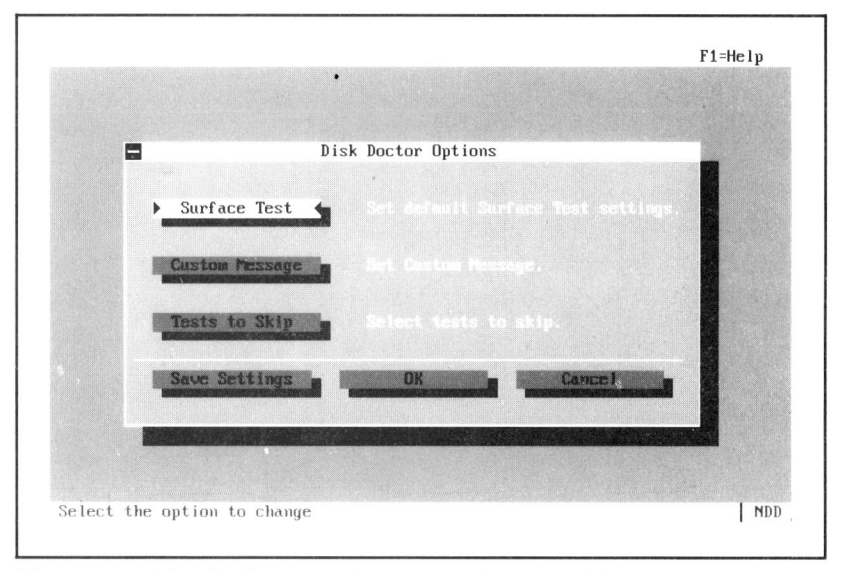

Figure 16.8: The Options selection screen, for customizing the program

DETERMINING THE SURFACE TEST

Select this option to enter your choices for the Surface Test. This screen is exactly the same as the screen shown in Figure 16.4. Make your selections from Test, Test Type, Passes, and Repair Settings.

MAKING A CUSTOM MESSAGE

If you are a network manager or are in charge of several computers in a department, you will find the Custom Message selection very useful. Here you can enter a message that Norton Disk Doctor will display if the program finds an error in the system area of a disk. Because this is the most important part of a disk, you might not want your users to proceed with repairs on their own. So you could enter a message that included your name, department name, and extension number, as shown in Figure 16.9.

After you have entered the text, press the F2 function key to set the display attribute of your message. Choose from Normal, Reverse, Bold, or Underline. This will add even more impact to your message. Don't forget to check the Prompt with Custom Message box, and

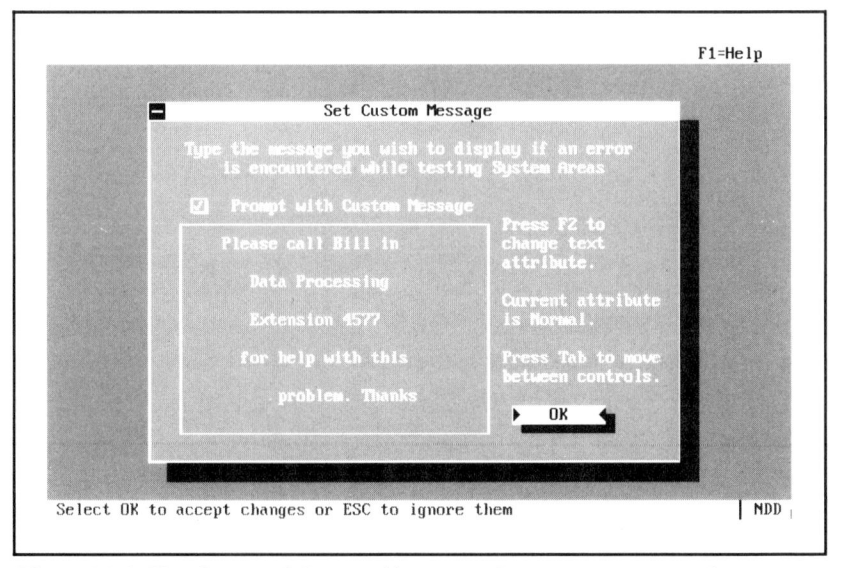

Figure 16.9: Use Custom Message if you are the system manager for a group of computers

then save this message by choosing or clicking on the Save Settings box in the Disk Doctor Options window.

After you have saved your custom message, the user's only option when NDD detects an error is to choose the Cancel Test button at the bottom of the screen. There is no way to continue with the NDD tests.

DECIDING WHICH TESTS TO SKIP

The Tests to Skip selection provides more configuration choices so that you can customize the program even further. This is particularly useful if your computer is not truly IBM-compatible. There are four options in Tests to Skip, as Figure 16.10 shows:

>**Skip Partition Tests.** If you use nonstandard hard disk partition software, Norton Disk Doctor might not recognize your partitions. Check this selection to turn off the partition table tests.
>
>**Skip CMOS Tests.** If your CMOS settings are nonstandard, check this selection to turn off the CMOS tests. (See Chapter 12 for more details about CMOS.)
>
>**Skip Surface Tests.** If you never plan to use the Surface Test, select this option. I recommend that you *not* check this box; the Surface Test is one of the program's most useful features and you should not ignore it.
>
>**Only 1 Hard Disk.** Check this box if your computer consistently reports that you have two hard disks when you know you only have one. For example, if you use an AT&T 6300, NDD will find two hard disks even though the computer only contains one. This is a problem with the computer, not a problem with Norton Disk Doctor.

When you have finished making your selections, save them by highlighting the Save Settings box and pressing Enter, or by clicking on the box with the mouse. The next time you run Norton Disk Doctor, the selections you just saved will be loaded into the program automatically. This way you don't have to reconfigure the program each time you run it.

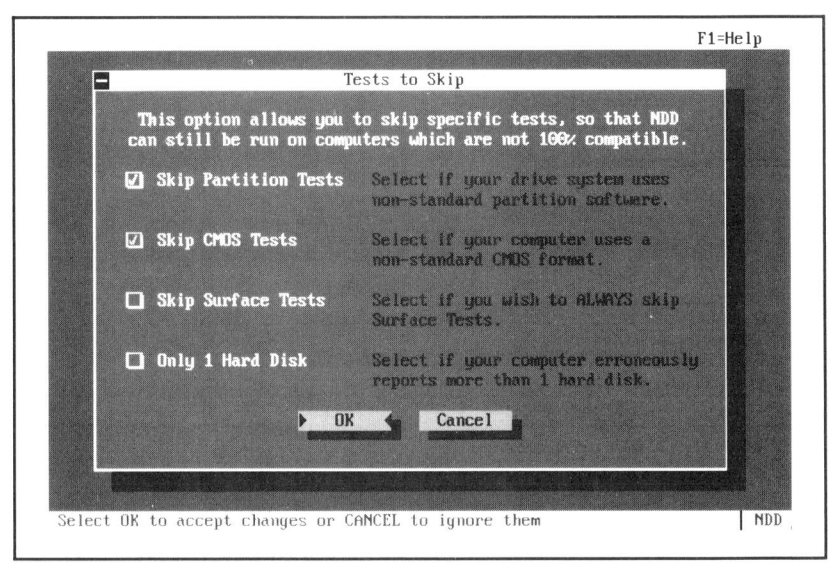

Figure 16.10: The Tests to Skip screen lets you configure NDD to your particular computer hardware

QUITTING THE NORTON DISK DOCTOR

The final menu selection is Quit Disk Doctor. Use this selection to return to DOS when you have finished running the Norton Disk Doctor.

UNDERSTANDING DISK ERRORS

If Norton Disk Doctor discovers an increasing number of errors, you should replace or repair your hard disk as soon as possible. How critical an error is depends on where the bad sector is on your disk. If the error is in the system area of the disk, the area containing the boot record, the FAT, or the root directory, you may lose all the data on the disk. In the case of a hard disk, this can represent a great deal of data. (This is another reason to be sure that your floppy-disk backups are always up to date.) If the bad sector contains the boot record, the hard disk may refuse to boot.

If NDD reports errors on a floppy disk, try cleaning the disk heads; then reformat the disk and run NDD on it again to see whether the problems have cleared up. If that does not work, throw the disk away. *Never* use a dubious disk as a backup disk for archive storage; make your backups on error-free disks and replace them periodically. When you need to reload your system from your backup disks, you can't afford to have any errors!

RUNNING NORTON DISK DOCTOR FROM THE DOS COMMAND LINE

You can also run the Norton Disk Doctor from the DOS prompt with one of two switches: /C (complete) tests every sector on the disk, and /Q (quick) tests only the system area of the disk. To run NDD on drive C without the data sector tests, type:

NDD C: /Q

(If you include the above line in your AUTOEXEC.BAT file, NDD will perform a brief analysis of your hard disk every time you boot up your computer.) To run NDD on drive C and test the entire data area, type:

NDD C: /C

> If you are working with a badly damaged disk, use NDD in full-screen mode rather than from the DOS command line.

The other command-line switches you can use with the Norton Disk Doctor are as follows:

/R:*filename*	sends the NDD report to the file specified by *filename*
/RA:*filename*	appends the NDD report to the file specified by *filename*
/X:*drive*	excludes the drive specified by *drive* from physical testing
/REBUILD	rebuilds an entire disk after it has been damaged

/SKIPHIGH   does not load the program into DOS 5 high memory

/UNDELETE   restores a DOS partition that you previously skipped

Unlike the Norton Disk Doctor for Windows, which can only find disk-related problems, NDD finds *and* fixes most problems you are likely to encounter. It fixes bad or corrupted partition tables, bad or missing boot records, and a corrupted BIOS Parameter Block. In the area of file-structure problems, Norton Disk Doctor repairs bad or corrupted file allocation tables, reconstructs cross-linked files, and fixes physical problems that prevent you from reading directories or files. Finally, NDD can reverse any changes that were made during the repair process and return the disk to its original state.

SEVENTEEN

Optimizing Your Disk Drives

FILES ARE WRITTEN TO YOUR DISKS IN A UNIT OF disk space known as a *cluster*. When you write a short file to a disk, it occupies the first available cluster. When you write another short file to the same disk, it occupies the next available cluster. Now if you modify the first file by increasing its size above one cluster and save it under the same file name, DOS cannot push the second file "up the disk" to make room for the larger first file. Instead, DOS has to *fragment* the first file by splitting it into two pieces, one occupying the first cluster (as before) and one occupying the *third* cluster. This is the way that DOS was designed to work.

The potential problem with such file fragmentation is that the disk heads have to move to different locations on the disk to read or write to a fragmented file. This takes more time than reading the same file from a series of consecutive clusters. By reducing or eliminating fragmentation, you can increase the performance of your disk substantially.

Another benefit of unfragmenting a disk is that DOS is less likely to fragment files that you subsequently add to the disk. Should you delete and then try to unerase any of these added files, your chances of success will be higher because unfragmented files are usually easier to unerase. On the other hand, unfragmenting, or *optimizing*, your disk will probably make it impossible to recover any files that were deleted before the optimization. The reason for this is that Speed Disk "moves" data by rewriting them to new locations, and so will probably write over any erased files in the process.

To remove the effects of file fragmentation, all the files on the disk must be rearranged so that they fill consecutive clusters. You can do this yourself by backing up all your files using Norton Backup for Windows, reformatting the hard disk, and reloading all the files back onto the hard disk—but that would be a tremendous amount of tedious work. It is much easier to use a program designed for eliminating file fragmentation—the Norton Speed Disk utility.

> If you need to recover erased files, do so *before* you unfragment a disk with Speed Disk.

PRECAUTIONS TO TAKE BEFORE RUNNING SPEED DISK ON YOUR HARD DISK

Before you have Speed Disk actually reorganize the files on your disk, you must take a few precautions:

> Be sure to use Norton Backup for Windows to make the full hard-disk backup.

- Back up your hard disk completely, in case your system and the Speed Disk utility are incompatible. Problems sometimes occur because of the enormous number of potential combinations of disks and disk controllers.

- Do not turn off your computer while Speed Disk is running. The only safe way to interrupt Speed Disk is by pressing the Escape key. Speed Disk will not stop working immediately but will continue to run until it reaches a convenient, safe point in which to do so.

- Be sure to disable any memory-resident software that might access the disk while Speed Disk is running. For example, some programs save your work to the hard disk at set time intervals. This type of software must be turned off.

- If you are using the DOS FASTOPEN utility or any other disk-buffering program, turn it off before running Speed Disk. Because Speed Disk changes directory and file locations on the disk when it optimizes the disk, FASTOPEN might not find the files where it expects to find them. If DOS displays the message **File not found** after you run Speed Disk, reboot your computer and try again.

> The Norton Disk Doctor is discussed in Chapter 16.

- Run the DOS CHKDSK command to remove any lost clusters and run the Norton Disk Doctor to find and fix any bad sectors on your disk. This gives Speed Disk a clean system to work with.

UNFRAGMENTING YOUR HARD DISK WITH SPEED DISK

Start Speed Disk from the DOS prompt by typing **SPEEDISK**. The program starts with the display shown in Figure 17.1.

OPTIMIZING YOUR DISK DRIVES   359

■ Although Speed Disk reports on specific files and directories, you cannot unfragment selected files or directories.

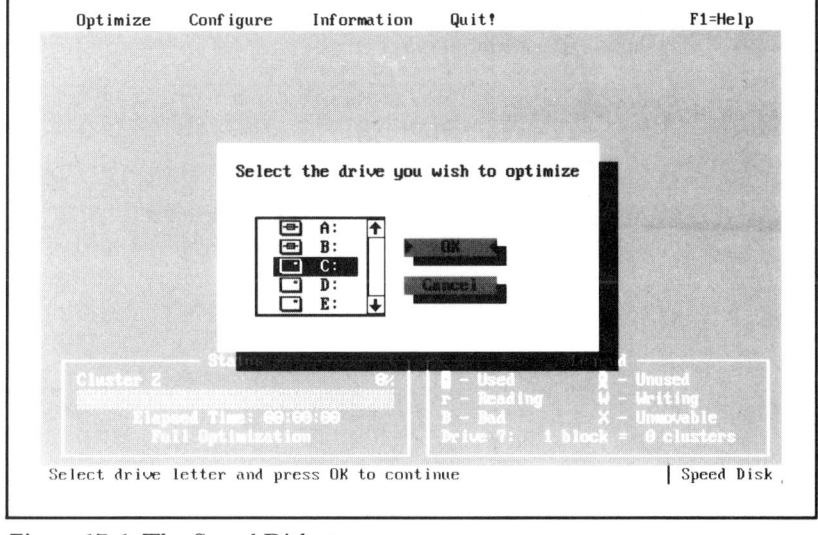

Figure 17.1: The Speed Disk startup screen

■ You cannot use Speed Disk on a network drive.

■ Speed Disk is smart enough to know when optimization is not needed and will display the message **No Optimization Necessary.**

Select the drive letter of the disk you want to optimize and press Enter, or double-click on the drive letter with the mouse. After Speed Disk reads and analyzes the data on the chosen drive, it visually displays memory usage and informs you which level of optimization is required. Figure 17.2 shows this display for a 33MB hard disk.

In Figure 17.2, Speed Disk shows the percentage of fragmentation for the 33MB hard disk and recommends an optimization method based on this percentage. The two boxes on the screen give you the choice of optimizing your disk or configuring Speed Disk. The first time you run Speed Disk, press the Escape key to go to the Configure menu. After you have examined all the possible options you can run the optimization.

The Legend box, at the lower-right corner of the screen, defines the graphic characters used to make the disk-usage map. The characters represent the following elements:

- The "used block" character designates the area of the disk currently occupied by files. It represents all the directories and files in the data area of the disk.

- The "unused block" character designates the area of the disk occupied by clusters but not allocated to files. Speed

```
                Optimize    Configure    Information    Quit!              F1=Help
```

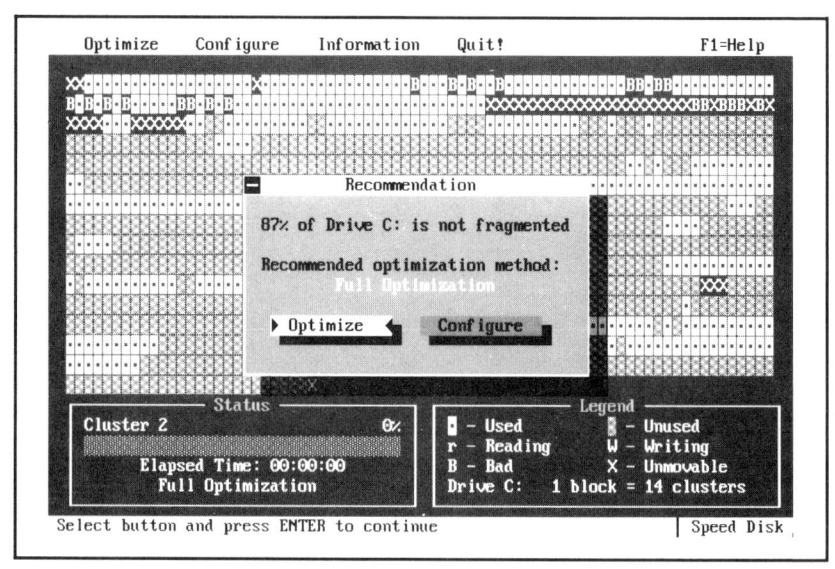

Figure 17.2: A Speed Disk map for drive C

Disk can consolidate this space and make it available as part of the unused disk space at the end of the files' area on the disk.

- The "bad block" character—a **B**—represents any bad blocks on the disk. Note that Figure 17.2 shows a disk with several bad blocks.

- The "unmovable block" character—an **X**—marks the position of any files or directories that Speed Disk cannot move. The **X** characters in the upper-left corner of the display in Figure 17.2 represent the hidden DOS system files. To avoid interfering with copy-protection schemes, Speed Disk does not move hidden files.

Depending on the size of the current disk, each one of these above characters represents a specific amount of disk space. In Figure 17.2 each character happens to represent 14 clusters.

The Status box at the lower left of the screen displays Speed Disk's progress after you start the optimization. The current cluster number and percentage-complete value are shown as numbers, along with the optimization type and the time that has elapsed so far. The horizontal bar displays the percentage of the operation completed.

CHOOSING THE RIGHT OPTIMIZATION METHOD

Speed Disk provides menus to let you configure the program and make the appropriate optimization selection. Selecting the Optimize menu displays three selections:

Begin Optimization (Alt-B) This begins the process of unfragmenting the drive. Don't select this option until you're sure that all the other options are set correctly.

> Don't start optimizing until you're sure that all options are set correctly.

Drive This lets you switch to another drive. It opens a window that is similar to the initial drive selection screen you used when Speed Disk first started. Use the arrow keys to highlight a new drive letter or type in the drive letter and press Enter. With the mouse, simply double-click on the new drive letter.

Optimization Method This lets you choose the type of optimization that Speed Disk will run on your disk. When you select this choice, the Select Optimization Method window opens, as shown in Figure 17.3. Choose the method that is best suited to your disk and the way you work with your system; you don't always have to use the same method every time. Here you can select one of the following radio buttons:

Full Optimization unfragments all your files, but does not move directories or files selected in the Files to Place First list. This option runs very quickly; when it is complete, there will be no unused areas of disk space between your files.

Full with DIR's First unfragments your files and moves directories to the front of the disk.

Full with File Reorder is the most complete option available in Speed Disk; it performs a complete optimization of your hard

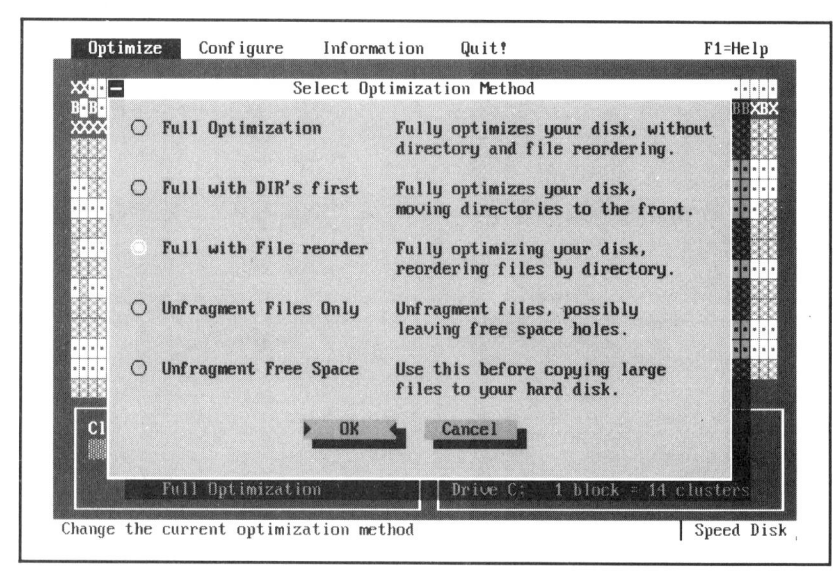

Figure 17.3: You choose Speed Disk's optimization method in this window

disk. It takes the longest to run, but also provides the greatest speed increase afterwards.

Unfragment Files Only unfragments all the files that it can, but may leave some unused space between files when it is complete. Some large files may remain fragmented even after Speed Disk has finished.

Unfragment Free Space moves files to fill the unused space left between them, but does not actually unfragment any files. You can use this selection to create a single large block of free space before you install a new software package.

CONFIGURING SPEED DISK

The Configure menu, shown in Figure 17.4, contains six options to complete the optimization setup:

Directory Order This selection lets you manipulate the order in which Speed Disk arranges the directories. You do this by working with a graphic display of the disk's directory, as shown in Figure 17.5. The

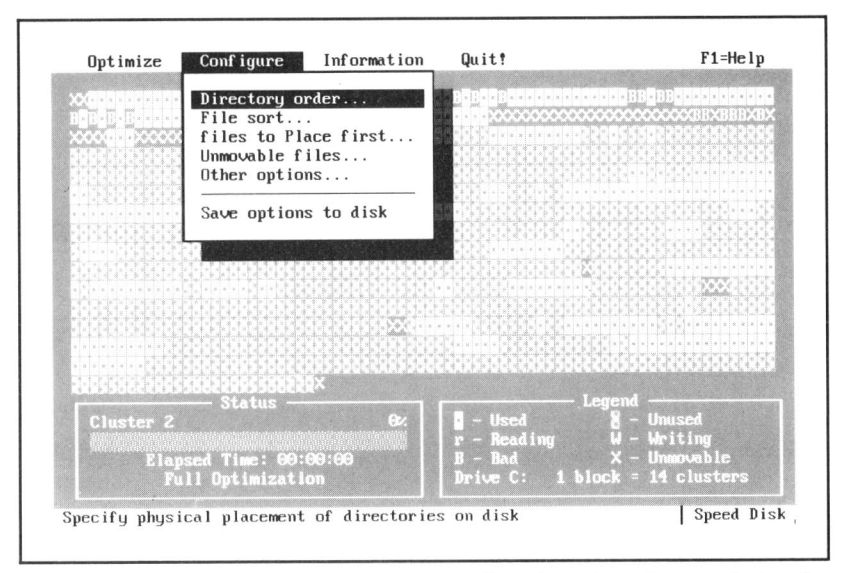

Figure 17.4: Speed Disk's Configure menu offers six options for completing the optimization setup

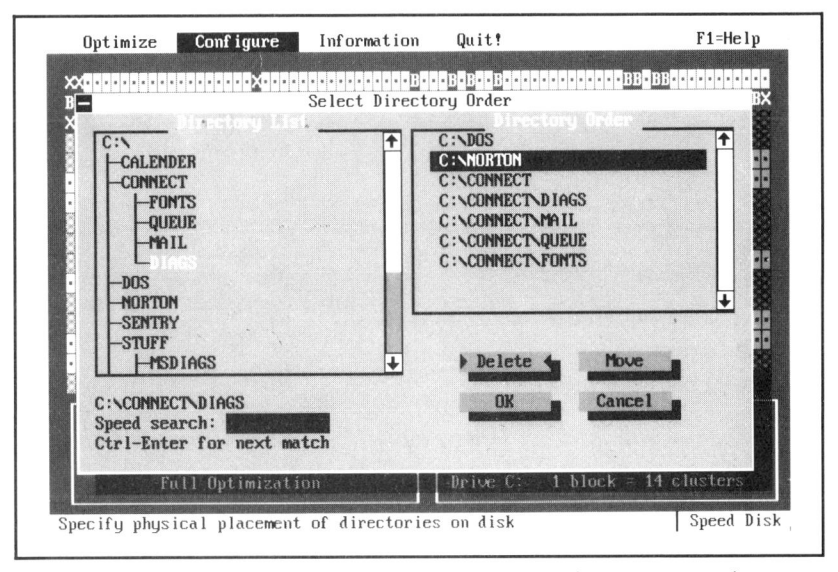

Figure 17.5: The Select Directory Order window lets you organize your directories

window is divided into two parts: the Directory List shows all the directories on your disk in a graphical form, and Directory Order shows the sequence in which the directories are arranged. The default directory order is taken from the path you established in your AUTOEXEC-.BAT file. To select a directory from the Directory List, use the up and down arrow keys to highlight the directory name and then press Enter or click on the Add box. You will see the directory name appear at the top of the list in the Directory Order display. You can also use the Speed Search box to move directly to a specific directory. Just type in enough letters to make the entry unique and Speed Disk will automatically select the right directory. Press the Ctrl and Enter keys together to move to the next match if you have several directories with very similar names.

Use the left and right arrows to move between the two windows. The Directory Order display provides more options:

Delete. To delete a directory from the Directory Order screen, highlight its name, move the cursor to the Delete box with the Tab key, and press Enter.

Move. To move a directory, highlight the name and press ↑ or ↓ to place the directory at a new location. Press Enter to confirm the position of the directory.

OK. When you are satisfied with the placement of directories, select OK to return to the main Speed Disk screen.

File Sort   Use this selection to specify the order in which you want your files arranged. The File Sort window is shown in Figure 17.6. File Sort arranges your files according to the selection in the Sort Criterion list. You can sort by name, extension, date and time, and file size—in ascending or descending order. You can also leave them unsorted. (Unsorted does not change the order of your files; it leaves them exactly where they are.) Select OK after you have made your choice.

Files to Place First   This lets you choose which files to put at the "front" or outer edge of the disk. Use this option to position your program files, which do *not* change in size, close to the FAT. The first time this window opens it contains two file specifications: *.EXE and

> Putting program files near the outer edge of the disk can help prevent further fragmentation.

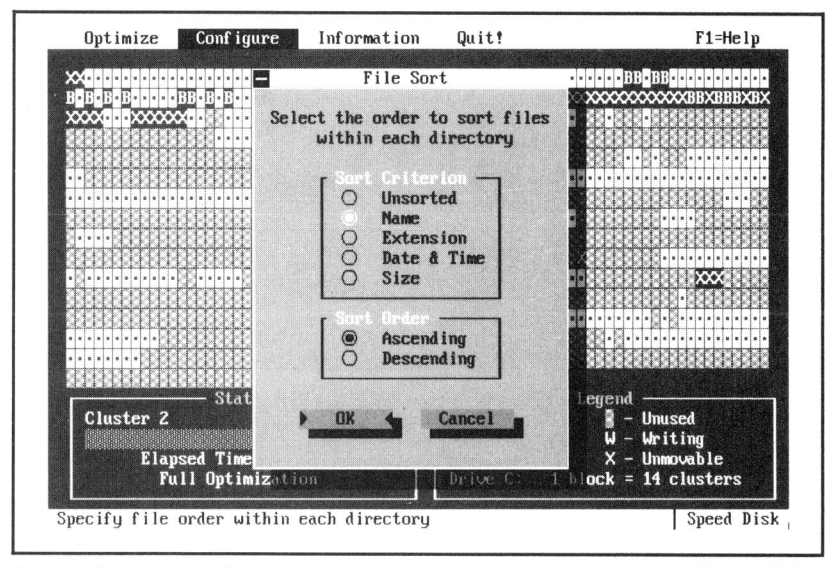

Figure 17.6: The File Sort window lets you choose how your files will be arranged

*.COM. Position your data files, which *do* change size when you modify them, after your program files. This arrangement avoids future file fragmentation by preventing space from opening up near the outer edge of the disk. The Files to Place First window is shown in Figure 17.7.

You can use wildcards to help relocate files. For example, to relocate all .EXE files, you would type *.**EXE** into the highlighted box. Use the Delete, Insert, and Move boxes to rearrange the entries in the list:

Delete. To remove an entry from the list, highlight the entry, move the cursor to the Delete box, and press Enter.

Insert. To insert a new entry, highlight the entry immediately below where you want to make the insertion, move the cursor to the Insert box, and press Enter. A blank space opens for you to add the new file specification.

Move. To move an entry, place the highlight over the entry, position the cursor in the Move box, and press Enter. Use the

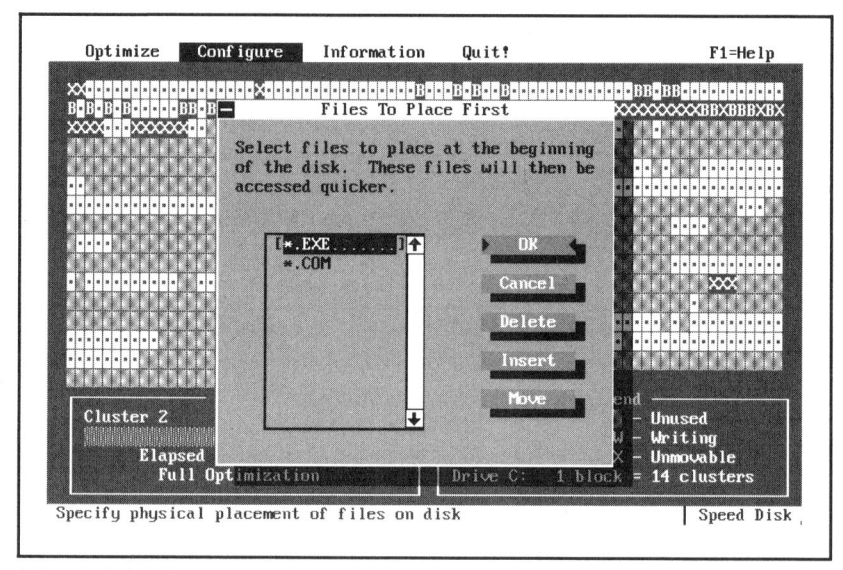

Figure 17.7: The Files to Place First window lets you position files where you want them

up and down arrow keys to move the entry to its new location and press Enter.

After you have completed your entries, select OK to return to the Configure menu on the main Speed Disk screen.

Unmovable Files Use this selection to enter the names of files that you do not want to be moved during optimization. This window holds only ten entries, but you can use the DOS wildcard characters to extend the selection to more than ten files.

Other Options This selection includes three options:

> You can choose more than one option from this list.

Read-After-Write. By default, Speed Disk uses this setting as a check for the optimization process. However, because it is such a rigorous check, it can take up to twice as long to perform the checks as the next selection.

Clear Unused Space. Speed Disk can wipe clean all areas of the disk that are not being used to store files or directories. The Clear Unused Space option writes zeros into all the unused clusters on the disk during the optimization process.

Beep When Done. Speed Disk will sound a tone when the optimization is complete.

Save Options to Disk   This selection saves the options you have chosen to a small hidden file (called SD.INI) in the root directory of the disk you are optimizing, and returns you to the main Speed Disk screen. The next time you run Speed Disk, these configuration options are loaded from the SD.INI file and used as the default startup settings.

SPEED DISK INFORMATION

The selections in the Information menu let you look at fragmentation and disk statistics:

Fragmentation Report   Choose this to check the degree to which a file, directory, or disk is fragmented before you decide whether to start the file reorganization process. Daily and weekly file fragmentation reports show you how fragmentation on your disk is changing over time and tell you how often you should run Speed Disk to get the best results.

The report is shown in Figure 17.8. The left side of the File Fragmentation Report window shows a graphical display of your directory structure and the right side shows the files in the directory. As you use the arrow keys to change to a different directory in the left window, the file display changes to show the files in the new directory. You can also use Speed Search to enter a directory name. A "percent unfragmented" figure is given for each file in the directory. A value of 100 percent means that the file is not fragmented and that all its clusters are consecutive. A value lower than 100 percent signifies some degree of fragmentation in the file. Fragmented files are bulleted and shown in a different color in the file list.

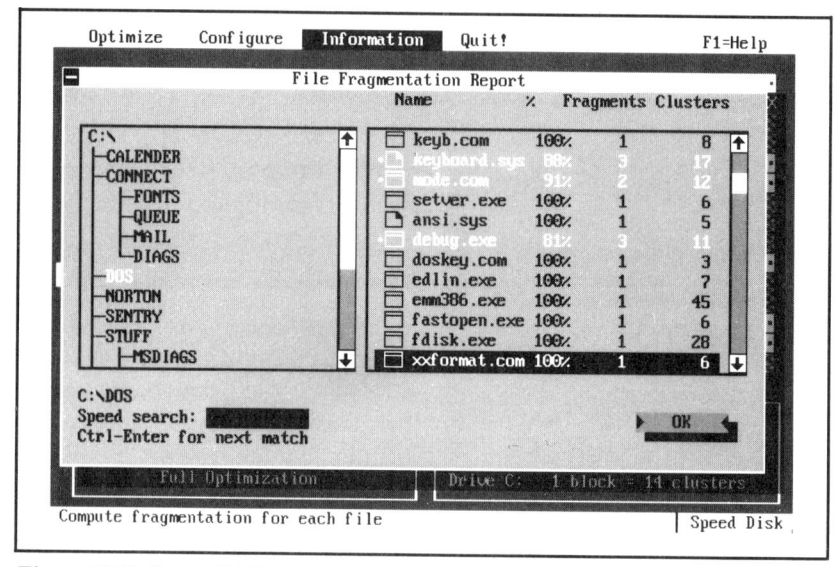

Figure 17.8: Speed Disk reports the percentage of fragmentation for all files in the directory

This window also shows the number of fragments into which each file or directory is broken, as well as the total number of clusters that the file or directory occupies. File names are shown in lowercase letters and directory names in uppercase letters.

Select OK to return to the main Speed Disk screen. The other selections in the Information menu provide useful information about files and disks:

Disk Statistics This provides detailed information about the drive you selected for optimization. Figure 17.9 shows the statistics for a 33MB hard disk, including disk size, amount of the disk used, number of files and directories, and percentage of unfragmented files. Also shown are details about the clusters allocated to movable and unmovable files, the clusters allocated to directories, the number of bad clusters, and the total number of clusters on the disk.

Map Legend This selection opens an information window that shows the characters used on the disk map display while the disk is being optimized. This window, shown in Figure 17.10, is more

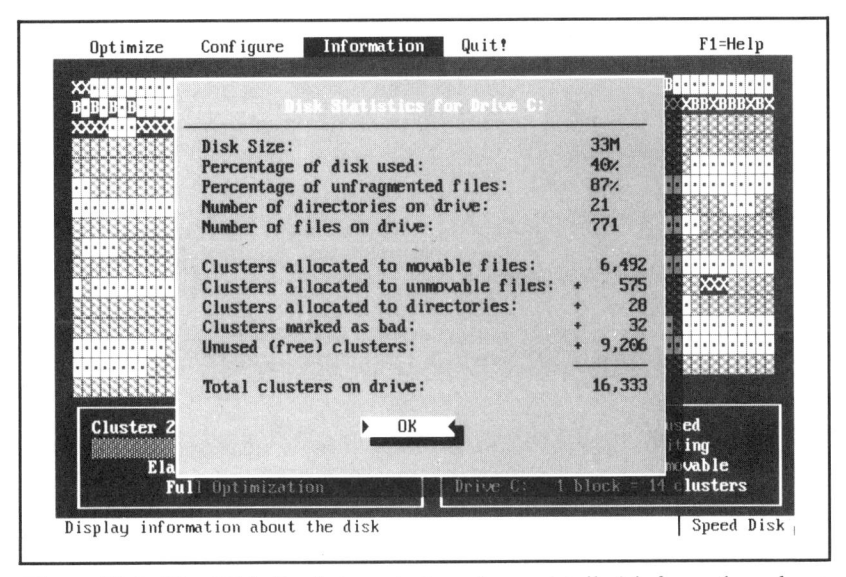

Figure 17.9: The Disk Statistics window shows detailed information about drive C

Figure 17.10: The Disk Map Legend shows the characters used during the optimization process

detailed than the Legend box displayed on the main Speed Disk screen. As the optimization proceeds, you will see different characters on the screen, each one representing a different part of the process. Disk space in use by files or directories is indicated by the block with a dot in the center, while unused disk space is represented by an unfilled block. Bad blocks are represented by a **B** and clusters occupied by unmovable files are marked with an **X**. An **r** shows the area of the disk currently being read, a **W** shows clusters being written, and a **V** shows that the data are being verified. If you selected Clear Unused Space under Other Options in the Configure menu, you would see a **C** to indicate clearing.

> The PC-DOS names for these two files are IBMBIOS.COM and IMBDOS.COM.

Show Static Files This selection opens the Static Files window, which lists all the files that Speed Disk cannot move, as shown in Figure 17.11. Figure 17.11 shows the DOS system files, IO.SYS and MSDOS.SYS, listed in the Static Files window along with several other files. These two files are position-sensitive; since they must be at a specific location on your disk, Speed Disk will not move them.

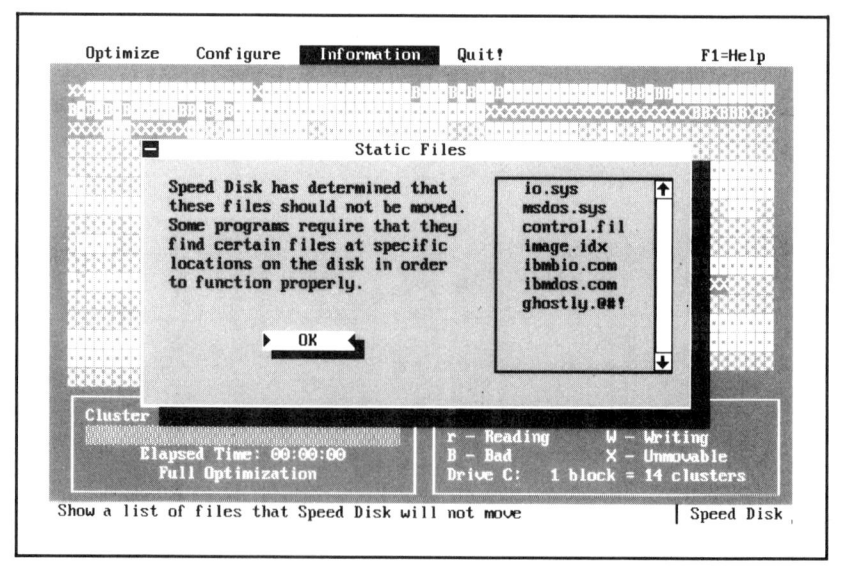

Figure 17.11: The Static Files window lists files that will not be moved during the optimization

Walk Map   This selection lets you use the arrow keys to move around the disk map and display which files occupy which locations on your disk. The cluster range represented by the block character under the cursor is shown at the lower left of the disk map screen. When you find an area of the disk you want to look at more closely, press Enter to open the Contents of Map Block window, as shown in Figure 17.12. If you use a mouse, just click on the area of the disk you want to examine.

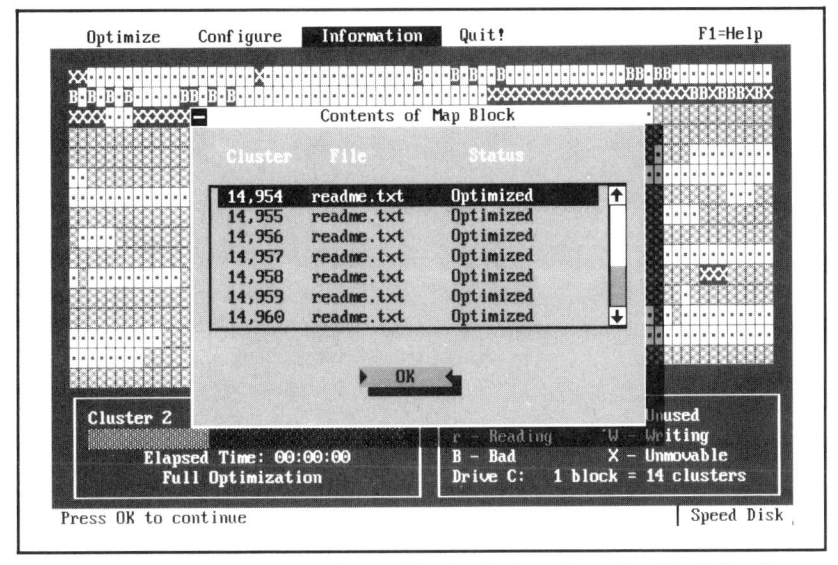

Figure 17.12: The Contents of Map Block window gives details of the chosen cluster range

The window includes three columns of information: Cluster, File, and Status. The Cluster column lists the cluster numbers, the File column displays the name of the file that occupies that cluster, and the Status column indicates whether the file is fragmented or optimized. You might also see a cluster labeled as "bad," "unmovable," or simply "not used."

Use the arrow keys or PgUp and PgDn to move through the display, or click on the scroll bars with the mouse. Press Enter to return to the Walk Map, and press the Escape key to return to the main Speed Disk screen.

Quit This returns you to the Norton shell program or back to DOS, depending on the method you used to start Speed Disk.

RUNNING SPEED DISK

When you are sure that all the options have been set correctly, choose Begin Optimization from the Optimize menu to start the process. Speed Disk unfragments the selected item(s), collecting all the free space and placing it at the end of the used blocks. The disk usage map shows you this process as Speed Disk works. As data are read from the disk, the r character moves across the screen. When they are rewritten to the disk, W is used to indicate writing. If you turn the Verify option on, V indicates the progress of the verification process. A C represents unused disk space that is being cleared.

You can press the Escape key if you want to interrupt Speed Disk, but Speed Disk might not stop instantly—it will take a few moments to complete the current operation and tidy up before stopping.

Speed Disk beeps when it is finished. This means you can focus your attention on more important work during the entire process and still know when the optimization is complete.

> Optimization can take a long time, especially if you are unfragmenting an entire disk. Monitor the Status box to get an idea of how long the entire process will take. Press the Escape key if you need to stop the optimization.

SPEED DISK AND COPY-PROTECTION SCHEMES

Some copy-protection methods that rely on hidden files insist that the hidden files stay in exactly the same place on the disk. For example, Lotus 1-2-3 Version 2.01 does this. If your copy-protection method uses hidden files and you move them to another location on the disk, your application program will often refuse to work—it thinks you are using an illegal copy. Speed Disk recognizes this problem and does not move hidden files in case moving them interferes with the copy-protection system. In fact, Speed Disk goes further than this: it will not move any .EXE file that does not have a standard file header. All such files are left alone. Also, Speed Disk will not move the hidden files—IBMBIO.COM and IBMDOS.COM, or IO.SYS and MSDOS.SYS—that DOS places at the beginning of all bootable disks. Even so, the only way to be *absolutely* sure that Speed

Disk will not interfere with a copy-protection scheme is to remove the software package completely before running Speed Disk, and then reinstall it after Speed Disk is finished.

RUNNING SPEED DISK FROM THE DOS PROMPT

If you run Speed Disk from the DOS prompt, you can take advantage of some of the special Speed Disk switches. For example, if you want to use the Unfragment Free Space option to collect all the free space on your C drive into one large piece, you can do so by typing

SPEEDISK C: /Q

from the DOS prompt. Speed Disk runs the optimization automatically, without any prompting. Many of these command-line switches are very powerful:

/B	reboots the computer when the optimization process is complete
/F	performs a full optimization
/FD	performs a full optimization, placing directories first
/FF	performs a full optimization, reordering files
/U	unfragments files only
/V	turns on the read-after-write verification. Each portion of each file is read and verified after it has been written to the disk
/SKIPHIGH	does not load into high memory

If you want to sort your files during the optimization process, use the following switches:

/SN	sorts files by name
/SE	sorts files by extension

/SD   sorts files by date

/SS   sorts files by size

You can reverse the sort order (making the sort descending) if you add a minus sign after the sort key letter. For example, /SN- instead of /SN.

EIGHTEEN

Recovering Files and Data

THIS CHAPTER CONCENTRATES ON TWO DIFFERENT aspects of data recovery: unerasing deleted files and rebuilding a hard disk after it has been reformatted accidentally. The last part of the chapter describes ways to minimize damage to floppy and hard disks.

Deleting files is easy, sometimes far too easy! You can easily find yourself carelessly ignoring the Desktop's warning screens and quickly erasing one file too many in your haste to get on to another task, for instance. If you use the * wildcard in a DEL operation from the DOS command line, you might specify more files than you intended and end up deleting too many files, maybe even the entire contents of a directory. Careful disk organization can help prevent some of these accidental erasures, but no matter how good your organization is, sooner or later you will accidentally erase a file or want to recover a file that you erased intentionally. If you can't recover the file using Norton Desktop and SmartErase, then this is where the UnErase program on the Emergency Disk comes into play. The program is famous for its ability to restore deleted files.

WHAT REALLY HAPPENS WHEN YOU DELETE A FILE?

When you delete a file, its bookkeeping entries are cleared from the file allocation table. DOS also changes the first character of the file name to a lowercase Greek sigma (ASCII E5 hex or 229 decimal) to indicate to the rest of the DOS commands that the file has been erased. However, the file's entry, including its starting location on the disk and its length, remain in their directory, hidden from view by DOS's inclusion of the sigma character in the file name. The data in the file itself remain in their original location on the disk. No data are erased until DOS writes another file on top of the original information on the disk. Thus a file can be found and recovered quite easily, as long as it has not been overwritten.

WHAT HAPPENS WHEN YOU SAVE A FILE?

> To learn how to reduce file fragmentation, see the discussion of the Speed Disk program in Chapter 17.

When you add a new file to your disk, DOS looks for the next available area of free disk space. If the file is small enough to fit into this space, DOS simply inserts it. However, if the file is larger, DOS splits it up into several pieces, recording it into areas on the disk that are not numbered consecutively. In other words, the file becomes *fragmented*.

Thus, saving a new file on the disk can destroy or overwrite some or all of a deleted file's data. If the new file is larger than the old one, the old file will be gone completely. If the new file is smaller than the old one, some unknown amount of the old file will remain on the disk until it is finally overwritten during a future write-to-disk operation.

The most important point to remember about file recovery is that you must not save anything on a disk until *after* you have completed the recovery operation. Do not even install the Norton Desktop for Windows on to your hard disk; instead, you should run UnErase directly from the Emergency Disk. Only install the complete Desktop package onto your hard disk after the recovery is completely finished. By following this advice, you will not overwrite the erased file's data and you will increase your chances of a successful recovery.

USING UNERASE TO RECOVER DELETED FILES

If the deleted file is a short file or is on a floppy disk, there is an excellent chance that UnErase will be able to restore it on the first attempt. If the file is badly fragmented, or part of it has been overwritten by another file, the chances of a complete recovery are substantially less.

To demonstrate how UnErase works, we will create a small text file, delete it, and then recover it using UnErase from the Emergency

RECOVERING FILES AND DATA 379

Disk. Follow these steps:

1. Create a small Windows Notepad file that contains the text:

   This is a short section of text.

2. Choose Save As from the Notepad File menu to call the file MYFILE.TXT, and check the Text Only box to save the file as a text file.

3. Return to the Norton Desktop, click on the drive icon that contains this new file, and drag the file to the SmartErase icon to delete it.

To run UnErase, exit Windows and type

UNERASE A:

at the DOS prompt. The main UnErase screen is shown in Figure 18.1.

In the center of the screen you can see information for any deleted files in this directory. Notice, however, that the screen shows the first character of the file name as a **?**. This reminds you that UnErase does not know what that first character should be (recall that DOS

> UnErase can recover deleted files from a network drive only if Erase Protect is installed for that drive.

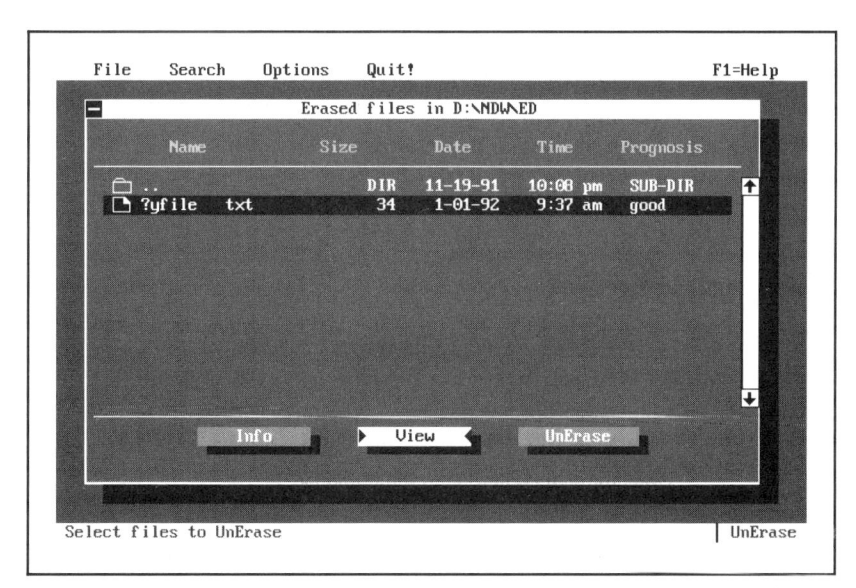

Figure 18.1: The main UnErase screen lists information about deleted files

CH. 18

> You will always be able to recover a file protected by the Erase Protect utility, mentioned in Chapter 11.

replaced this character with a sigma), so you will have to supply the original character during the next part of the recovery process. (If you are using Erase Protect, you will see the complete file name, with no missing letters.) Also in the display you can see the file size, creation date and time, and prognosis for recovery.

To see more information about MYFILE.TXT, choose the Info box below the main window. This displays a screen similar to the one shown in Figure 18.2, which shows the file name, creation time and date, as well as the file size in bytes, and the file attributes. All of this information helps you to identify this file as the correct file to unerase. The recovery prognosis is shown, along with the starting cluster number and the total number of clusters in the file. Clusters are the disk-allocation units that DOS uses when it stores files. A cluster represents the smallest single area of disk space that DOS can read from or write to at any given time. UnErase describes the chances of recovery of a file as excellent, good, average, or poor. (This column also might display the messages **Not Applicable**, **Recovered**, or **DIR**, depending on the status of the recovery process.)

UnErase also displays a short message describing the current status of the file. This message may be relatively optimistic about the

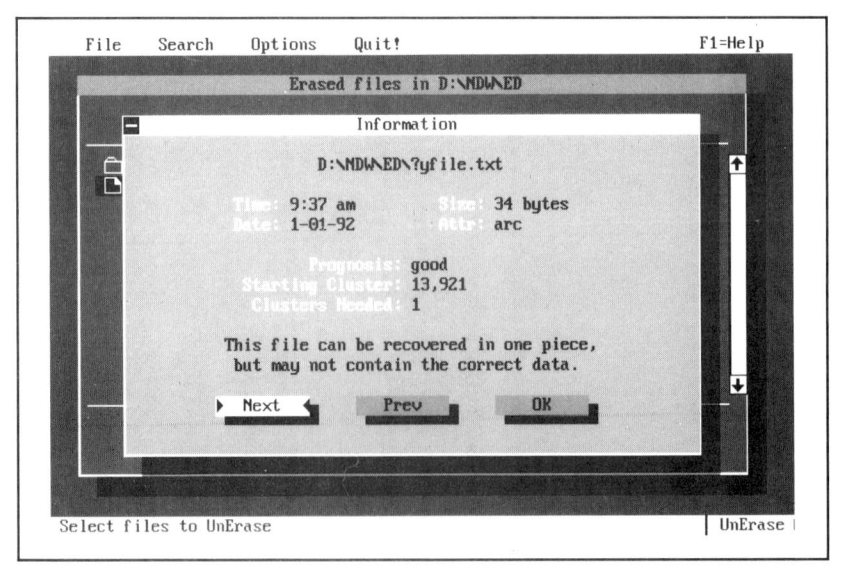

Figure 18.2: The Information screen displays details about the deleted file

recovery, such as:

> This file can be recovered in one piece,
> but may not contain the correct data.

or rather more ominous, as in the following case:

> The first cluster of this file
> is now being used by another file.

The message is directly related to the entry in the prognosis column.

Choose View to look at the contents of the file as text or in hexadecimal. For the sample MYFILE.TXT, you will see a display similar to the one shown in Figure 18.3. The View selection shows that the original data are still on the disk. Select Text or Hex to change the format of the display. The hexadecimal view shows the numeric values of the bytes on the left and the equivalent ASCII characters on the right. Figure 18.3 shows the file in hexadecimal view. Select the Next or Previous boxes to examine other deleted files on the disk, or select OK to return to the main UnErase screen.

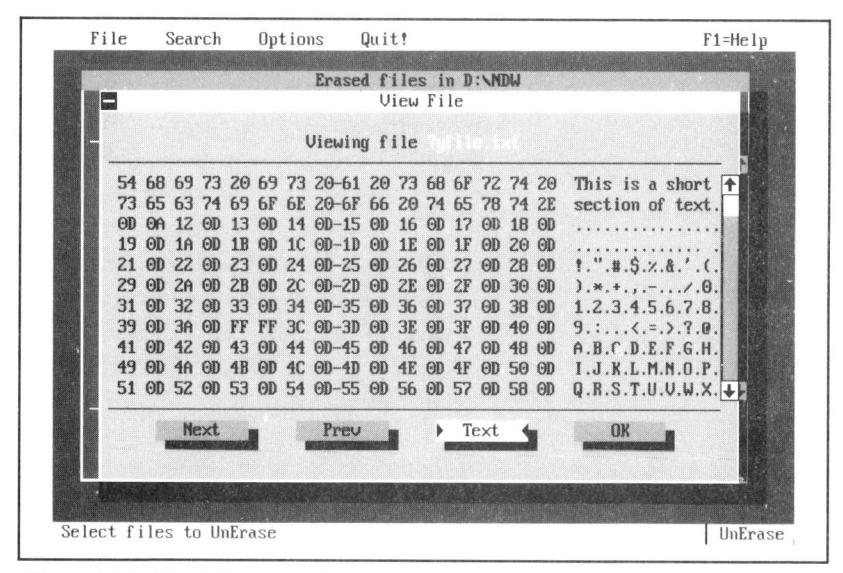

Figure 18.3: The View selection lets you look at the contents of the file as text or in hexadecimal

To recover the file, choose the UnErase option and you will be prompted to supply the first character of the file name. Use the correct character if you can remember it; otherwise, use any character for the first letter. Remember, you can always use the Rename option from the File menu or the DOS RENAME command to change the name later. As soon as you type the first character, the file is unerased, and the Prognosis column displays the status as **RECOVERED**.

RECOVERING GROUPS OF FILES

If you want to recover several files from the same directory, you can use the Select Group option from the File menu. Alternatively, you can use the + key on the numeric keypad. The Select window opens and prompts you to select the files. You can use file names, extensions, or any of the DOS wildcard characters to specify the files. For example, specify *.* to recover all the deleted files in the directory, or specify *.WK? to recover only your Lotus 1-2-3 spreadsheet files. When you select OK to return to the main UnErase screen, you will see arrowhead characters to the right and left of the files matching your file specification. To remove files from the list press the − key on the numeric keypad, or choose Unselect Group from the File menu.

After your selection is complete and you choose the UnErase box, a window opens to confirm the number of files you want to attempt to recover. This window also asks whether you want to be prompted to supply the missing first character of the file name. When this box has a check mark, UnErase prompts you to supply a beginning character for each file. If you clear the check mark from the box, UnErase does not prompt for a character—it simply inserts the first letter of the alphabet that results in a unique file name for each file. These names might look a little strange at first because most of them will begin with the letter *A* or *B*. Again, you can use the Rename command from the File menu to change the names to something more meaningful.

FINDING ERASED FILES

There are several options in the File menu that you can use to find erased files in other directories or on other disks. If you want to change to another drive, select Change Drive (Alt-D) and choose a drive from the list in the Change Drive window. Select View Current Directory (Alt-C) to display files in the current directory, or use View All Directories (Alt-A) to look at all the erased files on the current drive. To change to a specific directory, first select Change Directory (Alt-R); then locate the appropriate directory in the graphical display of directory names, or type the first few letters of the name into the Speed Search window. Remember that the Change Directory screen does not show deleted directories.

If the main window displays a large number of files, you can use the selections from the Options menu to arrange the files in a more convenient order. You can sort the files by name, extension, time, size, or prognosis, and you can choose to include or exclude existing files in the directory that have not been erased. A check mark appears next to your current selection in the menu. This sorting applies only to the files shown in the main UnErase window; the order of the files on your disk remains unchanged.

You have now completed a simple file recovery by unerasing MYFILE.TXT. With Erase Protect installed, you will always be able to recover the file completely. If Erase Protect is not installed on your system, then the chances of a complete recovery are somewhat reduced. However, as long as you start the recovery process soon after you have deleted the file, and the file is not badly fragmented or overwritten, the chances for recovery are often quite good.

MANUALLY UNERASING FILES

Now that you are familiar with unerasing files automatically, you are ready to learn how to unerase files manually. You should only use manual recovery methods if the automatic recovery mode does not work. Although it is considered an advanced technique, always remember that UnErase will provide help at every stage. In the following example, we will delete the README.TXT file supplied with the Norton Desktop and then use UnErase's manual recovery methods to restore the file. First, open the Norton Viewer and select the file README.TXT. Maximize the window to show as much of README.TXT as possible, as shown in Figure 18.4. Then delete the README.TXT file.

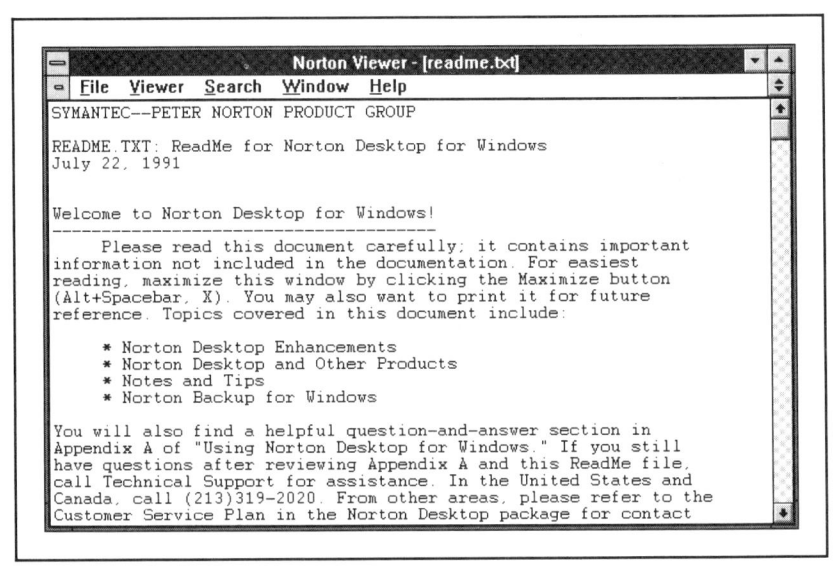

```
Norton Viewer - [readme.txt]
 File  Viewer  Search  Window  Help
SYMANTEC--PETER NORTON PRODUCT GROUP

README.TXT: ReadMe for Norton Desktop for Windows
July 22, 1991


Welcome to Norton Desktop for Windows!
----------------------------------------
     Please read this document carefully; it contains important
information not included in the documentation. For easiest
reading, maximize this window by clicking the Maximize button
(Alt+Spacebar, X). You may also want to print it for future
reference. Topics covered in this document include:

     * Norton Desktop Enhancements
     * Norton Desktop and Other Products
     * Notes and Tips
     * Norton Backup for Windows

You will also find a helpful question-and-answer section in
Appendix A of "Using Norton Desktop for Windows." If you still
have questions after reviewing Appendix A and this ReadMe file,
call Technical Support for assistance. In the United States and
Canada, call (213)319-2020. From other areas, please refer to the
Customer Service Plan in the Norton Desktop package for contact
```

Figure 18.4: The contents of the Norton Desktop README.TXT file

To restore README.TXT, exit from Windows and start UnErase from the DOS prompt by typing **UNERASE**.

Position the highlight over the ?EAD.ME file and press Alt-M or choose Manual UnErase from the File menu. UnErase asks you to enter a character to complete the file name. Enter **R** and you will see the Manual UnErase screen shown in Figure 18.5.

At the left side of the Manual UnErase screen the File Information box displays information about the README.TXT file, including its name, file attributes, file-creation date and time, and size in bytes. Below this information is the starting cluster number for README.TXT from the file-allocation table. Next, the Clusters Needed field reports the number of clusters that the file occupied before it was deleted; this represents the number of clusters that you must recover to unerase the file. On the last line, the Clusters Found count keeps track of the clusters you add to the file. This number is zero now, but it will increase as you recover clusters and add them to the file. In the center of the screen, the Added Clusters box displays the actual cluster numbers as you add clusters to the file.

From the selections at the right of the screen, choose Add Cluster, and you will see the display shown in Figure 18.6. You use the Add

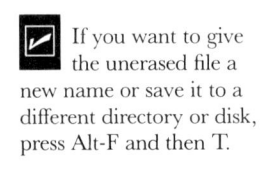

If you want to give the unerased file a new name or save it to a different directory or disk, press Alt-F and then T.

UnErase does not let you add clusters that are already allocated to another file.

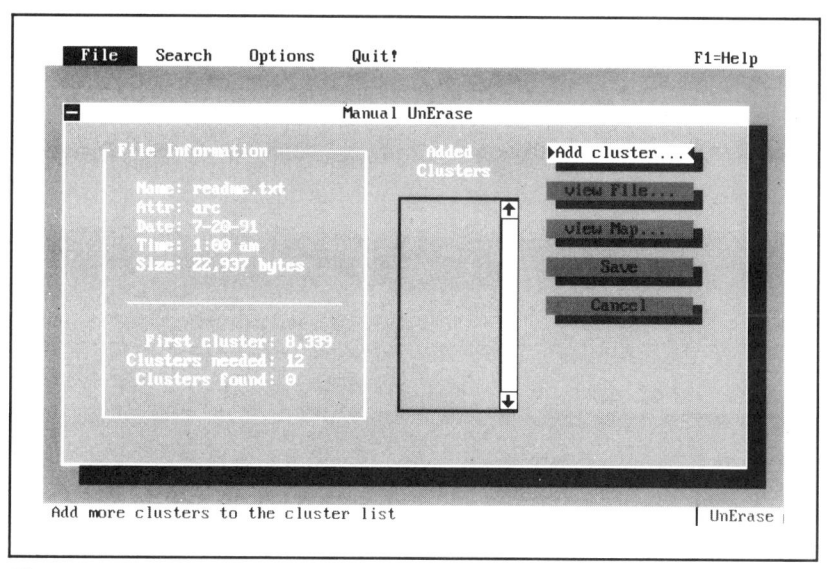

Figure 18.5: The Manual UnErase screen provides detailed information about the erased file

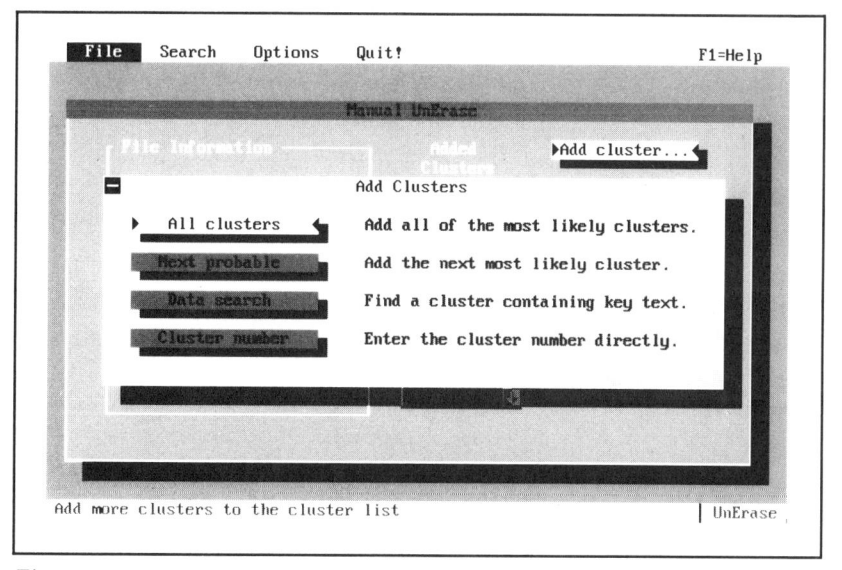

Figure 18.6: The Add Clusters screen allows you to specify the clusters to include in the file being recovered

Clusters screen to specify the clusters you want to include in the file you are recovering. Use the arrow keys to move the highlight from one box to another. Not all the clusters in the original file may be recoverable, of course.

To find the file's clusters, you can choose from the following options:

All Clusters automatically adds the most likely clusters to the file and provides the most straightforward method of recovering the file's data.

Next Probable Cluster lets UnErase choose the next likely cluster to include. (Clusters are chosen one at a time.)

Data Search lets you enter a search string of as many as 28 characters in either ASCII or hex. If you enter the search string in ASCII, it is translated into its hexadecimal equivalent and displayed in the hex window. To enter the search string in hex, use the Tab key or the arrow keys to move to the Hex box, and type in the search characters. Place a check mark in the Ignore Case box to find the search string irrespective of case, or clear the check mark to make the search case-specific.

Cluster Number requires that you know which cluster to add. At the top of the Add Cluster Number screen, UnErase lists the valid range of clusters for your drive. You can specify a single cluster or a range of clusters. Enter a starting cluster number and an ending cluster number. If the range you specify contains clusters already in use in another file, UnErase finds the first free cluster within the range.

The simplest way of finding the data for the file is to select All Clusters. Choose that option now. The program will find all the clusters that the README.TXT data now occupies and list them in the Added Clusters box. Before completing the recovery process by actually saving the file, you may examine the information contained in the found clusters or even remove or rearrange them.

VIEWING CLUSTERS

Be sure that the highlight is on the first cluster in the Added Clusters box, and select View File to examine the contents of this cluster. You will see a display similar to the one shown in Figure 18.7, but remember that your cluster numbers will be different because they refer to your own disk. Figure 18.7 shows the data as text; to see the display in hex, select or click on the Hex box. Use the up and down arrow keys, the PgUp or PgDn keys, or click on the scroll bars to move through the file. Cluster boundaries are marked in the file. Compare this figure with Figure 18.4 to confirm that what you see is indeed the start of the README.TXT text file. Select OK to return to the main Manual UnErase screen.

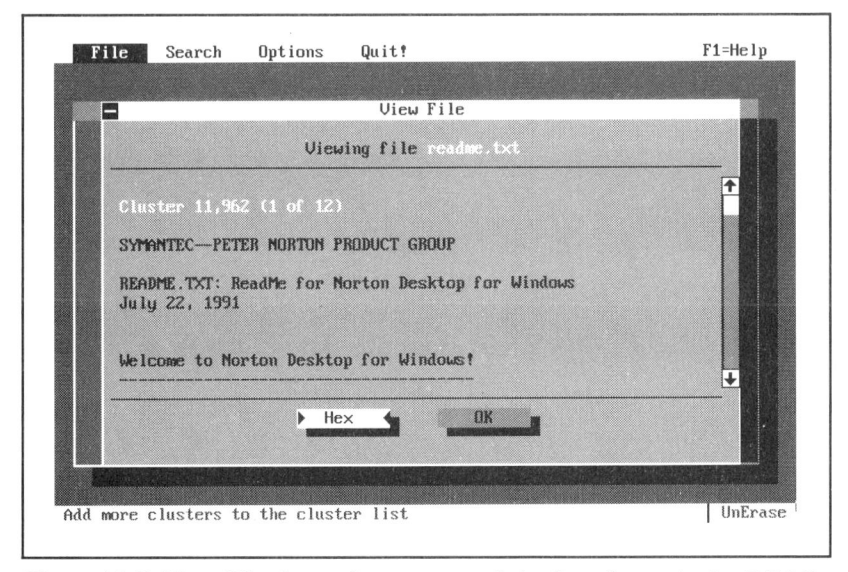

Figure 18.7: View File shows the contents of the first cluster in the README.TXT file

> Each block in the Disk Map display represents several clusters.

Select View Map to see the relative location and size of the data you have recovered so far. This information for our example is shown in Figure 18.8. The space occupied by this file is shown as an **F**. Disk space occupied by other files is shown as a block with a dot in the center, and unused disk space is shown as a solid block. Select OK to return to the main screen.

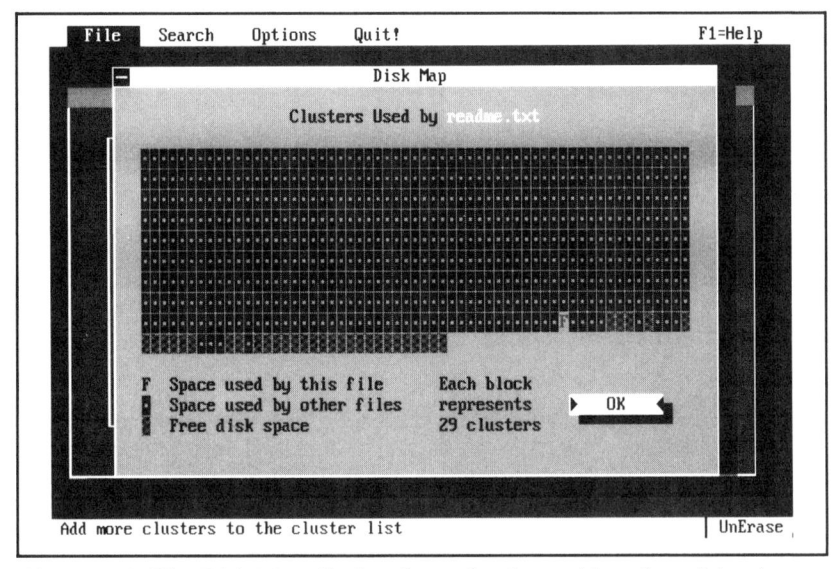

Figure 18.8: The Disk Map display shows the size and location of the clusters you have recovered so far

You can move a cluster within the Added Clusters box if you are unhappy with its current location. Move the highlight to the Added Clusters box, position the highlight on the cluster you want to move, and press the spacebar. A small arrowhead appears to the right of the cluster number and confirms your choice. Now use the up and down arrow keys to move the cluster to a new location in the list. Press the spacebar again to unselect the cluster at its new location. Select View File again to be sure that this new position is consistent with the rest of the file's contents.

Now that you're sure that you have selected the correct clusters to unerase, use Save to complete the recovery process. This menu selection stores the data in the README.TXT directory entry and also restores the file-allocation table data so that DOS can find the file again. Recovery of README.TXT is now complete.

RECOVERING PARTIAL FILES

Often, recovering files is not as straightforward as it was in the previous example. DOS may have overwritten all or part of the erased file with another file before you realized that you wanted to recover the erased file. Several factors determine whether recovery is possible, including the length of the new and erased files, and the existence or nonexistence of the erased file's directory entry.

If the file has been partially overwritten, you still might be able to recover some portion of the file, but there is a good chance that its original directory entry has been overwritten. If this is the case, you can use Create File from the File menu to create a new directory entry. You can now use Manual UnErase to search for clusters to add to the file. Note that in this kind of recovery, the Add Cluster screen contains only three selections: Next Probable, Data Search, and Cluster Number. You cannot use automatic recovery techniques under these circumstances.

If you are recovering files from a badly damaged disk, you probably don't want to store the recovered clusters on the same disk. Select the UnErase To option from the File menu to save the file to another disk. Choose the drive from the list of available drives shown in the UnErase To window, or merely type the letter of the drive you want to use. At the end of your recovery attempt, the clusters will be written to the drive you selected.

The single most important aspect of this kind of file recovery is how much you know about the contents of the erased file. If you know nothing about the file, it may be impossible to determine whether you have recovered it completely. If the file is a program file, running only the recovered portion can lead to unpredictable—and unpleasant—results. The only safe way to proceed in this case is to delete the partial file and restore the entire file from your backup set.

SEARCHING FOR LOST DATA

If you can't remember which directory an erased file was in, or if you are unable to recover the directory it was in, you can use the selections in the Search menu to locate clusters containing certain types of data. The Search menu contains the following options:

For Data Types This lets you choose from normal text, Lotus 1-2-3 and Symphony, dBASE, or other data types. Use the spacebar to make your selection, or click on the appropriate box with the mouse. Select Stop to abandon the search.

For Text This lets you enter a text search string. If you check the Ignore Case box, both upper- and lowercase strings are checked. The text you are searching for is shown at the top of the Search Progress window. A percentage-complete display shows the progress being made by the search. Select Stop to abandon the search.

As the search proceeds, the screen shows a list of the file fragments. UnErase names these fragments FILE0001, FILE0002, and so on. You can press the Escape key to stop the search at any time, highlight a file fragment, and use View to examine it. If the file fragment is the beginning of a file you want to recover, select UnErase.

For Lost Names This searches for inaccessible file names. Files may be lost if the directories that they were in are overwritten. Names of erased files are displayed on the screen; when you see a file name you recognize, highlight it and select the UnErase box in the lower-right corner of the screen.

Set Search Range This lets you specify the starting and ending cluster numbers for the search. The range of valid cluster numbers is shown on the Search Range window. You can use this selection to restrict the area of the disk that will be searched if you have an idea of where the missing file is located on the disk. You probably should use this selection first to restrict the search, and then specify the type of data you want to search for with one of the other selections.

Continue Search This resumes an interrupted search so you don't have to reenter the search criteria.

To save the file fragments found in this way, use the Append To selection from the File menu. Append To adds these clusters to an existing file.

RECOVERING AN ERASED DIRECTORY

Before deleting a directory, you must either move or delete the files in it. If you later want to recover a file, you may first have to recover the directory you deleted. You can use UnErase to restore deleted directories; in fact, the procedure is exactly the same as for restoring deleted files. After you have recovered the directory, you can restore all of its files.

DOS removes a directory in the same way that it removes a file. The first character is set to the same special character (a sigma), and the removed directory's entry remains in its parent directory (unseen, of course), exactly as a removed file's entry is. UnErase lists the names of directories that have not been deleted in capital letters, and lists the names of deleted directories in capitals with a leading question mark.

Let's look at an example to review this procedure briefly. Suppose you erased all your spreadsheet files that were in the 123 directory on drive C, erased the directory itself, and then realized that this was not the directory you should have deleted. The UnErase program will not be able to find the spreadsheet files because their names, starting cluster numbers, and file lengths are all stored in the 123 directory that has also been deleted. You must first recover the directory before attempting to recover the files. To run UnErase on the 123 directory, change to the directory that was the parent of the 123 directory (the root directory in this example) and type **UNERASE** at the DOS prompt. This displays the screen shown in Figure 18.9.

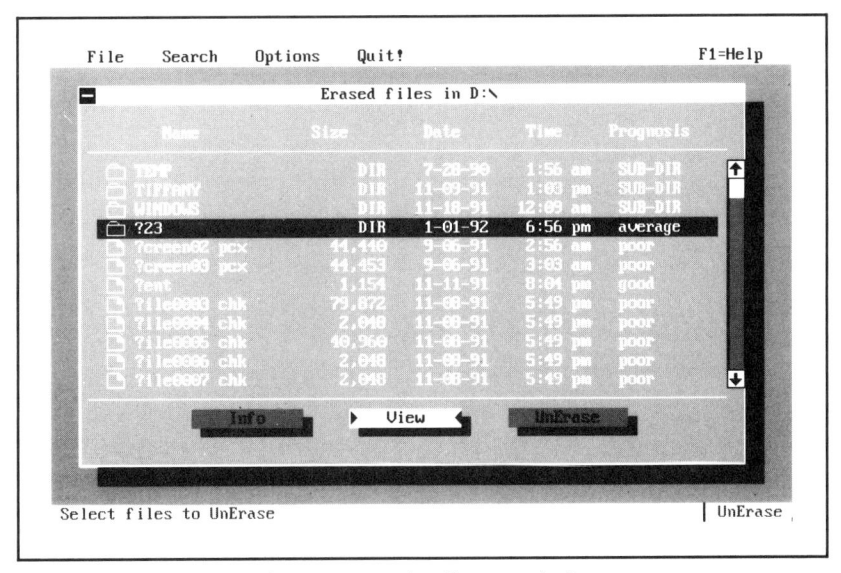

Figure 18.9: You must first unerase the directory before you can recover any files that were stored in it

UnErase asks you for the first character of the directory name, or uses information provided by Erase Protect to complete the entry. After you have recovered the directory, you can proceed to recover the files that were in the 123 directory. Because the files were all small, each a single cluster, your chances of recovering them are relatively good. Select Change Directory from the File menu. Using the graphical directory display, change to the recovered 123 directory. Select each of the files individually, or if you want to recover all of them at the same time, use Select Group to specify all the files.

UNERASING FILES WITH DOS 5

DOS 5 provides several utilities that can assist you in recovering files:

> Delete Tracking will not work on a network, or on any drive that has been redirected using the DOS JOIN or SUBST commands.

Mirror. This program creates a copy of the bookkeeping information on a disk, just like the Norton Image program.

Delete Tracking. Mirror also installs a memory-resident program called Delete Tracking. Delete Tracking is similar in operation to Erase Protect, but with one vital difference: it stores information about the deleted file, including the file name and starting cluster number, into a file called PCTRACKR.DEL, but it does not protect the file's data. Norton's Erase Protect stores the actual file itself, hence guaranteeing a complete recovery.

UnErase checks for files made by both Image and Mirror; if both file types are present, UnErase uses the most recent file. UnErase can also use information stored in the Delete Tracking file PCTRACKR-.DEL to help in recovering files.

The Norton Desktop Erase Protect and UnErase programs, together with a complete, up-to-date backup of all your important files made by the Norton Backup, offer the most complete solution to recovering deleted files.

USING COMMAND-LINE SWITCHES WITH UNERASE

There are several switches you can use from the DOS command line to help you get the most out of UnErase. You can specify the complete path to the file you want to recover from the command line, if you type:

UNERASE *path switches*

As long as the file is not badly fragmented or overwritten, UnErase will recover the file without going into full-screen mode. If you cannot remember the first letter of the file name, type ? instead and UnErase will open in full-screen mode, as usual. You can choose from the following UnErase command-line switches:

/IMAGE	uses information contained in the Image data file for file recovery and excludes the use of Mirror information
/MIRROR	uses information contained in the Mirror data file for file recovery and excludes the use of Image information
/NOTRACK	prevents the use of Delete Tracking information provided by DOS 5

As you now know, file recovery is by no means certain. Many aspects of the process influence the success of any recovery attempt, most of which you examined in this chapter. Although the file-recovery process can be more difficult than was shown in this chapter's examples (for example, recovering program files can be messy), you should have enough knowledge of the Norton UnErase program to attempt difficult recoveries on your own. Chances are, the file can't be recovered if you can't rescue it with the programs on the Norton Emergency Disk.

RECOVERING FROM FORMATTING PROBLEMS

One of the most appalling prospects for a hard-disk user is accidentally reformatting a hard disk, an operation that destroys all data and programs. With the UnFormat program contained on the Emergency Disk, however, you can recover data from a reformatted hard disk.

USING UNFORMAT

When you run the DOS FORMAT command on a hard disk, it clears the root directory and the file allocation table of their entries, but it does not actually overwrite the data area on the disk. The data are still there, but because the root directory and the file allocation table have been cleared, you normally have no way of getting to them. The UnFormat program provides an easy way of recovering these files. Note, however, that UnFormat cannot recover floppy disks formatted with the DOS FORMAT command, because then data *are* overwritten. However, UnFormat *can* recover floppy disks that have been formatted using the Format Diskette option from the Desktop Disk menu.

You should run the Norton Image program as a part of your daily operation. Doing so creates a file called IMAGE.DAT (and a copy called IMAGE.BAK) that UnFormat can use to recover the disk. The IMAGE.DAT file is compatible with the FRECOVER.DAT file made by Norton Utilities 4.5. UnFormat searches for either file. If it finds a copy of FRECOVER.DAT, UnFormat renames the file as IMAGE.DAT. Although these files' entries will be cleared from the root directory and file-allocation table should the hard disk be reformatted, running the UnFormat program from a floppy will let you recover their data and thereby recover your hard disk completely. You should add a separate Image statement for each disk partition or logical disk drive on your computer. For example, if you have a large hard disk divided into three logical drives—C, D and E—you need three Image statements in your AUTOEXEC.BAT file. Add the following lines to protect all three disk drives:

```
IMAGE C:
IMAGE D:
IMAGE E:
```

The Norton Desktop provides a safe formatting program, which not only helps to protect your hard disk from being inadvertently reformatted, but can also speed up the formatting process on floppy disks.

Some versions of DOS, including Compaq DOS 3.1, and DOS 2.11 from AT&T actually overwrite all the original data when they format a hard disk. UnFormat cannot recover files under these circumstances.

Include the Image utility in your AUTOEXEC.BAT file so that IMAGE.DAT is updated regularly.

After Image has created these files, you cannot delete them by accident—they are read-only files. The IMAGE.DAT file is also used by the UnErase program when you recover files and directories.

If you run UnFormat on a hard disk when the information contained in IMAGE.DAT is not up-to-date, the recovery will be less than complete. If you have added or removed files and these changes were not stored in IMAGE.DAT, UnErase will not know about them. For example, if you deleted files, UnFormat will assign data to those files even though they no longer exist. Furthermore, data in files created since IMAGE.DAT was updated will not be recovered. After UnErase has done all it can to recover data with an outdated IMAGE.DAT file, run Norton Disk Doctor from the Emergency Disk to sort out the few remaining file fragments.

If your hard disk has been reformatted with the DOS FORMAT command, insert the Emergency Disk into drive A; you have to run UnFormat from the floppy disk because your hard-disk copy can't be accessed. Do this immediately—before loading any backup copies to the reformatted hard disk. If you try to load other programs first, you may overwrite the IMAGE.DAT file, in which case a complete recovery will be difficult.

> Always run UnFormat before writing anything to the accidentally reformatted hard disk—otherwise you may overwrite IMAGE.DAT, making recovery difficult.

The UnFormat program is automatic and easy to use. You don't need to select options from pull-down menus; simply choose from two or three simple alternatives shown on the screen. To run the program from the DOS prompt, type **UNFORMAT** and the program will display the startup screen shown in Figure 18.10.

> You can run UnFormat from a network, but you cannot unformat a network file server.

Choose Continue to change to the drive selection window from which you can select a drive to unformat. In this example, we will use drive C. The next window asks whether you used IMAGE to save IMAGE.DAT for drive E. Answer Yes if you did or if you are not sure. If you answer No, the disk will be unformatted from scratch.

RECOVERING DATA WITH AN IMAGE.DAT FILE

If you previously used Image to save a copy of the system area of your disk, recovery after an accidental format should be fast and easy. The next window that opens is a warning screen that contains a list of the files in the root directory of the selected drive. These files will be lost if you unformat the disk.

> The combination of an up-to-date IMAGE.DAT file and a complete set of current backup disks made by Norton Backup for Windows greatly increases the chances of a complete recovery of all the files on your reformatted hard disk. Be prepared.

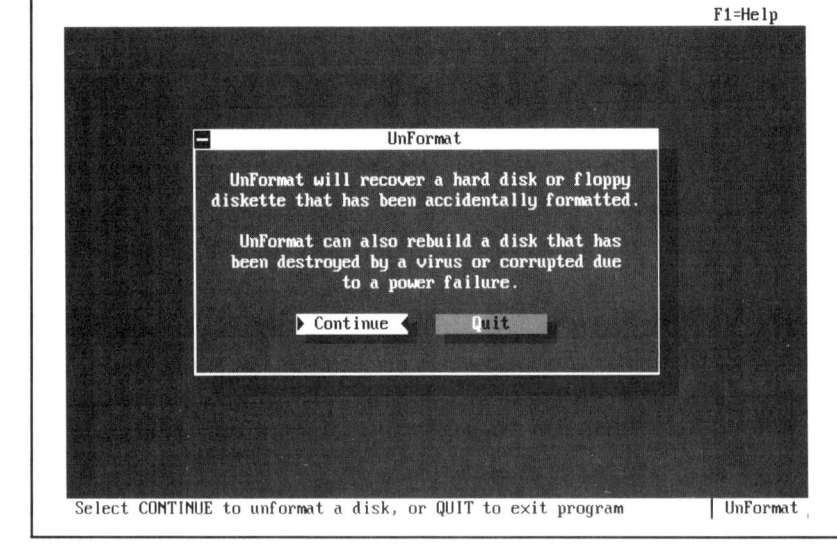

Figure 18.10: The UnFormat startup screen

Next, UnFormat looks for a copy of IMAGE.DAT on the disk. If it finds one, it opens the IMAGE Info Found window, as shown in Figure 18.11. The window shows both the most recent time that Image saved the IMAGE.DAT file and the previous time, and asks which version you want to use to unformat your hard disk. If you want to use the most recent copy of IMAGE.DAT to recover the contents of your disk, select Recent. If you want to use the previous copy, select Previous; otherwise select Cancel. If damage occurred to your disk after the last IMAGE.DAT file was created, you may not always want to use the most current version of this file to recover the hard disk. Obviously, any changes you made to the disk after the IMAGE.DAT file was created will not be recovered.

Restoring the data will overwrite the current data; if this is acceptable, select OK to continue. UnFormat now gives you the choice of a "full" restore or a "partial" restore:

> **Full** restores the entire system area, including boot record, file-allocation table information, and the root directory. If you are unsure of how to proceed at this point, selecting Full is the safest option.

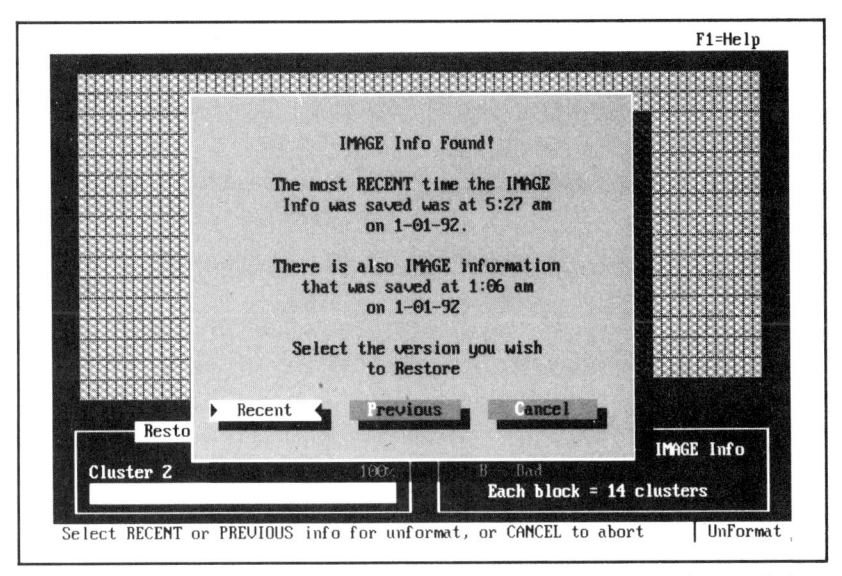

Figure 18.11: The IMAGE Info Found window displays the time and date that the IMAGE.DAT file was made

Partial lets you select the parts of the system area you want to restore—Boot Record, File Allocation Table, or Root Directory.

UnFormat reconstructs the data, and then opens a window to inform you that Drive C has been successfully restored. It also advises you to run the Norton Disk Doctor with the /QUICK switch selected as a final precaution against lost clusters or crosslinked files. If Norton Disk Doctor reports errors on your disk, the errors are a result of creating files after you last ran the Image Utility. In other words, IMAGE.DAT was not completely up-to-date.

RECOVERING DATA WITHOUT AN IMAGE.DAT FILE

Even if you do not have a suitable copy of IMAGE.DAT, you can still use UnFormat to recover much of the data on your hard disk.

When UnFormat asks if you have saved IMAGE.DAT for the drive, choose No. UnFormat then shows a map of the disk and displays the progress made during the unformatting process. When

UnFormat is finished, subdirectories will be called DIR0, DIR1, DIR2, and so on. All the files in your root directory will be missing. Use the manual UnErase techniques described in the first part of this chapter to recover these files.

Remember to run the Norton Disk Doctor to find any remaining file-allocation errors when UnFormat has finished. Then, check to see whether all your files and subdirectories are on the hard disk.

> UnFormat cannot recover files in the root directory; however, it can recover files in all other directories.

Finally, copy any files that you need for normal operation to the root directory. Be sure that AUTOEXEC.BAT, CONFIG.SYS, and COMMAND.COM are all present. If they are not there, copy them to the root directory from your backup floppy disks.

UnFormat returns to the opening screen to ask if you want to unformat another disk. Select Quit to return to DOS.

USING UNFORMAT FROM THE DOS 5 COMMAND LINE

DOS 5 provides protection against accidents in the form of the Mirror command. Mirror files are similar to Image files, in that they both save important information about a drive should it suffer an accident. UnFormat offers the best of both worlds, because it can use files made by Image or files made by Mirror to recover a disk. If both types of file exist on a drive, UnFormat makes use of the most recent file.

If you want UnFormat to use a particular type of file, you can include a command-line switch, as follows:

    UNFORMAT *drive* **/IMAGE**

forces UnFormat to use information contained in an Image file and ignore any Mirror files, while

    UNFORMAT *drive* **/MIRROR**

tells UnFormat to use a Mirror file for the recovery process and ignore any Image information. The *drive* variable represents the drive letter of the disk you are recovering.

TAKING CARE OF YOUR DISKS

In this final section, we'll take a look at ways to avoid mechanical damage to disks, since extended use can cause both hard and floppy disks to deteriorate. Floppy disks are especially prone to damage through mistreatment and careless handling.

SAFEGUARDING FLOPPY DISKS

The following suggestions for handling floppy disks will help you protect your data and prevent problems:

- When you are not using a floppy disk, keep it in its jacket in a disk storage tray or in its box.

- Do not expose floppy disks to high temperatures; for example, do not leave them on a window sill, on top of your monitor, or in a car parked in the sun. The disks will warp and become unusable.

- Keep disks away from objects that produce magnetic fields, such as motors, paper-clip holders, stereo speakers, magnetized screwdrivers, and magnetic keys.

- Do not touch the recording surface of the disk. This can transfer dirt and body oils to the disk's surface and destroy data.

- Label all your disks. Write on the label before attaching it to the disk. If you must write on the label after it is on the disk, use a soft felt-tip pen—not a ballpoint pen or pencil.

- Keep backup copies of all distribution disks, preferably in a different place than the original disks. Often, a local company will specialize in archiving data. Such places use precisely controlled temperature and humidity to ensure ong life of the media in storage. They also usually offer excellent security and fire protection.

PROTECTING HARD DISKS

Your hard disk is not immune to problems, either. The following suggestions relate to its care:

- When your computer is on, do not move the disk unit (if the drive is external) or the computer cabinet (if the drive is internal).

- To protect your system against power outages or "brownouts," use a voltage regulator, a surge suppressor, or a small uninterruptable power supply.

- Do not obstruct the air flow to the back of the computer; the air flow cools your system.

- Keep the card slots at the back of your computer covered. If you remove a card, replace the plate. An open slot directs hot air over the motherboard.

- Perform timely backups.

APPENDIX

Batch Builder Function Summary

THIS APPENDIX LISTS ALL THE COMMANDS AND functions available in the Batch Builder, grouped by task type, as well as a description of the predefined constants, math, relational, and bitwise operators, and the three different levels of error messages.

Each entry in the list of functions and commands includes a description, the syntax, a list of any optional parameters, and any returned value. Optional parameters are shown in square brackets and a variable number of parameters is indicated by an ellipsis. For example, the function that concatenates or joins two or more strings together, StrCat, must take at least two string parameters, but can take more. This is indicated as follows:

StrCat ("*string1* ", "*string2* "[, "*stringN* ",...])

RUNNING PROGRAMS

There are several different Batch Builder commands you can use to start an application program running. Choose a command depending on how you want to start the program and how well-behaved an application program it is.

RUN

Starts an application program running in a normal, non-maximized, non-minimized window.

Syntax

Run ("*program name* ", "*parameters* ")

Parameters

program name   The name of the application program to run. If you do not include drive and directory information, the current directory is searched, then the DOS path is used. If *program name* does not have an extension of .EXE, .COM, .BAT, or .PIF, it must be associated with an application program. In this case, the application program runs according to the settings in the [Extensions] section of WIN.INI, and any *parameters* you specify here may be ignored

parameters   Parameter required or accepted by the application program; can be null

Returns

@TRUE if the program was found, @FALSE if it wasn't.

RUNHIDE

Starts an application program running in a hidden window. RunHide tells the application program that you want to start the program in a hidden window. Whether or not the application does as RunHide requests is up to the application program and is beyond RunHide's control.

Syntax

RunHide (*"program name"*, *"parameters"*)

Parameters

program name   The name of the application program to run. If you do not include drive and directory information, the current directory is searched, then the DOS path is used. If *program name* does not have an extension of .EXE, .COM, .BAT, or .PIF, it must be associated with an application program. In this case, the applications program runs according to the settings in the [Extensions] section of WIN.INI, and any *parameters* you specify here may be ignored

parameters   Parameter required or accepted by the application program; can be null

Returns

@TRUE if the program was found, @FALSE if it wasn't.

RUNICON

Starts an application program running as an icon. RunIcon tells the application program that you want to start the program in a hidden window. Whether or not the application does as RunIcon requests, of course, is beyond RunIcon's control.

Syntax

RunIcon (*"program name"*, *"parameters"*)

Parameters

program name   The name of the application program to run. If you do not include drive and directory information, the current directory is searched, then the DOS path is used. If *program name* does not have an extension of .EXE, .COM, .BAT, or .PIF, it must be associated with an application program. In this case, the applications program runs according to the settings in the [Extensions] section of WIN.INI, and any *parameters* you specify here may be ignored

parameters   Parameter required or accepted by the application program; can be null

Returns

@TRUE if the program was found, @FALSE if it wasn't.

RUNZOOM

Starts an application program running in a maximized window. RunZoom tells the application program that you want to start the program in a hidden window. Whether the application program does as RunZoom requests is up to the application program to decide and is beyond RunZoom's control.

Syntax

    RunZoom ("*program name*", "*parameters*")

Parameters

program name	The name of the application program to run. If you do not include drive and directory information, the current directory is searched, then the DOS path is used. If *program name* does not have an extension of .EXE, .COM, .BAT, or .PIF, it must be associated with an application program. In this case, the applications program runs according to the settings in the [Extensions] section of WIN.INI, and any *parameters* you specify here may be ignored
parameters	Parameter required or accepted by the application program; can be null

Returns

@TRUE if the program was found, @FALSE if it wasn't.

ASKING FOR INPUT

Any batch program that talks to the outside world has to have a way of asking questions and choosing an item from a list of items on the screen.

ASKLINE

Opens a dialog box with a specific title containing a prompt and a text box that may contain an optional default string, prompting the user for one line of information.

Syntax

AskLine ("*title*", "*prompt*", "*default*")

Parameter

title Text to be placed in the title bar of the dialog box

prompt Question to be asked of the user, contained in the dialog box

default Default text that is placed in the dialog box. If left null, no default text appears in the text box

Returns

A string containing the user's response.

ASKYESNO

Opens a dialog box containing a specific title that prompts the user to click on the Yes, No, or Cancel buttons shown in the dialog box.

Syntax

AskYesNo ("*title*", "*question*")

Parameters

title Text to be placed in the title bar of the dialog box

question Question for the user to answer. It is small point, but remember to include a question mark at the end of the *question* text so that the user of your program is never in any doubt that you are asking a question

Returns

@YES or @NO, depending on which button the user clicked.

ITEMSELECT

Lets the user pick an item from a sorted list of items in a list box. This list box is contained in a dialog box that also has OK and Cancel buttons. The user selects one of the items in the list box by double-clicking on it, or by highlighting it and then clicking on OK.

Syntax

ItemSelect ("*title*", "*list*", "*delimiter*")

Parameters

title	Text to be placed in the title bar of the dialog box
list	String containing a list of items that the user can choose from
delimiter	A separate string containing the character serving as the delimiter character between items in *list*

Returns

A string containing the item the user selected from the items in *list*.

TEXTBOX

Displays a text file, like NDW.INI in a list box, and lets the user choose or highlight one line in the file. You can use this function to display multiline messages to the user, or as a multiple-choice question box.

Syntax

TextBox ("*title*", "*file name*")

Parameters

title	Specifies the text for the title of the text box
file name	Specifies the text file to open in the list box. If you do not include the drive and directory information with *file name*, the current directory is searched first, then the DOS path information is searched

Returns

A string containing the line that the user selected.

MANAGING INFORMATION

Any batch program that provides information to the user has to have a way of presenting that information in a logical, ordered way, usually by writing the information onto the screen.

BEEP

Sounds the computer speaker once with a tone of fixed duration and pitch.

Syntax

> Beep

Parameter

Beep takes no parameters.

DIALOGBOX

Opens a dialog box predefined by a .WBD template file, which is any ASCII file that identifies the structure of the dialog box, as well as the variables it uses. The .WBD file can be up to 15 lines long by 60 characters wide but no larger, and must not contain tabs; use the spacebar to insert the number of spaces you need. Each element in a .WBD file is contained inside square brackets and consists of a variable name followed by one of the following symbols:

- \+   checkbox
- #   text box
- \\   file selection list box
- ^   option button
- $ variable

If you use two of these symbols with a file selection list box variable of the same name, they take on special meanings: # becomes a text box that only accepts file names and $ becomes a directory variable.

The number that follows the checkbox and option button symbols is the value that is assigned to the variable if the corresponding box is checked or the button is selected. After the number, place any descriptive text that you want to see next to the box or button.

In each group of option buttons, the first one is always the default selection; keep this in mind when arranging your option buttons in the .WBD template file.

Syntax

DialogBox ("*title*", "*WBD file*")

Parameters

title	Text to be displayed in the dialog box title bar
WBD file	Name of the WBD template file

Returns

An integer equal to zero.

DISPLAY

Displays the text in a message box for the specified period of time, between 1 and 15 seconds. If you use a smaller number, Display treats it as 1 second; if you enter a larger number, Display treats it as 15 seconds.

Syntax

Display ("*seconds*", "*title*", "*text*")

Parameters

seconds	Number of seconds to display the message, from 1 to 15 seconds
title	Text to be displayed on the dialog box title bar

text Text to be displayed in the main part of the message box

Returns

@TRUE.

ITEMCOUNT

Counts the number of entries in a list. If you use FileItemize or DirItemize to create the list, it will be space-delimited, but if you use WinItemize, the list will be tab-delimited instead.

Syntax

ItemCount ("*list*", "*delimiter*")

Parameters

list A string containing the list of entries to choose from

delimiter A string containing the character that is the delimiter between the entries in the list

Returns

An integer containing the number of items in the list.

ITEMEXTRACT

Extracts and returns an item from a list. If you use FileItemize or DirItemize to create the list, it will be space-delimited, but if you use WinItemize, the list will be tab-delimited instead.

Syntax

ItemExtract ("*item position*", "*list*", "*delimiter*")

Parameters

item position The position in the list of the item to be selected

list A string containing the list of items to choose from *delimiter*   A string containing the character that is the delimiter between the entries in the list

Returns

A string containing the selected item.

MESSAGE

Displays selected text in a message box on the screen until the user clicks on the OK button.

Syntax

    Message ("*title*", "*text*")

Parameters

    title   Text to be used in the message box title bar

    text   Text to be displayed in the message box

Returns

    @TRUE.

PAUSE

Displays a message in a dialog box until the user clicks on either the OK button or the Cancel button.

Syntax

    Pause ("*title*", "*text*")

Parameters

    title   Text to be used in the message box title bar

    text   Text to be displayed in the message box

Returns

    @TRUE.

MANAGING FILES

Sooner or later you will want to store something on disk so that you can reload it later. There are several Batch Builder functions for accessing files.

FILECLOSE

Closes the file identified by the *file handle* parameter returned by the FileOpen function.

Syntax

    FileOpen (*file handle*)

Parameter

    file handle   The integer that was returned by the FileOpen function

Returns

    An integer equal to zero.

FILECOPY

Copies files with or without first displaying a warning message.

Syntax

    FileCopy (*"source list"*, *"destination"*, *warning*)

Parameters

    source list   A string containing the file names for copying; can include the ? and * wildcard characters, and groups of file names can be separated by spaces

    destination   String containing the target file name(s); you can only use the * wildcard character

warning @TRUE if you want a warning displayed before overwriting existing files, @FALSE if you don't want to see a warning message

Returns

@TRUE if all the files were copied successfully or @FALSE if one or more files were not copied successfully.

FILEDELETE

Deletes the specified files. You can use wildcards to extend the delete to include groups of files. As with any dangerous command, test the code very carefully before using FileDelete.

Syntax

FileDelete (*"file list"*)

Parameter

file list   A string containing one or more file names; you can use the ? or * wildcard characters in this string, or separate groups of files by spaces

Returns

@TRUE if all the files were deleted, @FALSE if a file does not exist or has the read-only attribute set so that it cannot be deleted.

FILEEXIST

Tests for the existence of a file. If you include complete path information for the file, then only the path you include will be checked for the file. If you do not specify complete path information, first the current directory will be checked, then all the directories in the DOS path statement will be checked.

Syntax

FileExist (*"file name"*)

Parameter

    file name   Either a complete drive, directory, file name, and file-name extension, or just a file name and extension

Returns

@TRUE if the file is found, @FALSE if it is not or if the path is invalid.

FILEEXTENSION

Isolates the extension part of a file name.

Syntax

    FileExtension ("*file name* ")

Parameter

    file name   Either a complete drive, directory, file name, and file-name extension, or just a file name and extension

Returns

A string containing the file-name extension.

FILEITEMIZE

Creates a list of file names in which each name is separated from the next by a space. Use this function with ItemSelect to let the user select an item from a space-delimited list.

Syntax

    FileItemize ("*file list* ")

Parameter

    file list   A string containing one or more file names; you can use the ? or * wildcard characters in this string

Returns

A string containing the space-delimited file names.

FILELOCATE

Finds a specific file and obtains the full path information for the file.

Syntax

    FileLocate ("*file name* ")

Parameter

    file name   A string containing the file name and extension. The current directory is checked first, then the DOS path is searched. FileLocate stops searching when it finds the first occurrence of the search file

Returns

A string containing the full path name for the first occurrence of the search file.

FILEMOVE

Moves file(s) to a new destination, with or without first displaying a warning message on the screen.

Syntax

    FileMove ("*source list* ", "*destination* ", *warning*)

Parameters

    source list   A string containing the file names for copying; can include the ? and * wildcard characters, and groups of file names can be separated by spaces

    destination   String containing the target file name(s); you can only use the * wildcard character

warning @TRUE if you want a warning displayed before overwriting existing files, @FALSE if you don't want to see a warning message

Returns

@TRUE if all the files were moved successfully or @FALSE if one or more files were not moved successfully, or if the read-only attribute was set, or if the destination file name was invalid.

FILEOPEN

Opens an ASCII file for reading or writing. This function returns a file handle that can be used by the FileRead, FileWrite, and FileClose functions.

Syntax

FileOpen ("*file name*", "*open type*")

Parameters

file name Name of the file you want to open

open type Either READ or WRITE, depending on what you want to do with the file

Returns

An integer containing the file handle.

FILEPATH

Obtains complete path information for a file.

Syntax

FilePath ("*file name*")

Parameter

file name File name for which you want to obtain path information

Returns

A string containing drive and directory information.

FILEREAD

Reads one line of information from an ASCII file.

Syntax

   FileRead (*file handle*)

Parameter

   file handle   Integer file handle returned by FileOpen when the file was last accessed

Returns

A string containing a line of data read from the file. This string contains *EOF* (End Of File) when FileRead reaches the end of the file.

FILERENAME

Renames one or more files.

Syntax

   FileRename (*"source list"*, *"destination"*)

Parameters

   source list   A string containing the file names for copying; can include the ? and * wildcard characters, and groups of file names can be separated by spaces

   destination   String containing the target file name(s); you can only use the * wildcard character

Returns

@TRUE if the file was successfully renamed, @FALSE if a source file was not found, or had the read-only attribute set, or the destination file name was invalid.

FILEROOT

Parses a file name and returns the name portion as a string.

Syntax

FileRoot ("*file name*")

Parameters

file name   A complete file name complete with drive and directory information, or just the file name with its extension

Returns

A string containing the name part of the file name, without the file-name extension.

FILESIZE

Finds the total size of a group of files.

Syntax

FileSize ("*file list*")

Parameters

file list   A list of zero or more file names, separated by spaces. You cannot use wildcard characters in this *file list*, but you can use FileItemize on a list of files containing wildcards, then use the resulting string as a FileSize parameter

Returns

An integer containing the total number of bytes occupied by the specified files.

FILEWRITE

Writes information to an open file, using the file handle obtained by FileOpen.

Syntax

    FileWrite ("*file handle*", "*output data*")

Parameters

    file handle   The integer file handle returned by the FileOpen function

    output data   The data you want to write to the file

Returns

    An integer with a value of zero.

INIREAD

Reads a specified string from the Windows configuration file, WIN.INI. The WIN.INI file has a consistent internal format of **[Section] key name = setting**. If the string is not found, IniRead can return a default string.

Syntax

    IniRead ("*section*", "*key name*", "*default*")

Parameters

    section   This is the name of the specified section in WIN.INI; examples include [Windows], [Desktop], [Extensions], [Fonts], and so on

    key name   Name of the item to be read from this section

    default   This is the string that IniRead will return if the item you specified is not found in WIN.INI

Returns

    A string containing information from WIN.INI.

INIREADPVT

Reads data from any (private) .INI file.

Syntax

IniReadPvt *("section", "key name", "default", "file name")*

Parameters

section	This is the name of the specified section in the .INI file
key name	Name of the item to be read from this section
default	This is the string that IniReadPvt will return if the item you specified is not found in the .INI file
file name	The file name and file-name extension of the .INI file you want to read

Returns

A string containing the data read from the .INI file.

INIWRITE

Writes a specified string into the Windows configuration file, WIN.INI. The WIN.INI file has a consistent internal format of [Section] key name = setting.

Syntax

IniWrite *("section", "key name", "data")*

Parameters

section	This is the name of the specified section in WIN.INI; examples include [Windows], [Desktop], [Extensions], [Fonts], and so on. The section is created in WIN.INI if it does not exist

key name Name of the item to be written to this section

data This is the string containing the data to write into the WIN.INI file

Returns

@TRUE.

INIWRITEPVT

Writes data to any (private) .INI file.

Syntax

IniWritePvt ("*section*", "*key name*", "*data*", "*file name*")

Parameters

section This is the name of the specified section in the .INI file

key name Name of the item to be written to this section

data This is the string containing the data you want to write to the .INI file

file name The file name and file-name extension of the .INI file you want to write data to

Returns

@TRUE.

MANAGING DIRECTORIES

Batch Builder offers a number of functions for managing directories.

DIRCHANGE

Changes the current directory, and can also change to another drive.

Syntax

    DirChange ("[d:] path ")

Parameter

    [d:] path   Specify the path of the directory to change to, and include the drive letter if you want to change to another drive

Returns

@TRUE if the directory was changed, @FALSE if the path was not found.

DIRGET

Obtains the current directory path information. DirGet is very useful when you want to change to another directory for a moment, then return back to your original starting directory.

Syntax

    DirGet ( )

Parameter

DirGet does not take any parameters.

Returns

A string containing the current directory information.

DIRHOME

Obtains complete path information for the directory that contains the Batch Runner executable files.

Syntax

    DirHome ( )

Parameter

DirHome does not take any parameters.

Returns

A string containing the path information of the directory that contains the Batch Runner executable files.

DIRITEMIZE

Compiles a list of space-delimited directory names.

Syntax

DirItemize ("*directory list* ")

Parameter

directory list   A string containing the directory names. You can use wildcards if you wish; in fact, *.* includes all directories

Returns

A string containing a list of directories.

DIRMAKE

Creates a new directory.

Syntax

DirMake ("[*d:*] *path* ")

Parameter

[*d:*] *path*   Path information for the new directory, including an optional drive letter

Returns

@TRUE if the directory was created successfully, @FALSE if it was not created.

DIRREMOVE

Deletes one or more directories. You cannot use wildcards with DirRemove.

Syntax

DirRemove ("*directory list*")

Parameter

directory list   String containing a space-delimited list of directory names

Returns

@TRUE if the directory was deleted successfully, @FALSE if it was not removed.

DIRRENAME

Renames a directory.

Syntax

DirRename ("*[d:]old path*", "*[d:]new path*")

Parameter

[d:]old path   Current directory name, including optional drive letter

[d:]new path   New name for the directory, including optional drive letter

Returns

@TRUE if the directory was renamed, @FALSE if it was not renamed.

MANAGING DISK DRIVES

These two functions are for organizing and changing disk drives.

DISKFREE

Obtains the amount of free space, in bytes, on one or more disks.

Syntax

DiskFree (*"drive list "*)

Parameter

drive list   List of drive letters, separated by spaces. Only the first character in each group is used to determine which drive to use, so you can use anything from just letters all the way to complete path statements, depending on where you obtain *drive-list*

Returns

The amount of free space on the disk, in bytes.

LOGDISK

Changes the current drive just as though you had typed a drive letter at the DOS prompt.

Syntax

LogDisk (*"drive "*)

Parameter

drive   The letter of the new disk drive, followed by a colon

Returns

@TRUE if the current drive was changed, @FALSE if it was not changed.

MANAGING WINDOWS

The Batch Builder would not be complete if it did not contain an extensive set of functions you can use to manage your windows.

WINACTIVATE

Activates an already running window or restores an icon to a normal sized window.

Syntax

WinActivate ("*partial window name* ")

Parameter

partial window name   Either a complete window name or the first part of it. This name must match the window name as it appears in the title bar exactly, including the case of the letters used and any included punctuation

Returns

@TRUE if the window or icon was found to activate, @FALSE if the window or icon was not found.

WINARRANGE

Arranges the first 12 open windows. Iconized programs are not affected.

Syntax

WinArrange (*style*)

Parameter

style   Can be one of the following:

@STACK overlaps the windows so that each title bar is visible.

@TILE resizes windows so that they are side-by-side.

@ROWS arranges windows in rows. If you use @ROWS when you have more than four open windows, WinArrange reverts to @TILE.

@COLUMNS arranges windows in columns. If you use @COLUMNS when you have more than three open window, WinArrange reverts to @TILE.

Returns

@TRUE.

WINCLOSE

Closes the specified window or icon and exits the application, just like choosing the Close command from the application's Control menu. Any closing messages from the application are displayed first, then the window is closed. WinClose does not close the window that contains the executing Batch Runner program, however; use End-Session for this task.

Syntax

WinClose ("*partial window name*")

Parameter

partial window name	Either a complete window name or the first part of it. This name must match the window name as it appears in the title bar exactly, including the case of the letters used and any included punctuation

Returns

@TRUE if the window was found and closed, @FALSE if the window was not found.

WINCLOSENOT

Closes all open windows, except those specified.

Syntax

WinCloseNot ("*partial window name1*[, "*partial window name2* ", ...])

Parameter

partial window name1, 2   Either complete or partial window name(s). Each name must match the window name as it appears in the title bar exactly, including the case of the letters used and any included punctuation

Returns

@TRUE if the window was found and closed, @FALSE if the window was not found.

WINCONFIG

Obtains the status of the Windows system configuration mode flags.

Syntax

WinConfig ( )

Parameter

WinConfig does not take any parameters.

Returns

The sum of the Windows system configuration mode flags, as an integer. You must use the bitwise operators to extract the status of individual bits from this integer:

1	Program running in Protected Mode
2	80286 CPU installed
4	80386 CPU installed
8	80486 CPU installed
16	Program running in Standard Mode
32	Program running in Enhanced Mode
64	8086 CPU installed
128	80186 CPU installed
256	Program running in Large Page Frame mode
512	Program running in Small Page Frame mode
1024	80x87 coprocessor installed

WINEXIST

Tests for the existence of a specified window or icon.

Syntax

WinExist ("*partial window name* ")

Parameter

partial window name   Either a complete window name or the first part of it. This name must match the window name as it appears in the title bar exactly, including the case of the letters used and any included punctuation

Returns

@TRUE if the window or icon is found, @FALSE if it is not found.

WINGETACTIVE

Obtains the title of the currently active window or icon.

Syntax

    WinGetActive ( )

Parameter

WinGetActive does not take any parameters.

Returns

The title of the window or icon as a string.

WINHIDE

Hides the specified window or icon.

Syntax

    WinHide ("*partial window name* ")

Parameter

partial window name	Either a complete window name, or the first part of it. This name must match the window name as it appears in the title bar exactly, including the case of the letters used and any included punctuation. If you set *partial window name* to a null value (" "), WinHide will hide the current active window

Returns

@TRUE if the specified window was found to hide, @FALSE if the window was not found.

WINICONIZE

Iconizes or minimizes the specified window.

Syntax

    WinIconize ("*partial window name* ")

Parameter

    partial window name   Either a complete window name or the first part of it. This name must match the window name as it appears in the title bar exactly, including the case of the letters used and any included punctuation. If you set *partial window name* to a null value (" "), WinIconize will minimize the current active window.

Returns

    @TRUE if the window was found, @FALSE if the window was not found.

WINITEMIZE

Obtains a tab-delimited list of titles of all the open windows. This function is useful, as window titles often contain embedded spaces.

Syntax

    WinItemize ( )

Parameter

WinItemize takes no parameters.

Returns

A string containing a list of the titles of all the open windows. Each window title is separated from the next by a tab, not a space.

WINPLACE

Changes the size and position of an open, non-maximized window. You can use this function to move the window to a new location, or to resize the window.

Syntax

    WinPlace (*x-ul, y-ul, x-br, y-br, "partial window name"*)

Parameters

x-ul	Position of the upper-left corner from the left side of the screen, 0–1000
y-ul	Position of the upper-left corner from the top of the screen, 0–1000
x-br	Position of the bottom-right corner from the left side of the screen, 10–1000, or @NORESIZE. Using @NORESIZE lets you move the window without changing the width or the height
y-br	Position of the bottom-right corner from the top of the screen, 10–1000, or @NORESIZE, or @ABOVEICONS. @ABOVEICONS positions the bottom of the window just above the icons along the bottom of the screen, without you having to know exactly where they are
partial window name	Either a complete window name or the first part of it. This name must match the window name as it appears in the title bar exactly, including the case of the letters used and any included punctuation

Returns

    @TRUE if the window was found, @FALSE if the window was not found.

WINPOSITION

Obtains the coordinates of the specified window.

Syntax

    WinPosition (*"partial window name"*)

Parameter

partial window name   Either a complete window name or the first part of it. This name must match the window name as it appears in the title bar exactly, including the case of the letters used and any included punctuation

Returns

A string containing the coordinates of the window, as described under WinPlace.

WINSHOW

Restores a window or icon to its normal or non-maximized size.

Syntax

WinShow (*"partial window name "*)

Parameter

partial window name   Either a complete window name, or the first part of it. This name must match the window name as it appears in the title bar exactly, including the case of the letters used and any included punctuation. If you use a null string with WinShow, the active window will be restored to normal size

Returns

@TRUE if the window or icon was found, @FALSE if no window was found.

WINTITLE

Changes the title of the specified window.

Syntax

WinTitle ("*partial window name*", "*new name*")

Parameters

partial window name   Either a complete window name or the first part of it. This name must match the window name as it appears in the title bar exactly, including the case of the letters used and any included punctuation

Returns

@TRUE if the window or icon was found to activate, @FALSE if the window or icon was not found.

WINWAITCLOSE

Suspends batch file execution until a specific window or icon is closed.

Syntax

WinWaitClose ("*partial window name*")

Parameter

partial window name   Either a complete window name or the first part of it. This name must match the window name as it appears in the title bar exactly, including the case of the letters used and any included punctuation

Returns

@TRUE if at least one icon or window was found, @FALSE if no window was found.

WINZOOM

Maximizes the specified window or icon.

Syntax

    WinZoom ("*partial window name*")

Parameter

    partial window name   Either a complete window name or the first part of it. This name must match the window name as it appears in the title bar exactly, including the case of the letters used and any included punctuation

Returns

    @TRUE if at least one icon or window was found, @FALSE if no window was found.

MANAGING STRINGS

Batch Builder offers a rich set of string-handling functions.

CHAR2NUM

> The first 128 characters in the standard ASCII table are the same as their ANSI (American National Standards Institute) equivalents.

Converts the first character of a string into its ASCII equivalent.

Syntax

    Char2Num ("*string*")

Parameter

    string   Any string

Returns

    The ASCII equivalent for the first character in the string.

ISNUMBER

Determines whether the specified string contains a valid number.

Syntax

    IsNumber (*"string "*)

Parameter

    string   Any string; this function is used to confirm that the user entered a valid number before proceeding to perform a calculation on that number

Returns

    @YES if the string contains a valid number, @NO if it does not contain a valid number.

NUM2CHAR

Converts an integer into its ASCII equivalent.

Syntax

    Num2Char (*integer*)

Parameter

    integer   Any integer from 0 to 255

Returns

    A one-byte string containing the ASCII equivalent.

PARSEDATA

Breaks down a string into smaller substrings, using the spaces in the original string as the delimiting characters.

Syntax

    ParseData (*"string "*)

Parameter

    string   Any string

Returns

An integer containing the number of elements in the original string and creates new variables to hold the string elements. The new substring variables are called param0, param1, to param*n*. Param0 always contains the count of the number of substrings derived from the original string. Param1 through param*n* contain the individual components of the string.

STRCAT

Joins, or concatenates, two or more strings together, one after the other.

Syntax

    StrCat ("*string1*", "*string2*"[, "*stringN*"...])

Parameters

    string1   The first, or root, string that the other strings will be joined to

    string2   The second string that will be joined to the first

    stringN   The other string(s), joined in sequence

Returns

A string containing all the joined strings.

STRCMP

Performs a case-sensitive comparison of two strings to determine their order in an ASCII sort.

Syntax

    StrCmp ("*string1*", "*string2*")

Parameters

    string1   The first string for comparison

    string2   The second string for comparison

Returns

−1 if string1 is less than string2, 0 if they are equal, and 1 if string1 is greater than string2.

STRFILL

Creates a string of a specific length, filled with copies of a substring.

Syntax

    StrFill (*"filler "*, *string length*)

Parameters

    filler   Any string that will be used in creating the return string; if *filler* is null, the return string is filled with spaces

    string length   The required number of characters in the return string

Returns

A string of the required length, containing a number of occurrences of the filler string

STRFIX

Truncates or pads out a string to a fixed length. The string is either truncated from the right, or padded out to the right by adding copies of the pad string until the required length is reached.

Syntax

    StrFix (*"base string "*, *"pad string "*, *length*)

Parameters

> *base string*   The original string whose length will be adjusted
>
> *pad string*   The string that will be appended to *base string* to achieve the required string length
>
> *length*   The required number of characters in the final string

Returns

A fixed length string as specified by *length*.

STRLCMP

Performs a case-insensitive comparison of two strings to determine their order in an ASCII sort.

Syntax

> StrlCmp ("*string1*", "*string2*")

Parameters

> *string1*   The first string for comparison
>
> *string2*   The second string for comparison

Returns

−1 if string1 is less than string2, 0 if they are equal, and 1 if string1 is greater than string2.

STRINDEX

Searches a string for the first occurrence of a substring.

Syntax

> StrIndex ("*string*", "*substring*", *start position*, *search direction*)

Parameters

string — A string to be searched

substring — A substring that will be searched for in the main string

start position — The character position in *string* where the search is to start (the first character in a string is at position 1)

search direction — Specifies the search direction. Use @FWDSCAN to search forwards or @BACKSCAN to search backwards through the string. For a forward search, a *start position* of 0 indicates that the search is to start at the beginning of the string. For a backwards search, a *start position* of 0 indicates that the search is to start at the end of the string

Returns

An integer containing the position of *substring* within *string*, or 0 if *substring* was not found

STRLEN

Determines the length of the specified string.

Syntax

StrLen ("*string*")

Parameter

string   Any string

Returns

An integer containing the length of the string.

STRLOWER

Converts all characters in a text string to lowercase.

Syntax

StrLower ("*string*")

Parameter

string   Any text string

Returns

A string containing only lowercase characters.

STRREPLACE

Replaces all occurrences of one substring with another substring.

Syntax

StrReplace ("*string*", "*old*", "*new*")

Parameters

string   The string to search for the *old* string

old   The string that will be replaced, if found

new   The replacement string

Returns

A string where *old* has been replaced by *new*.

STRSCAN

Finds the location of a specific delimiting character in a string.

Syntax

StrScan ("*string*", "*delimiter list*", *start position, search direction*)

Parameters

string	Any string
delimiter list	A string containing the delimiter character you want to search for, perhaps a period or a comma
start position	Byte location in the string where you want the search to start
search direction	Either @FWDSCAN or @BACKSCAN to search the string forwards or backwards. The search will stop when the first matching character is found or when the entire string has been searched

Returns

An integer containing the position of the first delimiter character found, or zero if the delimiter was not found in the string.

STRSUB

Obtains a substring from inside a string.

Syntax

StrSub ("*string* ", start position, length)

Parameters

string	Any string
start position	Character position within *string* where the substring you want to extract starts
length	Number of characters you want in the substring

Returns

A string containing the extracted substring. If you specify *length* to be zero, a null string is returned.

STRTRIM

Removes any leading or trailing spaces from a string.

Syntax

StrTrim ("*string*")

Parameters

string   Any string

Returns

A string with no leading or trailing spaces.

STRUPPER

Promotes a text string to uppercase.

Syntax

StrUpper ("*string*")

Parameter

string   Any string

Returns

A text string containing only uppercase letters

ARITHMETIC FUNCTIONS

Very often, you will need to perform some straightforward arithmetic in your programming. Batch Builder contains several commands to help you.

ABS

Returns the absolute value of a number, irrespective of whether the number is positive or negative.

Syntax

    Abs (*integer*)

Parameter

    integer   Any integer

Returns

    An integer containing the absolute value of the original integer.

AVERAGE

Computes the integer average from a list of integers separated by commas.

Syntax

    Average (*integer1*[, *integer2*,...])

Parameter

    integer1, 2   Any integer(s)

Returns

An integer containing the average. Because integers do not have any decimal places, there will be a level of inaccuracy associated with this calculation, due to truncation.

MAX

Determines the largest value from a list of integers separated by commas.

Syntax

    Max (*integer1*[, *integer2*,...])

Parameter

    integer1, 2   Any integer(s)

Returns

An integer containing the largest value found in the list of integers.

MIN

Determines the smallest value from a list of integers separated by commas.

Syntax

    Min (*integer1*[, *integer2*,...])

Parameter

    integer1, 2   Any integer(s)

Returns

An integer containing the smallest value found in the list of integers.

RANDOM

Computes a pseudo-random positive integer between zero and a specified maximum.

Syntax

    Random (*max*)

Parameter

    max   Upper limit for calculation of the pseudo-random number

Returns

A pseudo-random positive integer, between zero and *max* – 1.

HANDLING SYSTEM CONTROL

Batch Builder offers several different types of functions that operate at the system level.

CALL

Calls another .WBT batch file as a subroutine. The called file must end in a Return statement so that control can be passed back to the originating .WBT file.

Syntax

Call ("filename.wbt", parameters)

Parameters

filename.wbt — Name of the .WBT file to which you want to pass control; the .WBT file-name extension is required

parameters — Any parameters you want to pass to the other .WBT file, in the form of p1, p2, p3, p*n*. Parameter p0 always contains a count of the number of parameters passed. All variables are common or global between the calling and the called batch files; the called .WBT file can create or modify variables

Returns

@FALSE.

CALLEXT

Calls another .WBT file as a separate subprogram.

Syntax

CallExt (" filename.wbt ", parameters)

Parameters

filename.wbt — Name of the .WBT file to which you want to pass control; the .WBT file-name extension is required *parameters*   Any parameters you want to pass to the other .WBT file, in the form of p1, p2, p3, p*n*. Parameter p0 always contains a count of the number of parameters passed. All variables are local to the calling and the called batch files; the called .WBT file and the original program do not share variables.

Returns

@FALSE.

DATETIME

Derives the current system date and time.

Syntax

DateTime ( )

Parameter

DateTime does not take any parameters.

Returns

A string containing the date and time according to the format specified in the Windows Control Panel.

DEBUG

Turns the debug mode on or off. The default is off. When you turn debug on, the Debug dialog box opens. This dialog box shows the statement that was just executed, any error conditions, and a copy of the next statement due to execute. The dialog box also contains four command buttons, as follows:

Next executes the next statement in the file, staying in debug mode.

Run switches out of debug mode and runs the rest of the batch program normally until either debug is turned on again or the program ends.

Cancel terminates the batch program.

Show Var displays the contents of the variable whose name you enter into the text box.

Syntax

    Debug (*mode*)

Parameter

    mode   Either @ON or @OFF

Returns

    The previous debug mode.

DELAY

Pauses a batch file execution for a specified period of time, between 2 and 15 seconds.

Syntax

    Delay (*seconds*)

Parameter

    seconds   An integer number of seconds to wait, between 2 and 15 seconds

Returns

    @TRUE.

DOSVERSION

Returns the integer or decimal portions of the DOS version number on your system.

Syntax

    DOSVersion (*level*)

Parameter

    level   Either @MAJOR or @MINOR; @MAJOR determines the revision level before the decimal place and @MINOR determines the revision level contained in the decimal portion of the version number

Returns

An integer containing either the integer or the decimal portion of the DOS version number.

DROP

Removes one or more specified variables from memory.

Syntax

    Drop (*var1*[, *var2*,...])

Parameter

    var1, 2   Any variable name(s)

Returns

    @TRUE.

ENDSESSION

Ends the current Windows session, bypassing the normal Program Manager closing message. If auto-save options in the Desktop or in Quick Access are enabled, your changes will be saved before exiting Windows. Any other open windows will be closed and you will see their normal closing messages.

Syntax

    EndSession ( )

Parameter

EndSession does not take any parameters.

Returns

An integer value of zero.

ENVIRONMENT

Determines the value of a specified DOS environment variable.

Syntax

Environment ("*env variable*")

Parameter

env variable   Any defined DOS environment variable. This parameter is case-sensitive, so it must match the case used by DOS

Returns

A string containing the value of the environment variable.

ERRORMODE

Sets the error mode.

Syntax

ErrorMode (*mode*)

Parameter

mode   Can be set to one of the following: @CANCEL, @NOTIFY, or @OFF (see the discussion of errors under "Batch Runner Error Messages" at the end of this appendix)

Returns

An integer containing the previous ErrorMode setting.

EXCLUSIVE

Controls the amount of time other Windows programs have to execute.

Syntax

Exclusive (*mode*)

Parameter

> *mode* Either @ON or @OFF. @OFF is the default mode, and in this mode Batch Runner shares processing time with the other Windows applications running on your system. If you turn Exclusive on, Batch Runner takes more CPU time. Don't bother to use this if you have only a few Windows applications running, as it doesn't make a significant difference. Use it when you have a lot of Windows applications running and you want to execute several instructions very quickly

Returns

The previous Exclusive mode.

EXECUTE

Executes a batch statement in a protected environment, ensuring that any errors encountered are recoverable.

Syntax

Execute (*statement*)

Parameter

> *statement* Any statement you want to execute, including statements entered by the user

EXIT

Stops the current batch file running and exits.

Syntax

    Exit

Parameter

Exit does not take any parameters.

GOTO

Manages flow control in the batch file.

Syntax

    Goto *:label*

Parameter

    :label   Any text with a colon as the first character

IF...THEN

Provides for conditional branching in a batch file.

Syntax

    If *condition* Then *statement*

Parameters

    condition   If *condition* is true, then the Batch Runner will execute the command following Then; if *condition* is not true, Batch Runner will ignore this command

    statement   This *statement* is executed if *condition* is true

IGNOREINPUT

Disables the mouse and the keyboard.

Syntax

    IgnoreInput (*mode*)

> Be careful how you use IgnoreInput, as it is certainly possible to get to the point where the mouse and keyboard are both turned off and there is no way to talk to your batch file.

Parameter

   mode   Either @TRUE or @FALSE; the default mode is @FALSE

Returns

An integer containing the previous IgnoreInput mode.

ISDEFINED

Determines whether or not a variable is currently defined.

Syntax

   IsDefined (*var*)

Parameter

   var   Any variable name

Returns

@YES if the variable is defined, @NO if the variable was never defined or has been removed with the Drop function.

ISKEYDOWN

Determines whether or not the Shift key, the Ctrl key, or a mouse button is being pressed.

Syntax

   IsKeyDown (*key code*)

Parameter

   key code   Either @SHIFT or @CTRL; the left mouse button is treated like the Shift key and the right mouse button like the Ctrl key

Returns

@YES if the key is pressed, @NO if the key is not pressed.

LASTERROR

Obtains the error number of the last error that occurred during the processing of the current batch file.

Syntax

    LastError ( )

Parameters

LastError does not take any parameters.

Returns

An integer containing the number of the most recent minor or moderate error. When a fatal error occurs, batch file processing stops before the next statement can be executed, so there is little point in checking for fatal errors.

RETURN

Transfers program control back to the calling program.

Syntax

    Return

Parameter

Return does not take any parameters.

SENDKEY

Sends keystrokes to the active window, just as though they were coming from the keyboard.

Syntax

    SendKey (*"character string "*)

Parameter

    character string   Any string containing regular or special characters. Regular characters are the normal alphanumeric keys on the keyboard; special characters are shown in Table A.1 and must be contained in curly brackets

If you want to use a key combination using Alt, Ctrl, or Shift, use ! to represent Alt, ^ for Ctrl, and + for Shift. For example, Alt-E becomes SendKey ("!E"). You can also repeat the same character several times if you follow the character by a space and then a repeat factor. For example, SendKey ("{* 15}") sends 15 asterisks to the active window and SendKey ("{UP 20}") moves the cursor up 20 lines.

Returns

An integer with a value of zero.

SKDEBUG

Establishes SendKey's debug mode.

Syntax

    SKDebug (*mode*)

Parameter

    mode   One of the following modes: @OFF, @ON, or @PARSEONLY. The default mode is @OFF; when you use it, keystrokes are sent to the active window. If you use @ON, the keystrokes are sent to the active window and to a debug file called

Table A.1: SendKey Special Characters

KEY	SENDKEY EQUIVALENT
~	{~}
!	{!}
^	{^}
+	{+}
↑	{UP}
↓	{DOWN}
←	{LEFT}
→	{RIGHT}
Backspace	{BACKSPACE} *or* {BS}
Break	{BREAK}
Clear	{CLEAR}
Delete	{DELETE} *or* {DEL}
End	{END}
Enter	{ENTER} *or* ~
Escape	{ESCAPE} *or* {ESC}
F1 *through* F16	{F1} *through* {F16}
Help	{HELP}
Home	{HOME}
Insert	{INSERT}
Page Down	{PGDN}
Page Up	{PGUP}
Print Screen	{PRTSC}
Spacebar	{SPACE} *or* {SP}
Tab	{TAB}

C:\@@SKDBUG.TXT. You can use a different file if you change the entry under the [Batch Runner] heading in your WIN.INI file to include the new file name, as follows; SKDFile =*file name*, where *file name* is the name of the file you want to use. If you use @PARSEONLY, keystrokes are only sent to the file; they are not sent to the active window

Returns

The previous SKDebug mode.

VERSION

Obtains the version number of the currently running batch processor.

Syntax

    Version ( )

Parameter

Version has no parameters.

Returns

A string containing the current version number.

WALLPAPER

Changes the desktop wallpaper.

Syntax

    WallPaper ("*bmp name*", *tile flag*)

Parameters

bmp name		Name of the BMP wallpaper file you want to change to
tile flag		Either @TRUE if you want the wallpaper tiled, @FALSE if you don't

Returns

An integer with the value of zero.

WINVERSION

Returns the integer or decimal portions of the Windows version number on your system.

Syntax

   WinVersion (*level*)

Parameter

   level   Either @MAJOR or @MINOR; @MAJOR determines the revision level before the decimal place and @MINOR determines the revision level contained in the decimal portion of the version number

Returns

An integer containing either the integer or the decimal portion of the Windows version number.

YIELD

Gives up time for other applications to run.

Syntax

   Yield

Parameter

Yield takes no parameters.

WINDOWS CLIPBOARD FUNCTIONS

There are several very useful Batch Runner commands you can use with the Windows Clipboard.

CLIPAPPEND

Adds the contents of a string to the Clipboard if the Clipboard is empty, or to the end of any text already on the Clipboard.

Syntax

ClipAppend ("*string* ")

Parameter

string   Any string

Returns

@TRUE if the string was added, @FALSE if the Clipboard ran out of memory.

CLIPGET

Copies text from the Clipboard.

Syntax

ClipGet ( )

Parameter

ClipGet takes no parameters.

Returns

A string containing text from the Clipboard. Sometimes, if the Clipboard contains a very long string, a fatal out-of-memory error may occur.

CLIPPUT

Replaces the contents of the Windows Clipboard with the contents of a string. The previous contents of the Clipboard are lost.

Syntax

ClipPut ("*string* ")

BATCH BUILDER FUNCTION SUMMARY 461

Parameter

    string   Any string you want to place on the Windows Clipboard

Returns

    @TRUE if the string was copied successfully, @FALSE if the string was not copied because the Clipboard ran out of memory.

MATHEMATICAL, RELATIONAL, AND BITWISE OPERATORS

The Batch Builder includes support for mathematical, relational, and bitwise operators, as well as all the functions we have just looked at.

MATHEMATICAL OPERATORS

The following math operators are available:

*	Multiply
/	Divide
+	Add
–	Subtract
mod	Gives the remainder after an integer division

RELATIONAL OPERATORS

The following relational operators are available:

&&	Logical AND
||	Logical OR
!	Logical NOT
>	Greater than
>=	Greater than or equal to

      <   Less than
      <=   Less than or equal to
      ==   Equal
      !=   Not equal
      <>   Not equal

BITWISE OPERATORS

The following binary operators are available:

      <<   Left shift
      >>   Right shift
      &   Bitwise AND
      | Bitwise OR
      ^   Bitwise exclusive OR (XOR)

PRECEDENCE AND ORDER OF EVALUATION

The following priorities are used in determining which portion of a statement is evaluated first. Each line in the listing that follows is of a higher priority than the entry below it, and items at the same priority level are evaluated from left to right:

( )	Parenthetical grouping
~, !, −, +	Unary operators
*, /, mod	Multiplication and division
+, −	Addition and Subtraction
<<, >>	Shift operators
<, <=, ==, >=, !=, <>	Relational operators
&, ^, |	Bit manipulation operators
&&, ||	Logical operators

A simple example can demonstrate why it is important to know the order of evaluation. Consider the expression:

A = B + C/D

In this example, the result stored in variable *A* will be different depending on whether the division or the addition is done first. Since division has a higher priority than addition, variable *C* is divided by *D* first, then the result is added to the value contained in variable *B*.

PREDEFINED BATCH BUILDER CONSTANTS

The Batch Builder provides a set of predefined integer constants. The @ sign is always used as the first character of any predefined constant and you can type the constant name in uppercase letters, lowercase letters, or a combination of the two—it makes no difference.

LOGICAL CONSTANTS

The following logical constants are available:

@TRUE
@FALSE
@YES
@NO

WINDOW ARRANGEMENT

You can use the following predefined constants with WinArrange:

@STACK
@TILE *or* @ARRANGE
@ROWS
@COLUMNS

WINDOW PLACEMENT

You can use the following predefined constants with WinPlace:

@NORESIZE

@ABOVEICONS

STRING MANAGEMENT

You can use the following direction indicators with StrIndex and StrScan:

@FWDSCAN

@BACKSCAN

KEY CODES

You can use the following two constants with IsKeyDown:

@SHIFT

@CTRL

VERSION INFORMATION

You can use the following predefined constants with DOSVersion and WinVersion:

@MAJOR

@MINOR

PROGRAM EXECUTION

You can use the following predefined constants with Exclusive:

@ON

@OFF

ERROR HANDLING

You can use the following predefined constants with ErrorMode:

@CANCEL
@NOTIFY
@OFF

DEBUGGING MODE

You can use the following predefined constants with Debug and SKDebug:

@ON
@OFF
@PARSEONLY

BATCH RUNNER ERROR MESSAGES

Batch Runner provides for three kinds of error messages of increasing severity: minor, moderate, and fatal. The function Error-Mode controls what happens in the event of an error. It can be set to one of three states:

@CANCEL. All run time errors cause execution of the batch file to stop, and the user is notified which error occurred.

@NOTIFY. All run time errors are reported to the user, who can decide to continue if the error is not fatal.

@OFF. In this mode minor error messages are not reported, but moderate and fatal errors are reported.

MINOR ERRORS

If the error mode is set to @NOTIFY and an error occurs, you can continue with batch processing or cancel the batch file. If the error mode is set to @OFF, minor errors are ignored and you will not see an error message. Minor error message numbers start at 1000 and go to 1999.

Examples of minor errors include **Error 1040 WinHide: Window not found** and **Error 1900 WinExec 0: Out of memory**.

MODERATE ERRORS

When the error mode is set to @NOTIFY or @OFF and a moderate error occurs, you can decide whether to continue or to cancel the batch file. Moderate error numbers start at 2000 and go to 2999.

Error 2045 WinActivate: Window not found is one example of a moderate error you may encounter.

FATAL ERRORS

If a fatal error occurs, your batch file is canceled with an error message, irrespective of the current error mode. This means that the Last-Error function will not be accessible after a fatal error. Fatal error numbers start at 3000.

Error 3012 File Copy/Move: No room left on disk and **Error 3026 LogDisk: Illegal disk drive** are just two examples of some of the fatal errors you may encounter.

Index

A

Abs, 444-445
active window, 21
Alt-key combinations, 95, 113, 141
application windows, 19
archive attribute, 48
   set for backups, 160
   set for restorations, 198-199
archive files, viewing, 72
ASCII files, viewing, 79-80
AskLine, 318, 407
AskYesNo, 318, 407
associated documents, 106-108. *See also* file-name extensions, associations for
AUTOEXEC.BAT file
   device drivers statement in, 237
   Erase Protect statement in, 208-209
   IMAGE statement(s) in, 394
   modification during installation, 13-14
   PATH statement in, 112, 147, 149
   running Norton Disk Doctor from, 353
AutoStart, 118-119
Average, 445

B

backups, 157-159. *See also* restoring backups
   archive attribute set for, 160
   background running of, 204
   catalog files for, 168, 190-192
   command-line switches for, 202-203
   comparing files after, 172, 181, 185-190
   compatibility testing for, 164-166
   complete, 170-172
   configuring, 162-168
   data compression during, 181, 183-184
   data verification during, 181, 183
   floppy-drive configuration for, 167
   hardware, defined for 162-163
   log method before, 167-168
   macros for, 201-202
   Norton disk format and, 184-185
      options for, 180-185
      overwrite protection during, 184

partial, 173
file selection for, 174-180
include/exclude filters for, 177-180
printing log of, 175
selecting icons for, 176-177
types of, 173-174
Scheduler, used for, 203-204, 305-307
scheduling of, 159-160, 185
setup files for, 199-201
storage of, 161-162
target file size for, 184
target medium for, 160, 167
user level selection for, 166-167
bad clusters, 347
Batch Builder, 307-311. *See also individual command or function names*
   Clipboard operations with, 325
   command editing with, 311
   commands in, 315
   constants for, 314-315
   control passing with, 324
   Debug constants in, 465
   debugging batch files with, 324
   DialogBox function in, 321-322
   directory management with, 322-323
   DOSVersion constants in, 464
   drive management with, 323
   error messages in, 465-466
   ErrorMode constants in, 465
   Exclusive constants in, 464
   file commenting with, 314
   file management with, 322
   function editing with, 311
   function parameters in, 315
   identifiers in, 316
   IsKeyDown constants for, 464
   logical constants in, 463
   operators in, 316-317, 461-462
   program running and, 317-318
   running batch files with, 311-312
   SKDebug constants in, 465
   statement order of evaluation in, 462-463
   StrIndex constants in, 464
   string management with, 323
   string searching with, 309-310, 323
   StrScan constants in, 464
   user input functions in, 318-320
   variables in, 316
   WinArrange constants in, 463
   window management with, 323
   WinPlace constants in, 464
   WinVersion constants in, 464
batch files. *See* Batch Builder; Batch Runner
Batch Runner, 307-308
Beep, 409
benchmark information, 241-242
binary files, viewing, 73, 79-80
bookmarks, 37
boot record, 222, 343
bus type, 227
button bar
   customizing, 137-139
   in drive window, 45

C

calculators. *See* Scientific Calculator; 10-Key Tape Calculator
Call, 324, 447
CallExt, 324, 447-448
catalog files, 168, 190-192
Char2Num, 436
check boxes, 26

ClipAppend, 325, 460
ClipGet, 325, 460
ClipPut, 325, 460-461
clusters, 357, 380
    bad, 347
    lost, 223, 343
    searching for, 386, 388-389
    viewing, 387-388
CMOS summary, 240-241
command buttons, 27
comparing files after backups, 172, 181, 185-186
    complete, 187-189
    file selection for, 189-190
compatibility test, 164-166
compressed files, viewing, 72
computing index, 241-242
CONFIG.SYS file, 237
configuration file (NDW.INI), 83, 109, 149-153
confirmation configuration, 134-135
control-menu box, 22
copying
    directories, 54-57
    disks, 62-63
    files, 54-57
    groups, 116-118
Ctrl-key combinations, 94, 113, 141
Ctrl-Shift-key combinations, 95

D

database files, viewing, 72, 78-79
data compression, 72, 181, 183-184
data verification, 181, 183, 198
DateTime, 448
dBASE files, viewing, 72

Debug, 324, 448-449
    constants for, 465
default editor, 146-147
default viewer, 147
Delay, 449
Delete Tracking program, 392-393
deleting
    directories, 58-60, 391
    files, 58-60, 377-378
    groups, 116-118
destructive formatting, 65
device-based fonts, 280
device drivers information, 232, 237-238
DialogBox, 321-322, 409-410
dialog boxes, 26-31
    browsing in, 30-31, 53-54
    prompt, 132-133
dimmed command names, 25
DirChange, 322, 422-423
Direct Memory Access (DMA) test, 163
directories
    batch file management of, 322-323
    copying
        with the File menu, 55-57
        with the mouse, 54-55
    creating, 58
    deleting, 58-60, 391
    deselecting, 52-53
    moving
        with the File menu, 55-57
        with the mouse, 54-55
    recovering erased, 390-392
    renaming, 57-58
    selecting, 52-53
    Speed Disk sorting of, 362-364
DirGet, 322, 423
DirHome, 423-424

DirItemize, 424
DirMake, 323, 424
DirRemove, 323, 425
DirRename, 323, 425
Disk Change test, 163
DiskFree, 323, 426
disks
    bootable, 65
    capacity of, 66
    care of, 399–400
    copying, 62–63
    formatting, 64–66
    volume labels for, 67
disk summary, 229–230
Display, 410–411
display summary, 233–234
document windows, 20
DOD (Department of Defense) file overwrite standard, 145–146, 216–217
DOS boot record, 222, 343
DOS Delete Tracking program, 392–393
DOS Mirror program, 392–393
DOSVersion, 324, 449–450
    constants for, 464
drive icons, 42, 135–137
drive windows, 28, 44–45
    button bar in, 45
    closing, 51
    drive selection in, 45–46
    elements of, 45
    file display in, 47–50
    file pane in, 47–50
    resizing, 51
    speed searching in, 46
    status bar in, 46
    tree pane in, 46–48
    updating, 51
    view pane in, 51, 71–73
Drop, 450
drop-down list boxes, 27

E

editor, default, 146–147
Emergency Disk, 329
    help features of, 334–335
    menu selection in, 332–334
    Windows incompatibility with, 329–330
EndSession, 450–451
Environment, 451
Erase Protect. *See also* SmartErase
    configuring, 151
    network operation and, 215
    purging files and, 214
    in tandem with SmartErase, 208–210
    specifying file-name extensions for, 144
error messages, 465–466
ErrorMode, 451, 465–466
    constants for, 465
Exclusive, 452
    constants for, 464
Execute, 452
Exit, 452–453
expanded memory, 228–229
extended memory, 228
extensions. *See* file-name extensions

F

File Allocation Table (FAT), 222–223, 343
FileClose, 413
FileCopy, 413–414
FileDelete, 414
FileExist, 414–415

FileExtension, 415
FileItemize, 319, 415–416
FileLocate, 416
FileMove, 416–417
file-name extensions, 57
    associations for, 60, 72, 83, 87, 95–96
        adding, 96–98
        deleting, 98
        editing, 96–98
    of backup types, 188
    specifying for Erase Protect, 144
    viewing format specified by, 72–73, 83, 151–152
FileOpen, 417
file pane, 47–50
FilePath, 417–418
FileRead, 418
FileRename, 418
FileRoot, 419
files
    ASCII, viewing, 79–80
    batch. *See* Batch Builder; Batch Runner
    binary, viewing, 73, 79–80
    browsing for, 30–31, 53–54
    changing attributes of, 60–61
    comparing after backups, 172, 181, 185–186
        complete, 187–189
        file selection for, 189–190
    copying with the File menu, 55–57
    copying with the mouse, 54–55
    database, viewing, 72, 78–79
    deleting, 58–60, 377–378
    deselecting, 52–53
    drive window display of, 47–50
    editing, 61–62
    erase protection of. *See* Erase Protect; SmartErase
    erase standards for, 145–146
    formats of, 72–73
    fragmentation of, 357, 359, 367–368, 378. *See also* Speed Disk
    graphics, viewing, 80–81
    hidden, 48
    iconizing, 60
    moving with the File menu, 55–57
    moving with the mouse, 54–55
    naming, 57
    overwriting. *See* Shredder
    printing, 84–85
    read-only, 47, 60–61
    recovering with SmartErase, 211–213
    renaming, 57–58
    restoring. *See* restoring backups
    selecting, 52–53
    Speed Disk sorting of, 364–367
    spreadsheet, viewing, 73, 77–78
    string searching in, 81–83, 251. *See also* SuperFind
    unmovable, 360, 366, 370, 372
    viewing with Norton Viewer. *See* Norton Viewer
    viewing with view pane, 51, 71–73
file sets, 247, 249, 255–258
FileSize, 419
FileWrite, 419–420
fonts, 280
formatting, 64–66
fragmentation, file, 357, 359, 367–368, 378

frame, 22-23
function call, 239
function keys, 94, 113, 141

G

GoTo, 453
Graphics Device Interface (GDI)
 fonts, 280
graphics files, viewing, 80-81
Graphics Interchange Format
 (GIF) files, viewing, 72
grayed command names, 25
group box, 30
group items. *See* groups
groups, 106-108
 changing properties of, 116
 copying, 116-118
 creating, 109-114
 deleting, 116-118
 icons for, 24, 108-109, 113-115
 moving, 116-118
 password protection of, 113,
  115-116
 in Quick Access, 106-108
group windows, 20

H

hardware
 configuration information,
  225-229
 requirements, 6
Help system, 33-36
 annotating Help text, 36-37
 bookmarks in, 37
hidden file, 48

I

IBMBIOS.COM file, 370, 372

IBMDOS.COM file, 370, 372
.ICO files, 299-300
Icon Editor, 287-289
 choosing colors in, 291-292
 deleting icons with, 294-296
 editing tools in, 289-291
 exporting icons with, 296-297
 icon libraries and, 293-298
 icons in .EXE files, 298-299
 importing icons with, 296-297
 individual icon files and,
  299-300
 inserting icons with, 294-296
 modifying icons with, 294-296
icons, 24, 29
 changing, 114-115
 creating, 114-115
 drive, 42, 135-137
 editing. *See* Icon Editor
 group, 24, 108-109, 113-115
 printer, 84
 spacing of, 109
 tool, 133
If...Then, 453
IgnoreInput, 453-454
Image program, 209-210, 392-393
 UnErase and, 392-393
 UnFormat and, 394-398
IniRead, 322, 420
IniReadPvt, 322, 421
IniWrite, 322, 421-422
IniWritePvt, 322, 422
installation
 floppy-disk backup before,
  10-11
 hard disk, 11-15
 modifications to
  AUTOEXEC.BAT file
  during, 13-14
 network, 5, 16-17
 partial, 15-16

interrupt handler, 238
interrupt request (IRQ), 239
interrupt vectors, 235-236, 238-240
IO.SYS file, 370, 372
IsDefined, 454
IsKeyDown, 454-455
    constants for, 464
IsNumber, 437
ItemCount, 411
ItemExtract, 411-412
ItemSelect, 319, 408

K

keyboard shortcuts, 94-95, 113, 139-141
KeyFinder, 279-284
    Clipboard transfers with, 284-285

L

LastError, 455
launching programs, 87-88
    with custom startup command, 98-99
    with unassociated documents, 99-100
    using Quick Access, 88
    using the file pane, 88-89
    using the Launch List, 89-90
    using the Run command, 90-91
    using the Run DOS command, 91
Launch List, 89-90, 133
    customizing, 92-95
Launch Manager, 92-95
list boxes, 26-27
location sets, 247, 249, 255-258
LogDisk, 323, 426

lost clusters, 223, 343
Lotus 1-2-3 files, viewing, 73

M

macros for backups, 201-202
math coprocessor, 226-227
Max, 445-446
maximize button, 21-22
memory
    expanded, 228-229
    extended, 228
menu bars, 22
menus
    adding items to, 126-129
    customizing, 121-126
    editing commands on, 129-130
    elements of, 25-26
    full, 43, 121
    short, 43, 121
Message, 312-313, 315, 412
Microsoft Excel files, viewing, 73
Min, 446
minimize button, 21-22
Mirror program, 392-393
moving
    directories, 54-57
    files, 54-57
    groups, 116-118
MSDOS.SYS file, 370, 372

N

NDW.INI file, 83, 109, 149-153
network
    Erase Protect on, 215
    Norton Desktop on, 5, 16-17, 67-68, 136
    Norton Disk Doctor and, 346, 350
    Speed Disk illegal on, 359

UnErase and, 379
Norton Disk Doctor, 221-224,
    336. See also System Information
    customizing, 348-352
    disk diagnostics with, 341-343,
        351-352
    disk surface testing with,
        343-348, 350
    network operations and,
        346, 350
    running from the DOS
        command line, 353-354
    undoing repairs with, 348
Norton Viewer, 73-74
    configuring, 83
    image manipulation with, 81
    selecting files for, 74-75
    viewing binary files with, 79-80
    viewing database files with,
        78-79
    viewing graphics files with,
        80-81
    viewing spreadsheet files with,
        77-78
    window placement in, 75-77
Num2Char, 437

O

option buttons, 27

P

PaintBrush (.PCX) files, viewing,
    73, 80-81
parallel port, 227-228
ParseData, 437-438
partial backups. See backups,
    partial
partition table, 222, 343

passwords, 113, 115-116, 130-131
    with Sleeper program, 278
PATH definition, 15, 112,
    147, 149
Pause, 412
position-sensitive files, 360, 366,
    370, 372
printer summary, 234
printing, 84-85
    setup strings for, 150-151
prompt dialog boxes, configuring,
    132-133

Q

Quick Access, 103-105
    AutoStart and, 118-119
    configuring, 141-143
    groups in, 106-108
    as a shell, 105
quick formatting, 65
quick keys, 94-95, 113, 139-141

R

Random, 446
raster fonts, 280
read errors, 344
README.TXT file, 9, 15
read-only file, 47, 60-61
renaming files, 57-58
restoring backups, 192-194
    configuring options for,
        196-199
    data verification after, 198
    full, 192-194
    hard disk failure and, 196
    overwrite protection
        during, 198
    partial, 194-196

speed of, 192
Return, 455
ROM BIOS, 226
Run, 90–91, 317, 403–404
Run DOS command, 91
RunHide, 317, 404–405
RunIcon, 317, 405–406
RunZoom, 317, 406

S

safe formatting, 65
Scheduler, 151
    appointment tracking with, 300–304
    backups with, 203–204, 305–307
    reminder messages with, 304
    running a program with, 305
Scientific Calculator, 149, 151, 267–268
    Clipboard transfers with, 273
    conversion functions on, 271
    display functions on, 271
    error messages on, 273
    functions on, 269–270
    memory registers on, 271–273
    notation formats on, 270
screen saver. *See* Sleeper
scroll bars, 22
SD.INI file, 367
SendKey, 455–456
serial port, 227–228
shell definition, 105, 147–149
Shift-key combinations, 94, 113, 141
shortcut keys, 94–95, 113, 139–141
Shredder, 145–146, 216–219

SKDebug, 456–458
    constants for, 465
Sleeper, 273–274
    images for, 274–275
    password protection with, 278
    setup for, 277–278
    wake up from, 279
SmartErase, 207–208. *See also* Erase Protect
    configuring, 143–145, 151
    deleting files with, 210–211
    DOS 5 and, 214–215
    in tandem with Erase Protect, 208–210
    recovering files with, 211–213
software
    interrupts information, 238–240
    requirements, 6
special characters. *See* KeyFinder
Speed Disk, 336–337
    configuring, 362–367
    copy-protection methods and, 372–373
    directory order established by, 362–364
    file order established by, 364–367
    fragmentation report in, 359, 367–368
    illegal on network, 359
    optimization methods in, 361–362
    running, 372–374
spin buttons, 29–30
spreadsheet files, viewing, 77–78
startup files information, 242–243
StrCat, 438
StrCmp, 438–439
StrFill, 439

StrFix, 439-440
StrIndex, 440-441
   constants for, 464
string searching, 81-83, 251, 323, 440-441
   in batch files, 309-310
   in UnErase, 386
StrlCmp, 440
StrLen, 441
StrLower, 442
StrReplace, 442
StrScan, 442-443
   constants for, 464
StrSub, 443
StrTrim, 444
StrUpper, 444
SuperFind, 247-251
   file attribute searching with, 254
   file date searching with, 252-253
   file owner searching with, 254
   file sets used by, 247, 249, 255-258
   file size searching with, 253
   file time searching with, 253
   location sets used by, 247, 249, 255-258
   string searching with, 251
   using batch files with, 258-260
swap file, 229
system file, 48
System Information, 224-225
   benchmark information graphed by, 241-242
   CMOS summary shown by, 240-241
   device drivers information shown by, 232, 237-238
   disk summary shown by, 229-230
   display summary shown by, 233-234
   hardware configuration shown by, 225-229
   printer summary shown by, 234
   software interrupts listed by, 238-240
   startup files information listed by, 242-243
   system summary shown by, 225-229
   TSR program summary shown by, 234-237
   Windows memory usage graphed by, 230-233
SYSTEM.INI file, 148

T

Tagged Image File (TIF) format files, 73
Task List, 90, 133
10-Key Tape Calculator, 149, 151, 260-262
   Clipboard transfer with, 266-267
   data entry display on, 262-263
   memory functions on, 266
   setup for, 264-265
   tape display on, 263-264
   tape editing with, 265-266
terminate-and-stay-resident (TSR) program information, 234-237
TextBox, 320, 408-409
text boxes, 26
TIFF files, viewing, 73

title bar, 21
toggle, 25
tool icons, 133
Trashcan, 143, 207-213. *See also* SmartErase
  purging files from, 214
  storage limits in, 145
tree pane, 46-48
TSR program information, 234-237

U

UnErase, 337, 378-382. *See also* Erase Protect
  DOS 5 utilities with, 392
  Image program and, 392-393
  locating erased files with, 382-383
  manual operation of, 383-390
  partial file recovery with, 388-389
  recovering directories with, 390-392
  recovering from network with, 379
  recovering groups of files with, 382
  running from DOS command line, 393
  searching for clusters in, 386, 389-390
  viewing clusters in, 387-388
UnFormat, 337-338, 394-395
  running from DOS command line, 398
  with IMAGE.DAT file, 394-397
  without IMAGE.DAT file, 397-398
unmovable files, 360, 366, 370, 372

V

vector fonts, 280
Version, 324, 458
video adapter, 227
video mode, 233-234
viewer, default, 147
view pane, 51, 71-73

W

WallPaper, 458-459
warning signal configuration, 134-135
.WBT files, 311-312
wildcard characters, 31, 62, 248, 251, 256, 365
WinActivate, 427
WinArrange, 427-428
  constants for, 463
WinClose, 428
WinCloseNot, 429
WinConfig, 429-430
Window frame, 22-23
Windows memory usage information, 230-233
windows, 19
  cascaded, 23, 75
  dialog boxes in, 26-28
  drive access in, 28
  icons in, 24
  menus in, 25-26
  parts of, 20-23

size of, 21-23
tiled, 24, 75
types of, 19-20
viewing multiple, 23-24
WinExist, 430
WinGetActive, 431
WinHide, 431
WinIconize, 323, 431-432
WIN.INI file, 95-96
WinItemize, 432
WinPlace, 432-433
   constants for, 464
WinPosition, 433-434
WinShow, 323, 434
WinTitle, 434-435
WinVersion, 324, 459
   constants for, 464
WinWaitClose, 323, 435
WinZoom, 323, 436
WordPerfect Image Graphics
   images, viewing, 73

Y

Yield, 459

FREE BROCHURE!

SYBEX®

Complete this form today, and we'll send you a full-color brochure of Sybex bestsellers.

Please supply the name of the Sybex book purchased.

_____

How would you rate it?

_____ Excellent   _____ Very Good   _____ Average   _____ Poor

Why did you select this particular book?

_____ Recommended to me by a friend
_____ Recommended to me by store personnel
_____ Saw an advertisement in _____
_____ Author's reputation
_____ Saw in Sybex catalog
_____ Required textbook
_____ Sybex reputation
_____ Read book review in _____
_____ In-store display
_____ Other _____

Where did you buy it?

_____ Bookstore
_____ Computer Store or Software Store
_____ Catalog (name: _____)
_____ Direct from Sybex
_____ Other: _____

Did you buy this book with your personal funds?

_____ Yes   _____ No

About how many computer books do you buy each year?

_____ 1-3   _____ 3-5   _____ 5-7   _____ 7-9   _____ 10+

About how many Sybex books do you own?

_____ 1-3   _____ 3-5   _____ 5-7   _____ 7-9   _____ 10+

Please indicate your level of experience with the software covered in this book:

_____ Beginner   _____ Intermediate   _____ Advanced

Which types of software packages do you use regularly?

_____ Accounting   _____ Databases   _____ Networks
_____ Amiga   _____ Desktop Publishing _____ Operating Systems
_____ Apple/Mac   _____ File Utilities   _____ Spreadsheets
_____ CAD   _____ Money Management   _____ Word Processing
_____ Communications   _____ Languages   _____ Other _____
                                                          (please specify)

Which of the following best describes your job title?

____ Administrative/Secretarial   ____ President/CEO

____ Director   ____ Manager/Supervisor

____ Engineer/Technician   ____ Other _____
                                              (please specify)

Comments on the weaknesses/strengths of this book: _____

_____

_____

_____

_____

Name _____
Street _____
City/State/Zip _____
Phone _____

PLEASE FOLD, SEAL, AND MAIL TO SYBEX

SYBEX, INC.
Department M
2021 CHALLENGER DR.
ALAMEDA, CALIFORNIA USA
94501

SYBEX®

SEAL

Task	Program	Chapter
Arrange icons	Desktop	8
Back up a hard disk	Norton Backup	10
Calculate equations	Calculators	13
Calculate performance benchmarks	System Information	12
Cascade windows	Desktop	3
Change a volume label	Desktop	5
Change file attributes	Desktop	5
Clear the screen	Sleeper	13
Compare backed up files	Norton Backup	10
Configure Norton Desktop	Desktop	9
Connect to a network drive	Desktop	5
Copy disk	Desktop	5
Copy files	Desktop	5
Create a batch file	Batch Builder	14
Create a group	Quick Access	8
Create a directory	Desktop	5
Delete a directory	Desktop	5
Delete a file	Desktop	5
Disconnect a network drive	Desktop	5
Edit an icon	Icon Editor	14
Find disk problems	Norton Disk Doctor for Windows	12
Find lost files	SuperFind	13
Find text in a file	SuperFind	13
Fix a bad boot track	NDD	16
Fix a bad file allocation table	NDD	16
Fix a bad partition table	NDD	16